FREEDOM IS,
FREEDOM AIN'T

FREEDOM IS, FREEDOM AIN'T

JAZZ AND THE MAKING OF THE SIXTIES

SCOTT SAUL

HARVARD UNIVERSITY PRESS

Cambridge, Massachusetts, and London, England

2003

Quotations from *Ask Your Mama* from *The Collected Poems of Langston Hughes* by Langston
Hughes, copyright © 1994 by The Estate of Langston Hughes. Used by permission of Alfred A.
Knopf, a division of Random House, Inc., and Harold Ober Associates.

Publication of this book has been supported through the generous provisions of the
Maurice and Lula Bradley Smith Memorial Fund.

Library of Congress Cataloging-in-Publication Data
Saul, Scott.
Freedom is, freedom ain't : jazz and the making of the sixties / Scott Saul.
p. cm.
Includes bibliographical references and index.
ISBN 0-674-01148-1 (alk. paper)
1. Jazz—1951–1960—History and criticism. 2. Jazz—1961–1970—History and criticism.
3. Bop (Music)—Influence. 4. Arts, American—20th century. 5. African
Americans—Music—History and criticism. I. Title.

ML3508.S28 2003
781.65′0973′09046—dc21   2003051076

CONTENTS

ILLUSTRATIONS

PREFACE

This book may be seen as two books rolled into one—a history of one strand of jazz in the decade between the mid-1950s and mid-1960s, and a history of its uses. It tells, first, the story of jazz artists of the period, including Charles Mingus and John Coltrane, how their lives and music fed off one another; and, second, the story of postwar jazz's broader impact on intellectual and social life, as the values and practices associated with jazz—freedom, spontaneity, social and aesthetic experimentation, the rediscovery of one's roots—percolated through American culture at large. Book 1 aims to give the reader a thicker impression of the craft and power behind music like Miles Davis's *Birth of the Cool,* Max Roach's *Freedom Now Suite,* Charles Mingus's *The Black Saint and the Sinner Lady,* and John Coltrane's *A Love Supreme:* it guides the reader through the aesthetic choices (about arrangement, improvisation, genre, and so on) that these artists made and suggests how these choices were freighted with social as well as musical meaning. When Miles Davis put a mute on his trumpet, for instance, or Abbey Lincoln and John Coltrane started screaming on their respective instruments, they were not only opening up new musical vistas but also enacting new stances to the world. Part of the goal of *Freedom Is, Freedom Ain't,* then, is to describe these new stances—to break down jazz performances so that we can appreciate where they draw or depart from conventions, where they elaborate on old paradigms of music-making or create new ones, and to link these musical choices to the social world that these musicians shared.

Book 2, meanwhile, turns more explicitly to the social backdrop that helped give the music its meaning, charge, and relevance. The appeal of jazz in the 1950s and 1960s, for example, was undoubtedly tied to its sense of "cool," so the first part of this book gives an intellectual genealogy of this quicksilver concept, tracking the performance styles of jive-talking DJs, zoot-suited swing musicians, and the "signifying" hipsters of bebop and hard bop and keying into larger postwar debates about whether African-American bohemianism posed a promising or dubious alternative to the cultural mainstream. Likewise, the appeal of jazz in this period was also linked to its aura of rebellion, so I try to discern the various sorts of experimentation and protest that it inspired—everything from new rhythms in film and drama, new structures in poetry, and new palettes in painting and photography to new forms of collective organizing, new critiques of the shallowness or injustice of the status quo, and new visions of the "good life." In some sense, jazz-inspired artists such as James Baldwin, Langston Hughes, Roy DeCarava, and Sam Shepard were the most articulate members of the jazz audience, leaving a paper trail that testifies to the music's reach and, in crucial if complex ways, to how the music was received and understood.

Freedom Is, Freedom Ain't brings Book 1 and Book 2 together, but not without recognizing the tensions between the two. In many cases—for instance, Norman Mailer's notorious "White Negro" essay, Bert Stern's *Jazz on a Summer's Day,* and the youth riot at the 1960 Newport Jazz Festival—the jazz world was signified upon, but the actors had only a thin connection to the smaller insider community of jazz musicians, critics, producers, and devotees. Figures like Norman Mailer appropriated jazz for their own ends, made a certain amount of cultural hay, and then moved on, often without looking back. By contrast, musicians like Mingus and Coltrane were key presences within the jazz community and, quite rightly, continue to tower in most accounts of the music's history (Ken Burns's *Jazz* notwithstanding). They remain indispensable for what they have given us as artists and thinkers in their own right.

So why not write a history that focuses solely on the musicians themselves? Certainly this project would be impossible without the groundwork laid down by earlier such studies. Yet my interests have driven me to pursue different questions and methods. While artists like Mingus and Coltrane were often heroically determined and willful—in fact, much of the magnetism of their music comes from the way that they made palpable this act of self-concentration—they were also stuck in the familiar predicament of making history under conditions not of their own choosing. Moreover, these unchosen conditions often had such a powerful effect on the music that it is unwise to push them always to the background; certainly few jazz musicians could afford to do so in the context of their own life and work. As performing artists, they were very aware of how they played to an audience, sometimes flouting, sometimes corroborating, sometimes tweaking, sometimes transforming the expectations that were brought to their work. For a fuller understanding of their music, we need to grapple with this dialogue between artist and audience. So this project often listens to the music, but just as often it asks how the music was received and perceived and tries to unpack the sorts of enigmas that intrigue a cultural historian of the period. Why did the jazz hipster become attractive to progressive intellectuals who were running away from the label "Progressive"? Why did young white people riot at a jazz festival? Why did Mingus expend so much energy in his autobiography embroidering his romantic history and sex life? And why did Coltrane and Malcolm X become the twin guiding lights of the Black Arts movement, when Coltrane never identified himself with revolutionary nationalism or the Nation of Islam?

My goal in this project is to bring together several readerships—historians of American culture, jazz lovers, scholars of African-American life, literary critics—that rarely share a common conversation. I hope that social and literary historians, who rarely treat popular (much less unpopular) music in their overviews of the postwar period, will find in *Freedom Is, Freedom Ain't* new ways to incorporate jazz music into the broader stories of intellectual and avant-garde culture during the Cold War, into the narratives of civil rights and Black Power, and into the histories of youth culture and the New Left. I hope that jazz lovers and music scholars, the most discriminating of audiences, will not only discover new nuances in the art of Mingus and Coltrane but also be intrigued by Parts One, Two, and Five, which relate how generations of jazz aficionados—in intellectual and anti-intellectual circles—understood jazz as a language of dissent, the occasion for a subculture of cool, and a key medium of postwar leisure.

Partly because it tacks between the music and the culture inspired by the music, this book is prismatic rather than comprehensive, a way of looking at hard bop rather than a way of summing it up. Jazz readers may wish for more about particular figures—for instance, Sonny Rollins, Max Roach, Abbey Lincoln, and Randy Weston, to name four compelling artists who dealt forthrightly with issues of freedom and politics in music—or may long for a fuller treatment of the relationship, say, between the "freedom" jazz of hard bop and the free jazz that emerged especially in the mid-1960s. Coming from another angle may be readers who will question this book's scope: How can a single book address the relationship between jazz and civil rights, the New Left, the counterculture, and Black Power—some of the most complex changes that fall under the rubric of "the sixties"—all while trying to comment upon the fertile aesthetic transformations that make the period between 1955 and 1967 so crucial to the history of jazz?

Intellectual chutzpah can be enabling, yes, but not when it is so bound up with an outsized ambition that it becomes simply foolhardy.

From the outset, then, I should say that I am not so interested in constructing an airtight taxonomy of the genre of hard bop, a taxonomy that might then be used to divide the field of postwar jazz into more precise subgenres. By some lights, "hard bop" is a fuzzy and not-so-useful term since it errs on the side of inclusiveness, describing a music that sometimes borders the same kinds of jazz—modal jazz, free jazz, soul-jazz, action jazz, East Coast jazz—that it swallows at other moments. To me, the term appeals precisely because of its very looseness. Not only does it shelter a wide range of music from the late 1950s soul-jazz of Horace Silver and Cannonball Adderley to the more heterodox work of Mingus and Coltrane in their heyday, but also it suggests a web of affiliations that, notwithstanding the feuds that tore through the jazz community, become more clear with the passage of time. Hard bop musicians were, in the words of Benny Golson's tune, "stablemates": they shared a set of music labels (Prestige, Blue Note, Riverside, Candid, and so on), and they shared double and triple bills at nightclubs across the country like the Five Spot, the Plugged Nickel, the Village Vanguard, Lennie's-on-the-Pike, and the Blackhawk. They shared a sympathy with the civil rights movement and a desire to make music that drew upon and publicized the black community's deep reserves of joy, defiance, and self-respect: all of these artists participated in the broader cultural movement to rediscover and interrogate the "roots" of the black experience. While they did not make music that followed the same rules and conventions, they did share a field of argument over the origins, direction, and posterity of the music—where it came from, where it was going, and whether it was made to last. One of the most fascinating aspects of the jazz community in this slice of the postwar period is its almost compulsive desire to revisit and recast its own history, to define with jesuitical precision the exact balance between its debt to the past and its legacy to the future. Often in the very act of argument, hard bop musicians revealed their most profoundly shared assumptions and concerns. And all the while, through the play of their music and its range of reference, hard bop musicians were profound jazz historians as well, lucid in ways that challenge the most assiduous of listeners.

A final note on my title, itself a riff on the intellectual legacy of Ralph Ellison. In the prologue of Ellison's *Invisible Man* (1952), the nameless narrator lights up a reefer, starts listening to Louis Armstrong's "What Did I Do to Be So Black and Blue," and soon finds himself descending like Dante into the depths of an invented world, hallucinatory circles upon circles, each with its own staged performance and musical tempo. He comes to rest in front of a preacher, who announces that his text is—in an inversion of the usual Genesis story, where the world is generated in light—the story of the "Blackness of Blackness." The preacher does not deliver, however, what we might expect from such a title—either a hymn to the powers of blackness or a meditation on the dangers lurking in the darkness of the soul. Instead, he enters into a cryptic call and response with his congregation, a dialogue that searches for a definition of blackness but never comes to rest:

> *"Now black is . . ." the preacher shouted.*
> *"Bloody . . ."*
> *"I said black is . . ."*
> *"Preach it, brother . . ."*
> *". . . an' black ain't . . ."*
> *"Red, lawd, red: He said it's red!"*
> *"Amen, brother . . ."*
> *"Black will git you . . ."*
> *"Yes, it will . . ."*
> *"Yes, it will . . ."*
> *". . . an' black won't . . ."*
> *"Naw, it won't!"*

"Black is" and "black ain't": the sermon primes *Invisible Man's* reader for the half-painful, half-playful absurdities that keep the narrator running from misadventure to insight over the novel's next five hundred pages. "Black is": racial identity is irreducibly felt; the basic arrangements of American culture—where you live, what work you find, which communities welcome you, what resources you draw on to build your sense of identity—are structured along lines of race. "Black ain't": racial identity is the thinnest of fictions, a cover for power plays and an excuse for political complacency, a hard-and-fast line that hardens and moves according to those who have the power to control it, a socially invented check on an individual's ability to invent him- or herself. Ellison's achievement was, in part, to hold onto this tension between the reality and the fiction of race, to refuse to resolve it—and to suggest that living with its complexity involved both an act of virtuosity and a commitment to one's community. The preacher is necessary to give the sermon its text, but then it is the call and response between preacher and congregation that *enacts* the sermon, turning its tragicomic message into a form of lived ritual.

My title nods to *Invisible Man* because it seems to me that the jazz of the 1950s and 1960s was marked by an Ellisonian recognition of both the strength of African-American culture and the futility of race-hardened thinking, and was energized by an Ellisonian desire to marry virtuosity and community involvement. (At least in one case, the evidence of the affinity is quite concrete: Charles Mingus read *Invisible Man,* and Ellison hosted a 1965 TV special featuring Mingus's Jazz Workshop.) "Freedom is": freedom took sound and shape in the jazz performances of the 1950s and 1960s, which were exercises in reconciling liberation and discipline, self-expression and collective achievement. "Freedom ain't": the music understood freedom as something embedded in struggle, a hard-won realization rather than a gift with no strings attached. Dramatizing the social and psychological struggles necessary to achieve freedom during the heyday of the civil rights movement, jazz music offered a dynamic sense of freedom to its listeners—a barbed challenge as well as the most exhilarating of invitations.

INTRODUCTION

Hard Bop and the
Impulse to Freedom

There's a moment two minutes into the 1957 recording of Charles Mingus's "Haitian Fight Song" that never fails to unsettle me. The piece opens with a brief bass solo by Mingus, plaintive and blues-inflected, and builds in volume and complexity from there. One by one, the other members of Mingus's Jazz Workshop—Dannie Richmond on drums, Jimmy Knepper on trombone, Shafi Hadi on alto sax, and Wade Legge on piano—lend their voices to his G-minor blues. Then, just as Knepper's trombone and Hadi's saxophone play a set of interweaving melodies, and just as Legge pounds a ballast-like octave on the lower register of his piano, Mingus starts screaming for freedom. WOO-AAH-AYYY! WOO-AAH-AYYY! The screams slice through the Workshop's crescendo with an oddly disembodied, high-pitched power. Part of Mingus's aesthetic of excess, they help convert "Haitian Fight Song," which introduces itself as an ingenious eight-bar blues with canonlike melodies, into something less subtle and more extreme: a performance that aims to bury a world of convention, or at least force it into obsolescence.[1]

Why do Mingus's screams signal so much to me? Partly it's their religious resonance, the way they evoke abandon and humility, imposition and self-denial. Purposefully inarticulate, they recall the cries of the Holiness worshippers whom Mingus remembered from the Wednesday night services of his Watts childhood—"people . . . in trances," "women shout[ing] and roll[ing] on the floor." His screams sound like a new, jazz-inflected way of speaking in tongues, a new way of courting the flame of God. There is a surprising trade-off going on here, a kind of self-loss, with Mingus giving up the customary virtuosity of his bass work for another sort of power. Musically, this trade-off comes through in what one might call Mingus's technique as a screamer—a strange phrase, perhaps, but one that keeps us from underestimating the willfulness of his gesture. For all his two-hundred-plus pounds, all the fleshy heft that seems to make his bass playing sharp and authoritative, Mingus takes to screaming like a very thin man. We are as far from classical vocal technique, with its reliance on lung power and the use of the diaphragm, as could be imagined. The keening sound comes only from the throat, and for that reason it sounds thin even though it's burry and at full volume. It's more like a falsetto cry— a bellow stripped of its undertones but not its gravel, a man screaming unlike a man is supposed to scream.[2]

Which brings us to the obvious question about this moment in "Haitian Fight Song": Is a man supposed to scream at all? And behind that, these other questions: Why should music demand this kind of effort—this challenge to the moods of normalcy and the habits of convention, the way things are and have been? What sort of music puts tension, anger, and ecstasy at the heart of its aesthetic, and understands freedom as the sound of struggle?

This book seeks to explain how and why "hard bop," the loose genre of jazz that flourished alongside Mingus between 1955 and 1967, came to serve this role: as music of cultural burial and cultural awakening. Hard bop was the music of a generation, born in the 1920s and early 1930s, who imaginatively tried to recapture the roots of jazz in gospel and the blues while extending its ambition in the realms of art, politics, and spirituality (and often some combination of the three). Flowing in the postwar period out of cities like Chicago, Indianapolis, Pittsburgh, Detroit, and New York, it was unabashedly urban music, music that had a gemlike toughness and brilliance, a balance of glamour and grit. Jazz before had been "hot" or "cool," but hard bop was intense, soulful, unfussy, insistent—too agitated to be simply hot, too moody to be simply cool. The music crystallized in tandem with the civil rights movement and was in many ways its sonic alter ego. Like the movement, it grounded new appeals for freedom in older idioms of black spirituality, challenging the nation's public account of itself and testifying to the black community's cultural power. And, like the movement again, it worked through a kind of orchestrated disruption—a musical version of what civil rights workers called "direct action," which jazz musicians experienced as a rhythmic assertiveness and a newly taut relation between the demands of composition and the possibilities of improvisation.[3]

Freedom Is, Freedom Ain't bids to tell the story of these musicians and the culture around them. It describes how a generation of jazz artists built their music and their audience simultaneously, often in tension with that audience's own understanding of the music and its promise. In this story Mingus is a central figure, but he was far from alone in composing songs of freedom and wrestling with their aesthetic and practical challenges. His scream was echoed by the harrowing and annealing sound of John Coltrane's saxophone; by the exuberant riffing of Cannonball Adderley and his quintet; by the volcanic drumming that drove Art Blakey's Jazz Messengers; by the percussive, Monk-meets-Africa attack of Randy Weston's piano; by the buzzing inventiveness of Sonny Rollins's saxophone; by the mercurial timbre of Miles Davis's trumpet; by the harsh, declamatory singing of Abbey Lincoln; and by the trenchant and celebratory grooves laid down by Horace Silver's piano. The main point of convergence for this group was their imaginative reclamation of jazz's roots in the blues and in the gospel music of the black church, and their desire to explore these roots in an utterly contemporary form. Hard bop aspired to be music of roots and vision, new-time religion built out of old-time religion. It testified to a common past even as it underscored, with its feverish improvisations, the tremulous uncertainty of the present. Mingus said, typically, that "Haitian Fight Song" had a "contemporary folk feeling"; its innovations, as in much hard bop, were concentrated in the effort of reinventing roots music so that it could address the urgencies of the present and suggest a future beyond the crisis that the civil rights movement had so effectively dramatized.[4]

As a result of this impulse to be both backward- and forward-looking, hard bop was always tying together aesthetics and ethics, the style of soul and the mandate of soul. At the least it hoped to evoke a new mobilization of black energy; at the most it aspired to galvanize a larger "freedom movement" that extended from the early stirrings of the civil rights movement through the late-sixties' mobilizations of the black community under the signs of "Black Power" and "Soul Power." In thinking about why he started stretching musical form in Mingus's Jazz Workshop, pianist Mal Waldron observed, "We were talking about freedom, and getting out of jails. Bar lines was like going to jail for us. So everyone wanted to escape from that. There was a general feeling that everyone wanted to be free." Randy Weston remarked, "In the late Fifties to early Sixties, it was all in the air: the Civil Rights Movement, Malcolm X, Martin Luther King . . . we had that kind of energy, and it inspired me to compose what was in the air." Mingus himself said, with typical bite, that "Haitian Fight Song" "could just as well be called *Afro-American Fight Song*": he acted as if there wasn't much of a historical leap from the revolutionary Haiti of the 1790s, in the midst of its slave revolt, to the United States of the mid-1950s. Both ages demanded political struggle, and music that would propel it along.[5]

For hard bop musicians to realize these cultural ambitions, though, they needed to wrestle with a series of technical challenges—for instance, how to absorb the fervent passions of gospel without losing the velocity and self-conscious intelligence of postwar bebop; how to infuse the freedom of individual voices into the collective freedom of the ensemble; and how to invigorate a soul aesthetic that would testify to black strength without becoming so brittle or categorical that it bordered on the narrowmindedness that it sought to contest. Generally working within the instrumentation of the bebop small group—saxophone, trumpet, piano, bass, drums—hard bop players tried to tunnel through it toward a fresh rediscovery of elemental forms. Their goal was to reveal a tradition and—more—to make it convincing as a tradition, not simply a fabrication of convenience. At the same time, they also needed to meet the commercial challenge of building an audience that would support their livelihood and, perhaps, redeem their hopes of an arts community. In practice, this meant traversing the same racial minefield that gave urgency to their music—parrying stereotypes or plying them subversively for their own benefit, and maneuvering through the webs of structural discrimination that had long entrapped jazz musicians as outsiders not only in American culture but in their own industry as well.

Freedom Is, Freedom Ain't follows this music, and the various alliances and disputes that swirled around it, through the fifties and sixties. In order to understand the reach and contentiousness of the music, it examines those visual and literary artists who were inspired by the music's fusion of sophistication, spontaneity, and soul, and who shared its ambivalence about the state of the affluent society's conscience. Notably, these artists bridged several generations: many came of age during the Great Depression, where they often apprenticed in the radical culture of the New Deal, while another set came of age with the hard boppers themselves during the mid-fifties. A shortlist of crucial jazz-inflected works from this period would include, from the older generation, Langston Hughes's *Ask Your Mama*, Eugene Smith and Roy DeCarava's photographs of the working lives of jazz musicians, Romare Bearden's collages, and Ralph Ellison's essay collection *Shadow and Act*. From the younger cohort, such a list might begin with Bob Thompson's Fauvist-colored canvases, Allen Ginsberg's

Howl and Other Poems, James Baldwin's "Sonny's Blues" and *Another Country,* Amiri Baraka's *The Dead Lecturer* and *Blues People,* the early improvisational work of the Living Theater, Sam Shepard's first Off-Off-Broadway plays, director John Cassavetes's *Shadows,* and Shirley Clarke's films *The Connection* and *The Cool World.* Much of the power of hard bop lies in how it galvanized this lively cultural conversation about the value of dissent in American life, whether that dissent took the form of prophecy, insult, witness, insurgency, dropping out, or making do.

If we wish to understand how the Cold War thawed into the cultural tumult known loosely as "the sixties"—how black Americans and young people, in large part, helped force a new reckoning of the postwar consensus—we can learn much from this cultural community of literary, visual, and musical artists. In particular, the fortunes of hard bop were linked to the fortunes of the civil rights movement, and so the story of the one sheds light on the other. As a genre the music came together, then scattered to disparate ends in the twelve years between 1955 and 1967—which is to say, at the same time that the civil rights coalition progressed from the early triumph of the Montgomery bus boycott to the fracturing of its liberal-left alliance around the slogan of "Black Power" and the movement's decision to tackle nationally entrenched economic inequities. Around 1955, as the movement began asserting an unexpected kind of black grassroots power, jazz critics minted the term "hard bop" to describe how several new jazz combos—especially Horace Silver and Art Blakey's gospel-inflected Jazz Messengers—were tilting away from the well-tempered sound of cool jazz; Mingus's Jazz Workshop and Miles Davis's quintet with John Coltrane were also launched at this moment. Five years later, the flush of student sit-ins was also a moment of high tide for hard bop. The early 1960s incubated not only the innovations of modal jazz and John Coltrane's "classic quartet," but also several programmatic attempts to align jazz with the freedom movement, among them Max Roach's *Freedom Now* suite, Randy Weston's *Uhuru Africa,* and Oliver Nelson's *Afro-American Sketches.* Finally, the fracturing of the movement after the uprisings in Watts, Detroit, and forty other U.S. cities paralleled the fracturing of the hard bop coalition, its loss of a central sense of direction. After the death of Coltrane in 1967, a younger generation of free jazz musicians lost their most tangible connection to the jazz mainstream, Mingus and many others went into internal exile, and Miles Davis led another faction to pursue the electronic sound of rock-soul-jazz fusion.[6]

The connection between hard bop and civil rights was more, however, than the fact of cultural coincidence. I consider hard bop to be a musical facet of the freedom movement—an extension particularly of the idea of direct action into the realm of structurally improvised music. The hard bop group, with its loose, spontaneous interplay and its firm sense of a collective groove, modeled a dynamic community that was democratic in ways that took exception to the supposedly benign normalcy of 1950s America. Different ensembles might represent different kinds of publics and counterpublics—a congregation energized by a charismatic preacher, a crowd on the brink of riot, or a street-corner posse looking for the next hip thing—but the one assurance, given the diversity of attitudes struck by hard bop groups, was this: that the music would not sound like the quietly humming consensus deemed normative during the Eisenhower era. To be free in a jazz context meant being part of "the action"—a very simple point, perhaps, but also a challenging idea for a society struggling to reconcile democratic ideals with the increasingly bureaucratic order that Eisenhower, in his presidential farewell address, labeled "the military-industrial complex." Hard bop musicians seemed to innovate and collaborate on their art in real time, in ways that few citizens could be said to participate in the machinery of their own lives; their art was an attempt to capture in sound the freedom of collective animation. Just as so many political activists in the 1950s and 1960s tried to embody a prefigurative politics—creating counterinstitutions like freedom schools, grassroots political parties, and alternative media that would anticipate the world they desired—so the musicians of hard bop gave voice to a world beyond the Cold War consensus, where everyday people might be virtuosos and provocateurs at once.[7]

Hard bop was part of a budding critique of postwar American culture, one that elevated the values of collaborative freedom and creative spontaneity over the values of rational administration and collective security. The music spoke to the spirit of both the civil rights movement, which galvanized thousands to protest in a tradition of collective uplift, and the student-driven New Left, which tried to infuse American political life with ideas of grassroots action and shared decision-making. Though later in this introduction I contrast the practice of democracy in hard bop with the theory of democracy that prevailed in the affluent society, I hope to move beyond treating this aesthetic critique as a purely theoretical matter, an airy contest between different ideas about democracy and freedom; jazz music in this period is simply too diverse to be explained by any one theory of the fit between its aesthetic principles and its cultural role. The larger contest about the place of jazz in American culture was experienced through a set of more concrete and local battles—in the audiences of jazz festivals and nightclubs, in the pages of music and political journals like *Down Beat, Kulchur,* and *Liberator,* and in the lives of the musicians themselves. The five parts of *Freedom Is, Freedom Ain't* survey these battles, beginning with the invention of the hipster before World War II and ending with the ascendancy of separate white and black countercultures in the late sixties.[8]

Part One centers on the figure of the hipster, that flamboyant, jive-talking cat who seemed to escape the daily grind. From his origins in the cultures of swing and bebop, the hipster became a lightning rod for questions about radicalism of style, a vehicle for jazz musicians and intellectuals to prod one another about the meaning of jazz's dissent from mass culture. My first two chapters consider how white and predominantly Jewish intellectuals were attracted to jazz for the leverage it gave for a critique of culture at large, and how black jazz musicians parried by redefining hipness itself as a black vernacular, something no "white Negro" could capture. Along with the surprising vogue of Norman Mailer's "White Negro" essay, the arrival of soul-jazz in the late 1950s raised prickly questions for musicians and intellectuals alike: Did the commercialization of "the cool" blunt its power, reveal its aesthetic to be a sham? Or did it suggest simply that the real hipsters were finding new venues and new aesthetics—creating music, art, and poetry, like the group of bohemians in the East Village, under the radar of the advertising industry?

Part Two turns from the intellectual critique of mass culture to popular culture itself. Here I examine how the jazz festival became a magnet of postwar youth culture, one of the first places where young people could spend a weekend away from their parents in crowds of 40,000 or more. In particular I focus on the Newport jazz riot of 1960, where young white jazz fans vandalized the town after being shut out of the concert grounds, creating a crisis of respectability for the jazz community. Outside observers speculated that jazz music, like rock 'n' roll, had degenerated into an excuse for the hooliganism of the young. Meanwhile jazz critics and musicians lambasted the Newport Jazz Festival for sacrificing jazz's integrity to the mass market, indulging fantasies of leisure and not even delivering the goods. Also, as poet Langston Hughes adduced, the bottle-throwing battle at Newport involved a battle over racial representation. In his devastating dialogue of insult called *Ask Your Mama*, Hughes looked at Newport as a scrimmage where, as so often happens in American culture, white folks used blackness to work out their own questions of self-identity and, more specifically, to test the bounds and meaning of their privilege.

Parts Three and Four turn to Charles Mingus and John Coltrane, two of the most powerful, if heterodox, musicians of hard bop, two artists who took the music in utterly different directions. (Coltrane respected Mingus but had no desire to work with him, and Mingus returned the ambivalence.) Mingus was a musical magpie, an artist who tried to assimilate every genre he came into contact with—New Orleans jazz, Ellingtonian swing, bebop, mariachi, free jazz, cumbia, gospel—and often left them fascinatingly half-digested. His music was outrageous, joyful, difficult, militant in its ambition, forcefully out of scale, and marked by everything except restraint. Mingus himself was a fanatic for masquerade, someone who might appear suddenly in the garb of a British banker, a gunslinger, or even Robin Hood, complete with arrows. He seemed most comfortable among other boundary-crossers and spent much time in various interracial countercultural scenes. He frequented the Beat and mystic circles of 1950s San Francisco, saw his star rise in the Greenwich Village arts world of the early 1960s, and then hid out in the late 1960s in the bars of the Lower East Side, where he became just another regular. Yet despite his fondness for interracial worlds (and the ears of white women), Mingus was never reluctant to proclaim his blackness. Labeled "the Angry Man of jazz," he was hard bop's most visible scourge of the music industry and its institutional racism, a conspiratorial thinker whose suspicions were sometimes misplaced but often vindicated. Mingus's oversizedness—his embrace of hyperbole in art and life—marked him as hard bop's king of comedy. In Mingus's case, of course, the comedy was "as serious as your life"; his preferred means of overcoming cultural limitations was to explode them head-on, with satire, gusto, and manic creativity.[9]

Coltrane, by contrast, opened onto the serious side of hard bop. His seriousness was a matter of integrity even more than temperament: his music carried a singleness of purpose that refused the kinds of masquerade, the overt mixing of genres, that animated Mingus's work. His classic quartet worked like a crucible, melting together the various ingredients of its style: the three-against-four rhythms of Elvin Jones's drums, the quartal chords of McCoy Tyner's piano, the drone of Jimmy Garrison's bass, and Coltrane's own anguished vocalizing on saxophone. Rather than zigging and zagging between different styles as Mingus did throughout his career, Coltrane seemed to move in a straight line, focusing his musical intelligence on a single formal problem (for example, how his love of stacking different chords on one another in his 1959 compositions straitjacketed his improvisations) and then solving it with a new "sound"—which in turn led to another problem and, eventually, another solution. His movement from style to style was, depending on your perspective, a jazz version of higher mathematics, a story of spiritual struggle, a case study in negative dialectics, or a hurtling journey into deeper and deeper shades of blackness. Ironically, while Mingus was outspoken in his militancy, it was Coltrane who became the cultural saint of the late-sixties Black Arts movement, his ascension facilitated partly by his untimely death but even more by the shape of his career. Coltrane's music seemed to move forward in stages toward self-discovery and, for many, toward a fuller awakening of black consciousness. It was no accident that his most celebrated work, *A Love Supreme* (1964), had the upward arc of a pilgrim's progress.[10]

After concentrating on the music of Mingus and Coltrane and the cultural controversies they elicited, *Freedom Is, Freedom Ain't* widens the critical angle once again. Part Five examines the fate of hard bop in the late 1960s, and its legacies in the largely white counterculture and in the black community. Jazz festivals sprouted across the country in the late 1950s and early 1960s, regulating their spirit and incorporating their business side, and by the late 1960s these concerts had lost much of their novelty and draw for young white people, who were increasingly attracted to the rock festivals of the counterculture. This transfer of allegiance concealed several historical debts. The rock festival borrowed much of its ethic of anti-commercialism, for instance, from the fight over the Newport festival's incorporation—a point confirmed when the Monterey International Pop Festival borrowed its site and programming philosophy from Newport's leading challenger, the Monterey Jazz Festival. The legacy of jazz on the counterculture can also be traced biographically, and with this lens I look at the turbulent careers of two countercultural tribunes: playwright Sam Shepard, who moved from a jazz-inflected theater of spontaneity to a rock-inflected theater that lamented the disappearance of spontaneity; and John Sinclair, who began the 1960s as a free jazz partisan and ended the decade as a countercultural cause célèbre, the founder of the White Panther party and perhaps the leading advocate of "sex, drugs, and rock 'n' roll" as a revolutionary platform.

Freedom Is, Freedom Ain't ends with the mid- to late sixties attempts by jazz musicians to strengthen their base in the black community, both aesthetically by laying firmer claim to a soul aesthetic and practically by building community organizations. Often the cultural nationalist strain in the Black Power movement has been characterized as antiwhite and fascinated by the therapeutic value of righteous, revolutionary violence. In the final chapter I question this conventional wisdom. The late-1960s explorations of a soul aesthetic in jazz were both more militant and finger-pointing on the one hand *and* more open-ended and freewheeling on the other. Which is to say: jazz musicians and their partisans were struggling with several contradictory impulses at once. They hoped that the artistic work of "creative destruction" might challenge a white-dominated society to redistribute some of its power, and they had a skeptic's sense that art could not do the work of politics unless it was backed by force. They hoped to explore black pride and black identity, and they wanted to confirm a broader sense of human possibility. Utopian and skeptical, race-affirming and cosmopolitan, jazz musicians tried to create an art that would make uplift into something forceful, undeniable in its conviction and experimental in its search for new possibilities.[11]

That these musicians and critics did not resolve these tensions is no indictment of their intelligence or sophistication. Rather, it suggests the kinds of cultural pressure under which they—and other observers—labored. How is it possible to reconcile the realpolitik view that power is a zero-sum game, that people are made to suffer because their suffering is in someone else's interest, with Martin Luther King, Jr.'s injunction that if one person is oppressed, everyone suffers from the oppression? What sort of blind spot in American culture makes us suspect that someone cannot be both proudly black and proudly human? These are the contradictions that hard bop wrestled with, elegantly and powerfully. It is partly to the music's credit that these contradictions remain at the raw surface of American life. And it is part of the music's unfinished legacy that they still beg for a new reconstruction, a solution that would wed power and conscience.

Hard Bop, Civil Rights, and the Cold War

It is impossible to research the relationship between freedom and jazz in the 1950s and 1960s without crashing into a cultural riddle. Jazz artists gave scores of benefit concerts for the freedom movement—for the NAACP, the Congress of Racial Equality (CORE), the Urban League, the Student Nonviolent Coordinating Committee (SNCC), the Liberation Committee for Africa, and so on—and yet they were guarded about the freedom within their music, careful to claim freedom's mantle but also to question its exact meaning. While jazz musicians often spoke about the freedom of their music, they also took care to qualify the term, sometimes in the next breath. Free jazz pioneer Ornette Coleman typified this tendency when he asserted, "I let everyone express himself just as he wants to. The musicians have complete freedom"—and then went on to praise how his collaborators, while free, resisted the urge to grandstand and cultivate a "star-complex," and how their music was "at all times a group effort." Pianist Herbie Hancock, recalling the mid-1960s Miles Davis group, said that "we used to call [our aesthetic] 'controlled freedom'" and distinguished their playing from "total experimentation." Davis himself praised saxophonist and composer Wayne Shorter in similar terms: Shorter "understood that freedom in music was the ability to know the rules in order to bend them to your own satisfaction and taste." Cecil Taylor collaborator Sunny Murray, often held up as the leading drummer of the free jazz avant-garde, likewise contrasted his "controlled freedom" with the "complete freedom you could get from anyone who walks down the street." He stressed that in order to convey successfully the intense emotions of the moment—"humming and screaming and laughing and crying"—jazz ensembles needed to have the teamwork of a good crew on a boat. "There's the helmsman and a cat to put the coal in, but everybody can't be the captain." Such caveats about the spirit of freedom in experimental jazz ran the gamut from the adamant (George Russell: "I don't believe in freedom") to the cryptic (Sun Ra: "Look at the kind of people who say, 'I'm free, white, and 21.' Are they free? I see myself as P-H-R-E but not F-R-E-E. That's the name of the sun in ancient Egypt").[12]

Mingus's scored-poem "Freedom" (first performed in 1962, but written partly in response to the red-baiting of Paul Robeson) brilliantly captured some of the ambivalence of the jazz community to the term. Mingus recited the lines of his poem in alternating rhythm with a chain-gang chant from his band—a melismatic phrase followed by the 'huh' of the hammer swinging—so that for the duration of the performance, he seemed to embody freedom as his Workshop mimicked its brutal denial. Talking to himself about himself, with the pensiveness that comes to those engaged in hard labor, Mingus took stock of his predicament:

Stand fast young old mule
Soothe in contemplation thy burning hole and aching thigh
Your stubbornness is of the living
And cruel anxiety is about to die

There are a few certainties that you can take away from Mingus's performance, and far more ambiguities. Certainly Mingus was suggesting, with the figure of the mule who's "had some learnin', mostly mouth to mouth," that he might be treated as a beast of burden but that he was no beast: the oral tradition had given him resources, no thanks to the powers that be. His resilience—the better part of being mule-headed, so to speak—would be his salvation. And his poem very deliberately took on the practices of the Ku Klux Klan, yearning for a day when the burning of a cross was recognized as the work of "a madman in his most incandescent bloom."[13]

Yet like much of Mingus's music, the poem was enlivened by the play of contradiction, incongruous materials fused weirdly together. The image of a madman in "incandescent bloom" was supposedly hopeful but somewhat grotesque too, hinting at the Gothic horror of Billie Holiday's "Strange Fruit." Mingus's self-appraisal, repeated at the end of the poem, likewise gave reason for both optimism and caution. Addressing himself as a "young old mule," he balanced his anticipation of the long road ahead with the recognition that he was quite weathered already. "Stand[ing] fast," he hoped to move forward through the persistent effort to hold still. Perhaps most surprising of all is the poem's chastened sense of deliverance—the way it celebrates and chokes on the promise of freedom at once. At a cresting moment near the end, the band departs from the work-song chant and starts singing "Freedom for your mama, / Freedom for your daddy, / Freedom for your brothers and sisters"—all seems to be well, the movement is on the rise—but then with an unexpected reversal comes this stark announcement, punctuated by an emphatic return to the minor home key: "But no freedom for me." The mule is fated to wait—and to know, with bittersweet reassurance, that failure will not be his ultimate portion.

Taken together, the qualifications of Mingus, Davis, Sun Ra, and others are a sign of the stress that postwar jazz put on common understandings of "freedom": jazz artists wanted to claim the banner of freedom, but they also wanted to distance themselves from the term's association with individual license and whimsical choice. The pursuit of freedom, in Mingus's poem, is hard work if nothing else. Yet why did postwar American culture understand freedom as free choice in the first place? If we want to understand the ambitions and caveats of jazz artists, we need to step back a bit and probe into the different meanings that freedom assumed, on the one hand, for jazz musicians and, on the other, for the politicians, democratic theorists, intellectuals, and businessmen who defended the "American way of life" during the Cold War. Freedom has always been a cherished word in American life, but during the 1950s and 1960s it became a particularly contested term as well. American foreign policy became dedicated to promoting free enterprise and containing Communism, the civil rights movement pressed for "Freedom Now," and a host of artistic movements along with hard bop—abstract expressionism, method acting, the Beats, modern dance—justified their innovative work under the sign of free expression. Everyone aspired to freedom, but few agreed on the correct definition of the term, the limits that kept freedom from shading into anarchy or self-indulgence, and the enslaving power that freedom asserted itself against.[14]

In retrospect, we can see that postwar jazz and the civil rights movement together pulled against two intellectual axioms of 1950s America: first, that "freedom" was umbilically joined to the "free market," something guaranteed by your ability to buy whatever you could afford; and second, that the freedom of ordinary Americans was confirmed by the lack of strong dissent—the sense that a quiet, well-oiled consensus was the best consensus, since utopian dreams about reconstructing society were doomed to painful failure. In the context of the Cold War, these ideas about freedom had a strong geopolitical payoff. Government officials, business leaders, and newspaper editorials collaborated on the following cultural syllogism: if freedom was a product of individual consumer initiative and if politics was best where politics was least, then the West was clearly superior to the East with its grim factories, poorly stocked grocery stores, and insistent pursuit of egalitarianism.

Historian Eric Foner has ably traced this larger cultural turn—how the Cold War edged out broader understandings of American freedom as the U.S. government devoted itself, in the words of security document NSC 68 (1950), to the defense of "the idea of freedom" against the "idea of slavery under the grim oligarchy of the Kremlin." If anything, this militant rhetoric of freedom intensified in the early sixties. John F. Kennedy testified in his 1960 campaign that the Cold War "is not a struggle for supremacy of arms alone. It is also a struggle for supremacy between two conflicting ideologies: freedom under God versus ruthless, godless tyranny." Beneath the surface of Kennedy's speech, "freedom" was acquiring a more straitened meaning, since "freedom under God" was shorthand for the American system of postwar capitalism. The last two of Franklin Roosevelt's Four Freedoms—freedom from want and freedom from fear—were being eclipsed by "free enterprise," which hinted at a culture of abundance without guaranteeing its availability to all citizens. In the ongoing battle between the Free West and the Unfree East, it was free enterprise that carried the weight of American values, and behind it the sense that every individual had a freedom to consume, a freshly minted postwar "right." A 1958 opinion poll crystallized this conventional wisdom when it discovered that 82 percent of Americans agreed that "our freedom depends on the free enterprise system"; a Brand Names Foundation advertisement similarly opined that "without a free exchange of goods, you cannot have a free people."[15]

This celebration of free enterprise, endorsed by liberals and conservatives alike, led many Americans to conceive of freedom as the exercise of a private choice: being able to buy one product as opposed to another, to opt for one leisure pursuit as opposed to another. Atomic Energy Commissioner David Lilienthal wrote in 1952, "By freedom, I mean essentially *freedom to choose* to the maximum degree possible. . . . It means a maximum range of choice for the consumer when he spends his dollar."[16] Under the pressure of this redefinition, democracy itself began to be rethought too. A society was valued less for the way it inculcated the participatory or civic virtues of engagement and dissent and more for the way it respected the privacy of the individual and therefore held the totalitarian threat in abeyance. Somewhat to his chagrin, political philosopher Isaiah Berlin gave academic heft to this resorting of cultural priorities through his lodestar essay "Two Concepts of Liberty" (1958). Berlin distinguished between "negative liberty," the freedom to choose in one's private life aside from the interventions of the state, and "positive liberty," or the freedom to reach genuine self-fulfillment by transcending false needs.[17]

While Berlin framed "positive liberty" as an inner state of mind, his popularizers treated it as a fair description of how certain governments tried to mold their citizens, determining which needs were true and which were false. Soon after the publication of this essay, Berlin's distinction between negative and positive liberty became an organizing rubric of political philosophy and, not incidentally, a way of philosophically dividing the West from the East. The East's "positive liberty" was recategorized as a type of false liberty: too many totalitarian states, political scientists argued, had forced a specious obedience onto their citizenry, driven by such high-minded ideals of virtuous civic participation. The state was best when it promoted an "absence of interference," an "absence of obstacles to possible choices and desires"; the consent of the governed should be cultivated, of course, but the republican ideal of direct participation was deemed impracticable, even counterproductive. According to this strain of political theory, democracy had the best chance of thriving, in intellectual historian Howard Brick's words, "where there was a wide umbrella of consensus among leading political players, no astringent debate between political parties over fundamentals, lack of sharp divisions among elements of the population at large, and consequently a popular willingness, aside from electoral participation, to let politics go its own momentum."[18]

The year after Berlin's essay was published, negative liberty had its state-sanctioned, consumerist confirmation in the "kitchen debate" between Richard Nixon and Nikita Khrushchev at the 1959 American National Exhibition in Moscow. In this staged meeting of East and West, the conflict between America and Russia was not presented as a contest between two economic and political systems—a contest where the Soviets might have praised the virtues of solidarity and egalitarianism while the Americans might have spoken about the promise of individual achievement and the dynamism of free markets. Instead the conflict was reoriented around questions of material abundance: what kinds of kitchens were possible in the two worlds, and what kinds of family life followed as a result? The affair was less a debate than a stroll through consumer showrooms packed with home appliances, hi-fi sets, cars, and TVs. Nixon, for his part, extolled how American suburbia allowed people to choose from a wealth of appliances and other household goods while freeing housewives from their customary drudgery. Khrushchev meanwhile tried gamely to skewer the American fondness for household gadgets, but this was a small gesture in a spectacle designed by the United States. Its ground rules threw Khrushchev for a loss, since they presumed that social happiness could be measured by the quantity and quality of goods for sale—that consumerism and material wealth were at the root of freedom.[19]

Far from being outside this discourse, jazz—with its claim to improvisatory freedom—was enlisted by the federal government as an ally. Starting in 1956, the State Department sponsored "Goodwill Ambassador" tours by black jazz musicians such as Dizzy Gillespie and Louis Armstrong, who, it was hoped, would preach the gospel of American freedom to such Third World allies as Iran, Pakistan, Lebanon, and Ghana. By the late 1950s, the Voice of America's jazz program was reaching 80 million listeners, most of whom lived in Communist countries. "American jazz—hot, blues, Dixieland, bebop or rock 'n' roll," wrote the *Baltimore Afro-American* triumphantly, "has at last been publicly acknowledged as the principal asset of American foreign policy." Singer Frank Sinatra argued in the Cold War organ *Western World* that jazz was "the most American commodity we have outside of our wealth and power, which are much less loved. . . . [I]t causes millions of people outside the United States to believe that we are by no means as crude, mysterious, or childish as our foreign policy or its representatives have more often than not caused them to believe."[20]

The fit between American politics and jazz was even elaborated on at the level of aesthetic theory. U.S. Representative Frank Thompson, Jr., wrote in the 1956 Newport Jazz Festival program, "The way jazz works is exactly the way a democracy works. *In democracy, we have complete freedom within a previously and mutually agreed upon framework of laws; in jazz, there is complete freedom within a previously and mutually agreed upon framework of tempo, key, and harmonic progression.*" Thompson sponsored the Goodwill Ambassador legislation, and imagined that the individual "slave-state citizen takes heart" in jazz's "freedom of thought." Likewise the *New York Times* praised jazz as the United States' "Secret Sonic Weapon" and stressed that the music's "contest between musical discipline and individual expression comes close to symbolizing the conditions under which people of an atomic age live."[21]

Hard bop musicians put surprising accents on this Cold War linkage of jazz and American freedom. Along with the civil rights movement, they situated freedom within an arena of lively, unpredictable democratic participation: both musicians and the movement suggested that collective empowerment was indispensable to the advance of individual rights and that such freedom needed to be staked out through public struggles that were anything but tidy. Not coincidentally, for both jazz artists and civil rights workers the pursuit of freedom was set within a spiritual framework, a group of "higher laws" that validated the transgressions of direct action in music or politics. The art of hard bop, like the street choreography of the civil rights movement, was a kind of spiritual dramaturgy—one that tested principles in the heat of instigated group conflict.

Yet the challenge of hard bop and the civil rights movement was far from an unmitigated success in the culture at large, and as a result this collective sense of freedom seems almost counterintuitive now, so much so that we need to take a slight detour to spotlight two ways that it diverges from common uses of the term. First, the freedom of the civil rights movement and hard bop did not revolve around the desire to tap into a set of unbridled urges and give them free rein—what some parts of the counterculture later adopted as their freedom ethic, and what has haunted jazz writing as the myth of absolute improvisation. Hard bop soloists did not fling out their notes ex nihilo in an act of pure creativity or impulse, but rather engaged with the idioms and structures established by their fellow musicians; their freedom was not the freedom of the libertine. Musicologist John Chernoff's remarks about African music's commitment to social participation apply with equal force to hard bop: the music was "improvised in the sense that a musician's responsibility extends from the music itself into the *movement of its social setting*." Likewise, the movement situated freedom within the urgent needs of the republic, not the libidinal economy of Freud: civil rights partisans aimed to participate fully in American life—in schools, parks, public transport, and so on—not simply to indulge their preference for, say, one bathroom over another. As Martin Luther King, Jr., specified, "In speaking of freedom I am not referring to the freedom of a thing called the will." King disparaged how the abstraction of the "will" isolated the question of choice away from "the whole man," who, noted King, "is always subject as well as object." Neither hard bop nor the civil rights movement was driven by the promise of pure subjectivity, even as the music tried to dramatize acts of spontaneous creativity and the movement argued that individual black Americans needed more opportunities in life.[22]

Second—and this is a more subtle point—the jazz and civil rights movement sense of freedom was not primarily "rights talk," the equal right to act as you wished as long as you didn't infringe on the rights of others. Equal entitlement under the law may have been a means to the end of freedom, but it was not the end in and of itself. As intellectual historian Richard King suggests, it was primarily civil rights movement *observers* who were obsessed with the question of equal rights before the law or at the Woolworth's counter. For black people, the state of equality was presumed to be the case; what remained was its realization in the world of action—

that quality more aptly described as "freedom." Meanwhile, for jazz musicians, this sort of equal rights talk was almost counterintuitive to their aesthetic. The dynamism of hard bop depended on the tension and interplay between the members of the group; jazz musicians presumed that their bandmates would press upon their own sense of freedom. When one musician "infringed" on the rhythm or harmonic space of another musician, it was usefully reconceived as a provocation, a license for bold counter-response.[23]

If it was not about unbridled individual expression or equal rights, what *was* the civil rights and hard bop conception of freedom? Most strikingly, their freedom offered a profoundly social alternative to the Cold War conception of an individual freedom to consume or make a private choice. Freedom for them was rooted in collaborative action. This sense of collaboration was compounded by a faith in the virtue of struggle: as Martin Luther King, Jr., attested, "Freedom is won by a struggle against suffering." Whether in music or in the world of political action, their freedom existed in a perpetual state of tension—regulated by the bounds of convention and, just as necessarily, always testing these same limits. Radical sociologist C. Wright Mills converted this sense of freedom into an aphorism, writing in 1959 that freedom went beyond "the chance to do as one pleases"; it meant "the chance to formulate the available choices, to argue over them." While Mills emphasized collective argumentation, the movement tended to recognize a more metaphysical struggle at the heart of political experience. A favorite movement parable, elaborated in sermons and poems, was the story of Jacob wrestling with the angel. Awoken in the middle of the night by God's messenger, Jacob struggles with him until daybreak; finally, after having been lamed in the struggle, he forces the angel to bless him and his people. Movement workers were drawn to the story precisely because it intimated that people must win their blessing even from God, and that they would find their new promised name—Jacob's Israel—only by actively choosing their fate. This reckoning with struggle and its promise was the keynote of the movement, captured in the titles of Martin Luther King, Jr.'s books: *Stride toward Freedom, Why We Can't Wait,* and *Where Do We Go from Here.*[24]

The movement's novel sense of freedom was expressed most clearly in its strategic use of nonviolent, direct action, where civil rights workers reclaimed forbidden public spaces—the middle of the street, the voter registration booth at city hall, the county jail—for collective protest. The segregated South operated according to a rending logic of taboo, where blacks were intimately involved as a subordinate class in the lives of whites at the same time that they were quarantined in public. A black man could lather and shave a white man's face but not share the same drinking fountain; a black domestic could pat biscuits to feed a white family and care for the bodies of white children, but never be allowed to enter through the family's front door. Movement workers exploded these taboos by favoring acts of publicity and refusing en masse to comply with the logic of exclusion. They even reevaluated the Southern jail—the place where whites arguably held the gravest monopoly over black lives—as a space where they might exercise their right to protest unjust laws. The experience of being jailed, for all the terror that it still inspired, became an honorable test of full political participation.

Through these acts of solidarity and commitment, civil rights workers not only demonstrated that they deserved citizenship rights, but also reevaluated what citizenship might be. They suggested that even the most disenfranchised citizens might lead a life of action and participation and might openly contest the conventions of legal, political, and social institutions. The practice of direct action aligned the movement with another way of conceptualizing freedom, a countertradition often designated as "republican" (in reference to the classical republics of Athens and Rome), which linked the exercise of freedom to an expansive sense of political participation and self-rule. One motto of this tradition was Cicero's dictum, approvingly quoted by Martin Luther King, Jr., that "freedom is participation in power."[25] As Richard King has suggested, the movement's spirit dovetailed with republican philosopher Hannah Arendt's prescription for a healthy public sphere as one driven by the practice of political disputation and action. A Jewish emigré from Nazi Germany, Arendt refused to identify the public sphere with the state and its mechanisms of governance. Instead she understood political life as the performances of the people, the rituals of decision-making and influence that they chose, no matter how removed these performances might seem from the official levers of power. The polis, she wrote in *The Human Condition* (1959), was "the organization of the people as it arises out of acting and speaking together . . . no matter where they happened to be."[26]

By seriously revising the NAACP's strategy of legal action, the civil rights movement advanced this Arendtian conception of the public and its freedom. The boycotts, sit-ins, and marches all aimed to compel a reconsideration of her central question—What gives the people their power in a democracy?—and to answer it simply: direct, collective action. Yet it is also true that, in a brilliant and complex strategy, the movement rehabilitated "positive liberty" by orchestrating battles over "negative liberty." While its tactics gave rise to an expanded sense of the public sphere and a fuller vision of civic participation, the movement could also be seen as fighting for sturdy, consumer-based values: the freedom to consume a Coke at Woolworth's, the freedom to choose whichever seat on whatever bus, the freedom to swim in a lake or learn at a school financed by public funds. The movement revealed, against the polarizing rhetoric of the Cold War, that positive and negative liberty were not standoffish enemies in a zero-sum game but might actually be considered compatible. Negative liberties like the freedom to choose a bus seat could only be guaranteed through an active citizenry that fought for its right, in Mills's terms, "to formulate the available choices, to argue over them." As historian Ruth Feldstein observes, "By choosing to consume during sit-ins, and choosing not to consume when sit-ins became boycotts, activists transformed participation in consumer culture into a vehicle for demanding state activism to correct racial inequities."[27]

As an aesthetic, hard bop revitalized another sort of republican countertradition, this one carried through music. Like black music forms more generally, it broke down the presumed antithesis between social control and individual freedom. The music of hard bop did not work from the premise that individuals must compromise themselves within an antagonistic, preordained order, nor did it suggest that a group should be regulated through acts of clear-thinking, top-down orchestration.[28] To go back to the enlistment of jazz in the Cold War: the difficulty with Representative Thompson's description of democracy in jazz was that it threatened to turn the jazz group into a passive community—a society that recognizes laws, then discovers how to be playful and law-abiding—when in fact its "laws" were frequently under dispute during the music's performance. The *New York Times*'s appraisal of jazz as a "Secret Sonic Weapon" tipped in the opposite direction when it traced the power of jazz to its exposition of "musical individuality." The article hammered five times on the term "individual" and its cognates—for instance, in the tortuous expression that "individual Americans" (meaning jazz musicians with individual styles) would continue to lure Europeans to their performances. By understanding jazz's "universal" triumph as the result of its performers' Americanness and individualism, the article failed to appreciate the collaborative and volatile aspects of jazz performance—crucial qualities of its African-American musical aesthetic. Hard bop musicians struck a balance between these two understandings of jazz, one of which leaned to an excessively ordered vision of the music and the other of which underplayed the role of collaboration: these artists sought to mediate social and individual necessity, to bring them into an ever-dynamic state of equilibrium.[29]

The Sound of Self-Mastery

How, though, would musicians be able to achieve this utopian balance of self-expression and solidarity? A not altogether facetious answer is "practice; practice." Because the freedom of hard bop was tied less to the idea of being your own master (at liberty to choose among options, free from coercion) and more to the idea of mastering your self, self-discipline emerged as a key aspect of hard bop aesthetics. Even among jazz artists, hard bop musicians were particularly dramatic in their insistence that freedom and discipline were compatible values and that the extreme pursuit of individuality in matters of improvisation and style depended on the delimitations of a compositional framework, a sensitive handling of group interplay, and the complete control of one's instrument. Paradoxically, the jazz artists who were most fascinated with extending the boundaries of freedom were also fanatics for discipline—a discipline that could take many forms. With Mingus, it came through in his bruising regulation of his Jazz Workshop, where the rhythm section would suddenly shift gears as a test of alertness, and where dawdling improvisers might suddenly find themselves out of phase and possibly on the wrong end of Mingus's fist. With Coltrane, who was famous for his inability to stop practicing his instrument, his discipline had an inwardness, a quality of self-abnegation. His solos, taking their shape from his practice scales and exercises, operated on a similar timetable—which is to say, they had the devotional aspect of someone forever penitent. With Sun Ra—no hard bopper but an important contemporary experimentalist—his discipline suggested military and athletic analogies: he compared his Arkestra rehearsals to the "disciplined training" of the army and the "strict, disciplined rhythms" of a football team. The Arkestra itself lived together in an abstemious commune, where drugs and drinking were forbidden and sexual relations discouraged, especially if they crossed lines of race.[30]

Mingus, Coltrane, and Sun Ra may have been extreme disciplinarians, but their spirit of self-mastery infused all of hard bop: until the postmodern turn in late 1960s jazz, there were very few jazz musicians who embraced, in their lives or their art, the freedom of chance that John Cage's Dada-Zen spirit brought to an avant-garde group like Fluxus, also practicing in Greenwich Village in the early 1960s. The performers who gathered around the Fluxus project looked askance at instrumental mastery and the way it spun an aura around the artist. A typical 1960 "composition" by LaMonte Young called for butterflies to be set loose in the auditorium so that the audience could listen to the beating of their wings. By contrast, hard bop musicians inculcated a strict sense of craft and continued to make the subjectivity of the artist the source of a performance's expressive interest. When and if they came to Zen or other kinds of self-loss, it was through the Protestant work ethic and an often mystical devotion to the higher laws that bound together music, religion, and mathematics.[31]

Because discipline and self-mastery were linked to the idea of self-perfection—the idea of one's self at its best—all this hard work forced an even more difficult ethical question: What were the moral principles, beyond the laws of this world, that gave meaning to this effort? Hard bop musicians did not necessarily produce systematic answers to this question, but they were consistently drawn to the question itself, meditating on how freedom might work through the fulfillment of higher laws—laws that governed the world on a global level, as well as the jazz group on a local level. Like Martin Luther King, Jr., and a long line of mystics, many held that freedom thrived when individuals acted in accordance with the deeper workings of a shared, collective spirit. As if to prove this point, when hard bop artists were inspired by the story of black emancipation to compose extended works on the theme, they always put individual acts of improvisational testifying within a framework of collective deliverance. Programmatic works like Oscar Brown, Jr., and Max Roach's *Freedom Now Suite*, Oliver Nelson's *Afro-American Sketches*, Mingus's *The Black Saint and the Sinner Lady*, and Randy Weston's *Uhuru Africa* ("Uhuru" being Swahili for freedom) ranged in length from thirty to forty minutes in execution, bursting out of the confines of both the jazz single and the extended jam. Freedom in these works meant simultaneously extending musical structure and improvisational scope. The trick was to heighten the epic compositional ambition of the music—conveyed in *Afro-American Sketches'* "Freedom Dance," for instance, by an ingenious interweaving of themes earlier identified with yearning and disillusionment—while allowing each member of the group to shape the piece's spirit through their turns in the ensemble. It is striking that the story of the freedom movement did not inspire, say, solo meditations on the new horizons opened up to individual blacks. Rather, it led jazz musicians to imagine pieces that were heroic in intent but necessarily collaborative, compositions that modeled the quest for liberation as a collective journey toward a more uplifting, but also more indeterminate, endpoint.[32]

The impulse to collaborate toward freedom, then, was one with a questing impulse to understand the foundations beneath the foundations. "Scratch any musician," jazz scholar John Szwed has said, "and you find a crypto-Pythagorean." Szwed's adage applies with particular force to jazz artists like Mingus, Coltrane, Sun Ra, and composer-arranger George Russell, whose mysticism forcefully shaped the way that these artists impressed gospel music and the blues in the service of their experimental music. Russell's treatise *The Lydian Chromatic Concept of Tonal Organization*, circulated originally in 1953, is a perfect instance of this generative mysticism. A new approach to harmony, the "Lydian concept" was both an all-encompassing total system and a license for performers to do whatever they desired. "The scope of the Lydian Chromatic Concept," Russell wrote, "is as large as all of the music that has been written or that could be written. . . . It is an organization of all the tonal resources offered by equal temperament. It is free of rules, laws, and biases. There are no wrong notes or wrong progressions. It does not attempt to legislate or dictate, but merely to make the composer or improviser aware of the tonal and non-tonal resources of the chromatic scale." Russell's treatise was both a denial of freedom—there was no escape from the Lydian mode—and the unveiling of a new set of harmonic ethics that liberated the improviser from notions of right and wrong. Bridging theosophy and musicology, it led jazz improvisers to the simultaneous realization that they were always enmeshed in the system and that this system was the very guarantor of their freedom—a fair analogue to the ethical world of Martin Luther King, which also was governed by inescapable rules that ennobled the pursuit of freedom.

On a more down-to-earth level, Russell's Lydian system suggested the new approach to harmony that would underlie so many "modal jazz" pieces of the 1960s. Instead of seeing jazz songs as cycling between harmonic irresolution and resolution, the Lydian system implied that harmonies were always already resolved; such a solid-state view gave soloists permission to mix vertical and linear strategies of improvising, to meet the deadline of a background chord or to float on top of the chord as they so desired. With a bold theoretical leap, *The Lydian Chromatic Concept* claimed as normative what had previously been deemed impermissible. Six years after the *Concept's* original publication, Miles Davis's *Kind of Blue* perfectly illustrated its hypothesis that static background harmonies could free the soloist to a new errancy and performed a similar magic trick, converting the daring of modal jazz into the stuff of the inevitable.[33]

Of course most jazz artists expressed their devotion to higher laws not by composing musicological treatises like *The Lydian Chromatic Concept* but by composing music itself—and, more specifically, by creating music that seemed to be infused with the spirit of the blues and the black church. This was hard bop's signature as a genre: its translation of a "roots feeling," often identified with the sanctified ambience of the Holiness-Pentecostal church, onto the contemporary instrumentation of the small jazz combo. Hard bop was devoted to "feelin' the spirit," as guitarist Grant Green named his 1962 album of jazz-inflected Negro spirituals. The black church was considered the place where the "higher laws" were experienced at their greatest intensity, so hard bop sought sophisticated ways to mimic the experience of worshippers, the emotional spontaneity of spirit possession, and the sense of fellowship that enabled it. Strikingly, hard bop musicians turned not to the black church in toto but to the Holiness line in particular as a model for their aesthetic practice. Because they were interested in making jazz over as roots music, they looked to those areas of the black church that were considered closest to African and slave religious practices and furthest from the soul-deadening aspects of contemporary life. With its heavy use of music in worship and with its congregations of poor and working-class folk, the Holiness church was much more attractive than, say, the Methodist or even the straight Baptist tradition—this despite the fact that many jazz musicians themselves had personal roots in Methodist or Baptist churches.[34]

The cases of trumpeter Donald Byrd and Charles Mingus are illustrative here, suggesting some of the complicated ways that hard bop musicians reevaluated their own past as they reclaimed a new set of influences for their music. Byrd was not only raised in the Methodist church but raised in his *father's* Methodist church as the preacher's son. He was one of the most highly educated of hard bop musicians, attending the Manhattan School of Music in the 1950s and pursuing a doctorate in music education from Columbia University in the 1960s. Yet Byrd's music consistently tipped its hat to the sanctified church and its aesthetic of emotional intensity and release, through early 1960s recordings like "Amen," "Hush," and "Pentecostal Feeling" and through the popular 1963 album *A New Perspective,* whose five pieces aimed to be a "modern hymnal" scored for eight voices and a septet. *A New Perspective* featured "Elijah," a portrait of his minister father—but even here the piece did not try to emulate the Methodist hymnal, which Byrd recalled as "based on English tunes and Lutheran adaptations of drinking songs and that sort of thing." Rather, it took inspiration from the moments when "older visiting ministers came through Detroit" and the congregation "would abandon the formal hymnal and really go into the traditional, Southern spirituals that were first sung during slavery." Likewise, many of Mingus's most acclaimed pieces, from "Haitian Fight Song" to "Better Get It in Your Soul" and "Wednesday Night Prayer Meeting," drew on his recollection of trips to local Holiness churches in the company of his stepmother or his friend Britt Woodman. Yet the Holiness church had given Mingus only a small fraction of his religious experience growing up in Watts. Throughout his childhood, he had been a regular Sunday worshipper with his parents at a local African Methodist Episcopal church and had rarely crossed over to the less "respectable" Holiness denominations.

(His stepmother started attending other churches after Mingus's father took up with a member of the original church's choir.) Hard boppers like Byrd and Mingus mastered their craft, schooled themselves in all sorts of musical practices, and then and only then did they start emulating the spirit-possession and self-abandonment at the heart of Pentecostal worship.[35]

When jazz started "going to church," the music was transformed in two related ways. First, it became more dynamic and immediate: the practice of call and response, a key feature of black sermons, gospel, and the blues, came to the fore as an operational principle behind the music. Hard bop ensembles privileged a kind of loose, double-jointed interplay—an interplay popularized in the "blowing sessions" that were often typical of hard bop studio recordings, and an interplay that gave musicians room to roam in the extremely sophisticated compositions of figures such as Mingus, Benny Golson, and Wayne Shorter. Second, it became more intense: jazz opened itself to the sounds of rage, abandon, and ecstasy, even as it usually laced these emotions with a certain savvy or willfulness. Hard boppers exacerbated the vocal quality of their timbre, so that the instruments seemed to be involved in conversations, disputations, or even the glossolalia of spirit baptism. These artists chose to simplify and fortify the blues mode rather than complicate it as the beboppers had done: their blues were often set to a celebratory, toe-tapping backbeat (think Horace Silver's "The Preacher," Art Blakey's "Blues March," or Lee Morgan's "The Sidewinder") or, at the other tonal extreme, keyed to a series of minor chords that pulsed with a kind of forbidding energy. More generally, through choices of arrangement, rhythm, and song form, hard bop musicians heightened the melodrama and improvisational urgency within their performances. All these tendencies in hard bop separated its musicians from the early 1950s "cool school," whose music often toyed with the ironies of a muted sensibility and preferred to sizzle rather than combust.

We can deepen these general observations (and complicate the easy contrast between cool jazz and hard bop) by looking again at Mingus's "Haitian Fight Song." Mingus described the fight song's bass solo, perhaps the most famous bass solo in 1950s jazz, as a "deeply concentrated" act of moral witness, a call put out in hope of a sympathetic response: "I can't play it right unless I'm thinking about prejudice and hate and persecution, and how unfair it is. There's sadness and cries in it, but also determination. And it usually ends with my feeling: 'I told them! I hope somebody heard me.'" In "Haitian Fight Song," though, call and response is more than a matter of artistic aspiration, more than the hope that "somebody heard me." It is the modus operandi of the entire piece, beginning with Mingus's opening cadenza and the way that the players in the Workshop enter one by one in response to his bass's calisthenic eight-bar riff.

The piece's call-and-response dynamic is even more literal than usual in hard bop: the different Workshop players swap their melodies, quoting particular motifs back and forth with the insistence of a congregation stuck on a line from the gospel. Mingus had previously experimented much with the sort of contrapuntal exercises that marked cool jazz: on his album *Mingus at the Bohemia,* for instance, he combined the melodies of "September in the Rain" and "Tenderly" into "Septemberly," and fused "All the Things You Are" and the "Prelude In C# Minor" into "All the Things You C#." In "Haitian Fight Song," the contrapuntal melodies are less confined and more genuinely the basis for interaction, interjection, and the kind of thematic improvisation identified in the late 1950s with tenor saxophonist Sonny Rollins. Trombonist Jimmy Knepper comes into the piece by playing the piece's two motifs—one a salute, the other a spitfire triplet blast—and saxophonist Shafi Hadi follows by taking up the salute, playing it in alternation with Knepper's triplet figure. Then in the body of the performance, the different members of the Workshop quote from these two motifs in their solos, glossing the two melodies as they deliver their interpretation of the minor blues. A triplet fill by Dannie Richmond on drums inspires Hadi to consider the triplet figure himself; and at the end of his bass solo, Mingus breaks up the momentum of his eight-bar riff by quoting the triplet motif in the highest register of his bass—a gesture that is equal parts non sequitur and role-defying bluster. The piece ends by recapitulating its call-and-response opening. Once again, it builds from the individual bass riff to the overpowering assertiveness of the collective ensemble, with Mingus's scream adding the final layer of intensity.[36]

"Haitian Fight Song" gives us an exposition in music of the ethics behind call-and-response worship. It suggests that individuals need a collective in order to hear themselves, to express themselves fully; conversely, it also demonstrates how the redemption of the many is attained through the trials of the few and the one. The piece is less an existential drama than a sacramental one: the endpoint of its struggle is not self-enclosed mastery but collective deliverance. In this context, Mingus's scream is remarkable for how it combines strength and vulnerability, his desire to make himself heard and his urgent need for someone, somewhere, to scream back. Like much of hard bop, "Haitian Fight Song" both celebrates and worries the idea of freedom—and so models a community alive in its pursuit.

PART ONE

A New Intellectual Vernacular

1

BIRTH OF THE COOL

The Early Career
of the Hipster

In "But I Was Cool," one of the savviest send-ups of the late 1950s hipster vogue, singer Oscar Brown, Jr., is caught in a spiral of downward mobility that is more like a free fall. Over the course of three slinky soul-jazz verses, his wife deserts him; he gets drunk and totals his car; he's picked up by the police and sentenced to prison; and, last but not least, he tries to shoot his wife with a shotgun, but—in a cruel and fitting bumble—he pegs his trusty hound dog instead. The drama of the song, though, comes less from the misfortune itself and more from the singer's ridiculous attempt to cope with his misfortune through the hipster's "golden rule": "Whatever happens, don't blow your cool." At every chorus, after suffering the latest sling and arrow of outrageous fortune, Brown erupts into long howls of hilarious grief—"SHEEEEEEEAAAAH! AIEEEEEEE! HUH-AH-HAHAHA!"—only to cut himself off with the swift avowal "But I was cool." Exploding the cool pose for the sake of humor, the song suggests how absurd it is to deny suffering, how self-defeating it is to pretend that self-control can annihilate the pain of love lost. The tune ends, comically, with the hipster insisting as the authorities carry him away, "Be cool! Lay cool! Stay cool! Keep cool!"— a hysterical and terminal act of bravado.[1]

By the time that he started appearing regularly on national television with songs like "But I Was Cool," Oscar Brown was only one of many artists and intellectuals who took up, and took on, the charms of the hipster. The late fifties and early sixties were the moment of hip's ascent from the

Fingers snapping, toes tapping: Along with such figures as comedian Lenny Bruce, trumpeter Miles Davis, and novelist Jack
Kerouac, singer-songwriter Oscar Brown, Jr., came to be
identified with the 'hip' aesthetic of the late 1950s and early
1960s. A mercurial performer, onstage Brown would adopt personas—a stooped ghetto peddler with his pushcart, an auctioneer on a slave block, a convict breaking rocks on a chain gang, a
customer spellbound by his waitress's hips—and then shed
them in quick order. (Courtesy of Michael Ochs Archives)

underground to the mainstream, the moment when hipsters suddenly started making grand entrances in venues of high, low, and middlebrow culture. In intellectual journals such as *Dissent* and *Partisan Review*, Norman Mailer's "White Negro" and James Baldwin's jazz-shaped characters were at the center of debates over the possibility of interracial alliances and over the efficacy of nonviolent versus violent means of protest. In nightclubs Lenny Bruce perfected his own brand of "sick" stand-up humor, riffing over jazz while describing, say, his sexual attraction to a horse—and was arrested for offenses against public decency. Beat writers Jack Kerouac and Allen Ginsberg preached the joys of nonconformity in surprisingly popular fiction and verse, while their easy-to-mock doppelganger, the TV character Maynard G. Krebs, popped up on the primetime *Dobie Gillis* show with his snapping fingers, goatee, beret, and befuddled attempt at cool. In the space of four days in November 1959, for example, a TV viewer might have been treated to a hipster triple feature: Kerouac was a guest on Steve Allen's show on Monday, *Dobie Gillis* played on Tuesday, and two days later actor-director John Cassavetes starred in *Johnny Staccato* as a private eye who dabbled as a jazz pianist in a MacDougal Street joint. In the field of jazz, popular black musicians Cannonball Adderley and Ramsey Lewis tapped into the hipster's appeal with tunes like "Jive Samba" and "The In Crowd," while the appeal of Miles Davis was clearly tied to the way he both courted respectability (those elegant suits, the lush bachelor-pad collaborations with Gil Evans) and flouted it by turning his back to the audience, in more ways than one.[2]

As these examples suggest, jazz culture was the crucial source of the hip aesthetic, although the idiom of "cool" soon spread far beyond the confines of the jazz world. The figure of the hipster was a kind of cultural putty, to be shaped according to the aims of its handler. Outside of the consensus view that the hipster was male—a key, if often unnoticed, baseline for all speculations about the meaning of "hip"—few could agree on whether he was suave or icy, sly or clueless, black or white or both. At its most reductive, "hip" could mean simply the affectation of individuality. A 1958 Jules Feiffer cartoon, part of his "Hip World" series, registered early on this skepticism about what "hip" signified. In it, a grumpy middle-aged man tries to mimic a finger-snapping beatnik, wondering why he can't grow his sideburns or bring himself to enjoy jazz. The punch line is an ironic jab at the faddishness of outsiderhood: "What I wouldn't give," says the grump, "to be a non-conformist like all those others."[3]

Feiffer's middle-aged curmudgeon was obviously not supposed to be the chief audience for the hip aesthetic, but the cartoon suggested how "hip" would become something much more than an attribute of the jazz world.

In *The Conquest of Cool,* a groundbreaking history of the relationship between advertising style and the ethos of the counterculture, Thomas Frank has described hip as nothing less than "the public philosophy of the age of flexible accumulation"—by which he means that most acts of consumption are understood now as acts of individuality, an individuality colored by the rebelliousness of "cool" and "hip." Like Feiffer's grouch, the business community may not have seemed to be the intended audience of Lenny Bruce, Allen Ginsberg, or Miles Davis, but it was a very quick study. By the end of the 1960s, "hip" had moved from a form of African-American and bohemian dissent to become the very language of the advertising world, which took hip's promise of authenticity, liberation, and rebellion and attached it to the act of enjoying whatever was on sale at the moment. "Hip consumerism" became, in Frank's compelling interpretation, "a cultural perpetual motion machine in which disgust with the falseness, shoddiness, and everyday oppressions of consumer society could be enlisted to drive the ever-accelerating wheels of consumption."[4]

But here we are getting ahead of ourselves. This chapter and the next tell the prehistory of this complex (and by some lights unholy) marriage of the counterculture and the business world—not to summon up the 1940s and 1950s as a golden age of hip, an age before the co-optation of the style, but rather to understand some of the very local battles fought over the figure of the hipster at this formative stage in the history of cool. The story of the hip aesthetic—the attempts to create compelling and "cool" music and art, the roiling debates over who could aspire to hipness and whether hipness was a promising form of dissent or the trivialization of it—is a story first about how black Americans understood their place on the margins of American life, the value of this outsiderhood, and its challenges. Being hip, as cultural historian Andrew Ross has noted, began with a kind of refusal, a negotiated relation to black culture and mass culture that most often designated the latter as white, middlebrow, and deadeningly devoid of provocation. But hipsterism was more than a defiant attitude struck against mass culture in line with sociological worries about the soul-crushing pressures of conformity. Hipsters did not simply recoil from the culture at large but tried to assimilate, sometimes in a ragtag fashion, its most useful elements. "Hip" was a new vernacular, a new way of speaking and moving—and it offered the promise of a new way of living. As tough-minded as a hustler, as flamboyant as a dandy, the hipster reworked the dilemmas of urban manhood into the sensational art form that was his own life.[5]

The appeal of this aesthetic was tied to two of the most consequential phenomena of the postwar period: first, the public acts of African-American defiance that galvanized the civil rights movement; and second,

A NEW INTELLECTUAL VERNACULAR

the widespread concern with the power of social norms—everything that came together in that very 1950s word "conformity." In the drama that was the Movement, black Americans increasingly refused to wear the Sambo mask, the black face that smiled in the face of subordination. Their acts of organized noncooperation—boycotts, marches, sit-ins, freedom rides— disrupted the conventional expectations that white people had attached to the public selves of black people, rarely with their full consent. The hipster's cool pose was part of this Movement-related social dissonance, a posture to the world that defied easy interpretation and so begged to be deciphered. While this pose may not have been a postwar invention, it was a relatively new, and usually urban, form of emotional masking developed in response to the sorts of anonymous encounters that were meant to "put you in your place." The hipster was in some sense the civil rights movement's less charitable double, the face of a defiance that did not unconditionally turn the other cheek. He plugged into long-running debates in the black community about whether social protest should take direct or more evasive forms, whether it should be easily legible in its aims or should adopt the slyness of the trickster.[6]

The second trend—the questioning of conformity—had led, by the late fifties, to a burgeoning genre of "social problem" literature, which weighed how cultural norms imprisoned the individual psyche. The genre had an early start in Dwight Macdonald's writings on mass culture, David Riesman's *The Lonely Crowd* (1950), and C. Wright Mills's *White Collar* (1951), but crested later with works like William Whyte's *The Organization Man* (1956), Vance Packard's *The Status Seekers* (1959), Paul Goodman's *Growing Up Absurd* (1960), and Betty Friedan's *The Feminine Mystique* (1963). All these works shared a suspicion that Americans had, in historian Wilfred McClay's words, "succumbed to a collectivism of the mind, a dangerous susceptibility to the mass appeals of advertising and media, a deification of organizational life, and a social ethic that . . . enshrined as the American Way the bland and anxious conformism of the new white-collar personality-selling occupations." By the end of the 1950s, serious doubts about the suburbanization of American life were being regularly aired, as "the man in the grey flannel suit" began to seem horribly colorless and "the crack in the picture window" became a major cultural faultline.[7]

The hipster was born, we might say, at the crossroads—at the place where the civil rights movement met these works of social criticism. He seemed to have some crucial, if puzzling, answers for those seeking to understand the newest forms of political dissent and to translate cultural critique into subcultural practice. For leftist intellectuals who prized cultural engagement, the hipster was a paragon of improvisatory existential action—someone who lived by his wits and not by cultural convention, and who took inspiration from an art form (jazz) that was populist but not popular. At the same time, for those looking to criticize the Cold War domestic ideal, the hipster offered a model of tough urban manhood and gave a powerful counterimage to the suburban dad minding his barbecue and commuting dutifully to work. It was no coincidence that *Playboy* magazine was founded just as the hipster was breaking through to the culture at large, nor was it surprising that the magazine became a key sponsor of jazz, building a nationwide circuit of music festivals starting in this period.[8]

Much of the jazz audience in the late 1950s came from this *Playboy* generation of young men, working at new white-collar professions or priming themselves for such jobs. A 1960 *Down Beat* questionnaire discovered that an astonishing 92 percent of the jazz magazine's readers were men; that the reader's average age was twenty-eight, with very few middle-aged men (less than 4 percent over fifty); and that most of the readers (65 percent) fell into five job categories: office worker, student (high school and college), musician, salesman, and engineer. The *Down Beat* readership thus fell largely into the demographic category addressed by *The Lonely Crowd, The Status Seekers,* and *Growing Up Absurd*—new men of the service economy, working for a salary but aspiring to a life that was not batch-processed. The struggle to be hip, for some *Down Beat* readers at least, meant imagining how they might break out of their white-collar blues by redefining their sense of manhood, how they might trade in their salary for the more elusive bits of cultural capital to be found in the black community. Although intellectuals turned to the hipster partly to distance themselves from the labor metaphysic of the 1930s Popular Front, the hipster's appeal was tied to new kinds of working conditions, namely the expansion of the clerical and service professions in America's postindustrial economy.[9]

This chapter traces the first arc in the hipster's career, starting with his origins in the swing and bebop eras, when entertainers and DJs began to experiment with jive and its playful ironies. It examines Mezz Mezzrow and Bernard Wolfe's *Really the Blues* (1946), the first "white Negro" biography and a brilliantly cockeyed tale of the slumming Jew. I then turn to the challenge that bebop's more cryptic "coolness" posed to postwar intellectuals, who conceived of themselves as the nation's specialists in alienation and yet were puzzled by how jazz hipsters seemed to express this quality. Lastly, I look at two almost diametrically opposed explorations of the cool aesthetic: Jack Kerouac's *On the Road* and Miles Davis's *Birth of the Cool.* The differences between *On the Road* and *Birth of the Cool* suggest the different values that black and white artists imported into the idiom of cool in the late 1940s, as well as the different battles they waged in their art.

Jive Talking: Hip Onstage and on the Airwaves

The hipster from the beginning was tied to the idiolect of jive, the code language that was often offered as the proof of streetwise credentials. At least two dictionaries of jive, Cab Calloway's *Hepster's Dictionary* (1938) and *Dan Burley's Original Handbook of Harlem Jive* (1944), were published to popularize the lingo, the latter featuring a quasi-scholarly introduction that theorized jive back to "revolutionary times when it was necessary for the Negro to speak, sing, and even think in a kind of code." By virtue of their appearance, though, these dictionaries signaled a shift away from such strategies of secrecy. They were designed to commercialize the dialect that was gibberish to untrained ears, to make a buck by bridging the gap. Burley—a popular columnist for the *New York Amsterdam News,* a paper that served the black community—was crossing over; later he would act as a bop-friendly DJ for New York radio station WWRL. Calloway followed up his dictionary with *Professor Cab Calloway's Swinginformation Bureau* (1939), which promoted the jazz musician as a "new hero in public life," "a happy-go-lucky artist who [gives] his entire life to his music." Readers were directed to become "interheptuals" entitled to a "catskin hiploma" by deciphering samples of jive and quizzing themselves on industry trivia like the nicknames of jazz musicians. The adjective "happy-go-lucky" intimated that there were no deep secrets buried within the hipster's act, nothing the dedicated "interheptual" would have trouble picking up. Jive for Burley and Calloway had evolved from the secret language of the slave South into the colorful patter of the Harlem street corner, but it would not remain there, either. It was designed to become the adopted tongue of the jazz aficionado, the swing jitterbug.[10]

By far the most renowned ambassador of hip was Calloway, the "Professor of Jive" who led perhaps the most popular black band of the swing era. A crack unit with some of the most complicated jazz charts in the business, Calloway's band held down a long-term residency at Harlem's Cotton Club through the 1930s, crisscrossed the nation on a regular basis after 1931, starred in ten Hollywood vehicles, and at one point was featured three nights a week on national radio. A crisp and strong tenor with an astounding vocal range, Calloway himself ruled with an iron fist and a silky touch: he played the sporting man as virtuoso, an amalgam of flash and discipline. At the same time that he directed his band with a drillmaster's preci-

The hipster as extrovert: In the 1930s and 1940s, bandleader Cab Calloway was the most renowned ambassador of hip. He played the sporting man as virtuoso, an amalgam of flash and discipline. Here he is pictured in one of his signature outfits—white tie with tails—and with the gleaming smile of the crowd-pleaser. (Courtesy of Michael Ochs Archives)

sion, Calloway beguiled the crowd in flamboyant garb—white tie and tails in the 1930s, and a sombrero-sized fedora and a wide-shouldered zoot suit in the 1940s, purchased for $185 supposedly before the wartime material rationing orders had been introduced. Smiling toothily and flipping his hair, he was given to oversized gestures that turned his bandstand into a striking tableau. Often he closed his songs on an extended high note, one arm raised to the ceiling and the other pointing to the floor, his body arched with tense ecstasy. At least at the Cotton Club, such virtuosity was framed by scenery that put Calloway and his band back in the mythic Old South—and that allowed the white patrons of the Cotton Club to delight in the old-time comforts of minstrelsy alongside the up-to-date showmanship of Calloway's band. "The whole set was like a sleepy-time down South during slavery," Calloway remembered, "[and] the idea was to make whites who came feel like they were being catered to and entertained by black slaves." Blacks might be virtuosos at the Cotton Club, it seems, but only if they invested some of the cultural capital that they accrued in a more familiar tale of mammies, sambos, and high-yaller gals.[11]

Calloway's greatest crossover success, however, came through a distinctly Northern and urban tale, one that played on the power of jive and brought his listeners into palpable contact with it. "Minnie the Moocher" became Calloway's signature tune with white audiences, one of several Calloway touchstones, like "Boo-wah Boo-wah," that parlayed the nonsense syllables of scat into the memorable material of a song's refrain. On the call-and-response chorus of "Minnie," Calloway traded a famous set of scat syllables—"Hi-de-hi-de-hi-de-ho," "Hee-dee-hee-dee-hee-dee-hee"—with his band and audience, while the band hung steady on an E-minor vamp. Calloway used the language of jive to connect with his band and, in turn, his audience, who enthusiastically echoed his impromptu scats in live performances. While the song exoticized those drug-using Manhattanites who "kicked the gong around" in Chinatown, it also encouraged its audiences to join in its nonsense-loving fun.[12]

Although "Minnie the Moocher" was far from the first hit song to get its charge from a foreign-sounding refrain—Al Jolson's "Yaaka Hula Hickey Dula" (1916) springs to mind—it juiced up its idiom with a newly sensational story of drug use and seduction. The strange magic of "Minnie the Moocher" comes from how it uses the infectiousness of Calloway's scat to mimic, and comment on, the addictiveness of getting high through music, love, and drugs. A "red-hot hootchie-cootcher" with a "heart as big as a whale," Minnie is someone caught up in a chain of desire; in her search for the "King of Swing," she falls for a man who is "tokey" and who leads her instead to the dens of Chinatown. The song, like jive itself, points in two directions at once. It could be heard as a mournful lament for a fallen woman—an understanding reinforced by its dour pace and stomping emphasis on the E-minor chord—or it could be heard as a siren call itself, one that might lead other Minnies to fall for another "King of Swing," this time by the name of Calloway. In a version recorded in 1942, Minnie never suffers a fall and never gets jilted. The last verse has her lounging in a townhouse, eating twelve-course meals and counting Smokey's millions—not too shabby for a moocher who goes tokey.[13]

In the mid-1940s, Calloway's hip persona was reprised in the sensational small combo acts of Henry "the Hipster" Gibson and Slim Gailliard. Mislabeled "the big-wig of be-bop" by *Time* and known otherwise as the "Man from Another Planet," Gibson helped translate black subculture for a mainstream audience through a repertoire that tipped its hat to the legacy of Fats Waller. Born Harry Raab, he became the Hipster when he dropped the Jewish surname and patented a unique performance style—one that involved, according to one account, "slamming out a rumbling boogie and mugging at the audience like a maniac, eyes rolling, eyebrows wiggling, fingers flying, suddenly jumping up and smacking the ivories with his elbows when he took a notion." Gibson's most notorious number, "Who Put the Benzedrine in Mrs. Murphy's Ovaltine?," was a sort of sequel to Calloway's "Minnie the Moocher": like "Minnie," it was driven by a hip narrator who straddled the line between the drug-addled and the straight. Wondering wryly about the effects of narcotics on "squares," it allowed its audience both to laugh at drug culture and to sample its mind-altering benefits.[14]

Slim Gailliard was a more substantial successor to Calloway, an artist whose equal-opportunity spirit of satire led him to develop his own pan-ethnic R&B repertoire. A fine guitarist and a fantastic showman, Gailliard pared down Calloway's big band to a jump combo while highlighting the nonsensical and ethnic elements within jive. His *Vout Dictionary*, an offspring of Calloway's *Hepster's Dictionary,* turned any phrase into a Pig Latin–like chain of "oroonies." In performance, he was apt to parody Yiddish ("Mishugena Mambo"), Arabic ("Yip Roc Heresi") and Japanese ("Gomen Nasai"), as well as street-corner and barnyard slang ("Cement Mixer," "Chicken Rhythm"). While Gailliard did share the stage with Charlie Parker and Dizzy Gillespie, and while his musical partner, Slam Stewart, recorded often with Gillespie, his own music had little of bebop's melodic discontinuity, fast tempos, or harmonic flair. Yet perhaps for this very reason—Gailliard's music could be pigeonholed more easily than the work of Parker or Gillespie—the guitarist was identified as an icon of bebop: *Life* magazine's first coverage of postwar jazz consisted of a photo essay on Gailliard's white fans, two hundred college men and women who were self-described "Voutians." In *Life*'s photo shoot, the white students at Tulane and Sophie Newcomb College married bebop to two collegiate rituals, the sock hop and the school play. The first panels showed a couple performing a series of acrobatic dance steps that conveyed little physical intimacy and had names like "Put it in your pocket but don't rocket." Another series of

A NEW INTELLECTUAL VERNACULAR

photos illustrated a jive version of *Romeo and Juliet* with a disconsolate Romeo soliloquizing on his wounded lover, "Woe is me, chick, thou hast cut out right on our wedding night." This all-white collegiate jive was understood by *Life* as good-natured parody—done in the spirit of youthful hijinks, with no sense of racial taboo busting. If bebop could find its most faithful expression in the extracurricular escapades of white New Orleans undergraduates, the article seemed to imply, then jive might simply be a low-risk social lubricant for the young; and the zoot suit, which had incited race riots during wartime, could be understood as a kind of sartorial goof. The challenge of bebop, and the largely black subculture that gave birth to it, would not be aired in the publishing empire of Henry Luce.[15]

The jive of Calloway, Gibson, and Gailliard was exported in the late forties to an even larger mass audience by a pack of hep-talking DJs—some white, some black—who found a new niche in urban locales across the country. Between 1946 and 1954, the number of small and independent radio stations mushroomed as the FCC actively broke up the domination of radio by newspaper publishers. With their number tripling from 948 to 2,824, AM radio stations became increasingly independent in their tastes, giving more play to the four hundred recording companies that had been founded in the 1940s. The chief pitchman in this effort, establishing intimacy with listeners and courting their loyalty to his station, was the disc jockey, a startling new personality of the postwar era. While swing-era emcees spoke a plummy "announcer speak" and maintained a calculated, genteel distance from their listeners, postwar radio DJs cultivated a sense of loose familiarity. Trying to establish a cult of their own personality, they adopted nicknames like Hot Rod, Bear Cat, Wolfman, and Moondog; they established an ongoing imaginary dialogue with listeners "out there," using the second-person address; and they fielded listener phone calls and played requests.[16]

Jive was the language of this new invisible intimacy. Participating in a racial ventriloquism that descended from the minstrel show but had several new kinks, white listeners bonded with black DJs, black listeners bonded with white DJs, and—most commonly, as R&B segued into rock 'n' roll—white listeners bonded with white DJs like Alan Freed, who specialized in "talking black." In every part of the United States, DJs brought irreverent black rapping and rhyming games into their dialogue with listeners (much of which centered around promotions of their own show or of the products advertised on it). In Austin, Texas, Albert Lavada Durst—better known as Dr. Hepcat—became the city's first black DJ in 1947 and soon found fame for his *Rosewood Ramble,* a show where he peppered R&B, jazz, and blues music with a surreal, rhyming patter perfected in an earlier career as a Negro League announcer. In New Orleans, white-owned radio stations refused to hire a black DJ, but one station did hire Vernon Winslow, a black journalist and professor, to teach its DJs the art of jive and to write and direct a show called *Jam, Jive, and Gumbo*, which had a black-sounding DJ nicknamed Poppa Stoppa. Once in the door, Winslow broke the larger barrier at New Orleans's WJMR: a few years later, in 1949, he landed his own show as "Doctor Daddy-O" and remained on the air until the 1980s.[17]

After nearly a million black southerners migrated to the North during World War II in search of factory work, the airwaves of cities such as Chicago and New York were thick with the banter of jive. In Chicago, Holmes "Daddy-O" Daylie, after serving as bartender of the El Grotto Supper Club, became an announcer for the club's radio show in 1948. His bartending gig was then subsumed by a thirty-nine-year career as one of Chicago's most prominent black radio personalities, a DJ who addressed the programming abyss between the white pop favored on the radio and the R&B audience on the South Side. In New York, meanwhile, Al "Jazzbeaux" Collins found favor by announcing his jazz show from an imaginary Purple Grotto, a candlelit bohemian underground where Collins traded quips and shucked jive with Harrison, the purple Tasmanian owl. Formerly a bluegrass DJ in West Virginia, Collins became the lovable beatnik of national radio in the late fifties—a more knowing version of *Dobie Gillis*'s Maynard G. Krebs. Collins even scored a hit record of sorts with Steve Allen's *Bop Fables* (1955), which brought Grimm's fairy tales into the world of the hipster, updating the archaic with touches of the faddish. In the Allen-reworked fable "Crazy Red Riding Hood," the wolf sneaks into the grandmother's cottage by posing as a Western Union deliveryman with free tickets for Dizzy at Birdland; "Crazy" herself is a dotty gal with an affection for beatnik clichés like "Real gone, daddy."[18]

All told, the efforts of radio pioneers such as Durst, Winslow, Daylie, and Collins helped spread the gospel of jive far from its origins in black urban crucibles like Harlem and Chicago's South Side. They reached out to home listeners, who mimicked the DJs' speech patterns as the rhythm of cool, even as they uprooted jive from its base in drug culture. Later supplemented by a wave of white rock 'n' roll DJs, they turned the airwaves into a carnivalesque session where black urbanity crossed over to listeners of all colors.[19]

The First White Negro: Mezz Mezzrow, Bebop, and the Art of Signifying

While jive was establishing itself on the air, it was also making a spectacular debut in the more hallowed sphere of literary production, where it retained

A NEW INTELLECTUAL VERNACULAR

its seriousness of purpose and its connection to the underworld. The literary history of the white Negro is justly traced back to Mezz Mezzrow and Bernard Wolfe's *Really the Blues,* published by Random House in 1946 and touted in promotional ads as "an upside down success story," the story of a man who "crossed the color line, *backwards.*"[20] The book is an autobiography, rich in invention, of a crime-savvy Jewish boy whose career as a jazz clarinetist takes him on a journey of racial transformation. Published as bebop was emerging as a music of studied dissonance and athletic improvisation, *Really the Blues* charts the progress of an older musical generation, the white "Austin High Gang," who emerged from a Chicago suburb in the late 1920s and championed New Orleans combo jazz through the swing era and into the forties.

Although Mezzrow became something of a musical reactionary—"modern jazz," he said, was "no more jazz than a mixture of Chinese and English is good French"—he was also a countercultural pioneer who refashioned the story of the slumming bohemian. The book's influence in the postwar period—on the Beats, the jazz audience, and American culture more generally—should not be underestimated. Poet Allen Ginsberg testified that the experience of reading the book, at Columbia University's bookstore in the mid-forties, was for him "the first signal into white culture of the underground black, hip culture that preexisted before my own generation." While Ginsberg was led by the book into a realm of "angelheaded hipsters" and "hot cooking pederasty," the book had other buried lessons and other sorts of reception, too. In December 1953, NBC aired a TV drama based on the book as an installment of the Robert Montgomery–hosted Johnson's Wax program, a teleplay whose triumphant moral was that "Jazz means America . . . and all the people in it." What is undeniable is the book's popularity as an exemplum of jazz literature. Jazz writer and future record producer Orrin Keepnews estimated in 1952 that the book had sold 20,000 to 30,000 copies. Even in the late fifties, over a decade after its original publication, the book continued to sell at a rapid clip: *Down Beat* reported in 1958 that it towered in sales—along with Billie Holiday and William Dufty's *Lady Sings the Blues*—above all other jazz books, and critic Leonard Feather estimated in 1960 that one in five *Down Beat* readers had read the book.[21]

The book's success was undoubtedly a function of Mezzrow's extreme claim about the distance between white and black culture, and his equally extreme claim to have jumped the divide. Unlike earlier white slummers such as turn-of-the-century sociologist Walter Wyckoff or 1920s aesthete Carl Van Vechten, Mezzrow dedicated his entire adult life to a race and class masquerade—a commitment telegraphed by the fact that Milton

Mezzrow became forever "Mezz," in an echo of the music he loved. His career as a professional jazz musician and marijuana seller swept him deeper into the ghetto's most segregated spaces, from Al Capone's cabarets to Harlem and New York's Bunk, a den for heroin addicts where Mezzrow spent four half-lit years. And as he camouflaged himself in the black community, Mezzrow believed, he had soaked up not only the culture that sustained the blues but also some extra melanin as well. Mezzrow observed that he had physically become black—that his lips had become fuller, his hair had frizzed and thickened, and his skin had turned darker (*RTB*, p. 390). And if he is to be believed, his racial masquerade was convincing enough that the guardians of state authority followed his lead: when he served a mandatory nineteenth-month sojourn on Riker's Island for drug possession, he was confined on the Colored Cellblock; when he was discharged from prison, he was classified as "Negro" on his draft card.

As might be inferred by Mezzrow's Zelig-like claims, the musician based his appreciation of black urban culture in some of the oldest racial fictions in the book. He had near-total faith in his own individual adaptability, yet he matched it with a creed of racial determinism—that blacks had bred in their bones a pagan appreciation of the world's pleasures. This tension led his autobiography to become, in critic Gayle Wald's acute phrase, "a conversion narrative about the impossibility of conversion."[22] Yet Mezzrow himself did not acknowledge the tension: as cowriter Bernard Wolfe explained, Mezzrow believed "he had scrubbed himself clean, inside and out, of every last trace of his origins in the Jewish slums of Chicago, pulped himself back to raw human material, deposited that nameless jelly in the pure Negro mold, and pressed himself into the opposite of his birthright, a pure Black" (*RTB*, p. 390).

Mezzrow was an aficionado of the "primitive"—a blues spirit that he paraphrased as

> *Life is good, it's great to be alive!* . . . That was what New Orleans was really saying, it was a celebration of life, of breathing, of muscle-flexing, of eye-blinking, of licking-the-chops, in spite of everything the world might do to you. It was a defiance of the undertaker. It was a refusal to go under, a stubborn hanging on, a shout of praise to the circulatory system, hosannas for the sweat-glands, hymns to the guts that ache when they're hollow. (*RTB*, pp. 323–324)

Jazz music for Mezzrow gave expression to all those body parts, those organs, that high culture never recognized—not the head and the heart, but the lungs, muscles, nerves, tongue, blood, sweat glands, and intestines. His

A NEW INTELLECTUAL VERNACULAR

own metamorphosis from white to black, from straight hair to crimped Afro, was an extension of this logic, another example of peripheral body parts acting on their own initiative. Taken as an aesthetic principle, Mezzrow's primitivism led him to believe that jazz musicians were creatures in tune with their own inner urges and wounds. They were great artists, of course, but they were largely engaged, like Bessie Smith, in acts of natural self-exposure: "She *lived* every story she sang; she was just telling you how it happened to her" (*RTB*, p. 114; emphasis in the original).

Ironically, while Mezzrow based his musical analysis in instinctual drives that were beyond analysis, he also was an avid student of the street culture of the inner city. His picture of Harlem jive not only shares much with the aesthetic of bebop but also anticipated the urban anthropology of the 1960s, such as Roger Abrahams's study of the Dozens in Philadelphia. Mezzrow understood the jive talking of the street corner neither as a pathological response to a racist white culture nor as the wiles of a happy-go-lucky race, but rather as a satiric, inventive response to the power of institutional culture. With a little pressure, his sense of the connection between lived experience and art—exemplified in his appraisal of Bessie Smith's "liv[ing] every story she sang"—could shade into the famous aphorism of Charlie Parker: "Music is your own experience, your thoughts, your wisdom. If you don't live it, it won't come out of your horn."[23] Following this line of thought, Mezzrow suggested that jive "was jammed with a fine sense of the ridiculous that had behind it some solid social criticism" (*RTB*, p. 228).

On street corners across the urban North, Mezzrow was saying, educated whites were the targets of that oblique, teasing mockery known to African Americans as the art of "signifying":

Deny the Negro the culture of the land? O.K. He'll brew his own culture—on the street corner. Lock him out from the seats of higher learning? He pays it no nevermind—he'll dream up his own professional doubletalk, from the professions that *are* open to him, the professions of musician, entertainer, maid, butler, tap-dancer. . . .

The hipster stays conscious of the fraud of language. Where many ofays will hold forth pompously, like they had The Word, the Negro mimics them sarcastically. As a final subtle touch, his language is also a parody, a satire on the conventional ofay's gift of gab and gibberish.

For Mezzrow, jive was a "professional" idiom, a language that helped entertainers, porters, and maids comment on the white world that they had to defer to: it reflected high culture's esteem for technical expertise even as it converted its own expertise into a form of doubletalk. As doubletalk, jive was meant to accomplish two ends: to nod to high culture, then to establish an alternate kind of knowledge, one based in worldly experience.[24]

Although Mezzrow huffily denounced bebop, his conception of jive brought him close to bebop musicians like Charlie Parker, Dizzy Gillespie, and Thelonious Monk, who practiced a more aggressive act of signifying than performers like Cab Calloway and Slim Gailliard. The term "bebop" itself might have had several derivations—it could have come from the abrupt sequence of two distant eighth notes that was the music's signature or the sound of the policeman's billy club on a Harlemite's head (as Langston Hughes contended)—but Ralph Ellison was certainly right when he noted that the word "throws up its hands in clownish self-deprecation before all the complexity of sound and rhythm and self-assertive passion which it pretends to name." The music of bebop married the comic and the complex, the extroverted and the introverted; it replaced Calloway's brilliant smile and elegant antics with a flagrant act of signifying, where the musical expectations of the audience were teased, courted, and flouted at once. It was Mezzrow's "fraud of language" brought onto the bandstand.[25]

Gillespie—the most energetic showman of the bunch and the most successful black bebop big-band leader—is a fertile case in point. On the one hand, he learned much from his brief stint (1939–1941) in Calloway's band. He magnetized the media with the richness of his shtick, what he called "my own way of 'Tomming.'" His beret, smoked glasses, leopard-skin jacket, goatee, and ballooning cheeks became bebop's trademarks in the print media. Onstage, he pursued broad comedy (saying "I'd like to introduce the band," then having the saxophonists stand up to shake hands with the trombonists), and he sprinkled his repertoire with novelty numbers like "Ooop-Bop-Sh'bam" and "She Beeped When She Should Have Bopped." Gillespie remarked in 1950 that "if you want to make a living at music, you've got to sell it," and he also admitted that he steadied his tempos so that his music would remain danceable. On the other hand, Gillespie's antics had a harder edge, just as his dance music insisted on new chromatic harmonies and new Afro-Cuban rhythms. For every "Ooop-Bop" there was a "Manteca" or a "Night in Tunisia," where insistent bass ostinatos underscored feverish and aggressive improvisations. Gillespie's solo style emphasized headlong rushes of notes and intervallic leaps in the high register; "Manteca" featured flashy brass punctuation that built up with abrupt crescendos, then dropped out to isolate the underlying rhythm. Likewise, when Gillespie bowed to Mecca in a now-infamous 1948 *Life* photo spread, he sent mixed signals to middle America: were these new beboppers flamboyant stuntmen willing to spoof exotic religious commitment, or were they strange characters prey to "outside" allegiances? Gillespie later rued the gesture since it mocked Islam, but the threat behind the gesture was part of his appeal: his wry smirk and dazzling revisions of popular song were at considerable distance from Louis Armstrong's head-on enthusiasm and wrap-your-troubles-in-dreams spirit.[26]

This modern hipness did not merely seduce and entertain with its surface nonsensicality and rhythm: both Mezzrow and the beboppers advertised hipness as a deep mental strategy, a form of psychological complexity. Which is to say: in the postwar period, the hipster became increasingly "cool," with all that the term hazily implies. As Joel Dinerstein has suggested, the cool pose in the 1940s was an aesthetic accomplishment as well as a form of everyday resistance to a society that tended to pigeonhole its black citizens. It effectively synthesized Anglo-American ideals of cool (exemplified by the existential loner—the detective, the gunslinger—who repressed emotion and resisted temptation "in exchange for an unimpeachable reputation for straight talk") with West African ideals of cool as a form of "relaxed intensity," the ability to take part in community rituals with simultaneous passion and detachment. Like much of jazz itself, the cool pose was an inventive synthesis of Anglo and African cultural materials and aesthetic practices—a celebratory but barbed form of integration.[27]

With bebop, "cool" became not just an aesthetic but a kind of shared atmosphere, a principle of community. Bebop musicians dressed their music with academic suffixes that hinted at whole systems of secret knowledge: thus song titles like "Anthropology," "Ornithology," "Epistrophy," and "Crazeology." Drummer Kenny Clarke remembered that bebop was "different from the 'swing' music that had preceded it, the technology of the whole thing . . . it was the most intelligent era of jazz." The music of bebop was understood to derive from those after-hours moments ("'Round Midnight") when the jam sessions began, the professionals talked to themselves in their own quasi-Masonic language, and time itself seemed to dilate according to the moods of the musicians. In the 1948 *Life* photo spread, Gillespie and Benny Carter gave each other a highly involved, entirely bogus "secret" handshake—a sure stunt for a white public raised on the lodge of *Amos 'n' Andy*, but not without a symbolic truth. The pioneers of bebop were, by and large, a black brotherhood who played music according to still-unwritten rules. Being "hip" was to practice a form of "Crazeology": one codified a type of knowledge that, while institutionally unaccredited, tapped hidden mental reserves. The lifestyle could appeal to those blacks who were excluded from the middle class by Jim Crow conventions and cultural snobbery, or it could appeal to those—like Mezzrow, the Beats, and their adepts—who disparaged "making it" as "selling out" and who looked to black subcultures for intense personal transfiguration.[28]

Mezzrow, having forsaken the traditional nice Jewish boy's options for success (law school, a career in business), retold the Horatio Alger story as a descent into the slums and an exercise in self-authentication. Leaving behind a family who "all worked hard to make a solid citizen of me," Mezzrow testified briefly to the spiritual aridity of his family life and much more extensively to the pull of black culture. But if the enemy of hipness was clear (white middle-class society, with the premium it placed on respectability and refinement), the strategies for becoming hip were morally ambiguous. For one thing, becoming hip meant defrauding your own kin—and, more specifically, the women who represented the straight life of a steady job and proper manners. Mezzrow recounts how he bought his first alto saxophone by stealing his sister's seal-fur coat and hawking it to a local madam for $150—an act he understands as poetic justice, since he had earlier asked his sister (who worked as a secretary) to transcribe Bessie Smith's lyrics. Remembering that she had insisted on correcting Smith's grammar and polishing her prose, Mezzrow remarks, incredibly, that he has "never felt friendly towards her to this day, on account of how she laid her fancy high-school airs on the immortal Bessie Smith" (*RTB*, p. 54). Unlike the Jewish sons who populate other memoirs of the 1940s, Mezzrow leaves his family and does not seem much motivated to look back.[29]

By contrast, Mezzrow's pride surges whenever he believes he has been accepted across the color line—when he plays in a largely black band at the Pontiac Reformatory at age sixteen; when he finds "mezz" listed in Cab Calloway's *Hepster's Dictionary* as "anything supreme, genuine" and in Dan Burley's *Original Handbook of Harlem Jive* as "tops, sincere"; when he joins the "brotherhood on The Corner," where he pushes the fat joint known as a mezziroll; and at the end of the book when he discovers at a jam session that he can play the New Orleans blues (*RTB*, pp. 5, 14–15). This last jam session, where Mezzrow emerges reborn from his incarceration, serves as the climax of the entire book: through his clarinet playing, Mezzrow comes to feel that he has transcended himself and found himself at the same time. "Somebody else had taken over and was directing all my moves," he writes as the band translates the Sousa march into the "ageless language of New Orleans." For Mezzrow that "somebody else" was the pantheon of great black New Orleans musicians: "I was Jimmy Noone and Johnny Dodds and Sidney Bechet, swinging down Rampart Street and Basin Street and Perdido Street, stepping high and handsome, blowing all the joy and bounce of life through my clarinet" (*RTB*, p. 322). Far from simply incar-

A NEW INTELLECTUAL VERNACULAR

nating other clarinetists, Mezzrow imagined himself living a dream of collective improvisation, becoming one with an entire musical community—in this case, black jazz giants in the thick of Mardi Gras.

Strikingly, Mezzrow's hunger for transcendental pleasure made him tone-deaf to the appeal of the jazz styles that followed his own adopted New Orleans idiom. He attacked swing, jump, and bebop as music that, rather than transcending the neurosis of modernity, symptomatized it through its "tics" and "mania." Drawn to metaphors of war and disease, he wrote:

> If you let yourself get all split up and pulverized inside, maybe you can make "modern" music, the music of tics, the swing and jump and rip-bop. . . . Modern swing and jump is frantic, savage, frenzied, berserk—it's the agony of the split-up, hacked-up personality. It's got nothing in common with New Orleans, which by contrast is dignified, balanced, deeply harmonious, high-spirited but pervaded all through with a mysterious calm and placidity—the music of a personality that hasn't exploded like a fragmentation bomb. (*RTB*, p. 327)

In hindsight Mezzrow's musical argument seems off-base: swing band-leaders like Duke Ellington, Benny Goodman, and Count Basie certainly prized the control of a well-calibrated arrangement, and the new four-four pulse of swing might easily be considered *less* frenzied or berserk than the rollicking rhythms of New Orleans. Yet Mezzrow's critique, while musicologically obtuse, was an innovative slander: it updated a long-standing smear against black music (its "savagery," its "frenzy," its "mania") with a more novel emphasis on the fragmented personality. Mezzrow's swing musicians were at war with themselves, bombing themselves into oblivion. In the language of psychology, they were not "well adjusted."

Mezzrow's choice of words—"split-up," "hacked-up"—left central questions unanswered: Who and what were doing the hacking? Might these performers be signifying on the bandstand—mimicking a societal neurosis—just as Mezzrow had noticed, in their cutting contests and jive lingo, that they had appropriated and satirized the "jawbusting" talk of elite culture? Mezzrow was not an apologist for Jim Crow or the dominant culture generally, but he did presume that black music was either "really the blues" or inauthentic—all or nothing at all. While he was a shrewd observer of street-corner life, he never wrote an ethnography of the bandstand and its audience. He approved of the ironic senses of jive as street-corner banter, but he diagnosed such irony on the bandstand as split-level neurosis, a spontaneous expression of self-lacerating agony. Yearning for interracial bandstand solidarity, he found it only by moving backward in time, to the "balanced" collective improvisation of New Orleans jazz.

Analysis Interminable? Early Partisan Reviews of the Hipster

While Mezz Mezzrow was the first white Negro in print, his cowriter Bernard Wolfe can claim a similar distinction: first highbrow critic of the white Negro, first intellectual to anatomize the hipster as a cluster of interracial longings and psychosexual drives.[30] After *Really the Blues,* Mezzrow exited the world of literature for a career as a working Dixieland musician. Meanwhile Wolfe became obsessed with the allure of subcultural solidarity and the value of nonconformity in an unjust, underachieving America, turning shortly after the Mezzrow book to a 200-page meditation on bebop. Though Wolfe figures at best as a sideman in the full-dress histories of the New York intellectuals, his career as Trotskyite activist in the 1930s, bebop theorist in the 1940s, and sexual polemicist in the 1950s illustrates the shifting agenda of these thinkers who staffed such journals as *Partisan Review* and *Commentary* and who flirted with the hipster in the postwar period. The watchwords of this intellectual generation, according to sociologist Daniel Bell (one of their own), were "irony, paradox, ambiguity, and complexity." Such cultural values helped shape a postwar politics of disenchantment and reflection, albeit one spiked by an uncompromising anti-Communism. The New York intellectuals were successful in the sense that they achieved greater and greater access to power and its spoils—migrating to university chairs, think-tank appointments, and government offices—so their confrontation with "hip" provides an interesting case study in how one upwardly mobile intellectual subculture confronted a possibly rival intellectual subculture in its very midst. The confrontation was both a skirmish between a community of largely Jewish intellectuals and their black counterparts and a form of shadow boxing, with the New York intellectuals using the figure of the hipster to interrogate and, more often, fortify their own preconceptions about themselves.[31]

The hipster was one of a number of "types" that were anatomized in the pages of *Partisan Review* and *Commentary:* he took his place alongside the Communist, the Fellow Traveler, the Artist, the Jew, the Inauthentic Negro, and (that master term) the Intellectual as a figure that seemed to offer himself up for portraiture. He might have come from the field of jazz, but he made sense to these commentators largely insofar as he tied into prevailing discourses about the banality of mass culture, the trap of "ideological" thinking, the promise of a more pragmatic liberalism, and so on. *Commentary* editor Eliot Cohen, sketching a profile of the "typical Jewish intellec-

A NEW INTELLECTUAL VERNACULAR

tual of the late 1940s," situated him as "a cultural child of the Great Depression, of the defeat of social reconstruction that followed it, of the great human cataclysm of World War II, and of the present period of peace which is not peace." Under these conditions, Cohen suggested, the Jewish intellectual had become "wary, unhopeful, isolated, and alienated. . . . Rather than ranging the whole country or the many continents, he is thrown back on himself. Skeptical of large claims of political ideologies, he is neither a joiner not a devotee."[32]

Cohen was here describing the early stages of the New York intellectuals' transformation from partisans of the working class into cultural critics of the great American middle. In place of their earlier broadsides against the brutalities of American capitalism and the threat of Stalinist aesthetics, they turned to the difficulties of what *Partisan Review* editor Philip Rahv called "the *embourgeoisement* of the American intelligentsia"—the dilemmas that came from identifying with a centrist American liberalism but not the cultural tastes of its constituency. How does one reconcile the political promise of mass democracy with the cultural "domination of the 'masses'"? How does one stanch the flow of kitsch culture? As *Dissent* editor Irving Howe remarked, "If you couldn't stir the proletariat to action, you could denounce Madison Avenue in comfort." Howe's skepticism about this postwar turn has a certain justice, but it is also true that in the mid-1940s the New York intellectuals were less triumphalist than they would become, less sure of their place in the social and economic settlements of the postwar period. Howe himself observed in 1946 that the young Jewish intellectual was trapped in a pitiless self-awareness, cut off both from his Jewish heritage and the movement cultures that had earlier sustained him. A "victim of his own complexity," the intellectual had to "turn to his own inner resources for intellectual and emotional sustenance," but the more he did so, the more he felt "unhappy about his withdrawal and desires a sense of community." The result boiled down to one word that seemed to sum up the postwar mentality: "angst."[33]

The work of *Really the Blues* coauthor Bernard Wolfe attests to the complicated ways that these Jewish-American intellectuals turned to black life for critical leverage on American culture as a whole. A fringe member of the New York intellectual clique—he made his living as a writer for *Nugget, Playboy,* and other newsstand magazines rather than as an in-house intellectual—Wolfe was one of the few Americans whose writings were eagerly picked up by psychiatrist and black liberationist Frantz Fanon. The son of working-class Jewish immigrants in New Haven, Wolfe was radicalized by the Depression's effect on his parents: his father lost his job as factory foreman and became so depressed that he needed to be institutionalized, and his mother struggled to keep a neighborhood grocery afloat. Soon after, Wolfe was introduced to the two paradigms that would explain this economic trauma and mark the rest of his career: the darkly pessimistic psychoanalysis of Freud and the cultural, class-based politics of Trotsky. While studying psychology at Yale in the mid-thirties, he taught at Bryn Mawr's summer College of Women Trade Unionists and contributed to Trotskyite publications *The Militant* and *The New International.* After graduating from Yale in 1936, he headed down to Mexico where he served for a year as Trotsky's bodyguard and secretary, an experience that later served as the basis for his novel *The Great Prince Died.* During the forties, Wolfe drifted away from Trotskyist circles and toward Greenwich Village bohemia, apprenticing to literature by writing pornographic novels under the recommendation and tutelage of Henry Miller.[34]

Really the Blues was Wolfe's first full-fledged literary project, but he soon used his jazz expertise to leverage himself into the postwar intellectual circles of New York and Paris. In the late forties, he composed what he called a "study of the role of the Negro in popular culture"—his work "From the Solid to the Frantic: The Somewhereness of Bop," which was published in fugitive excerpts in *Commentary* and Jean-Paul Sartre's *Les Temps Modernes.* Though the larger manuscript was never published, Wolfe continued to ground his novels in dissident subcultures—pacifists in the science-fiction *Limbo* (1952), Broadway lowlifes in *The Late Risers* (1954), political exiles in *The Great Prince Died* (1959), and Greenwich Village hipsters in *The Magic of Their Singing* (1961).[35]

As an intellectual, Wolfe struggled to reconcile his social egalitarianism, which asserted the value of black culture and the necessity of legal equality, with his psychoanalytic paradigm, which labeled the "cool" emotional management of bebop as a form of repression. Perhaps his greatest intellectual achievement was his pioneering analysis of the minstrelsy embedded in American popular culture: a decade before Fanon (who cited Wolfe in *Black Skin, White Masks*) and a half-century before historians Eric Lott and David Roediger, Wolfe argued that American music, dance, art, and literature were built on the fault line of their racial fictions. White Americans embarked compulsively on the pursuit of happiness, but they could only find such ecstasy in minstrelized forms like black jazz and black dance, which relied on the character of the "happyifying Negro." In his study of bop, Wolfe maintained that blacks had historically performed their laughter—a laughter primed with ambivalent gestures—even as mainstream culture flattened "dark laughter" into a happy-go-lucky smile: "The truth about the Negro performer, as about the Negro in general," he wrote, "is that he is required to be a Negro impersonator." Br'er Rabbit was a time-honored example of the black trickster, who disguised malevolence behind a simpleton's mask; a much more recent example was the bop trickster, whose "mask begins to be at odds with the racial image to which the white man clings." With a nod to the postwar literary-critical interest in levels of ambiguity, Wolfe even anatomized bop's laughter, "the most complicated laughter heard in America," into its six different forms ("genuine gusto," "calculated naivete," "a gibe at the Machine," and so on).[36]

Bop remained for Wolfe, however, a kind of subcultural delusion for both black and white America. The white fan of bop—the "jazzuit"—clung to this latest of fictions, the black bopper whose cool demeanor was no act. Meanwhile the black musician was trapped by the Freudian axiom that "culture is built on the ruin of the instincts": Wolfe's bop attained aesthetic status only when blacks internalized the psychology of their colonizers and bound their frenetic impulses to the "coolness" of the Brooks Brothers commercial man. In a psychoanalytic echo of Mezz Mezzrow, Wolfe argued that bop was a neurotic music that symptomatized a larger American disease. For Wolfe, the disease was the "caste" divide between black and white; bebop as an art form took measure of the distance between mainstream and margin and then performed the social gap through its ambivalent ecstasy.[37]

Wolfe's sense that bebop was an expression of psychological paralysis became, in the pages of *Partisan Review* and *Commentary*, something like a party line—or as much of a party line as possible, given the journals' infrequent attention to black music. *Partisan Review* music critic Weldon Kees attacked bebop as a false refuge from the culture of conformity, a facile indulgence dressed up in the language of revolt. Kees described bebop's fans as "iconoclastic and compulsive types . . . [who] extend their interests beyond music—to drug-addiction, abstract painting, and the theories (and for all I know the practice) of Wilhelm Reich, philosopher of the orgasm." The threat of Wilhelm Reich seems to have unlocked other anxieties in Kees, who ended with his own fantasy of cross-racial identification: "I can only report, very possibly because of some deeply buried strain of black reaction in me, that I have found this music uniformly thin, at once dilapidated and overblown, and exhibiting a poverty of thematic development and a richness of affectation not only, apparently, intentional, but enormously self-satisfied."[38]

A much more intriguing set of writings on bebop and the hipster came from then-unknown intellectual Anatole Broyard. While Mezzrow built his literary career out of his fantastic claim of becoming black, Broyard staked out the opposite territory: after initial forays as a black author writing as an insider about black culture, he succeeded in passing as white. By the 1970s, he had become a staff book reviewer and essayist for the *New York Times,* famous for his Olympian dispassion, wit, and cultural conservatism.[39] In his earlier work and life, however, Broyard had written for *Partisan Review* and *Commentary* as a court expert on the inner life of black people. There is a double sense of peculiarity to these early essays. The work of a young and ambitious writer, they tend to be overstuffed with incongruous metaphors, contradictory insights, literary allusions that gesture more than they add up. In addition, the details of Broyard's biography—the fact that he was in the process of severing his connections to his family, the fact that he razored out the biographical note from his personal copy of one of these essays because it referred to his firsthand knowledge of the black community—lend an extraordinary poignancy to these writings, even when they are at their most evasive or impersonal. When Broyard writes disapprovingly of the hipster as someone who has abstracted himself from the community he once belonged to, or of "coolness" as a self-defeating "attempt to move from the performer to the omniscient and superior spectator," we as contemporary readers may have the strange sense that he is signifying on himself—and that he wanted no one to be clued into the painful joke.[40]

Like Wolfe, Broyard was interested in the Negro as someone fated to perform his racial identity for an audience that consistently failed to read the performance *as* a performance. And like Wolfe again, he used existential frameworks to argue that blacks had become inauthentic and unfulfilled, so embattled that they did not adhere to their true selves; they were trapped into unconscious defensiveness and "personality distortion," a coolness that kept them from accepting the terms of engagement with the world. In a 1950 piece for *Commentary* entitled "Portrait of the Inauthentic Negro," for instance, Broyard argued that the most pressing problem for blacks was not racism but "their own authenticity," by which he meant the "stubborn adherence to one's essential self, in spite of the distorting pressures of one's situation." Their personalities had been "lost in the shuffle, a shuffle with marked cards, dealt from the bottom of the deck."[41]

While other writers would use this analysis of black psychological difficulties to make a case for social remedies—social psychologist Kenneth Clark took this tack four years later, when he offered testimony about black children's self-esteem in the *Brown v. Board of Education* case—Broyard's early writings always halted at the brink of prescription. He was more interested in self-authentication than in racial affirmation or social justice. Yet "authenticity," in Broyard's early writings, was quite a conflicted term, one that oscillated between two different meanings. On the one hand, Broyard was attracted explicitly to the Sartrean sense of authenticity as the personal acceptance of one's freedom. "Authenticity," wrote Sartre in *Anti-Semite and Jew* (a work Broyard valued highly and openly used as his theoretical framework), "consists in having a true and lucid consciousness of the situation, in assuming the responsibilities and risks that it involves, in accepting it in pride or humiliation, sometimes in horror and hate." But on the other hand, along with this sense of authenticity as the anguish and power of existential freedom Broyard was attracted to the idea of authenticity as a kind of community engagement that was so absorbing, so fulfilling, as to be cathartic—action *without* self-consciousness. In his capsule history of black music-making, he spoke positively of Jazz styles that came before swing: "getting hot"—the alternative to laying cool, in Broyard's mind—was "a spontaneous, unself-conscious tribal activity having little to do with white society," "a release, a letting off of steam after hundreds of years of suppression." Mezz Mezzrow could not have said it much better.[42]

Judged according to either of these modes of authenticity, Broyard's hipster was a failure. His irony, his ambiguity—terms that were used to validate the modernist literature that Broyard loved—were precisely what kept him from Sartrean self-acceptance. Writing shortly after the conclusion of World War II, Broyard described the hipster as "a pacifist in the struggle between social groups—not a conscientious objector, but a draft-dodger." The bebop dodge, in Broyard's mind, kept the hipster from truly confronting the racial stereotypes that he objected to; he had removed the minstrel mask but could get no true self-image because he had entered a world of abstraction, a house of mirrors:

> The élan of jazz was weeding out of bebop because all enthusiasm was naive, nowhere, too simple. Bebop was the hipster's seven types of ambiguity, his Laocoön, illustrating his struggle with his own defensive deviousness. . . . It presented the hipster as performer, retreated to an abstract stage of *tea* and pretension, losing himself in the multiple mirrors of his fugitive chords. . . .
>
> [The hipster] no longer had anything relevant to himself to say—in both his musical and linguistic expression he had finally abstracted himself from his real position in society.

Far from being a formula for artistic distance and critical energy, alienation turned into a successful marketing strategy, and transformed the hipster into a company man. "The frantic praise of the impotent meant recognition—*actual somewhereness*—to the hipster," Broyard wrote. "He got what he wanted; he stopped protesting, reacting. He began to bureaucratize jive." Strikingly, while Jewish intellectuals were praised for being perennial outsiders—and were thought to bring a critical point of view even as they caught the ear of the powerful—the black hipster was someone who could succeed only as long as he remained unrecognized. And while it's difficult to imagine other artists and intellectuals being attacked for modeling a heightened self-consciousness or resorting to "abstraction" in art (Clement Greenberg would soon tout abstract expressionism as the great American contribution to the modernist avant-garde), this abstraction was for Broyard the crux of the hipster's lack of relevance.[43]

Broyard may have explicitly attacked the hipster for his pursuit of abstraction, but his harshest words were reserved for his judgment of the hipster's manhood. Behind Broyard's logic of authenticity stood a set of charged assumptions about masculinity and femininity. Labeling hipsters as impotent and bureaucratic, Broyard drew on the conventional distinction between the manly, commerce-scorning intellectual and the effeminate, pandered-to audience—a distinction on which he insisted. He ended his piece with a startling metaphor for the hipster's acceptance: the hipster, he wrote, "was *in-there*. . . . [H]e was back in the American womb. And it was just as unhygienic as ever." The note of sexual alarm here is palpable, and it carries over into Broyard's later memoir *Kafka Was the Rage,* where bebop comes in for a harsh drubbing—its technique likened at one point to the off-putting sexual technique of one of Broyard's lovers.[44]

In both Broyard and Wolfe's writings, then, a seemingly astute analysis of the performance of race coincided with a seemingly tone-deaf dismissal of the performance style that was bebop. How to explain this? One answer is that the aesthetic of bebop challenged not only the "entertainment" principle of swing but also the "authenticity" principle of Wolfe and Broyard's existentialism, which valued commitment and full-on engagement rather than the ironic style suggested by the cocked beret and the tilted trumpet. A related answer is that the postures of bebop did not fulfill Broyard's and Wolfe's prescriptions for a heroic postwar masculinity. Either too cool or too compromising, their hipster had made a complicated pact with mass culture, and his instinctive drives had paid the price. Profoundly influenced by Sartre, Broyard's and Wolfe's writings were case studies edging toward social criticism: they sought to diagnose the type that was the hipster, to diagram the impulses and pressures that he felt, to uncover the acts of bad faith where the hipster's style led him to diminish himself. Yet for all the premium that Wolfe and Broyard placed on authenticity, their acts of judgment hover in a vacuum of social documentation. Wolfe's 200-page manuscript on bop, for instance, mentions bebop performers in only the most cursory fashion, such as when he riffs on the ascetic connotations of Thelonious Monk's surname. Indeed, this absence

A NEW INTELLECTUAL VERNACULAR

of documentary depth may help explain why these commentators were drawn to sounding the hipster's psychological depths: by turning inward to the unconscious script of bebop, Broyard and Wolfe established intellectual authority over an area (music of great abstraction and subcultural distance) that might have seemed beyond their expertise. They could address the most disputed of topics—the sexual health of black men—while pretending to be above mere sensationalism. And in the process they could distinguish between a successful form of intellectual activity and its counterfeit, between the act of reflection they modeled in their own writing and the hipster's failed gestures of detachment and abstraction.

Underground in the Late 1940s: *Birth of the Cool* and *On the Road*

Despite the disapproving glances of Wolfe and Broyard, the hipsters of America's cities did not exchange their zoot suits for coats and ties, their cool pose for straightforward civic engagement. But the hipster as a cultural figure did tend to remain underground in the late 1940s and early 1950s—a fact underscored by the belated reception of two landmarks of "cool" culture, Miles Davis's *Birth of the Cool* and Jack Kerouac's *On the Road*. Both works were grounded in artistic subcultures of New York in the 1940s—Davis's in the group of bebop musicians who gravitated to arranger Gil Evans's 55th Street apartment, searching for ways to extend bebop's harmonic and rhythmic complexity and to develop a new balance between group arrangement and individual improvisation; Kerouac's in the embryonic Beat subculture, which drew together the bohemians of Greenwich Village and the urban-outlaw hustlers of Times Square. Yet both Davis and Kerouac had to wait until 1957 for their work to be received and absorbed by the public. *Birth of the Cool* earned its title, unsurprisingly, only in retrospect: the twelve tunes, recorded in three sessions under Davis's name in 1949 and 1950, quickly faded from view when they were released as a set of singles, and were only re-released—and baptized with the zeitgeist-sensitive title by Capitol Records producer Pete Rugolo—after "cool jazz" had become a best-selling genre and Davis had magnetized 1955's Newport Jazz Festival with his spellbinding version of "'Round Midnight." Meanwhile *On the Road* had to run the book trade's version of the gauntlet: six years of publishers' rejections (Harcourt Brace; Knopf; Dodd Mead; Farrar Strauss; E. P. Dutton; Little, Brown) and stop-and-start negotiations between Kerouac and his skeptical editor, Viking's Malcolm Cowley. In the process, the novel shifted titles ("The Heroes of the Hip Generation," "Anywhere Road," "Beat Generation") and was transformed from its famous first draft—125,000 words typed on a continuous stretch of paper that resembled a ribbon of highway—into the book hailed by the *New York Times* as "the most beautifully executed, the clearest and most important utterance yet made by the generation Kerouac himself named years ago as 'beat.'"[45]

Despite these parallels in reception history, however, Kerouac and Davis might be said to have staked out opposite ends of the hipster continuum. Kerouac was dedicated to Mezzrow-like ideals of spontaneity and free impulse, with the twist that he saw these ideals embodied in the bebop music that Mezzrow so abhorred. His early manifesto "Belief and Technique for Modern Prose" was half-parodic ("Like Proust be an old teahead of time"), but most of its thirty bulletlike points suggested that "modern prose" should dedicate itself to unmediated expression: "Remove literary, grammatical, and syntactical inhibition"; "Write what you want bottomless from bottom of the mind"; "Composing wild, undisciplined, pure, coming in from under, crazier the better"; and included a helpful reminder for outsiders to the literary establishment: "You're a Genius all the time." The equation "Freedom = Spontaneity = Authenticity = Open Form" governs many of Kerouac's theoretical writings, with jazz musicians enlisted as its most faithful exponents. In "Essentials of Spontaneous Prose," the act of "blowing (as per jazz musician)" is taken as exemplary: just as jazz musicians work to achieve an effortless flow of notes, so writers should open up to the "undisturbed flow from the mind of personal secret idea-words"; just as jazz musicians draw breaths without slowing their momentum, so writers should minimize punctuation and opt for the "vigorous space dash" over "false colons and timid usually needless commas"; and finally, just as jazz musicians do not revise their playing after the fact, so writers should not "afterthink" ("blow!—now!—your way is your only way").[46]

Kerouac's *On the Road* breathed cultural life into this ethic of postwar spontaneity—hitched it, in a sense, to a fully revved automobile and took it cross-country. The vagabonds that populated the proletarian literature of the 1930s became, with the embrace of an improvisatory outlook and the ownership of a car engine, the road-tripping adventurers of the 1950s as the bop ethic of heroic spontaneity was translated into a new type of "modern prose book." Yet the book's reception as an untroubled tribute to youthful spontaneity did a double disservice—to the black Americans who were assumed to embody its spirit of spontaneity and to Kerouac's full literary achievement. The *Village Voice*'s Ned Polsky called Kerouac's romantic appraisal of black inner vitality "an inverted form of keeping the nigger in his place," and he was joined in his damning assessment of Kerouac's racial politics by critics as diverse as James Baldwin, anarchist-poet Kenneth Rexroth, and *Commentary*'s Norman Podhoretz. The sense of Kerouac's

A NEW INTELLECTUAL VERNACULAR

blindness on this score has not softened over time. James Campbell, a sympathetic historian of both the Beats and the black writers who exiled themselves in Paris in the 1940s and 1950s, remarks that "there is a striking absence, in [Kerouac's] letters and books, of the sociology of black music, of the history that brought it into being. Nor is there much appreciation of the complexity of black taste and black life. . . . The 'essential American' [the black American] is spotted in a variety of guises in early Beat Generation traffic, sometimes as an object of fear or revulsion, sometimes of condescension, sometimes of romantic affiliation, but rarely just as himself or herself, as an American." And as Campbell notes too, the cross-country kicks of *On the Road* were strictly for whites only—a fact that seems to have escaped Kerouac's notice. Two black buddies in the late 1940s would hardly have been able to cruise from one end of the country to the other, sampling all the pleasures (food, drink, music, sex, companionship) on offer by the side of the road or in town—not unless they wanted to court a jail sentence and possibly even more severe reprisals.[47]

Yet if *On the Road* is weakened by its false idealization of black inner life, it is partly redeemed by its less noticed undertow, the creeping desperation that haunts its characters and drives their search for ecstasy in the form of jazz, drugs, women, whatever. "Where we going, man?" asks Sal Paradise in a typical moment—to which Dean Moriarty responds, "I don't know but we gotta go." The pressure to keep moving, always, is behind the book's restless plot and its highly rhythmic prose, which carries the reader along when the book's racial clichés (not to mention its misogyny) give much reason for pause. Should we pause, or should we go with the jazz-inspired flow? Most likely we end up doing both: close to fifty years after its original publication, *On the Road* inspires a conflicted reading experience, one that derives in part Kerouac's own creative struggle to get the "black dog" of depression off his back by plunging into a fiction of who he might be. The book's readers are asked to throw themselves into a set of identities that are an escape and obviously no escape at the same time. For all its recourse to an aesthetic of spontaneity and uncensored expression, the book remains surprisingly earthbound. Refusing the consolations of fantasy and enchantment, as well as the authorial prerogatives that marked the postmodernism of the 1960s, *On the Road* is ultimately not that far removed from the sobering stories of vagabondage and cross-country migration that marked 1930s fiction such as *The Grapes of Wrath*.[48]

Without recourse to explicit manifestos, Miles Davis shredded many of the fictions of black life and culture that Kerouac leaned on. *On the Road*, for all its flurry of movement, is populated by characters who are largely and often poignantly static; Davis's career, by contrast, is the story of an artist who regularly transformed his aesthetic and self-conception as a matter of principle, and who did so with such freshness, charisma, and collaborative brilliance that the rest of the culture followed him in hot, if sometimes confused or querulous, pursuit. Even his forbidding persona was, in its own way, an inspiration—testimony to the power of badness. The *Birth of the Cool* sessions stand only at the beginning of a journey that took Davis from cool jazz to hard bop, modal jazz, the "no-time" quintet sound of the mid-1960s, and the many kinds of fusion he cooked up after the late sixties, but they speak to the force of Davis's musical imagination as well as his upending of racial expectations. In the music of *Birth*'s Nonet, Davis found a way to marry the prewar cool aesthetic of Lester Young—a laid-back, floating approach to the beat, an elliptical statement of melody, a softer tone that suggested introspection and self-editing—with his interest in chamberlike arrangements that stood between the symphonic template of swing's big band and the stripped-down instrumentation of bebop's small group.

Davis was the catalyst behind the organization of the Nonet: in fellow arranger Gerry Mulligan's words, Davis "put the theories to work"; he "called the rehearsals, hired the halls, called the players, and generally cracked the whip." Yet at the same time, the Nonet's work was remarkably collaborative from start to finish—fittingly so, given that its music redefined the terms of jazz ensemble playing. The music was largely inspired by the example of Gil Evans, who had arranged such Charlie Parker touchstones as "Anthropology" and "Yardbird Suite" for the Claude Thornhill orchestra and who had developed a rich harmonic palette on more meditative Thornhill numbers. The music of *Birth of the Cool* came about when a wide number of arrangers—Mulligan on four tunes, pianist John Lewis on three, Gil Evans, Davis, and Johnny Carisi on the rest—decided to see how Evans's style might translate for a midsize combo. Their goal, according to Evans, was to shrink the Thornhill big band to "the smallest number of instruments that could get that sound and still express all the harmonies (the band) used." Many commentators have remarked on the unusual timbres produced by the instrumentation of the Nonet—the French horn, which brought together the brass and reeds; the tuba, which gave a deep bottom to the Nonet's texture. Perhaps even more crucial to the group's sound, though, was the way that these instruments were introduced. In the process of miniaturizing the Thornhill big band into a nonet, the principle of blend trumped the customary jazz principle of call-and-response part writing. As jazz historian Ted Gioia notes, "For a quarter of a century, jazz big bands had been built on the opposition of sections. Reeds, brass, rhythm: these served as separate, quasi-equal forces employed in musical jousting. . . . Davis, in contrast, conceived of his band as a single section. The model was not a classical orchestra, but ensemble singing." Davis himself wrote that he "wanted the instruments to sound like human voices . . . it had to be the voicing of a quartet, with soprano, alto, baritone, and bass voices. . . . I looked at the group like it was a choir."[49]

The idea of a jazz choir, with its voices often blending so well that they were subsumed in the cumulative effect of the ensemble, was a far cry from the bop ideal of Jack Kerouac. Instead of stressing immediacy and spontaneity, the Nonet put a premium on the art of arranging. Instead of setting soloists up front and giving them the freedom to blow as long as the spirit moved them, the Nonet emphasized the interplay of soloists and background and gave them a fairly rigorous time limit. Only a few tracks, like the Lewis-arranged "Budo," allowed their soloists to stretch out over the typical bebop rhythm section of piano, bass, and drums. More commonly, solos were short—often less than a chorus—and were set in counterpoint to the chords being blocked out by some combination of trumpet, trombone, French horn, tuba, and alto and baritone sax. On Carisi's "Israel," the solos of Davis's trumpet and Lee Konitz's alto sax take up only a third of the song's brief two minutes, and Davis's solo seems to have been constructed so as to end with an effortless transition into the precomposed tag that joins his solo to Konitz's. On Gil Evans's suave, limpid arrangement of "Moon Dreams," Konitz seems at one point to be playing a chastened and affecting solo—until we hear Gerry Mulligan's baritone doubling Konitz's every note in a lower register and realize just how well Evans has hidden his own precomposed handiwork.

All this musical craft was enough to draw the admiration, bafflement, and hostility that often accompany the making of a new genre. *New Yorker* classical music critic Winthrop Sargent wrote that "the music sounds more like that of a new Maurice Ravel than it does like jazz. I, who do not listen to jazz recordings day in and day out, find this music charming and exciting. . . . If Miles Davis were an established 'classical' composer, his work would rank high among that of his contemporary colleagues. But it is not really jazz." More recently, critic Stanley Crouch has called the Nonet's work "little more than primers for television writing," "another failed attempt to marry jazz to European devices." In any case, the recordings remained fairly obscure until their re-release and retitling in 1957—at which point they seemed to tell the first chapter in the history of cool jazz: the story of Gerry Mulligan before his pianoless quartet with Chet Baker, the story of John Lewis before the formation of the Modern Jazz Quartet, the story of trombonists J. J. Johnson and Kai Winding before the duelling-trombone sound of their quintet, and the story of French horn player and arranger-scholar Gunther Schuller before he coined the term "Third Stream" to suggest a school of jazz that blended jazz and classical idioms.[50]

But were these recordings the first chapter in the story not only of cool jazz but of "the cool" in toto? The claim is, in some large part, only defensible when measured by the standards of advertising hyperbole. Many blacks besides Davis had in the 1940s started to wear, in Ralph Ellison's words, the "bullet-proof vest known as cool." The writings of Broyard and Wolfe attest, with some blend of insight and miscomprehension, to the new visibility of the cool pose as a stance toward the world. Even within jazz, cool had been modeled by Lester Young before Davis, and the word "cool" had popped up in titles by such disparate artists as trumpeter and big band leader Erskine Hawkins (1941's "Keep Cool, Fool"), Count Basie (1946's "Stay Cool"), and Charlie Parker (1946's "Cool Blues").[51]

Yet there is a way that Davis brought a new genre of cool to the culture at large, even as he dramatically turned away from the sound of the Nonet in favor of the more blues-inflected, heavily improvised, and aggressive sound of his mid-fifties quintets. His form of cool persisted in the often feverish music of hard bop. As jazz critic Gary Giddins writes, in a bit of music criticism that has its own cool economy:

> though Davis rejected cool jazz, he came to personify jazz cool. Miles looked cool, dressed cool, and talked cool—in a guttural, foul-mouthed sort of way. His posture was cool as he approached the mike or turned away from it. His notes were cool: fat voice-like plums sustained in a siege of meditation or serrated arpeggios ripped into infinity. Cool, too, were his rests, those stirring oases enacted with flashing eyes and shrugged shoulders. Miles was an ongoing musical drama. In the world of Marlon Brando and John Osborne, he was the angry young trumpeter: handsome, unpredictable, and smart, driving fast cars and squiring beautiful women. Miles was the first subject of a *Playboy* interview. Miles didn't need a last name. Miles was an idiom unto himself.[52]

To which one might add: an idiom unto himself, yes, but also an idiom that many performers and listeners would try to adopt, adapt, and speak as their own, as the ventriloquism of cool became, in the late fifties, a cultural fixation.

2

RADICALISM BY ANOTHER NAME

The White Negro Meets
the Black Negro

In a 1959 column in the *Village Voice*, pacifist-socialist and *Liberation* editor David McReynolds fantasized about a solution to the paralysis of the left in New York City. "We live in a city," he said, "where the poor are driven legally from their homes to make way for the apartments of the wealthy; a city where the lives of our youth are so bleak and devoid of purpose that they turn to gang war and brutal murder . . . [a] city, in short, from which justice has taken a holiday and compassion is on an indefinite leave of absence." The traditional devices of political organizing had done little to halt the bulldozers, much less the powers behind them, so McReynolds proposed a spiky alternative: a hipster general strike. Granted, the hipsters of Greenwich Village had a reputation for holding politics at arm's length, but McReynolds suggested that their general strike would be less a work stoppage and more a public carnival. Following Allen Ginsberg's adage (via Plato) that "when the mode of music changes, the walls of the city shake," the strike would be masterminded by musicians and poets. Well before the strike, such artists would start "fashioning exciting new visions and drafting incomprehensible manifestos"—all of which would be scattered across New York by leafletting motorcyclists.[1]

As McReynolds imagined it, the strike itself would gather its power by drawing together hipsters from black and white New York, Harlem and Greenwich Village alike. From Harlem, "which is born hip," a first column of marchers would descend toward City Hall, "preaching great New

Orleans truth into every door and window" of Madison Avenue. Spanish Harlemites would "sheath their weapons" in honor of the occasion's jubilee; gang warfare would make way for class spectacle. In Greenwich Village, meanwhile, every cafe would field a strike-happy contingent, and these squadrons would march towards Washington Square and City Hall to the accompaniment of bongo drums and poetic incantations. At this moment, "special hip agents" would seize control of TV and radio stations, and jazz would become the city's new music, "alerting the city to the Revolution at hand." In all, McReynolds hoped, a crowd of hundreds of thousands would be "sustained and inspired by magic horns of jazz," "the walls of indifference would crumble," developer Robert Moses "would agree to be sheathed in concrete and set in Central Park as a monument," and "at last the back of the Tammany Tiger would be broken." After this great buildup, though, McReynolds admitted that his hipster general strike was "nothing but fantasy"; his hipsters "would be no more effective with their General Strike than we politicos have been with our General Elections." He had merely pitched the event in a spirit of humorous consolation.[2]

McReynolds's fantasy tapped into a deep well of intellectual sentiment, one that foreshadowed his own involvement in the bohemian and pacifist circles of the War Resisters League and later his leadership of the Socialist Party. His pessimism—his sense that political organizing had hit a point of diminishing returns and that ideologies like socialism no longer carried people into the streets—echoed the conventional wisdom of the liberal left. Norman Mailer's "The White Negro" (1957) had crystallized this disenchantment two years earlier by arguing that straightforward electoral solutions had to give way to the crabwise guerrilla maneuvers of the hipster. The hipster certainly did not organize himself or anyone else toward collective political action; he promised to transform American culture only by infusing it with a chaotic, if liberating, impulse—the ethic of spontaneous action that he had learned from the predatory, self-preserving world of the slum.[3]

But McReynolds also moved, albeit with humor, away from "The White Negro" and toward a future politics. His optimism—his hunch that hundreds of thousands of people were disaffected with the trials of modern life and needed only a broader rallying call, his faith that black and white would collaborate politically if they could hear each other through a common cultural language like jazz, his enthusiasm for the power of media-savvy spectacles—suggested the cultural politics that would typify the 1960s. In the coming decade, his intimation about a political rhetoric of self-fulfillment would reverberate in the Port Huron statement of Students for a Democratic Society (SDS), which argued that "the search for truly democratic alternatives . . . is a worthy and fulfilling enterprise"; his hope for interracial alliance would be fulfilled in civil rights projects like Freedom Summer and through musical genres like Motown; and his blueprint for a hipster general strike would have a carbon copy in mass media stunts like the Yippies' attempt to levitate the Pentagon as a Vietnam War protest. "If we want to involve youth in politics," McReynolds wrote presciently, "we must develop a politics of action." So his dream of a hipster general strike links the straitened radicalism of the mid-fifties to the provocative and often spectacular radicalism of the next decade.[1]

This chapter will excavate that brief period, roughly between 1957 and 1961, when the hipster's cultural stance suddenly had political appeal for a wider swath of intellectuals, and when black intellectuals struggled with the contradictory ways that the hipster was used to represent ironic detachment and spontaneous violence, racial authenticity and interracial rapport, existential alienation and bohemian play. The disputes over hip were on one level an effort to monkey-wrench the machine of liberal politics; hipsterism promised to be a visionary, existential politics, one that would not be corrupted by the routines of power-sharing because it was based in the authenticity of the self. At the same time, though, the hip was an aesthetic, a matter of style and taste, a performance that usually aimed to seduce through its perfectly calibrated ratios of emotional heat and stylish nonchalance. The hip pose always risked being dismissed as a kind of triviality, a form of decadence, or a political joke, but it offered a promise that would resonate especially in the 1960s: that a vanguard style, emerging from everyday life, would be the point of origin of far-reaching transformations in politics and art.

The Freedom of Pathology: Mailer's White Negro

In 1957 the hipster flashed with new intensity across the intellectual radar, a fact illustrated by the summer issues of *Commentary, Dissent,* and *Partisan Review.* In each journal, a figure on the fringe of the New York intellectual movement—someone who shared this group's concern with mass culture, individual alienation, and racial conflict but did not move in their inner editorial circle—staked a claim for the hipster. *Commentary* published Isaac Rosenfeld's posthumous "Life in Chicago," a subdued piece of urban sociology that lamented how Chicago's cultural vitality had been sapped in part by college students who had adopted the "anti-social" demeanor of jazz musicians. Meanwhile in *Dissent,* a magazine founded in

1954 to revive democratic socialism, Norman Mailer published "The White Negro." Few essays have generated as much heat as "The White Negro," which took a fairly standard critique of affluence—that white American men were sapped by bureaucratic etiquette and the comforts of conformity—to a provocative conclusion. A true dissident, according to Mailer, had to embrace the ethic of the "white Negro" and "encourage the psychopath in [him]self" (*AFM*, p. 292). Lastly, in *Partisan Review*, the flagship journal that balanced modernist aesthetics with anti-Communist politics, James Baldwin published "Sonny's Blues," a short story that imagined the reconciliation of a "straight" black schoolteacher and his jazz-pianist, heroin-addicted brother. The story gave a distinctly modernist spin to the traditional tale of African-American cultural uplift. While it began with Sonny in jail on a heroin rap and his brother sick at heart, it ended, ecstatically, with Sonny's nightclub performance and his brother's near-conversion to Sonny's code of improvisatory aesthetics.[5]

Together, Rosenfeld, Mailer, and Baldwin staked out the major intellectual positions in the late-1950s romance with the "hip" ethic, and their choice of medium (sociological sketch, existential manifesto, Jamesian short story) reflected each writer's degree of embattlement and affection. Rosenfeld's piece carried the sense of unease that was familiar to intellectual worrying over Mass Man; like David Riesman in *The Lonely Crowd* (1951), Rosenfeld discovered that young Americans were using culture to ingratiate themselves with others rather than to express themselves. Between the 1946 publication of his novel *Passage from Home* and "Life in Chicago," Rosenfeld had gone from being the great literary hope of the New York intellectuals to just one of many utility players, scraping by on an adjunct professor's wages at the University of Chicago's downtown campus.[6] His faith in cultural solidarity had declined along with his fortunes: while Rosenfeld's youthful alter ego in *Passage from Home* imagines a web of fellowship with anonymous black Americans, "Life in Chicago" found fault with collegiates who became jazz enthusiasts and adopted black lingo as their own. Rather than taking comfort in the new social diversity to be found at coffeehouses around Hyde Park, Rosenfeld diagnosed it as a sign of the new conformity:

> One meets types in the varied off-campus dives whom one would mistakenly warrant as students, and students on campus who would seem, by nature, to belong on a motorcycle or behind a counter, tending bar. The shrinking of the distance between extremes has produced a student culture typical, as a particular, and lower, social level, of the amalgamations taking place all over society in our conservative time.

For Rosenfeld jazz was, if not the chief culprit behind the cultural homogeneity of the young people around him, then at least its great accomplice. The "universal solvent of jazz," he observed, had leveled an earlier set of social and political discriminations and replaced them with the "least common biological denominator"—an ethos he saw (perhaps too cleverly) reflected in the way collegiates addressed each other as "man." Rosenfeld's jazz-loving collegiate was a poorer, less respectable cousin of the middlebrow reader who appears often in debates over mass culture: the student's mistake was to "chatter" and "drone" on about culture superficially, without allowing it to transform his life. In another contemporary (and posthumously published) article, Rosenfeld argued similarly that the "dominant values" in coffeehouses were "taken over from jive—where the key words and the key metaphors are . . . 'cool' and 'crazy,' 'gone,' 'gas' and so on. The dominant metaphors therefore are of insanity and death." Rosenfeld had been stupefied by the coffeehouse ambience, which seemed so different from the political, not to say sectarian, conversations that buzzed around the cafeteria alcoves of New York's City College and the University of Chicago in the 1930s. In these new cafés, he wrote, "you get a headache from the din, but nevertheless, you can't find anyone talking to anyone else."[7]

Echoing the analysis of Bernard Wolfe and Anatole Broyard while maintaining a more explicit connection to the engaged politics of the 1930s, Rosenfeld argued that the University of Chicago had given these students "no adequate idea" of what "cultural life . . . should be." Unlike his own generation, for whom "politics was form and substance, accident and modification, the metaphor of all things," these young people had abandoned "politics as an active vocation" in favor of calypso music, "bop-talk," and the "dead-pan Afro-Cuban mask." They aimed for a "passionless, 'cool' life, exposed, but uncommitted, to many worlds and to be *au courant* in them all." For Rosenfeld, as for Broyard and Wolfe, the cool pose was a faddish way to default from intellectual obligations—a failed attempt to create politics by other means.[8]

On the other end of the spectrum, Baldwin and Mailer stood as the primary intellectual partisans of hip, its main exegetes and egg-headed, streetwalking embodiments. For Mailer and Baldwin both, the hipster was heroic because he confronted his own psychological limits and shattered them through concerted action—direct action imbued with the risk-taking spirit of postbop jazz. Writing in the mode of an existentialist manifesto, Mailer argued against liberal platitudes of reasoned, articulate dissent; he envisioned a company of hipsters "trying to create a new nervous system for themselves," engaged in psychological and even physical combat with anyone who might constrain their free will. Against the "sunlit playpen" that Baldwin saw as mass culture, and against the "slow death by conformity" that Mailer diagnosed in "every pore of American life," the hipster offered a guerrilla solution. He recognized an underground economy of scarcity, long familiar to black communities living with hardship, where suffering was indiscriminate and authority had to be seized by zero-sum force. Baldwin contrasted the American dream of affluence with the American Negro's general "experience of life," which he saw as a daily grind against "the force of the world that is out to tell your child that he has no right to be alive."[9]

Yet while Mailer and Baldwin's hipsters were adversaries of society at large, they also were moving toward self-actualization; and here it was that Mailer and Baldwin shared a common psychological framework that grafted Sartrean existentialism onto the American therapeutic ethos. Both Mailer and Baldwin saw the hipster thrust into a world that would deny his humanity, forcing him to improvise an identity as a technique for survival itself. As Baldwin wrote in his essay on Mailer:

> To become a Negro man, let alone a Negro artist, one had to make oneself up as one went along. This had to be done in the not-at-all metaphorical teeth of the world's determination to destroy you. The world had prepared no place for you, and if the world had its way, no place would ever exist. Now, this is true for everyone, but, in the case of a Negro, the truth is absolutely naked: if he deludes himself about it, he will die. (*NKMN*, p. 183)

The hipster, then, lived with an ongoing sense of personal crisis—a neurosis that Mailer viewed positively as "an undeniably dynamic view of existence for it sees every man and woman as moving individually through each moment of life forward into growth or backward into death" (*AFM*, p. 295). The hipster was a man who needed to act—not to move toward some collective political goal (as older ideologies of intellectual commitment would have it), but merely to wrest his individuality from a prejudiced and bureaucratized world. While the system squeezed, the hipster maneuvered. As Beat writer John Clellon Holmes explained in the wake of Mailer's essay, "In the wildest hipster, there is no desire to shatter the 'square' society in which he lives, only to elude it. To get on a soapbox or to write a manifesto would seem to him absurd."[10]

The scandal of Mailer's essay, though, came through his compact phrase "the white Negro," which crystallized the dominant postwar racial division (white-black) even as it encouraged the "pathology" that set whites to adopt black streetwise attitudes. The starkness of Mailer's black-white contrast was conveyed in the City Lights 1960 pamphlet's cover, a photographic negative that inverted the white face and gave it a space-alien stare, a klieg-bulb keenness. The use of the doctored *individual* face was telling: although "The White Negro" was written ostensibly as a brief for racial integration, it understood integration as a psychological and self-enclosed effort. Integration for Mailer meant white men embracing a scorned culture for existential ends, not a community project of joint uplift and understanding. Here he swerved away from Baldwin, who took respectable white readers on a guided tour of black life but never asked them to emulate blacks.[11]

Mailer's most sensational move, however, was to describe integration in the very sexual language that drove the more vicious rhetoric of white supremacists. What had been decried as "miscegenation" was here recast, in spicier and less pejorative language, as an all-male *"ménage-à-trois"* between juvenile delinquents, bohemian Beats, and black urban men, or as a subcultural "wedding" where "the Negro . . . brought the cultural dowry." Mailer's free-ranging metaphors (what kind of *"ménage-à-trois"* was also a "wedding"?) indicated a larger ambiguity about the terms of the black-white exchange he was describing. His black men were both more self-possessed (they had the dowry) and more feminized (they stood in for the women in the marriage). Meanwhile the marriage of black and white, since it was plainly a symbolic affair between men, left plenty of room for heterosexual cruising; both black and white Negroes were free to flout the rule of monogamy. Here jazz—as music of "Saturday-night kicks," music that "relinquish[es] the pleasures of the mind for the more obligatory pleasures of the body"—became a necessary medium. In Mailer's infamous phrase, jazz was "orgasm . . . the music of orgasm, good orgasm and bad," and it was just what American rebels needed, since they not only distrusted the country's power elite but also "knew almost as powerful a disbelief in the socially monolithic ideas of the single mate, the solid family and the respectable love life." Jazz, in Mailer's account, allowed men to discover a more intense private life that was free from the presumption of monogamous commitment (*AFM*, pp. 292–294).

"The White Negro" sent ripples of titillation and some shock waves through American intellectual culture. More inflammatory than *Dissent's* usual academic fare, it prompted outrage from black intellectuals and fine-toothed critiques from white ones, and it confirmed Mailer's literary identity as an intellectual gadfly unafraid to attack liberal pieties or engage in absurd blowhardism.[12] Perhaps most surprising, in retrospect, is the general intellectual enthusiasm for Mailer's gambit: Mailer scorned white liberals, but in turn they indulged him as the postideological flavor of the month. Existentialism had seasoned New York intellectual writings from Dwight Macdonald's "The Root Is Man" (1946) through Harold Rosenberg's "The American Action Painters" (1952), and these intellectuals treated Mailer as a somewhat cockeyed follower of the grace-under-pressure Hemingway.[13] George Steiner saluted Mailer in *Encounter* as one of "the honest men" and praised hipsterism as "a doctrine of vehement candour and a bizarre yet compelling attempt to reassert the sanctity of private life against the pressures of a mass technocracy." *Commentary*'s F. W. Dupee, preferring detachment to solemnity, called the hipster "a charming but probably doomed phenomenon of recent years." Norman Podhoretz, in an extensive appraisal, sized up Mailer with the highest compliment ("a major novelist in the making") and welcomed hipsterism as a renunciation of ideology itself. For Podhoretz, Mailer's hip ethic was "as much a repudiation of ideological thinking in general as of Marx and Trotsky." For all his apocalyptic rhetoric, Mailer was admitting the failures of radical politics: "what else is Hip," Podhoretz asked, "but a means of turning away from despair . . . from the problems of the world and focusing all one's attention on the problems of the self without admitting that this must automatically entail a shrinking of horizons, a contraction of the sense of possibility, a loss of imaginative freedom?" The hipster, understood as the man who beat the most anguished retreat into his private life, deserved our sympathy, our appreciation, and our forbearance. By and large, the white intelligentsia recognized in "The White Negro" a class warrior's admission of defeat.[14]

Jazz critics were more apt to see Mailer as a threatening figure. Nat Hentoff criticized Mailer for inflating the acumen of hipsters, whose "reactions" to jazz were "as superficial and unknowledgeable" as those of white "adolescents" who loved the onstage hamming of Stan Kenton. He also took up Mailer's equation of jazz with music of Saturday night kicks and orgasm. "The music of jazz," Hentoff wrote, "is much too pragmatic, too variegated, and too unpredictable to support such over-simplified romanticizations of the 'holy' role of jazz." Some of its practitioners, he added evenhandedly, led itinerant lives of adventure and disrepute, but many were "cigar makers, dock workers, artisans, sons of small businessmen," even "the children of the middle class." Read as an analysis of the jazz scene, "The White Negro" could not fail to disappoint: it limited the musicians to an underworld clique and flattened the music, as Mezzrow's autobiography had done, into a single-minded quest for ecstasy.[15]

The most astringent criticisms of "The White Negro," however, came from the corner of black intellectuals, who seized on Mailer's assumptions about class, race, and sexuality. The essay prompted future author and then jazz pianist Claude Brown to enter the world of intellectual writing through a letter to *Dissent*'s editor about the piece.[16] Ralph Ellison picked up on Hentoff's defense of the work ethic in jazz culture and attested that "most Negroes can spot a paper-thin 'white Negro' every time simply because those who masquerade missed what others were forced to pick up along the way: discipline—a discipline which these heavy thinkers would not undergo even if . . . it would make of them the freest of spirits, the wisest of men and the most sublime of heroes." In his private correspondence with fellow writer Albert Murray, Ellison was even more blistering. Lumping Mailer with Jack Kerouac, he called the hipster vogue "the same old primitivism crap in a new package":

> These characters are all trying to reduce the world to sex, man, they have strange problems in bed. . . . That's what's behind Mailer's belief in the hipster and the "white Negro" as the new culture hero—he thinks all hipsters are cocksmen possessed of great euphoric orgasms and are out to fuck the world into peace, prosperity, and creativity. . . . It makes you hesitant to say more than the slightest greetings to their wives lest they think you're out to give them a hot fat injection. What a bore.

In another letter, Ellison suggested that Mailer's primitivism, for all its machismo, was just a retread of white aesthete Carl Van Vechten's writings during the Harlem Renaissance: "Mailer would be quite surprised to see that the crap he's selling is actually V's leavings."[17]

Lorraine Hansberry, author of the acclaimed Broadway play *A Raisin in the Sun*, uncorked her anger four years after "The White Negro"'s original publication, provoked by Mailer's review of Jean Genet's *The Blacks*. In an extended essay, she wrote that "it has had a numbing effect, the creation of 'the hip' into an expanded formalized idea. Negroes seem to have met it mainly with a crowning silence because who knew *where* to begin in the face of such monumental and crass assumptions." Hansberry charged Mailer as the leader of "the New Paternalism," a movement of left-leaning intellectuals who redeemed "romantic racism" as the inside knowledge of "the most inside of insiders . . . [the] obscure undefined universal outsider who may be known as 'the hipster.'"[18]

The argument between Mailer and Hansberry was, in large part, an argument about class in America. Following the logic of such cultural critics as Vance Packard and William Whyte, who criticized the suburban ideal for its mass production of status seekers and organization men, Mailer was moved to write that "the real horror worked on the Jews and the Negroes since the Second World War is the *mass-communication* of nothingness into their personality. They were two of the greatest peoples in America, and half of their populations sold themselves to the suburb, the center, the secure." In response, Hansberry asked what it meant to preserve suffering in the name of the sufferer's best psychological interests: "Negroes of *all* classes have made it clear that they want the hell out of the ghetto just as fast as the ascendancy of Africa, the courts, insurance money, job-upgrading, the threat of 'our image overseas,' or anything else can thrust them. . . . Misery may be theatrical to the onlooker but it hurts him who is miserable. That is what the blues are about." Just as Hansberry's most famous play used the genre of family melodrama to make an eloquent argument for black social mobility, here she defended the black middle class and those who aspired to join it. It was an intellectual luxury, she suggested, to attack those who joined the middle class after the fact—and to pass over in silence the injustices that constrained life in the ghetto.[19]

James Baldwin had a more vexed relation to Mailer than Ellison or Hansberry, perhaps because the same cultural forces that turned "The White Negro" into a succès de scandale also elevated Baldwin into the race man of the moment: their careers both peaked between 1955 and 1965. Well before "The White Negro" and well after it, Baldwin wrestled with its admixture of righteous energy, sexual struggle, and existential soul-searching. Recognizing such a shared agenda—and perhaps attuned to the homoerotic undertones of Mailer's essay—he introduced his own trenchant "The Black Boy Looks at the White Boy" as a "love letter" (*NKMN*, p. 170). At the same time, Baldwin came to loggerheads with Mailer over some of the most substantial questions regarding the hipster. First, was the hipster's sexual style worthy of emulation (Mailer), or was it the figment of racially driven fear and envy (Baldwin)? And second, was he the prototype for successful dissent (Mailer), or was he a suicide waiting to happen (Baldwin)?

The first question was the more sensational and immediate one. According to Mailer, the hipster compensated for his general lack of power through the insistent chase of sexual power; his life was the pursuit of love of a distinctly unsuburban variety—the "search for an orgasm more apocalyptic than the one which preceded it" (*AFM*, p. 300). No families were to be raised, no questions of commitment to be introduced; the white Negro lived in an existential present that foreclosed these questions and made the latest orgasm appear on the same spectrum as the most recent testing of the H-bomb. With much verbal enthusiasm if not much clarity, Mailer tried in "The White Negro" to reverse the punishing language of diagnostic psychiatry that infused the analysis of intellectuals like Bernard Wolfe and Anatole Broyard. Here liberal pop psychologist Robert Lindner, who coined the term "rebel without a cause," was Mailer's source of theoretical inspiration and his sparring partner. While Lindner had lamented both delinquency and conformity and then instructed the mature man "to identify the psychopathic antagonist and to struggle against the conditions that produce him," Mailer cited Lindner but then asked his audience to embrace the psychopath within them, to turn to spontaneous action—not incremental environmental reform—as the most heroic response to a conformist age.[20]

Baldwin sympathized with Mailer's frank fascination with power, but he lambasted Mailer for reviving one of the oldest racial fictions: that black men were devil-may-care studs with no interest in long-term intimacy and its emotional risks. The "glorification of orgasm," Baldwin wrote, was merely "a way of avoiding all the terrors of life and love"; he rued that Mailer, like so many white men, was forcing black men to "pay[,] in [their] own personality, for the sexual insecurity of others" (NKMN, pp. 180, 172). A black and openly gay writer, Baldwin questioned the mythologies of black potency that Mailer had elaborated, to almost cartoonish lengths, in his manifesto. Such mythologies had taken root not only among segregationists, who saw the threat of miscegenation in any act of black self-assertion, but also among postwar liberal sociologists, who viewed black life as a dysfunctional response to the humiliations of segregation and the deprivations of poverty. For Baldwin, the rebuttal of Mailer's program took on an extrasexual significance, one he would enlarge upon as he became a prophet for the rage brewing among blacks in the urban North.[21]

The second question—was hipsterism a viable alternative or a recipe for failure?—was answered largely over the course of the next decade, as Mailer and Baldwin moved into the media mainstream and invented new fates for their improvisatory antiheroes. As Mailer grew into a media pundit, writing commentary for Esquire and the recently founded Village Voice, he began to see his hipster taking on a larger cultural mandate. The liberal intelligentsia had its first impressions confirmed: Mailer's hipsters began evolving into more palatable, less violent figures of cultural leadership. In "Superman Comes to the Supermarket," a 1960 piece for Esquire, he cast presidential candidate John F. Kennedy in the role of hipster politician, a man whose conventional politics masked his unconventional style—the existentialist solution to the nation's failure of nerve.[22] In retrospect, Mailer's love affair with Kennedy seems seeded in "The White Negro," which everywhere emphasizes charismatic leadership over community building. Mailer's controlling metaphor, in fact, is the undeclared warfare between an unrecognized elite and a stultified majority. Calling hipsters an "élite with the potential ruthlessness of an élite," Mailer predicts that

America's collective violence "must either vent itself nihilistically or become turned into the cold murderous liquidations of the totalitarian state"—Armageddon scenarios of chaos or martial law (*AFM*, pp. 296, 310). Similarly, his "marriage" of bohemian, juvenile delinquent, and black hipster revolves around the compulsion "to open the limits of the possible for oneself, for oneself alone, because that is one's need" (*AFM*, p. 307). Even his orgasms are individual triumphs, apocalypse served up for a party of one.

Baldwin, meanwhile, never imagined another jazz success story like that of "Sonny's Blues," even as he became *the* American black intellectual celebrity through his TV appearances and best-selling essays and fiction. His later jazz hipsters were martyr figures whose deaths mobilized the surrounding community—Rufus in the million-selling novel *Another Country* (1962), Richard Henry in the Broadway play *Blues for Mister Charlie* (1964). Whereas Mailer baptized the hipster with mainstream success, Baldwin built his own celebrity on a genre that might be called the hipster elegy. Both *Another Country* and *Blues for Mister Charlie* began with riddles of alienation and death (Rufus committing suicide, Richard killed by a bigoted assassin), then proceeded to unravel the mysteries of guilt and despair behind the corpse. Ultimately, Baldwin envisioned a sort of beloved community rising out of his artistic postmortems—a fallible but strong community of lovers, friends, and family. His hipsters died without meaning, alone; but these tragedies had the ironic effect of gathering together a community, chastened and schooled by its loss. "Sonny's Blues" marked the beginnings of this trajectory; in this story, Baldwin tried to understand why a diseased society fastened so much attention—so much hope and so much despair—on the black men in jazz.[23]

James Baldwin's Street Corner: Ray Charles, Meet Henry James

In "Sonny's Blues," James Baldwin took a nearly opposite tack from Norman Mailer. While "The White Negro" explained the hipster as a pathological individual whose violence was necessary to the culture as a whole, Baldwin sought to normalize the hipster by drawing him into the meshes of family, vocation, and tradition. When, in the first scene of the short story, the narrator reads his brother's name in the paper and discovers that he is accused of heroin peddling, it comes as a shock because he sees Sonny as "a good boy" who had never "turned hard or evil or disrespectful, the way kids can, so quick, so quick, especially in Harlem." The newspaper launches an act of defamiliarization that the whole force of the short story will work to reverse: Sonny has been transformed from a "good boy" to a crime statistic, but the narrator will work to recover Sonny as a brother, a man, an artist, and finally an avatar for his race. In this effort Baldwin marshals the tradition of the Jamesian psychological novel—its spectatorial point of view, its gradual unraveling of recrimination and compassion, its respect for the deeper and elusive springs of human motive. A schoolteacher and straight man, Sonny's brother gives the hipster a kind of accreditation that far outranks what can be gained from the knowledge of algebra (the narrator's specialty in the classroom). First likened to the boys in his brother's charge, whose heads "[bump] abruptly against the low ceiling of their actual possibilities," Sonny becomes a virtuoso of his own intensity, translating his frustration into the blues idiom and claiming a spiritual family in the process (*GMM*, pp. 103–104).

Although Baldwin never displayed any technical familiarity with jazz music, he did claim the jazz aesthetic for himself and even made a sly connection between jazz and Henry James, the most prestigious American literary presence of the 1950s. For Baldwin, the ambition of his prose was to fuse the psychological inwardness of James with the ecstatic compassion of jazz-gospel. It was an incongruous match, but one elicited when Baldwin was asked about his artistic aims; Miles Davis and Ray Charles, he said,

> sing a kind of universal blues . . . , they are telling us something about what it is like to be alive. It is not self-pity which one hears in them, but compassion. . . . I think I really helplessly model myself on jazz musicians and try to write the way they sound. I am not an intellectual, not in the dreary sense that word is used today, and do not want to be. I am aiming at what Henry James called "perception at the pitch of passion."[24]

"Perception at the pitch of passion" was a high-toned translation of the blues riff, which often has accompanied more earthy pleasures. Baldwin was interested in identifying the suffering and empathy within jazz. In the distinction between "self-pity" and "compassion," he found the difference between exhibitionism and a moral engagement with the community. Perhaps for this reason, he was drawn to the music's call-and-response modes, which figured a more responsive community, rather than to the virtuoso flights of its soloists.[25]

His hipster, unlike Mailer's white Negro and unlike blues figures from Ma Rainey to Chuck Berry, represents no affront to the politics of respectability. In fact, in Baldwin's account, every black character—no matter how religious or secular, no matter how hip or square—is linked by a chain of suffering, one that binds them in mutual empathy. The plot of the story is punctuated by instructional flashbacks of grief. For instance, the narrator's mother reveals that her husband was mentally wracked by the murder of his brother, and the narrator is spurred to take care of Sonny. Similarly, at a later point, the narrator's daughter dies of polio, and the narrator sees that "[his] trouble made [Sonny's] real" (*GMM,* pp. 116–118, 127).

For Baldwin, who saw the horizon of "actual possibilities" dimming throughout the ghetto, Sonny was caught in a vocational dead-end: he was trapped between the sellout that had no sublimity (his brother's teaching job) and the cop-out that gave an ecstatic charge (his heroin addiction). In this sense, "Sonny's Blues" foreshadows later works, such as Paul Goodman's *Growing Up Absurd* (1960), which criticized the mass production of young men without a sense of purpose. A dialogue between Sonny and his brother, in the aftermath of their mother's funeral, captures the friction between the narrator's good-thinking liberalism and Sonny's bitter conviction that he needs to pursue a career in music. The nudnick, focused on the steady job, meets the rebel, whose cause is self-fulfillment:

"Doesn't this take a lot of time? Can you make a living at it?"

He turned back to me and half leaned, half sat, on the kitchen table. "Everything takes time," he said, "and—well, yes, sure, I can make a living at it. But what I don't seem to be able to make you understand is that it's the only thing I want to do."

"Well, Sonny," I said, gently, "you know people can't always do exactly what they *want* to do—"

"*No,* I don't know that," said Sonny, surprising me. "I think people *ought* to do what they want to do, what else are they alive for?"

"You getting to be a big boy," I said desperately, "it's time you started thinking about your future."

"I'm thinking about my future," said Sonny, grimly. "I think about it all the time." (*GMM,* pp. 121–122)

In this dialogue Baldwin wrestled with a question central to jazz music as it gained critical and popular ground in the 1950s: Was it music of spontaneous impulse, as it had been considered by a long line of popular Negrophilic writers including Mezz Mezzrow? Or was it music of profound, self-exploring rumination, as modernist-influenced critics like Martin Williams had begun to appraise it? Sonny's shallowness or profundity hung in the balance. The main thrust of Baldwin's tale is to redeem

Sonny from his purported pathologies, to establish the ruminations within the emotional anguish. Thus the narrator sets their reconciliation in motion by considering anew the depths of Sonny's personality:

> [I] had begun, finally, to wonder about Sonny, about the life that Sonny lived inside. This life, whatever it was, had made him older and thinner and it had deepened the distant stillness in which he had always moved. He looked very unlike my baby brother. Yet, when he smiled, when we shook hands, the baby brother I'd never known looked out from the depths of his private life, like an animal waiting to be coaxed into the light.

Baldwin works to establish Sonny's interior space through the dominant metaphor here, the lonely and dark proscenium in which Sonny moves, thinks, and looks out from his depths. By recognizing this world of emotional secrecy, the narrator begins to unriddle Sonny, to see the "baby brother I'd never known"; yet at the same time, Baldwin's narrator is limited by the furtiveness of the signals—smiles, handshakes—which bear an enormous emotional freight. Throughout the story, Baldwin's narrator wrestles awkwardly to characterize a figure who, like the movies' Marlon Brando or James Dean, communicates his depth through gestures of partial inarticulateness, through the surface struggle to represent his own emotions. The halting rhythm of the back-and-forth exchange over Sonny's vocation reappears throughout the story's dialogue.

Ultimately, the power of Sonny's nightclub performance in Greenwich Village awakens the narrator to his brother's grace and gift: he realizes that Sonny's music allows him at once to raise himself up and establish a deeper connection to the struggles of his family and his race. Baldwin reworked the conventional (and conventionally male) African-American narrative of emancipation, which sees freedom won through an often physical, often violent confrontation with one's oppressor. In "Sonny's Blues," by contrast, the first struggle occurs within the individual's mind, and freedom is capped by the achievement of intimacy; self-knowledge must be conveyed through a confessional art so that it can be understood sympathetically by its audience. In the course of Sonny's performance, bonds of familial sympathy are rediscovered everywhere: between the bassist Creole and Sonny and the rest of the bandstand, between the narrator and his brother, even between Sonny and his now deceased mother and father. The art of the blues revives the community by allowing its members to share formerly private struggles (*GMM*, pp. 139–140).

Prodded by Creole's bass and Sonny's elaboration of the blues theme, the narrator writes:

> Freedom lurked around us and I understood, at last, that he could help us to be free if we would listen, that he would never be free until we did. Yet, there was no battle in his face now. I heard what he had gone through, and would continue to go through until he came to rest in earth. He had made it his: that long line, of which we knew only Mama and Daddy. (*GMM* 140)

Baldwin echoed this conception of freedom in "Nobody Knows My Name," where he called freedom "a complex, difficult—and private—thing," "the fire that burns away illusion" from one's self-conception (*NKMN*, p. 99).[26] The Sonny who has "no battle in his face" has achieved a preternatural calm. The crucial twist in "Sonny's Blues," however, is the mutual dependence between Sonny and his audience, their inability to discover freedom without each other. For Baldwin, the power of jazz lay not in the soloist's authority nor even in the camaraderie across the bandstand; it was the music's capacity to suggest collective emancipation as a kind of shared empathy. Sonny's individual performance had the virtue of reestablishing a common "inside" space, an "us" beyond estrangement, a circle of listeners and performers all engaged in a collective act of introspection. Jazz for Baldwin promised to knit together a community of common sentiment through a paradox: the shared discovery of a private freedom (*GMM*, p. 140). The spirit of Henry James, connoisseur of psychological nuance and the pained logic of renunciation, hovered over the conundrum.

Bohemian Rhapsody: Robert Thompson's Village Art

Ironically, the site of this euphoric black reconciliation was a jazz club in Greenwich Village, not Harlem. Baldwin's community of lovers had its roots in tradition, but it also reinvented that tradition in a bohemian crucible that was both old-fashioned and entirely novel—a neighborhood that went by the gemeinschaft name the Village. Baldwin's later novel *Another Country* was similarly centered around Greenwich Village: all of its characters meet there even as their lives radiate out to the South, Harlem, and Paris. Together, Mailer and Baldwin confirmed Greenwich Village as the crossroads where black and white artists could explore the vicissitudes of a hip life—the cafés and bars, where much mingling took place; the rent parties, where cocktails mixed with the latest gossip; the cramped apartments, where men and women shared their art as well as their bodies; and the bathrooms and lofts, where drugs (mostly pot and heroin) could be smoked, spiked, or otherwise ingested. Indeed, between 1958 and 1963, the Village thrummed with artistic experimentation at coffeehouses like the Hip Bagel, bars like the Cedar Tavern, community centers like the Judson Church, and jazz clubs like the Village Vanguard. Literary types could stroll the "Elephant Walk," a daisy chain of cafes and bookshops that featured regular poetry readings by younger writers such as Allen Ginsberg and Frank O'Hara. The Off-Broadway theater movement, epitomized by the Living Theater (which had an uptown venue), thrived alongside the Off-Off-Broadway movement, launched by the Open Theater, Caffe Cino, and Café La Mama. Interested avant-garde partisans could sample the pleasures and confusions of "happenings"—live gallery exhibitions that would later be deemed "performance art"—at the Delancey Street Museum and the Reuben Gallery. Along with such creative ferment came a fair amount of hype, as developers tried to milk the new ambience. Would-be renters along Avenue B were lured by the real estate slogan "Join the Smart Trend."[27]

For most black jazz artists and fans, however, this bohemian world was a faraway place. Exact numbers are elusive, but one statistic strikes pointedly at the myth of Village interracialism: writer Hettie Jones estimated that in 1957, there were fewer than half a dozen steady interracial couples in the Village. Still, the early 1960s also witnessed a sizable migration of black intelligentsia into Greenwich Village, especially the just-dubbed East Village. Writers Lorraine Hansberry, Claude Brown, James Baldwin, LeRoi Jones/ Amiri Baraka and A. B. Spellman; saxophonists Marion Brown and Archie Shepp; drummer Sunny Murray; painters Bob Thompson and William White—all took up residence in the Village, and many of them (Baraka, Spellman, Hansberry, and Thompson at least) settled into interracial marriages there. The jazz club the Five Spot, through its sponsorship of Ornette Coleman, Thelonious Monk, and John Coltrane, wielded an almost totemic charm. Meanwhile, a group of young black poets, including Calvin Hernton, David Henderson, Ishmael Reed, and Lorenzo Thomas, formed the tempestuous fellowship called Umbra on the Lower East Side and published a magazine by the same name in 1963 and 1964.[28] The question might then be posed: Did these black bohemians share the white Negro's proposal of a powerful, even violent, primitive consciousness among them? Or did their art and criticism reflect Baldwin's more humane world of empathy, sacrifice, and reconciliation?

There is perhaps no better self-image of this nascent black bohemianism than Bob Thompson's monumental, jazz-inspired canvas *Garden of Music*. The painting not only strikes a balance between Mailer's primitivism and

Baldwin's sense of community but also injects a welcome note of absurd humor. Thompson's life fit the hipster prototype to a tee. Taking a page from existentialism, he described himself to his mother as "a man who changes constantly," and added breathlessly that change "means progression in my book as long as one progresses there is no stopping." Baraka recalled that Thompson "had a gigantic jet engine driving him. He took everything to extremes. He had a passion for life." Practically, this life of extremes involved great turmoil and itinerancy: by May 1966, when he died from an apparent drug overdose at the age of twenty-eight, he had hustled from his native Kentucky through the artistic colonies of Provincetown, Greenwich Village, Paris, Ibiza, and Rome. He threw himself into the multimedia avant-garde, participating in the earliest happenings (sometimes playing bongo drums) and frequenting jazz performances at the Five Spot, the Jazz Gallery, and Slug's. Charlie Haden, Ornette Coleman's bassist and a friend of Thompson's, remembered his Greenwich Village digs as the very image of the bohemian at work. Thompson squatted rent-free in a loft without heat or hot water, approached through an unlit stairwell, in a building that risked being condemned. There were few furnishings, just a portable heater, a chest of drawers, and a couple of chairs; the artist's paints, canvas, and blasting record player dominated the room. Addicted, like Haden, to heroin, Thompson was nonetheless a dynamo who, in Haden's words, "would not sleep for days" but would "just paint, rest for a couple of hours, and get up again."[29]

Garden of Music was the fruit of Thompson's many hours at jazz clubs, a resplendent homage to the music's powers of fantasia. Six feet tall and twelve feet wide, it refused the stigma of a lesser, minority art. As Thompson announced to Haden as he worked on Haden's portrait, "I'm painting my favorite musicians, the ones who inspired me!" Thompson carried his enthusiasm to one other canvas—his 1965 *Homage to Nina Simone*—but these jazz paintings were a small part of a larger oeuvre in which he reworked classic European paintings (Géricault's *Le Radeau de la Méduse,* Goya's *Los Caprichos,* Tintoretto's *St. George and the Dragon*) through the Fauvist color palette that was his signature.[30] While *Garden of Music* swerved away from the usual topics of his painting, it evoked the jazz community via an intermediary European tradition, namely pastoral painting. Outrageously, it recast the urban-jungle primitivism of Mailer's "White Negro" as a jam session in the Garden of Eden. On the garden's verdant stage, Thompson drew together the all-stars of the jazz avant-garde—from left to right, Ornette Coleman on alto sax, Don Cherry on toy trumpet, Sonny Rollins arching under his tenor, John Coltrane playing straight-on. This was a jam session, notably, where all artists could solo at once; their

Bob Thompson, *Garden of Music* (1960): Six feet tall and twelve feet wide, with a Fauvist-influenced palette, *Garden of Music* was Bob Thompson's resplendent homage to the jazz musicians he loved (and associated with). Pictured in various states of whimsy and concentration—though all in a full state of nudity—are Ornette Coleman, Don Cherry, Sonny Rollins, John Coltrane, Ed Blackwell, and Charlie Haden. (Courtesy of the Wadsworth Atheneum, Hartford, the Ella Gallup Sumner and Mary Catlin Sumner Collection Fund)

instruments may have pointed in different directions, but their bodies formed a semicircle that welcomed the audience and centered the picture. Meanwhile, the rhythm section meditated and frolicked. Drummer Ed Blackwell sat on his haunches, whittling his own drumsticks; bassist Charlie Haden could be found in the background, his back turned, engaged in the fantastic act of balancing his immense instrument by its bottom point.

Garden of Music celebrated the eros of jazz even as it obeyed its own absurd laws of discretion. Thompson responded to the urban spirit of jazz by taking the music on a nudist field trip, with the only piece of clothing being a crushed hat that suggested Lester Young's famous porkpie.[31] Against "The White Negro"'s dictum that "jazz was orgasm," the painting was frank but judicious, hiding the sexes of its performers. A yellow lollipop of shrubbery conceals Ornette Coleman's genitals; Coleman's horn obscures Don Cherry's; Sonny Rollins is enveloped in his blackness; John Coltrane has his saxophone strategically placed; Ed Blackwell works on his whittling project; and Charlie Haden has his back to the viewer. Such compositional decorum, however, is loosened by the eroticism of the musical poses themselves. The central figure of Coltrane, eyes lowered on his instrument, is diligently administering to his own satisfaction. Likewise, Ed Blackwell's exercise in drumstick whittling—decipherable as such only because Haden has remarked on Thompson's fascination with Blackwell's instrument-making—might easily be viewed as an exercise in self-pleasure. Overall, Thompson effectively conveys that, for these artists, their instruments are their sources of sublime satisfaction: eyes shut, they are completely absorbed. As the Bible says, paradise is a place before sex and its knowledge, before the curses of toil and procreation.

At the same time that *Garden of Music* establishes the ideal of a worker's playtime, it also discovers a less obvious utopia for its audience. Here Thompson avoids the cliché that we might expect, and that a jazz artist like Charles Mingus had demanded on occasion from the bandstand: an audience magnetized by the music to the exclusion of all else. Indeed, a good fraction of the audience in the painting is as distracted as the performers are absorbed. In the left foreground, a milk-chocolate figure hugs a tree. On the right side of the canvas, a dark-haired woman peeks slantwise away from the musicians; a faceless woman kneels and clutches her hands as if praying toward the viewer; an emerald-skinned woman stares straight out to the bottom-right corner; and a cluster of three men—critics?—share looks that are half-blasé, half-surly. The woman on the right edge offers oblique caution. Perhaps most strikingly—altering the mood of the canvas—the example of Charlie Haden, an escaped fugitive from the bandstand, underscores the pull of entropy and self-diversion.

At the same time, there are a number of exceptions to the rule of distraction. A triad of three women—one burnt umber, one deep blue, one terracotta red—sit and stand diminutively in the center, offering their backs to us and their attention to the musicians. Seemingly more passive—and yet also more unknowable, their faces unseen—they offset the circle of male critics and suggest that listening can be a devotional art. Such is the range of choices offered by Thompson in his nudist jazz festival: we may be spellbound by the music, spellbound by ourselves, caught in our own reflections, or searching for something new, outside the frame. A generous painter, Thompson bestows on everyone the same vibrancy of color, an equal share of light. The small field in the high left background looks suspiciously like an artist's palette, and its rich spots of color match up with the flesh of musicians and audience alike.

For all its exuberance, though, *Garden of Music* also offers a frank and disquieting view of the sexual roles that inspirited the bohemian project of personal liberation. There is a stark contrast between the line of female fans, each diminutive and looking up to the jazz heroes, and the pack of male critics who, compositionally speaking, come at us as bulging heads. The *Garden*'s women generally pose submissively—for instance, the burnt-umber woman sitting on the grass and the blond woman, mysteriously faceless, who kneels and has her hands locked in prayer at the base of a tree. Similarly, there is only one exception to the *Garden's* rule of genital discretion: the black woman with a flaming copper afro on the right edge. She comes at us with the force of a reproach, an exception disguised as an offering. Her arms are unnaturally tense and hang in anticipation of doing something; her gaze is aimed at us but she seems to be staring through us, distracted. She has a highly ambivalent relationship in the painting, both marginal and magnetic, pulling us in and pulling us away. She does not conceal herself, but neither does she offer herself; she confronts us but does not recognize us. Such ambivalence reflected the difficulty that Thompson had in placing women—particularly black women—alongside his improvisatory jazzmen and surly critics. Writer Joyce Johnson has recalled how Beat women figured only as "minor characters" in the Beat story of personal liberation: in part, Beat men like Jack Kerouac imagined themselves as liberating themselves and their art *from* the clutches of women, who were viewed as the enforcers of the cultural rule of monogamy, the steady job, and the nuclear family. Thompson shared the larger Beat limitation inasmuch as he gave his women no active vocation for themselves, nothing besides their bodies and their affection to offer—in effect, no license for heroic improvisation.[32]

Created in 1960, *Garden of Music* also gave a snapshot of the black bohemian avant-garde at a moment before the militant racial politics of the mid-sixties, when black artists would root themselves in vernacular models and seek a direct social application for their art. Thompson himself was uncomfortable with the frank politicization of cultural nationalism. Although he later drew portraits of Amiri Baraka and civil rights diva Nina Simone, he had little interest in activism as such. He did not join Baraka and A. B. Spellman in a proto-nationalist group called the Organization of Young Men, formed in 1961 as a civil rights adjunct in New York, and a move to Europe allowed him to evade the most pressing political dilemmas of the Lower East Side—some of which, for instance, led Umbra to dissolve in a round of bickering and physical abuse, and provoked Baraka in 1965 to leave his wife and children and choose Harlem as the home of the Black Arts Repertory Theater School. As Judith Wilson comments, "Thompson was loath to relinquish a mythic 'universalism' that has had special force for academically trained black practitioners of the visual arts." The *Garden of Music* is a desegregated recreational area—a mirror image of the integrated swimming pools, beaches, and parks that the civil rights movement fought for. Its white and black men and women have no hostility to one another; in fact, the dominant ethos is a simple epicurean one: fulfill thyself. Similarly, Thompson's figurative expressionism aimed to show that European and African-American artistic practices could commingle in rough-edged but pleasurable harmony. He reworked the genre of the pastoral with a palette that established wide swaths of high-contrast colors in the landscape—setting the garden on fire in its outer reaches and turning human figures into bold impresarios of the land. His celebration of jazz no doubt "classicized" the music and kept its women as minor characters, but it also did not lose sight of one of this music's cardinal virtues: its fusion of discipline and diversion, concentration and reverie.[33]

The Riddle of Killer Joe: Soul-Jazz and the Rise of the Hippie

Question: What was the hippie before he was a long-haired flower-child?
Saxophonist Benny Golson's answer, circa 1960: A womanizing hustler.[34]
Saxophonist Cannonball Adderley's answer, circa 1961: A jazz fan posing as an intellectual.[35]

Here is one of those etymological riddles that stand for a larger cultural puzzle. Names are often weapons aimed by one group at another, and the arrival of the hippie in jazz subculture suggested that jazz artists were targeting those camp followers who poached on their presumed hipness and soaked in their subcultural authority. Such poachers were not hard to find. In March 1958, San Francisco columnist Herb Caen had performed a consequential act of renaming, coining the term "beatnik" to describe those members of the Beat generation who were as "far out" as the Russian Sputnik satellite. Caen's Slavic suffix smeared the beatnik as an unwitting conformist, someone whose flamboyant rebellion was a cover for his or her fashionable, and possibly un-American, smallmindedness. The beatnik was a close relative of the hipster—in many popular magazines the two were interchangeable—and by 1959 the two were staples of national magazine coverage, pulp novels like *Beatnik Wanton* and *Bongo Gum,* schlocky B-movies like Roger Corman's *A Bucket of Blood* and Albert Zugsmith's *The Beat Generation,* and TV cop dramas and sitcoms. From *Life* and the *New York Herald Tribune* to *Playboy* and *Mad Magazine,* hipsters and beatniks appeared in their obligatory garb and gear: loose-fitting T-shirt, beret, sunglasses, poetry books at the ready. All beatnik men, it seems, had goatees while all beatnik women wore deep fringe and the blackest of eye shadow.[36]

Such mass-media attention helped bring the hipster new allies and, from the ranks of many avant-gardists and jazz critics, many new enemies as well. The hipster's success was so diffuse that his spirit started appearing in non-jazz contexts—for instance, in the reflections of student radicals like Tom Hayden. One of the founders of SDS and the main author of the Port Huron Statement, Hayden argued in 1961—a year before Port Huron— that the New Left would be distinguished by its "radicalism of style." Mailer's white Negro reappeared, without the color cues but with his strutting existentialist bravado, in Hayden's description of the New Leftist: radicalism of style meant "to be exposed always to the stinging glare of change, to be willing always to reconstruct our social views. In its harshest consideration, radicalism of style demands that we oppose delusions and be free. It demands that we change our life." Hayden's dream of a radical style echoed David McReynolds's earlier fantasy of a hipster general strike; like many New Leftists, Hayden and McReynolds hoped that a politics of personal authenticity could launch a moral renewal and provide an alternative to the zero-sum equations of interest-group politics. These new radicals approached politics through their direct experience of the world. They might later entertain the art of compromise, or search outside the self for the class or community that would be the engine of revolutionary change, but their politics would be grounded in the good conscience of the individual.[37]

Within jazz, the hipster took on a second life through the burgeoning category of soul-jazz, a subgenre of hard bop popularized by such figures as Cannonball Adderley and Oscar Brown, Jr., pianists Horace Silver and Bobby Timmons, saxophonists Gene Ammons, Eddie "Lockjaw" Davis, and Stanley Turrentine, and organists Jimmy Smith and Shirley Scott. Soul-jazz transparently incorporated more gospel and rhythm and blues (R&B) techniques into the music: it brought back the showmanship of the honking tenor and the funky-lick pianist, often setting them to an emphatic backbeat and the waves, rolls, and patches of a churchy Hammond organ. Soul-jazz hipsters could never be mistaken for hipsters of the cool school. Instead of modeling ironic detachment and emotional self-editing, they opened jazz up as an idiom of earthy delights, impromptu feeling, and blues conjugations. The pleasure principle behind the music—equal parts gospel possession and get-down groove—was advertised by album titles like Adderley's *What Is This Thing Called Soul* (1960); Ammons's *Funky* (1957); Brown's *Sin and Soul* (1960); Davis's three-volume *Cookbook* (1958); Smith's *The Sermon* (1958), *Houseparty* (1958), and *Home Cookin'* (1959); Scott's *The Soul Is Willin'* (1961) and *Soul Shoutin'* (1961); and Timmons's *Soul Time* (1960).[38]

The cover of a November 1960 issue of *Down Beat* raised some of the basic questions about this emerging genre: "What's all this talk of Groove,

Funk, and Soul? Is this Down Home feeling a new force in jazz? An infusion of Gospel flavor, a true Spirit Feel? Is it a manifestation of the rising tide of racial protest? Or is it merely current argot for an earthy flavor that has always been in the bloodstream of jazz but used to be called gutbucket, dirty, in the gutter, or in the alley?" The lead article was simply titled "funkgroovesoul"—a combination of three words that cut to the heart of this new, emphatically black, and vernacular aesthetic, three words that would only become more prominent over the course of the next decade. *Down Beat* issues from 1960 regularly carried full-page ads from Riverside Records and Prestige Records, the two labels that trumpeted their sponsorship of soul-jazz. Signifying on the gospel spiritual "Everybody Talking about Heaven Ain't Going There," Riverside proclaimed that "Everybody's talking about soul . . . but Riverside's got it!" and judged soul-jazz "the most discussed (and most widely enjoyed) jazz form of 1960." Prestige took a more embattled tone, promoting albums by Ammons, Davis, and Scott with the motto "Despite opposition of critics Prestige gave birth to soul jazz!"[39]

Soul-jazz was an indisputable popular success, and it helped to revive the connection between jazz and popular music that had been frayed since the end of the swing era. The jazz single, bought by jukebox operators and young people, returned after 1958 largely on the strength of such releases as Ray Bryant's "Little Susie," Ramsey Lewis's "The In Crowd," Jimmy Smith's "Midnight Special," and Adderley's "This Here" and "African Waltz," the latter of which outsold every other record in Riverside's catalog at 175,000 copies. Riverside Records's Bill Grauer and legendary A&R man John Hammond both speculated in 1960 that rock and roll had merely filled a vacuum in the late fifties and that the return of the jazz single would shift popular taste back in the direction of jazz. They were half right: the success of these jazz singles did signal a revival of interest in less "poppy" ballads, but jazz was a decidedly junior partner in a more general trend towards R&B and, later, soul music. While some jazz singles crossed over into the R&B audience, many of the most prominent hard boppers—for instance, Horace Silver, always a steady seller on LPs—never cracked the singles market. Soul-jazz remained a borderline genre, halfway between hard bop and R&B, boosting jazz sales but never capturing a new audience.[40]

At the same time that jazz industry executives were thrilled by the possibilities of crossover success, of singles pressed in quantities of between 5,000 and 15,000, critics and fellow musicians were often suspicious of soul-jazz as a genre. *Down Beat*'s cover story about soul-jazz failed to ask the most pointed question about the music, perhaps in deference to the re-

A NEW INTELLECTUAL VERNACULAR

cord labels that had bought so many pages of advertising in the issue: Was soul-jazz simply a manufactured trend, the latest attempt by record labels to commodify blackness and sell it to the broadest audience? Soul-jazz artists like Adderley had to parry the possible criticism that a "blacker" jazz was a less innovative or less authentic music—in effect, that soul-jazz musicians had surrendered the modernist imperative to "make it new" by indenturing themselves to a perfunctory hipsterism. Bebop enthusiast Barry Ulanov wrote in an early broadside against the "funky" school that, while the "down-home," "backwoods feeling" might always have its place in jazz, the "modernist" violated his own sense of self by indulging it too much. Ulanov asserted that the "modern jazzman is not, properly speaking or properly playing, a funky musician, not all that much of the time, anyway. He doesn't belong amid the alien corn." *Down Beat* editor Gene Lees likewise attacked soul-jazz as ersatz spirituality and invoked, for comparison's sake, the ghost of British iconoclast William Blake. For Lees, the example of Blake revealed how "the current talk about 'soul'" was "cheap and shallow," how "so much Gospelized playing" was "false," and how "the current jazz esthetic" was merely "precious and pretentious."[41]

After the success of the single "This Here," soul-jazz musicians—and the Adderley quintet in particular—bore the brunt of an increasingly hostile attack, which expanded beyond the older, white critics of *Down Beat* and into more bohemian critical circles. The Adderley group was charged with "contrived funk" by a musician who had worked with the group, while Charles Mingus claimed that the group had stolen the rhythmic principle behind his "Better Get It in Your Soul" but got it wrong, turning swinging gospel 3/4 time into a metronomic dead-end. In 1963 *Kulchur* editor Gilbert Sorrentino judged that "'professional' hipsterism" had bound jazz musicians and fans in a stultifying embrace, and he pointed a finger at the soul-jazz of Adderley, adducing that "there is more 'soul' in almost any two bars of a blues by Bird or Prez than in [Adderley's] entire life output." Sorrentino lamented the institutionalization of "the 'hipster,' complete in Ivy League suit and accoutrements, snapping his fingers to [Horace Silver's] *Señor Blues,* or similar junk." Black avant-garde enthusiast A. B. Spellman wrote that "soul, which means in jazz a proclivity to express a blues feeling in everything you play, became a commodity rather than the bones of a music." Amiri Baraka agreed, writing that "funk (groove, soul) has become as formal and clichéd as cool or swing" and observing acidly in his classic *Blues People* that there was even a bug repellent named "Hep." Years later, Adderley himself admitted that his "soul" bona fides had been foisted on him by hit-craving record executives: "we were pressured quite heavily by Riverside Records when they discovered there was a word called 'soul.' They kept promoting us that way, and I kept deliberately fighting it . . . Everybody in the record industry laid that label on thick to make it more durable, and especially more salable. But that was all foreign to the musicians."[42]

With hipsters proliferating wildly on TV, movies, and pulp fiction, and with soul-jazz attracting both the love and the loathing of the jazz community, it is no surprise that jazz musician-intellectuals began raising questions about the vogue that surrounded them—and turned partly to the epithet "hippy" to do so. The term had come into circulation in the immediate postwar period. Malcolm X provided a typical use in his *Autobiography:* he remembered throwing the epithet of "hippy" on "a few of the white men around Harlem, younger ones . . . [who] acted more Negro than Negroes." More generally, according to novelist and lexicographer Clarence Major, the postwar "hippie" was "a person who trie[d] without success to be hip; over-blasé; a would-be hipcat." Ten years after Malcolm's zoot suit days in Harlem, however, hard boppers Benny Golson and Cannonball Adderley had different targets and quite different analyses of how hipness had devolved into hippiedom—differences that illuminate how the jazzman's cultural influence ricocheted throughout the black and white communities. As Oscar Brown, Jr., had hinted in "But I Was Cool," the pursuit of the cool was criticized by jazz musicians themselves, who inventively signified on their aficionados, both black and white.[43]

Golson found the hippie in the black community's Killer Joe, a ladykiller who reprised Cab Calloway's seductive persona. Like Smokey Joe, he was a male fashion plate from head to toe and an inveterate trickster and gambler. In fact, the first half of Golson's soliloquy introducing Killer Joe on a 1960 recording might read, with a few snips of the tailor, as a description of the 1930s Calloway:

> We'd like you to meet a friend of ours who goes by the name of Killer Joe.
>
> Picture a so-called hippie or hipcat, standing on a corner in a neatly pressed double-breasted, form-fitted pin-striped suit, a pair of pointy-toed shoes with bowl-white stitches around the soles, a black shirt, long white tie, a black pencil moustache, and of course a very wide-brimmed felt hat.
>
> Killer Joe always has a pocketful of loot, but only the kind that jingles. (You see, he likes to play the horses.)
>
> He is most certainly a ladies man. As a matter of fact, he is always willing to accept cash contributions from them, for any cause—namely, his own.

A NEW INTELLECTUAL VERNACULAR

The most important thing about Killer Joe that you have to know is that he is very much against manual labor.[44]

The second half of Golson's soliloquy drew some sharp differences between Killer Joe and the Calloway persona, who had lured Minnie the Moocher to a townhouse and wealth as he had drawn her into the world of opium addiction. Killer Joe was himself the mooch—a figure much like the Philadelphia barkeep who inspired Miles Davis's "Freddie Freeloader" (1959).[45] Loving the kind of money "that jingles," Killer Joe spends endlessly. Opposed to manual labor, he makes a living by exercising his charms on women. Golson's wry talk about "cash contributions" clarifies that Killer Joe considers himself a charity case, a worthy "cause" rather than a shameless sponge. A black dandy in a world where work is scarce, he is a peerless consumer who follows Oscar Wilde's dictum "To do nothing is the most difficult thing of all."

Yet although "Killer Joe" could hardly be called a defense of this idle hippie, neither was it a tweedy attack. An act of musical portraiture, it lightly mocked the hippie's pretensions but then took joy in creating the easygoing, loping groove that was his life's rhythm. Like "Romance without Finance," the Tiny Grimes vehicle from Charlie Parker's early recording session with Savoy, "Killer Joe" took delight in ventriloquizing the womanizer who was both powerful and pathetic, at the mercy of his own spiel. "Romance without finance is a nuisance": so goes Tiny Grimes's 1944 refrain, and its goofy syllabic repetition is echoed in the melody of "Killer Joe," which also embraces repetition as the founding principle of wit.[46]

The provenance of this wit was suggestive: by 1960, Golson had made a name for himself as a hard bopper of exceptional finesse. Part of a generation of star Philadelphians that included John Coltrane, Lee Morgan, Philly Joe Jones, and Red Garland, he served as chief arranger and writer for Art Blakey's Jazz Messengers in the late 1950s. His compositions "Along Came Betty," "I Remember Clifford," "Are You Real," and "Whisper Not" became, like "Killer Joe," part of the jazz standard repertoire, in no small part because of his original voicings and arrangements. In this context, "Killer Joe" is a remarkably streamlined, even simple, composition, one taken at an easeful tempo. During its first section, the underlying chords shift between a measure of C7 and a measure of B♭7 for eight bars; meanwhile, the lead melody consists of rudimentary two-note and three-note phrases, which conjugate five notes into spirited salutes that hold onto the last note for a whole measure. The bridge carries forward this sense of salute, as the drums cut out and the brass section winds through a stop-time fanfare that modulates smoothly back to the tonic. Compared with the other selections on the album *Meet the Jazztet*—an "Avalon" with a finger-busting piano solo by McCoy Tyner, a "Serenata" that sparkles with Latin rhythms—"Killer Joe" knows the uplifting pleasure of relaxation. Paced midway between the ruminating balladry of "I Remember Clifford" and the fury of "Avalon," its solos are puckish and brief, enlivened by a series of riffs colored by a trumpet-mute.

Surely a great irony was embedded in this suavely professional tribute to the shiftless, gambling lothario. Golson's Jazztet, founded in 1959 with trumpeter Art Farmer, embodied the professionalism of the hard bop scene: the Jazztet combo spiced up the informal "blowing sessions" associated with hard bop (and pioneered by Miles Davis's mid-fifties quintet) with an emphasis on innovative ensemble arrangement and voicings. Golson's "Killer Joe" was a double-voiced tale, a droll portrait that appreciated Joe's flash *and* went beyond the "manual labor" that he refused. Its joyful lilt suggested that there was a type of work between wage labor and the hustler's full-time sponging: the discipline of art.

While Golson aimed his satire at the hustler—a figure who would later turn up in the rearview mirror of the two 1965 landmarks of black urban literature *Manchild in the Promised Land* and *The Autobiography of Malcolm X*—Julian "Cannonball" Adderley took on the know-it-all jazz fan. In one of his first "Jazz Scene" columns for the *New York Amsterdam News,* Adderley aimed to dissect the jazz audience as a whole, but he glossed over the two most obvious subgroups that he named—the "serious jazz enthusiasts" and the "squares" who "come out of curiosity." Instead he devoted the bulk of his column to the "type . . . known in the trade as Hippy," who Adderley said was "one of the world's most exacting conformists." Standing between jazz ignorance and knowledge, Hippy was the representative jazz fan, "an accurate popularity barometer" who "may directly influence how a musician plays in public." Adderley took care to disabuse his readers of some of the reigning stereotypes: "Hippy comes in all ages and all colors of the spectrum. . . . He also runs the occupational gamut. He may appear as a 'beatnik' or a Madison Avenue advertising executive in a continental suit." He could be found in Saudi Arabia, "Red China," and Australia, as well as the more traditional New York venues.[47]

This transnational jazz fan had an abiding interest in transnational affairs—a political hunger that Adderley poked fun at. "Hippy is usually prepared to hold conversation with you," he wrote, "so long as it's related to modern jazz, Communism, Africa, Fidel Castro, or race relations in general." Hippy, that is, was not unlike Norman Mailer: an intellectual who appreciated jazz in the context of a brewing radicalism, as a form of cultural politics. He was interested in jazz for what it signified about the world shared by jazz fan and musician alike. One can only speculate on the topics that Adderley's Hippy could *not* talk about, although certainly his own emotional investment in certain fictions of black life would seem to be one of them. Adderley suggested as much when he named Adlai Stevenson— the liberal standard-bearer who chose segregationist John Sparkman as his running mate for the presidency in 1952—as an "intellectual hippy." Here Adderley was cultivating an insider relationship with his black readers, who could understand—in W. E. B. Du Bois's famous words—what it meant to be considered a problem, an abstraction in the nagging form of flesh. A jazz educator who had taught high school in Florida, Adderley had at the same time pioneered the ostensibly "blacker" style of soul-jazz: he tried to legitimate the music as an art form, establish its racial bona fides, and sell millions of records all at once. His column for the black weekly *New York Amsterdam News* worked similarly on different levels. It educated his audience on the protocols of jazz listening even as it drew on a sense of shared racial rapport.[48]

Clarence Major defined the postwar hippie as "a would-be hipcat," and we can see in Golson and Adderley how this essentially negative definition of the hippie—the hipster manqué—allowed them to balance the competing allures of respectability and notoriety in hard bop. Golson and Adderley aimed to show that the pursuit of the hip could be a self-conscious enterprise; they were alert to possible dangers (indolence, snobbery) and able to spoof them. Criticizing the hippie, they authorized themselves out of the aesthetic dilemma peculiar to soul-jazz, which traded on the authenticity of its black vernacular. As "soul" became both a trademark of quality and a sign of commodification—and as "blackness" became a recognizable quantity in music—black musicians tried to steer a middle course where they might bring vernacular rhythms back to jazz without simply reiterating rifflike clichés and accommodating record-label expectations, and where they might reassert their own authority over their art. As a Harlem record store owner confided to Nat Hentoff, "I think most of that soul music is now being manufactured rather than felt . . . , but at least this is one time in jazz history when the Negroes are popularizing their own music. It would take a lot of courage for Stan Kenton or Shorty Rodgers [white musicians identified with "progressive" jazz] to call one of their albums *The Soul Brothers*." The "hippie" was a shadow image for black musicians, the counterfeit in their midst, as they defined their music as a defiance of expectations rather than a pat fulfillment of them.[49]

Kicks and Screams: Oscar Brown's *Sin and Soul,* Max Roach's *We Insist*

The career of singer-songwriter Oscar Brown, Jr., might be profitably viewed as an illustration of the possibilities and difficulties of performing hipness in the late 1950s and early 1960s—and of the political stakes involved for an artist who made no secret of his commitment to the civil rights movement. One of the delights of Brown's music from this period is the nimble way that he approaches the question of black identity, adopting personas and shedding them in the next song or the next breath, summoning up a musical genre with a riff or vocal style and then adapting its formulas with such panache that they no longer seem like formulas at all. Certainly few other performers seemed so ever-hip and mercurial at the same time. One can understand why Langston Hughes originally wanted Brown to take on the part of Simple in a production of the musical *Simply Heavenly,* since the singer seemed—like Simple himself—the most supple Everyman. In the space of a typical performance, Brown might play a stooped ghetto peddler with his pushcart, a father dwelling on his child's beauty, an auctioneer on a slave block, a convict breaking rocks on a chain gang, a customer spellbound by his waitress's hips, and a small boy who hopes his parents will make him a present of a nearby elephant. And while he shifted roles, Brown would also shift musical gears: his music synthesized the material of black folktales, early blues, jazz cabaret, and postwar R&B with the funky-lick style of soul-jazz. It was fitting that one of his great musical settings was a version of the folktale "The Signifying Monkey," in which the trickster monkey outwits the more powerful lion by playing him off the still more powerful elephant. Brown was a signifier par excellence, a trickster who could switch codes, deflate clichés, and mock the powerful—all while swinging to the beat.[50]

One set of clichés that Brown deflated was the cluster of expectations that Mailer and others had attached to the black hipster—namely, that he was a sexual and economic predator and that his power was inextricably tied up with his exclusion from the respectable middle class. Brown's song "But I Was Cool" was, as noted earlier, a send-up of the cult of cool. The hipster was assumed to be a combustible mixture of slang, rebellion, and violence, and Brown irreverently turned the violence into a cartoon and the rebellion into a repeated act of self-repression. Engaging in a simultaneous act of cultural and self-parody, Brown refused to be hipper-than-thou. "But I Was Cool" was just one of several songs in Brown's repertoire that performed hipness and satirized it at the same time. Other examples include "Somebody Buy Me a Drink," where the waggish narrator can't help but buttonhole the listener; "Dat Dere," where the elephant-besotted

A NEW INTELLECTUAL VERNACULAR

kid is both a source of wonder and a source of aggravation; and "The Signifying Monkey" itself, where the narrator admires the monkey's resourcefulness more than his mischief in toto—refusing, as it were, to lionize him.

Yet while Brown was a master of the satiric portrait, he was also indebted to ideas of respectability and dignity that have marked a tradition of black (and often women-led) activism and art. As Brown's album title *Sin and Soul* suggested, "sin" would find its moral balance in "soul": his trickster tales were twinned with another set of songs that spoke with little irony about the joys of love and parenting (two of the most famous being "Afro-Blue" and "Brown Baby"), and even his juiciest tales of seduction often sneaked in a hidden moral. In the process, Brown's working-class hipsters, watermelon sellers, and junk peddlers found their place in a community whose class accents were more ambiguous. Brown's performance style spoke to his ability to imagine solidarity across conventional class lines— an ability that may have been rooted in his family history. Like playwright Lorraine Hansberry, he was the child of a prominent Chicago realtor who had spearheaded antidiscrimination efforts. In 1934 Oscar Brown, Sr., had founded the National Movement for the Establishment of a Forty-Ninth State, which demanded commonwealth status for a new state whose principal residents would be black. Brown, Jr., similarly balanced black demands for integration and nationalism, middle-class decency and racial self-respect. When he was profiled in the press, he seemed always to strike this balance—for instance, in the 1961 *Ebony* feature, which both testified to his hip credentials and posed this unabashed family man at home with his wife and their five children. In a 1965 children's TV special, he sang of black pride and resistance to a multiethnic group of kids—all while wearing a cardigan sweater that would have made Mr. Rogers proud.[51]

Family-loving yet militant, Brown was a natural candidate for a mass media hungry to understand black life and black protest in the upsurge of the civil rights movement, and for a brief moment in the early 1960s he exploited this cultural opening. Tagged as "the best entertainer since Belafonte," he seemed poised to join such culture heroes as Sidney Poitier, James Baldwin, and Jackie Robinson. After several appearances on the *Ed Sullivan Show* and the *Steve Allen Show,* he was commissioned to host *Stars of Jazz,* a series of 117 half-hour shows that were to be broadcast nationwide. And yet the failure of his most ambitious project in this period—an original musical titled *Kicks & Co.*—speaks to the difficulty of Brown's balancing act. The musical itself was pitched as "a morality play with a beat": it traced the efforts of Mr. Kicks, a high-living magazine publisher and "modern Mephistopheles," to seduce upstanding black folk and, more

The hipster in the cardigan sweater: A regular on TV in the early 1960s, Oscar Brown, Jr., is shown here hosting a 1965 episode of CBS's Sunday morning program *Look Up and Live*. The episode, billed as "a profile in song of Negro Americana from slave days to the present," suggests how musicians like Brown bent hipsterism to their own uses. Note the multiethnic composition of the group of children. (Courtesy of Michael Ochs Archives)

specifically, black students who had been radicalized into launching a series of sit-ins. Like much of Brown's work, and like Benny Golson's "Killer Joe," the play recognized both the pull of the hipster's charms and his limitations. Brown's career arguably reached its high point when he mounted an unconventional live TV fund-raising campaign for the musical. Dave Garroway, himself a former jazz DJ, gave his *Today* show completely over to Brown, who staged an unprecedented two-hour telethon performance that put *Kicks & Co.* $100,000 over the top. Even Martin Luther King, Jr., was moved to call the musical "a great work," one that would "affect vast numbers with the moral force of our young people today."[52]

Unfortunately for Brown, the musical was a success in previews only. It bombed at its premiere at Chicago's Arie Crown theater, and soon Brown was back to a career outside of the national spotlight. Undeterred, he turned in the mid-1960s and 1970s to the kinds of community theater productions that sprang out of the Black Arts movement—enlisting Chicago's

Blackstone Rangers in "Opportunity Please Knock," collaborating with the students of Malcolm X College on his musical "Slave Song," and working with residents of the city's public housing projects in "Great Nitty Gritty." The lines between the respectable and disreputable, the aspiring middle class and the so-called underclass, were never assumed by Brown to be absolute.[53]

Yet if *Kicks & Co.* was a failure with the public, Brown also lent his songwriting talent in the early 1960s to one of the most indelible musical projects of the period: the Max Roach album *We Insist! The Freedom Now Suite*. Brown had started collaborating with Roach in 1959 on a longer choral work, to be performed four years later on the centennial of the Emancipation Proclamation, but that project was soon overtaken by the urgency of the civil rights agitation of early 1960. Inspired by the wave of sit-ins that swept from a lunch counter in Greensboro, North Carolina, to other points in the segregated South, Roach decided to record a version of the suite posthaste. Despite the accelerated schedule, the album still lived up to Brown and Roach's original ambition to compose a synoptic work of black history: *We Insist!* began by exploring the African-American experience of slavery and emancipation ("Driva' Man" and "Freedom Day"), then linked this cycle of bondage and liberation to contemporary freedom struggles in the American South, South Africa, and the African continent more generally ("Triptych: Prayer/Protest/Peace," "All Africa," "Tears for Johannesburg"). And it did so while experimenting with novel musical forms that might match its programmatic intent. "All Africa," for instance, used the interplay between three sets of drummers—jazz drummer Roach, Afro-Cuban drummers Ray Mantilla and Thomas Du Vall, and Nigerian drummer Olatunji—to convey both the disparate ways that African peoples understood freedom and the syncretic possibilities of an African-derived aesthetic.[54]

Much could be said about the collective artistry behind *We Insist!*—about how "Driva' Man" models the punishing violence of slavery through its off-balance 5/4 beat, mournful horn voicings, and Abbey Lincoln's clipped vocals; about how "Freedom Day" manages to capture both the anticipation and anxiety of the moment of emancipation ("Can't conceive it, don't believe it, but that's what they say / Slave no longer, slave no longer, this is freedom day") by setting its minor-blues solos over a feverishly paced rhythm section; or, more generally, about how Roach's polyrhythmic drumming interlocks with the sinuous front-line playing of Booker Little on trumpet, Walter Benton on saxophone, and Julian Priester on trombone. But as an endpoint for this discussion of the jazz hipster, it's perhaps

Abbey Lincoln and Max Roach: The vocalist and composer-drummer, a married couple in the 1960s and two of the most prominent activists in the jazz world, collaborated on the indelible *Freedom Now Suite* (1960). The pose of this photo—Roach steely and staring into the camera, Lincoln looking up to Roach—suggests some of the gender politics that informed the jazz militancy of the 1960s. (Courtesy of Michael Ochs Archives)

most important to note how the album, in its reaching for a more militant political statement, also created a striking musical alternative to the cool pose. As its title suggested, the point of the music was to "insist"—not to make a point obliquely, not to engage in an artful form of shadow play, but to lay out the story of the liberation struggle with a confrontational sense of urgency. The album cover was dominated by a photograph from the

Greensboro sit-ins, in which two of the students turned their bodies away from the Woolworth lunch counter and looked the viewer straight in the eye.

This directness demanded, among other things, a new vocal style, and Abbey Lincoln responded imaginatively to the challenge. Sometimes she seemed to be almost spitting out her words ("Driva' Man"); at other moments she brought a spirit of incantation to the music ("All Africa"). Her most breathtaking move, though, was to push her voice to the sort of instrumental limits that had previously been explored by saxophonists like John Coltrane, Ornette Coleman, and Jackie McLean. As jazz horns were turning to the sound of pealing and screaming, so Lincoln in "Triptych: Prayer, Protest, Peace" explored her voice at its most eerie and wrenching. A spare duet between Lincoln's voice and Roach's drums, "Triptych" takes both voice and drums into unconventional areas; there are no words to speak of, and no steady beat for the first two sections of the triptych. While "Prayer" and "Peace" are meditative in character, with Lincoln singing open vowels with heavy vibrato over a generally steady pentatonic scale, "Protest" may be the most hair-raising ninety seconds of jazz in existence. Lincoln screams with uninterrupted fury and at high volume, in an act of aggression that doubles as the sound of hurt. *We Insist* producer Nat Hentoff suggested that this movement in the triptych was "a final, uncontrollable unleashing of rage and anger," a "catharsis" that spoke to "all the accumulated fury and hurt and blinding bitterness." He added, significantly, for those listeners attuned to debates in the black community about the efficacy of nonviolent protest: "It is all forms of protest, certainly including violence."[55]

While Oscar Brown, Jr., silenced his hipster's yelps of pain in "But I Was Cool," turning the cool mask into a joke, Roach and Lincoln's "Protest"— recorded within two months of the other song—gave full vent to the anger of the moment and discarded the cool mask in its entirety. The result of this catharsis was a haunting sense of resolution, not the reassumption of the mask. In "Peace," the last movement of "Tryptch," the work gains a sense of steady and controlled momentum: for the first time, Roach adopts a regular beat on his high hat and adds spare, coloristic rimshots and raps on his toms. Yet "Peace" does not model an untroubled movement forward, the triumph of progress. Lincoln's vocals turn the joyful noise of scat into something altogether more earthbound and guttural; she gives a performance that suggests that the very material of singing—the breath of the voice—is beyond her control. She begins "Peace" with a set of phrases that all end in exhalations of fatigue, and closes it with an exhalation that has a ritual finality. In between, she improvises a series of slow, floating phrases with heavy vibrato, none of which seem to come to any melodic closure. If this is "Peace," it is peace with gothic undertones, as if the ghosts of the past might be appeased for a moment but never exorcised in their entirety.

We Insist! might seem far from the lighthearted comedy of Oscar Brown, but it would be a mistake to deny the jazz hipster's complementary role as a figure of black self-assertion. While many portraits of the hipster—from intellectuals like Broyard, Wolfe, and Mailer, in the pages of *Partisan Review* and *Dissent* as well as *Beatnik Wanton* and *Bongo Gum*—often settled for a cartoonish image, performers like Brown dedicated themselves to creating a vernacular art that would not be one-dimensional. Black roots were being rediscovered and reinvented, and soul-jazz musicians were leading figures in the cultural end of this project: they hoped to create music that would flesh out disreputable words like "groove," "funk," and even "black" and bring them into the accepted lexicon. In a telling incident in 1962, Brown sent up a flare when his recording of Gwendolyn Brooks's "Elegy of a Plain Black Boy" was banned by Chicago radio station WNEW for its insistent phrase "a plain black boy." The phrase was deemed too offensive to "Negroes," who preferred their art separate from their politics; Brown was pushing the boundaries of the very middle class whose allegiance he courted in the pages of *Ebony*.[56]

The controversy over "Elegy of a Plain Black Boy" was part of a general sea change, as the word "black" was questioned, then adopted with pride by the radical edge of the civil rights movement. In 1963, high school students in Toledo, Ohio, held a mass protest after an administrator referred to them over the intercom as "black" students; the term was understood as an insult in the mouth of whites. By contrast, in the same year at the March on Washington, the word "black" was taken up by perhaps the least centrist speaker to assume the podium. Representing the student wing of the Movement, SNCC president John Lewis favored phrases like "black people" and "the black masses" in his speech, and was alone in not using the term "Negro." The examples of Brown and Lewis suggest how "Negroes" became "blacks" under pressure from within their own community, around 1962 and 1963, as soul-jazz entertainers like Brown aimed to capture a spirit of protest and challenge. The phrase "black boy" hit the airwaves, firing the language of loss with indignation, paving the way for soul music's late-sixties avowals of black pride. The hipster, as he always hoped, was ahead of the crowd.[57]

PART TWO

Redefining Youth Culture

3

RIOT ON A SUMMER'S DAY

White Youth and the Rise
of the Jazz Festival

On July 2, 1960, white teenagers rioted for the sake of black music. Or, to put it more crudely: on this summer night, thousands of white youth were inspired by black culture to do something that very few black folks were predisposed to do. The hipster general strike that had fired David McReynolds's socialist fantasies did not materialize, but in its place came another prefigurative event: a youth riot fought over the issue of consumer freedom.

In its bare anatomy, the "riot" was a problem of jazz crowd control. While fifteen thousand jazz enthusiasts were listening in Freebody Park to Dakota Staton and Horace Silver at the Seventh Annual Newport Jazz Festival, twelve thousand young people were gathering in the narrow streets outside of the gate, ticketless and barred from the jammed concert grounds. The outsiders started pushing toward the gate en masse, and soon the force of the crowd crashed through the gate—at which point a squad of police rushed in and kept them from entering, and a fire truck was propped as an obstacle directly in front of the gates. What followed was, depending on your point of view, a blow to the dignity of jazz music, a tragedy of America's misbegotten youth, or a carnival of misrule. Retrenched in the streets outside Freebody Park, the youths turned more violent. They brandished torn tree branches as clubs; hurled beer cans, stones and whiskey bottles at the police; and started tearing up the town, knocking over cars and smashing windows.

Directing traffic: During the riot at the Newport Jazz Festival in 1960, young whites tore up the town after being informed that the festival was sold out, battling a large contingent of state and local police, firemen, Marines, and National Guardsmen. Here at the height of the riot, a bare-chested reveler directs traffic with a parking cone atop his head. (Courtesy of *Providence Journal*)

The police wired for reinforcements, and Newport's mayor put out a call to the governor of Rhode Island. Soon Newport's fire and police departments were supplemented by fifty Marines from the Newport Naval Base next door, a hundred National Guardsmen carrying clubs, and carloads of state troopers summoned by the governor. The forces of law and order tried their best to disperse the crowd and push it away from the concert grounds, which were only a quarter-mile from "Millionaire's Row," the set of regal estates along the cliffs of Newport. With the mansion of tire manufacturer Harvey Firestone in the most immediate danger, police cars moved forward in flying wedges, officers tossed barrage after barrage of tear gas bombs, and firemen turned high-pressure hoses on the crowd. Police blockades were thrown up at every entrance to Newport, and would-be festivalgoers were stopped from entering the city. After a few hours of maneuvers, with the crowd launching fusillades of beer cans in response to the fusillades of tear gas, half of the group had been driven into the downtown area, and the other half had been driven to the public beach, where fifteen hundred of them proceeded to crash for the night. Millionaire's Row remained safe.[1]

The aftermath of the riot was, in many respects, as taxing as the riot itself. Over two hundred rioters were arrested and transported by police caravan to various holding tanks at Newport's police station, courthouse, and jail. One hundred seventy were booked on charges of disorderly conduct; soon the three Newport jails, like the previous night's concert, had standing room only. When the vast majority pleaded innocent to the charges, they were held in a detention cage in the courthouse basement. On another side of the ledger, at least one hundred twenty-five festivalgoers and police-men reported injuries of various sorts—many resulting from the high-ve-locity collision of beer bottle and flesh. Newport's city officials imposed a "cooling off" period, sealing the two bridges leading into Newport, placing guards on ferryboats to ensure that no one except longtime residents en-tered the city, and banning the sale of liquor for two days. The circle of vic-tims extended to the festival entrepreneurs themselves when the City Council revoked the license of the Newport Jazz Festival and forced the or-ganization to cancel two days' worth of performances, including the much-anticipated shows of John Coltrane, Count Basie, and Nashville star Chet Atkins. The festival's board of directors struck back against the City Coun-cil by filing a $4 million lawsuit against the city. "The city had ample warn-ing that trouble was brewing, but didn't take the proper measures to pre-vent it," said festival director Louis Lorillard, attempting to shift the blame away from his own enterprise. That same day, in a more prosaic mop-up operation, two parties grappled with the litter that blanketed the city streets: packs of ten-year-olds scavenged for bottles to recycle for the de-posit, while a fleet of bulldozers worked to clear the ankle-high debris of beer cans and assorted trash.[2]

Along with the ten-year-olds and the bulldozers, several sets of com-mentators sifted through the debris of the festival, asking the more sym-bolic questions: who were the rioters, and why did they tear up the streets of Newport during a jazz festival? For its part, the jazz press moved quickly to disown the disturbance and the rioters behind it. Every music press ac-count, from *Metronome* to *Down Beat*, distinguished between the jazz aficionados in Freebody Park, toes tapping peacefully to Ray Charles and Horace Silver, and the jazz flunkies outside the park. "What the rioting mi-nority came to enjoy," wrote critic Leonard Feather, "was not the voices of Lambert, Hendricks & Ross, blended at Freebody Park, but the effects of malt, hops, sugar and yeast, brewed in Milwaukee." The festival's board of directors took a similar line, blaming the city police for their poor han-dling of "non-ticket holding people outside the Park" and lamenting that "the true jazz lovers" were the ones punished. Langston Hughes wrote in the *Chicago Defender* that "the rioters were not lovers of jazz, but young beer drinkers who had nothing better to do than throw their beer cans at the cops." Hughes added parenthetically, but significantly, that "there was not a single Negro among them." The remark was a bit of public-relations adjustment on behalf of black jazz musicians: if jazz had been linked in the white mind to sexual license and general impropriety, then the Newport ri-ots demonstrated that this notion was a self-serving fiction propagated by college-age whites to justify their own alcohol-lubricated good time.[3]

The morning after: A festivalgoer surveys the beach on the morning after the 1960 Newport festival riot. Thousands of teenagers crashed on the beach in the early years of the festival; in 1965, the city formally banned festivalgoers from sleeping there. (Courtesy of *Providence Journal*)

For jazz musicians and critics, the Newport riot suggested the perils of opening up jazz to the masses—a "lowest common denominator" identified almost exclusively in the late 1950s and 1960s with rock 'n' roll. In the seven years since its 1954 inception, the Newport festival's attendance had skyrocketed from 13,000 to between 50,000 and 60,000. This expansion was deliberate: in a memo circulated among the festival's board of directors in January 1960, Voice of America DJ Willis Conover laid out a business plan that would allow the festival to thrive on the grandest scale. The board, he wrote, needed to accept that the festival's target audience included both a good number of "general, not too hip, jazz fans" and a group he categorized as "vacationers; college crowd; people seeking entertainment; curious first-timers." The aims of the concerts were to "attract large enough crowds to meet expenses"; to "stay above minimum standards of quality"; to "please the audience, once it comes"; to "reverse the tide of trade criticism"; and lastly "to provide innovations, in keeping with Newport's first-festival status."[4]

Conover added that these aims were listed in no particular order, but many critics within the jazz community would have disagreed. By the late 1950s, jazz partisans were raising questions about the bigger-is-better corporate logic that seemed to be driving the festival. In 1957 the *New Yorker*'s Whitney Balliett noted the festival's "bulging, General Motors proportions" and described the event as a "vast and steamy musical circus." A year

REDEFINING YOUTH CULTURE

later he called the festival "a statistician's dream" and gave a catalogue of its scale: "over thirty-five solid hours of music and talk; approximately two hundred and fifty musicians, including five big bands, sixteen singers, and a welter of small groups; and a total attendance of sixty thousand." Jazz critics and musicians went so far as to claim that the riot was a form of payback for the festival's indifference to jazz as an art form. Critic Nat Hentoff suggested that the festival had surrendered jazz to "the status-grubbing, money-mesmerizing compulsiveness that has characterized the culture at large" and had then paid the price: "In grabbing for more and more bigness each year, [the festival] had encouraged the conviction among thousands of teenagers that Newport had become a carnival town over the July 4 weekend. Neither the beer-drinkers nor the musicians had any illusions left that the N.J.F. had anything basically to do with 'art.'" Charles Mingus quipped that the festival "deserve[d]" the riot "because they confused rock 'n' roll with jazz. They lost their identity with jazz." Murray Kempton offered in the *New York Post* that "the issue here is the dignity of a trade" and suggested that jazz musicians were nowhere more disrespected than at the festival that ostensibly celebrated them.[5]

For those observers with less investment in jazz as an art form, the riot was a sign of an alarming new type of American delinquency, one that seemed to emerge, counterintuitively, from an era of economic security. The mainstream news coverage of the riot was nagged by the same doubts that turned the phenomena of juvenile delinquency, comic book reading, and teen romance into the stuff of congressional hearings and much socio-logical literature. The mysterious conjunction of affluence and delin-quency, the strange attraction of black subculture, the long shadow cast on America's future by the recent launching of the Sputnik satellite—these were the themes that echoed through the media's coverage of the riot.[6] Al-most all press observers noted that the rioters were affluent: they drove convertibles and wore college sweaters from locales as diverse as Boston University, Villanova, Lehigh, the University of New Hampshire, and the United States Military Academy. As the *New York Journal-American* wrote, the "Newport rioters were definitely not delinquents with holes in their pockets. These were 'good' boys and girls from 'better' families and col-leges." They were also, perhaps as a function of their affluence, casual in dress and dubious in their sexual attitudes. The *New Yorker*'s Balliett called them "amusical yahoos of college age—many of them barefoot, loutish, overvitamined, and, in the case of men, effeminately dressed in pedal-pushers." *Variety*'s reporter noticed that the rioters were "clad usually in Bermuda shorts, weird shirts, white sneakers and crazy hats," and carried "on their arm, if they can pick them up, . . . young girls as bizarre in their dress." *Metronome's* Ted White struck the loudest note of sexual alarm: "What didn't frighten me sickened me . . . countless near-rapes and orgies, all consummated by partners too benumbed to be really aware of their actions."[7]

The composite portrait suggested that these young Americans were financed well beyond their worth, and dangerously so. Father Norman O'Connor, known as the Jazz Priest for his musical sponsorship over the years, not only chastised the rioters but also blamed their parents for their loose values. "It was a crowd that had money because the great share of them were traveling the streets in . . . sports cars . . . and convertibles," he wrote in the *Boston Globe*. "Parents must not care if sons and daughters sleep out all night on beaches, in cars, or not at all. Parents no longer care if teenagers come home at night or not. Parents no longer care about the drinking habits of their children." While jazz musicians like Charles Mingus blamed the grubbing commercialism of the festival, which invited more people to Newport than the city could sustain, commentators like O'Connor used the riot to reflect on the moral loosening of the American family.[8]

When taken as a flare in the twilight struggle of the Cold War, the riot took on a significance even beyond such gloomy insights into family mores. For the *New York Herald Tribune,* the riot was "an orgy of pointless destruction" that carried the disquieting international message that American youth was becoming ideologically flabby. "Perhaps the most discouraging aspect of the whole sorry mess," the paper editorialized, "was the emptiness and futility of it all. American youth hit some sort of a new low in Newport this week end. Here was mass violence—vicious violence, potentially lethal missiles hurled at total strangers—with neither point nor reason, done by several thousand of those bright college students who supposedly are our hope for tomorrow." Having dug at the privilege of the rioters, the *Herald Tribune* compared them unfavorably to student demonstrators abroad—presumably including the South Korean students who had helped topple an American-sponsored regime, the Okinawa students who heckled President Eisenhower on his recent Asia tour, and the Tokyo students who had torpedoed the tour entirely by leading a four-day anti-American demonstration. A few months later, radical sociologist C. Wright Mills would use the still-novel phrase "the New Left" to describe these international student demonstrators; they were his clinching evidence that the "end of ideology" was a hollow intellectual fiction.[9]

The *Herald Tribune* did not approve of these events abroad but was even more disheartened by the native protesters' seeming lack of ideology: "In capitals around the world, desperately earnest students have lately been demonstrating, often rioting, for causes . . . [I]t is as if a contagion of violent fervor were overleaping national boundaries and spreading from university to university. But these young Americans had no cause. They were rioting for nothing but the perverse pleasure of violence. Theirs was hedonism gone wild, an irresponsible animal self-indulgence that reflects discredit on their generation." Smaller newspapers across the country echoed the *Herald Tribune*'s anxieties about the decadence of the West. North Carolina's *Shelby Star* worried that America's "enemies" would exhibit footage of the youth riot as evidence of "a culture of booze and bop that places frantic values on getting close to the blaring trumpet and the busty blues singer." Washington's *Olympian* adduced that "in at least all the Western world, the pattern is a sickness of moral chaos and lack of discipline. . . . We seem almost to have reached the point where disorder and rudeness are acclaimed as 'human' while their opposites are 'inhuman.'" *Metronome*'s Ted White joined this chorus, writing, "It is one thing to read of student demonstrations in Japan, Korea, or Africa, to look at the ugly faces in newspapers or newsreels. It is quite another to be personally a part (if only peripherally) of an army of drunken college kids taking over a normally quiet, small town hosting a *jazz festival*."[10]

The Newport riot, then, was taken as a cautionary tale with two basic angles: for musicians and music critics, it was a case study in the decadence that threatened jazz if its entrepreneurs pandered to the profit motive; and for other editorialists largely outside the jazz press, it was proof of the younger generation's inane, dangerous combustibility. Both angles, however, shared a certain indifference to the rioters' motivations. Rather than consider what the riot may have expressed, however destructively, about this new youth culture, the commentators merely argued that the violence was pointless and somehow linked to rock 'n' roll, that it had no proximate cause except the depravity of these particular youths. But the riot did occur at a jazz festival, and it did occur in the fabled sanctuary of Newport, and so we might consider how the Newport festival seeded the riot—by setting up cultural expectations that could not be met, by following an economic logic that dictated what kind of music would be offered and that suggested how it would be consumed, by bringing together different audiences whose tastes and values could not be reconciled. Between the inauguration of the festival in 1954 and the riot of 1960, the festival's organizers, the press, and other cultural impresarios had collaborated on a new form of postwar leisure, a kind of luxury for the masses. Through Newport they had constructed a late 1950s model of the weekend getaway, an unstable compound of cultural uplift and carnivalesque indulgence, adult satisfactions and even-more-adult excesses. In brief, they had *sold* Newport as an exemplary site for a festival weekend, using the cultural materials at hand. Newport had once been a monument to exclusivity, the leisure of the very rich. Festival boosters helped the city give rise to a more expansive, even riotous, sense of consumer freedom—but they needed jazz, and black musicians, to accomplish this conjuring trick.

City in Decline or Resort in the Saddle?

In 1954 jazz was largely considered an urban and black music; Newport was largely considered a resort colony of wealthy and white America. Out of this contrast—or to be more exact, out of the injection of the music into the sinking prestige of the colony—came the great novelty of Newport's jazz festival. A deal was struck: the festival would help jazz purge itself of the taint of urban nightclubs, while the music would help refurbish Newport's antiquated image and pump money into its troubled local economy. This social experiment prompted a series of cheeky reports by journalists fascinated by the exchange of cultural capital, though it should be noted that the reports were lopsided toward one side of the exchange: they focused almost exclusively on the skirmish between Newport's jazz aficionados and its old guard, while rarely soliciting the perspective of the jazz musicians themselves. Instead of considering how these urban musicians felt about transporting jazz from nightclub to high-class resort, the press focused on the battle within Newport, the one fought by Louis and Elaine Lorillard against the highbrow biases of the Newport elite. As the Newport couple who underwrote the festival, the Lorillards were understood to be leading a sneak attack on the provincialism of the very rich, and jazz was understood to be music that could seduce its enemies through enlightened contact. A "festival," modeled after the classical-music annual concerts at Tanglewood, was thus the perfect weapon in the Lorillards' cultural war.

Festival promoter George Wein recalled in *Playboy* how the idea for the festival was incubated over the course of leisurely cocktail conversation. "I was relishing a tumbleful of fine old Kentucky sour mash at a Boston house party one evening in February, 1954," he recalled. "The conversation bounded from subject to subject as it is wont to do at affable gatherings and finally alighted on music." In just such an ambience, the Newport festival would be first entertained as an idea: "I learned . . . that the Lorillards were still in the market for financial grief, this time in the form of a jazz concert. . . . [I]t was a jolly evening: the whiskey was hearty, the music good, the guests convivial, and the conversation rosy and rich in wondrous imagination." Part of the early appeal of Newport jazz was this image of high-society millionaires descending from a nearly Olympian place of detachment and assuming the financial and social risks of the festival.[11]

Wein's dapper cocktail party had many echoes in the coverage of the *Saturday Review* and the *New Yorker,* which patched together absurd snippets of Newport small talk in a spirit of gently humorous hyperbole. Newport's social world relied on the dinner party as an instrument of social leverage, and so the press simply seemed to eavesdrop over dinner on the brittle exchanges between Newport's old and new guards. The *Saturday Review* article opened with a high-society matron gabbing about Newport's legendary resistance to modernization—how, for instance, a proper airfield had never been built because Mr. Phelps worried that the airplanes would disturb his cows; and how her friends were now boycotting the festival by hosting dinner parties that clashed with the concerts. Another woman remarked, "I just couldn't sleep. . . . The whole thing upset me so much. The party and everything. Too queer. Blacks and whites all together." It was this sort of talk, lifted from Newport's Spouting Rock Clubhouse, which dramatized the old-line resistance to the festival. Both articles, however, were slanted toward more optimistic Newporters, who remarked on the town's capacity to endure and flourish, despite the introduction of the income tax and the latest popular onslaught. The *New Yorker's* Lillian Ross highlighted the efforts of the Lorillards to sway the Newport old guard, which meant covering the dinner party thrown by their one ally in the community. Lifted out of their nightclub element, Ross's jazz musicians come across as a deferential yet irrepressible lot—the sort of folks who, like Gerry Mulligan, would query a high-toned Newport resident about his feel for jazz with "You dig it, sir?" The arrival of jazz at the resort community was framed as a story of the music's upward mobility: Newport tribune Cleveland Amory said forthrightly that "Jazz has made the grade—from Storyville to Newport in fifty years."[12]

Jazz might have been making the grade, but the burghers of Newport were profiting as well, using the festival to fend off doubts about the city's ability to thrive in the postwar period. The doubts had been sounded in establishment journals like *Business Week,* which pronounced that the "summer colony's illness is prolonged. It's also fatal." By the 1950s, the myth of Old Newport—the Newport where the Vanderbilts mingled with the Belmonts and Mrs. Stuyvesant Fish over ten-course meals—was being punctured on three fronts. First, as the press noted, the wealthy were no longer the glamorous engines of city life. In fact, they could hardly sustain their own lavish investments in real estate, much less the rest of the Newport economy. In the postwar period, while Newport's population grew from 30,532 in 1942 to 38,500 in 1954—an increase of 26 percent, typical of the suburban boom—the summer colonists, with their Italianate palazzos and retinues of servants, were a shrinking class. The four hundred social register families of the prewar period had dwindled to half that number by the fifties. Meanwhile the mansions on the coast were increasingly pressed into service as apartment houses, prep schools, Roman Catholic women's colleges, and—most aptly for the postindustrial economy—tourist magnets open to public inspection. In 1954, the Jazz Festival's inaugural year, the Preservation Society of Newport County was formed to renovate the city's mansions and colonial buildings. The Breakers, a sixty-room mansion that formerly served as the summer home of Cornelius Vanderbilt and his family, was opened to the public, who for only $1.75 a head could sample the glories of Old Newport. Some 50,000 day-trippers made the Newport rounds every year. Fittingly, the Breakers also served as the on-location set for the 1956 movie *High Society,* where Bing Crosby wooed Grace Kelly with the support of Louis Armstrong and Frank Sinatra. Whereas Old Newport had once prided itself on its fantastic insularity, in the fifties the city began to market itself as a public commodity—a spectacle of high living with fewer and fewer actual residents.[13]

The second factor that cracked the myth of Old Newport was the emergence of the U.S. Navy as the chief financial player in the region. The Atlantic Destroyer Force, a presence that included some 108 ships and 24,000 sailors shipping out, was headquartered after World War II in Narragansett Bay, north of the city. Not even counting the 3,000 servicemen and women who were stationed on the base, 3,400 of Newport's skilled working-class civilians were employed by the navy, and another 1,400 were on other federal payrolls. When Dwight Eisenhower decided in 1957 that Newport was the perfect locale for a presidential summer vacation, he marked the fusion of Old and New Newports: the city had become the kind of place where high-ranking naval buddies could play golf at the Newport Country Club in the morning, then survey the fleet and its servicemen in the afternoon. Ike the military man did not even reside in the summer colony known as the Gold Coast, choosing instead the residence of the naval base commander as his Summer White House. The spectacle that greeted Ike's arrival suggests how much the Newport economy was swerving in the direction of a tourist economy, geared not to the exclusivity of the very rich but to the inclusivity of the very famous. The city manager closed the town dump so that the President could avoid the city's fouler odors; able-bodied city residents were put to work raking leaves; a bandstand was erected in a main square. Ike's mere presence was hailed as an economic boon that would translate into $1 million worth of publicity for the town.[14]

A third, less publicized factor undermining Old Newport was the presence of a struggling working class. Certainly the turn-of-the-century mansions had been staffed by the financially strapped, but in the 1950s, 5 percent of Newport's families lived on welfare and another 7 percent lived on poverty-level incomes of less than $1,500 a year. *Business Week* illustrated its 1957 feature on the town with images of a tattoo parlor and a vacant shopping district, and reported that unemployment was up 55 percent in the past year. Compared to the city's impoverished minority, the city's majority population—the 72 percent who worked in wholesale and retail trade, service industries, construction, manufacturing, and fishing—fared well. But compared to the fortunes of other middle-class suburbanites, they were at a distinct disadvantage: their median family income of $2,859 was, according to historian John Ashton Worley, only half of what Rhode Island's other middle-class suburban families took home in pay.[15]

Writer Joan Didion shrewdly grasped how Newport's cultural capital was depreciating when she visited the "summer cottages" a decade later: Old Newport, she observed, could not keep up with the ethic of consumption that was transforming earlier ideas of virtue and the good life. The mansions—"those vast follies behind their handwrought gates"—were "the products of the metastasis of capital, the Industrial Revolution carried to its logical extreme." Old Newport represented the values of an age that consecrated "production" industries like steel and railroads; it was "a fantastically elaborate stage setting for an American morality play in which money and happiness are presented as antithetical." It was this equation that the Newport Jazz Festival sought to reverse, by infusing the luxurious life with the casual vibes of liberation. If the captains of industry had built "a place which seems to illustrate, as in a child's primer, that the production ethic led step by step to unhappiness, to restrictiveness, to entrapment in the mechanics of living," the festival's boosters remade the city as a zone of escape, a place where life's annoyances might be tossed to the fair winds.[16]

"No Hipsters but a Healthy Group of Youngsters"

The Newport Jazz Festival hoped to provide both new kinds of leisure and new sources of revenue—high-profile swankiness along with high-volume sales in package stores, restaurants, and hotels. The boost in sales is easier to document with precision than the boost in swank. In 1958, the year that the festival expanded to include a blues night featuring rock 'n' roll star Chuck Berry, the Newport Chamber of Commerce estimated that the affair injected $500,000 into the local economy. The following year, when the

Kingston Trio and Pat Suzuki were imported into the festival, *Down Beat* estimated that the figure was closer to $1 million. The price of food and lodging doubled and tripled during the festival weekend, with those dispensing alcohol profiting especially from the upturn in sales. The local Kiwanis Club, which managed the alcohol concession booth, sold 2,000 bottles of beer an hour during the concerts, then split their profits three ways between themselves, the Newport Boys Club, and the festival. Meanwhile, local liquor stores stayed open until 5:00 A.M., when would-be patrons finally checked out for the night. According to all accounts, local merchants were not inclined to enforce the laws relating to drinking age.[17]

The new sexiness of Newport, although it cannot be captured with statistical exactitude, left its fair share of traces in public iconography. The festival became a magnet for youth culture, and a highly visible one at that. By the late 1950s much of the world press corps, stretching from the *New York Times* and the *Pittsburgh Courier* to Britain's *Melody Maker* and France's *Le Figaro,* was sending out its correspondents to the resort city. In 1958, a peak year for the festival, *Variety* estimated that 720 jazz writers and broadcasters were in attendance. Before the 1960 riot, the media focused almost uniformly on the sunny side of youth; their reports offer some sense of the allure of Newport, the advertised promise that brought so many young people there. This promise, however, was a dangerous thing: not only could healthy amusement shade easily into sick fun (sick sexually, sick alcoholically, sick racially), but also—as the riot would demonstrate—a broken promise could detonate the materials at hand.[18]

Before the promise could explode, however, it had to be negotiated; and starting with the first festival, professional observers used Newport to model an image of youth at play. The ideal image of male Newport youth appeared in Edgar Z. Friedenberg's *The Vanishing Adolescent* (1959), which recalled nostalgically how the first festivalgoers had prized "competence" over "eccentric dress or behavior, or exhibitionism." Friedenberg was a psychologist of youth behavior, heavily influenced by Harvard sociologist David Riesman. (In the 1960s Friedenberg would become a regular contributor to the *New York Review of Books* and would lend his support to, among other things, the legal defenses of Black Panther Eldridge Cleaver and the Chicago Eight.) Published nine years after Riesman's *The Lonely Crowd,* *The Vanishing Adolescent* argued that adolescence was being squeezed into nonexistence by the competing pressures of the mass society, which made childhood increasingly precocious and adulthood increasingly infantile. Just as Riesman, who provided the introduction to *The Vanishing Adolescent,* had described the replacement of an "inner-directed" individual with a peer-influenced "outer-directed" counterpart, so Friedenberg saw post-

REDEFINING YOUTH CULTURE

war youth unmoored from the traditional task of adolescence, which was "self-definition." Instead of cultivating their own competence ("the foundation of autonomy"), American youths were being stranded in "the desert of standardization." In the area of musical taste, they were being manipulated by the "infant industry" of "Elvises," which was itself "protected by the major radio, phonograph, and television companies from the competition of more specialized appeals."[19]

For Friedenberg, the first Newport Jazz Festival beckoned as an oasis of self-educating consumption. The Newport festivalgoers, he noted, actually learned from bandleader Stan Kenton's spiel of jazz history, and they took their learning seriously. As he observed rhapsodically:

> The first annual Newport Jazz Festival (1954) . . . was a moving experience, and in many ways a unique one. . . . Here was none of the intensity of basketball; the occasion did not demand it. But it was serious in the way I should suppose a cabinet meeting would be serious at a time when there was no special crisis. These people knew what they were there for, and they knew what they expected.

Friedenberg's youngsters were the soul of professionalism and commitment—as tightly knit, self-respecting, and hard-thinking as Cabinet members were presumed to be in the age before *Dr. Strangelove*. And Friedenberg denied exactly what later observers would highlight—the "eccentric dress," the "exhibitionism" of the young. His Newport festivalgoers were so focused on self-improvement that they felt no need to draw attention to themselves; he noted that they did not even protest when a five-hour rain dampened their seats.[20]

As the festival expanded in the mid-1950s, Friedenberg's competent, Cabinet-like youngsters started dropping out of press reports, to be replaced by the fun-loving masses. By 1957, the Newport Jazz Festival had become a northeastern version of Fort Lauderdale, a summertime ritual whose attendance swelled from 13,000 in a casino to 50,000 in an open air park. Accordingly, the first story of Newport—the Lorillards and jazz musicians fighting a cultural battle against the fusty old guard—became triangulated through the appearance of massive numbers of white youth. The 1957 festival programming, for instance, spotlighted a high school youth band who cast a powerful spell over *Time, Life, The Nation,* and other media in attendance. Thus *Life* magazine's first coverage of the festival featured not a single African-American face or body; instead, the photo essay followed Long Island's Farmingdale High School Jazz Band as these healthy young tyros scored a "jazz hit" with the festival audience. "The

"A healthy group of youngsters": Much of the early coverage of the Newport Jazz Festival focused on the promise of white youth at play. This Suzanne Szasz photograph from *Life* accompanied a story on Long Island's Farmingdale High School Jazz Band, whose 1957 performance at Newport delighted critics from publications as diverse as *The Nation, Saturday Review,* and *Time*. (Courtesy of Photo Researchers)

prodigies who had rivaled the pros," wrote the *Life* correspondent, "were no hipsters but a healthy group of youngsters who prefer to tranquilize their preshow jitters on the beach. Their solid musicianship is largely the work of Bandmaster Marshall Brown, who trains his team with the devotion of a football coach." Lest the reader doubt that jazz was discipline-building concert music for young amateurs—the musical equivalent of spinach—the *Life* coverage was dominated by a beach shot that fairly glimmered with good health.[21]

At a moment when musicians like Gerry Mulligan, Art Pepper, and Tadd Dameron had famously—and criminally—"tranquilized" their jitters through drugs like heroin, these youngsters were a shining counterimage

REDEFINING YOUTH CULTURE

of innocent stress relief. The fifteen-year-old female vocalist performed a handstand on the beach—looking healthy and gymnastic in the right foreground—while her male cohorts cheered along from behind, their bodies sending shadows that dappled up the wet strand. These young people resembled the dancers who twisted to the latest records on Dick Clark's *American Bandstand,* the "Bandstand Kids" who, as historian Grace Palladino writes, "embodied the values of good clean fun (like dancing to records that were available to purchase), an attractive appearance (that could be attained through products advertised on the show), and fitting in with the crowd (the real essence of the teenage market)." Jazz music, like rock 'n' roll, was being retooled aggressively—to be made safe.[22]

Perhaps the most powerful iconography of youth at Newport was the documentary film of the 1958 festival, Bert Stern's *Jazz on a Summer's Day.* Stern was a successful commercial photographer with little previous connection to jazz. His chief editor, Aram Avakian, had become involved with the project through his older brother George, a Columbia Records producer who served as the film's musical director. Stern and Aram Avakian shifted the focus of their music documentary away from the performers themselves, turning the film into a swooping, Technicolor ethnography of the Newport audience. Filmed with experimental, fast positive-reversal 35-mm color stock, *Jazz on a Summer's Day* was, in Avakian's words, "a subjective documentary-feature of a public event, a new concept in the U.S. at the time." The film stands as a telling evocation of that new institution of late-fifties youth culture, the festival weekend, in three related ways. First, it affords indispensable glimpses into the party atmosphere of the festival—in the audience-pit, on the beach, and even in the corridors of a house party; the filmmakers enjoyed remarkable access to the world-in-motion of this new event. Second, through its editing and point of view, the film models a new kind of glossy interiority, an intense but diffuse attention that reflects the attitude of the festivalgoers. Alternating between close-up absorption in the music and a blithe, jump-cutting search for kicks, the film technique mimics the distracted subjects it is trying to capture. Finally, as critic Kenneth Tynan noted in a contemporary review, the film stands as a "pictorial embodiment of the white (or 'ofay') attitude towards [jazz]." Through its identification with the mainstream Newport audience, the film describes a fantasy of black bodies at work (often sweating profusely on the bandstand) and white bodies at frolic. More than perhaps any other document left by the festival, *Jazz on a Summer's Day* captures the unique amalgam of delight, uplift, and intoxication that Newport jazz held for its white audience in the late 1950s.[23]

Not surprisingly, film critics found much to celebrate in the documentary, while jazz critics were more queasy. The *New York Times*'s Bosley Crowther praised the film in a Sunday lead article for its promise of "our own 'New Wave.'" Juxtaposing Stern's film with the blockbuster *Ben Hur,* Crowther claimed that "some modest hope for the future of American motion pictures" might be found in independent films like *Jazz on a Summer's Day.* "This picture has an easy, rhythmic flow, a lively grab for the vivid and colloquial, and a skillful blending of colors and sound," Crowther wrote. "[Stern's] color is absolutely brilliant, his subjects have humor and point, and his feel for jazz as an amalgam of oddities and cranks is good." Jazz critics took umbrage, however, at this assemblage of "oddities and cranks" that presumably extended to themselves. If the film was understood as a skirmish between its auteurish technique and its jazz subject matter, surely the jazz would be seen to suffer. Boston jazz critic John McLellan wrote, "Watching the film was alternately a stirringly beautiful and painfully repugnant experience. The reason is that the producer of the film, Bert Stern, is a skillful photographer, but no lover of jazz." In the *Jazz Review,* the most musicologically serious journal devoted to jazz, pianist Dick Katz offered likewise that "a requisite for enjoying this film is that one not be a jazz devotee. Although it is a semi-documentary of the 1958 Newport Festival, the music in it, what little quality there was, functions mainly as a prop for spectacular visual effects. . . . I came away from the theatre feeling that jazz was once again the butt of a bad joke, and as a jazz musician, I felt I indirectly had been had."[24]

Jazz on a Summer's Day should not, however, be understood simply as a war between its subject matter and its technique. Stern's technique expressed with apt flamboyance the transformation of the Newport Festival into an occasion for massive white jamboree; and his silences—his decision not to interview jazz musicians, his decision not to understand the worlds that filtered into Newport (for instance, Harlem or Newark)—expressed with telling understatement how the large part of the jazz audience, even after the efforts of bebop musicians and critics, could remain insulated from the music's intended social charge. The film used its jazz to create, on the one hand, an exercise in technicolor abstraction and, on the other hand, an ethnography of the leisure patterns of the jazz audience. Neither approach led to much insight into the plight or intention of jazz musicians, but the film gives us two significant, and compatible, takes on jazz music in the late 1950s. Jazz was both a jumping-off point for experiments in intense abstraction (thus "jazz" action painting), where "pure" sound was translated into "pure" color, and a medium of impulsive celebration (like rock 'n' roll for a slightly younger crowd), with no aspirations to high art but with an implicit protest against the restraint of an older crowd.

The film's first few minutes work as a microcosm of this first tendency toward abstraction, where a play of light on natural surfaces is taken as a visual corollary to the jazz soundtrack. The documentary begins with an image of peaceful repose, of bodies at rest. In the opening shot, the camera is trained on the ripples of the Newport harbor, while the soundtrack is cued to the pulsing harmonies of the Jimmy Giuffre Three. Although Newport had survived economically as the port city for the U.S. Navy, the film prefers the peaceful image of a dock at rest—a harbor deserted by sailors, dockhands, and other workmen. The camera lingers on the reflecting colors of the water as they ripple and modulate with deeper and lighter blues. A swab of red—presumably from a boat in dock—washes into the frame, and we are meant to notice the detail; our eyes are meant to be lost in looking. The camera continues to inch along in the water, until the first word ("Newport") appears from the dock sign, its characters dancing in their reflection. At this point, the film cuts to the Newport stage where the Giuffre Three, like the Newport harbor, are entranced by the droning interharmonics. Giuffre's music is taken as the functional equivalent of those rippling waters: the instruments interweave, but no lead melody asserts itself; rather, Giuffre's arpeggiating tenor bounces against the subtle guitar voicings of Jim Hall and the legato trombone of Bob Brookmeyer. Here the choice of Giuffre speaks to Stern's opening gambit. A supreme eclectic, Giuffre composed anything and everything but dance music; when his contemporaries groped for a classification to describe him, they chose "Third Stream" because Giuffre seemed to fuse jazz, classical music, and what is now called world music. For *Jazz on a Summer's Day,* Stern chose Giuffre's music at his most meditative, its beat submerged in arpeggios. He also chose not to pan outward to the audience, whose behavior may not have conformed to the peacefulness of that opening shot of Newport at rest. His jazzfest might heat up into a rowdy night, but it would begin in the contemplative ebbtide of a leisurely day, with an experiment in cool.[25]

Throughout the film, jazz performances serve as the soundtrack for Stern's fascination with photographic surfaces, the play of summer light dappling across the water. And not just any water, but water in the service of leisure: although the film is drawn to the Narrangansett Bay, it never admits the Navy's presence, preferring instead the more leisurely phenomenon of the America's Cup, the yacht race that was also located off the coast of Newport. Fifteen minutes into the film, in one of its most striking sequences, the camera cuts from the music of the Sonny Stitt–Sal Salvatore quintet to a series of high-altitude shots of America's Cup sailboats. As in the opening sequence, the camera lingers, but does so with a certain dandified flamboyance: it has cruised deep into the bay and now seems to perch from atop a crow's nest, where it views the other boats from a highly tilted angle. Again the high-contrast film turns the surface of the water into a kaleidoscopic spectacle. The sun plays fantastically against the waves; the foam of the waves churns with a distant pattern of ripples; and when the full force of the sun hits the metallic blue-gray water, the waves seem to give off sparks. The intensity of this spectacle—its mind-bending, almost psychedelic quality—has some sort of assumed correlation with the mindset of the jazz musicians, who are filmed, like the waves, from strange angles and are cropped weirdly. The camera contributes to this sense of intensity through long close-ups of the musicians, where every bead of sweat is allowed to glisten and every tooth is allowed to shine. Kenneth Tynan compared the camerawork on vocalist Anita O'Day to dentistry, and he was not far from the mark. At times (with Chico Hamilton, with Mahalia Jackson, with an unnamed half-naked cellist playing Pachabel's Canon, for example), the camera focuses with a nearly merciless fixity, modeling the deep concentration of the musician being filmed.[26]

While some segments of *Jazz on a Summer's Day* pointed to an analogy between the jazzfest and the yacht race—both strenuous experiments in the pursuit of cool—the bulk of the footage took as its model another kind of leisure: the white man's jamboree. In program notes to the film, Stern wrote that "we wanted to make a happy jazz film, a film showing musicians and audiences enjoying . . . the wonderful experience of jazz." The film bears out his intentions. On the level of musical selection, the film focuses on the celebratory, rather than the meditative, strains of jazz. Partly as a result of the crew's technical failure on their first day of filming to capture Duke Ellington and Miles Davis, the final cut is skewed to the "Blues Night" that drew howls from purist jazz critics. Artists such as Big Maybelle, Dinah Washington, Chuck Berry, and Louis Armstrong set the tone for much of the film.[27]

Even more significantly, the film depicts an audience half in the throes of Dixieland jive, half in the thrall of rock 'n' roll. The film's only recurring characters are a group of young white musicians, who play Dixieland jazz as they tool around Newport in an antique car. Their arrival marks the beginning of the film; their performance of "Bill Bailey" on an amusement park train, sandwiched into the miniature cars, marks the middle; and their exit from Newport, crashed out on the backseat, marks the end. These Dixielanders, testifying to the clean-cut appeal of old-time jazz, are joined at Newport by the rock 'n' rollers, whose behavior would prove so threatening at the 1960 riot. Even in *Jazz on a Summer's Day*, which labors hard to establish Newport music as good-time music, this rock 'n' roll audience ventures into provocation. The film cuts from the safety of the Dixieland "Bill Bailey," performed among tots and the elderly, to a house party where young people are drinking Budweiser in darkly lit hallways, and where one couple is the image of decadent nonchalance, twisting the day away on the house's mansard roof, wearing shades and holding cigarettes in the crook of their fingers. During Blues Night, this same segment of the Newport audience is on display again—sometimes jitterbugging in couples, sometimes shaking their bodies with great funk, sometimes smiling with dreamy abandon, but always on their feet and transported by the music.

Yet for all their provocative moves, the film accepts the young people in the Newport audience. It refuses to pass judgment through any intrusion of narration; it seems as devoted to their pleasure as they are. It does not turn away from them in a show of prudery, nor does it try to investigate why they are so transported by the music. Instead, it respects their amusement as a surface phenomenon, one that fascinates—like the waters of Newport—with its rippling moods. In fact, the film seems pulled along by their magnetism. In its choice of music (the prominence of Blues Night), the film follows the box-office tastes of the youthful multitudes. In its choice of locales (the house party, the town, the beach), it follows their extramusical interests. And, most powerfully, in its swing between close-up absorption and cross-cutting distraction, it follows their line of vision: while it absorbs the spectacle of the festival, it also takes the festival as a sufficient world of information; it is more curious about the pores of jazz musicians than about their lives beyond this summer day in a resort town. If *Jazz on a Summer's Day* was "a subjective documentary-feature of a public event," as editor Aram Avakian claimed, then it succeeded by capturing a particular mind-set in a state of delighted self-enclosure.

"So Fashionable and So Squalid"

Two years later, the Newport festival's youth culture moved from jamboree to riot, as its consumer fantasy collided with the logistics of an overcrowded, overinstitutionalized event. The fantasy did have some basis in fact: between 1954 and 1960, the Newport Jazz Festival had pioneered a new form of mass leisure, converting jazz from the ubiquitous dance-hall music of the swing era into the occasion for a weekend blockbuster blowout, with more traces of Elvis and Fort Lauderdale than of Count Basie and the Savoy. In the absence of sufficient accommodation, the beach became a mini-colony of crashed-out young people; alcohol was sold freely and consumed liberally, under the open encouragement of Pabst Blue Ribbon, Budweiser, and Schlitz. For much of the festival audience, however, the

Newport affair not only gave them a good time, but also suggested other splendid truths about their America, truths that invited them into a new public. Remade in the attractive light of the festival, Newport was neither an exclusive resort nor a struggling blue-collar town with rising unemployment, but a tourist magnet renewing itself through its landscape, its past, and its welcome to one and all. Likewise, jazz was neither intimidating music for highbrows nor an exclusive vernacular of the black community, but a swinging beat that verged on the audacity of rock 'n' roll. The clincher was that these two formerly exclusive communities, Newport and the world of jazz, did not require much sacrifice as the price of admission. In fact, the Newport Jazz Fest promised simultaneously the fantasy of slumming and the fantasy of upward mobility; it allowed its patrons to indulge their corresponding fantasies about the immorality of the very poor and the decadence of the very rich. As columnist Murray Kempton observed with his usual loftiness in January 1960, "Was ever anything in America at once so fashionable and so squalid?"[28]

It is only when we understand the dreamwork of the festival—the images and tropes that it produced for mainstream consumption—that the motives for the riot become clear. Jazz critics may have been right that the Newport patrons were not primarily concerned with jazz music, but they would have been wrong to assume that these youths were unfamiliar with the myths that rode on the coattails of Newport jazz, or that the rioters were sharply different from the jazz fans peacefully enjoying the music in Freebody Park. As journalist Steve Gelman wrote in the most in-depth account of the riot, "Most of the 12,000 people outside, like most of the 15,000 people inside, were in their late teens or early 20s, dressed in Bermuda shorts and on vacation from a hundred or so colleges. They were outside because they couldn't get inside (it was a sellout) and they wanted to get in because 'digging the sounds' is a 'must' for campus status-seekers. They can be classified as pseudo-jazz fans, perhaps, but fans nevertheless, because a fan is measured by his enthusiasm, not his sincerity or knowledge." There was a gap, no doubt, between the average *Down Beat* reader and the average Newport rioter: the age of the first group was mostly late twenties, for instance, while that of the latter was late teens and early twenties. But the Newport riot was one of the most striking expressions of jazz's greater youth audience in the postwar period, the larger circle of fans that radiated out from the inner circle of gigging jazz artists, critics, nightclub stalwarts, and amateur musicians. The riot also coincided with the emergence of soul-jazz as a subgenre that resuscitated the connection between jazz and mainstream popular music. The double bill on the riot evening— Horace Silver and Ray Charles—were both identified with soul-jazz, and their appeal came from the imaginative way they remade African-American roots music. The Newport festival was thus attracting a larger audience at the very moment that jazz was attracting a larger audience (as measured by the revival of the jazz single) through an infusion of R&B.

Newport ignited into riot when this white fascination with "getting down" coalesced with a rising sense of consumer entitlement. When the crowds were rebuffed at the festival gates, they were being instructed that Newport was not the open city they had imagined, that in fact they had better respect the authority of its gatekeepers. At first, in the early evening, a steady trickle protested by simply scaling the walls of Freebody Park and occupying vacant seats. Later, the crowd responded en masse by turning the open promise of Newport into a reality of free entrance: denied admission, they crashed in the gate and tried to open the concert to everyone. Here the alcohol may have lubricated the riot—a fact borne out by the use of beer bottles and cans as artillery in the battle against the police—but despite the put-downs of the editorial writers, it was not the lure of alcohol that drove the riot. Beer was generally cheaper outside the festival than inside it. On the night of the riot itself, all fans who wished to enter Freebody Park had to submit to the confiscation of their beer cans, bottles, and flasks.[29]

While the riot was not a pointless act of rebellion, neither was it a purposeful attack on middle-class corporate society, as scholar John Ashton Worley has suggested in the most sustained interpretation of the event. Worley is right that the festival by 1960 had become a textbook case of the working principles behind postwar corporate gigantism: it created franchise festivals in Boston, Toronto, and Indiana; it included non-jazz acts, such as the Kingston Trio, Eartha Kitt, and a fashion show, in order to attract larger crowds; and it subcontracted the work around the festival (the sale of alcohol to the local Kiwanis Club; the sale of "live" albums to Verve, Columbia, and Atlantic; the publishing of the program to *Down Beat* magazine) in order to maximize profits and minimize accountability. Rather than being a protest of this corporate gigantism, however, the riot sprang out of the festival's central tension: the Newport fest had grown rapidly by promising a new public freedom to its audience at the same time that it hoped to leash this freedom to a corporate ideal of orderliness. The youths did not want to destroy the institution of the festival (in fact, they vandalized the town rather than the park); they simply wanted it to live up to its self-image.

The Newport streets became the scene of a riot when this sense of consumer entitlement was sharply rebuffed by a testy and overstressed police force. Like many of the urban disturbances of the mid- to late 1960s, the

Newport riot took hold in an atmosphere of extreme distrust between the forces of law and order and those "dancing in the streets." A Newport gas station owner testified, "There was no violence until the cops got here. The kids were singing, dancing, and drinking beer. But there were no fights, no bloodshed, nothing real bad." A local reporter wrote that the police "had done this crowd duty before, and hated it with the memories of men who have endured the taunts of wise youths for years." One of Newport's councilmen called the police work "worse than useless," and the police chief himself threw up his hands to the charge: "What could we do? We were in the middle of a riot. We grabbed whoever gave us any kind of a hard time. . . . We just wanted to get them into jail, and when the mess cleared, we wanted to get them out." In practice, getting the "mess cleared" meant that many young people were wrongly charged. For instance, a pair of Northwestern students came to the police station to report a stolen car, and were instead lumped in with the rioters and clapped into a five-by-six-foot cell, which they shared with students from Princeton, Penn State, and Miami University. More commonly, young people were thrown in jail when police officers judged that they were not hustling along as quickly as the situation demanded. Civil liberties were sacrificed to crowd control.[30]

Ironically, from the narrow point of view of the police, the large scale of the Newport disturbance seemed to prefigure the civil disobedience actions that would flood jails in cities like Albany, Georgia, in 1961 and Birmingham, Alabama, in 1963. The two hundred Newport rioters—transported in police caravans to jails so overcrowded that simply booking everyone was an onerous task—suggested how numbers could clog a penal system habituated to compliance. The Newport clerk was not able to process the complaints in one night's time, and the police were not able to substantiate all the charges. As a result, only seven rioters were fined between $20 and $50 for disturbing the peace, and only one had to stand trial on charges of assault. From the side of law and order, the Newport riot proved to be an instructive parable about underpreparedness in volatile situations. According to Worley, "in police academies across the country in 1978 police were still citing Newport as an example of police being unprepared for mass demonstrations and mass arrests in 1960."[31]

Yet while the police may have drawn analogies in retrospect between the Newport riot and acts of civil disobedience, the connection was a perverse one. While the white youths in Newport and the civil rights activists might have shared certain common antagonists (law-and-order policemen, an opportunistic corporate structure), they did not share a common sense of mission. In fact, the Newport riot pointed to a cleavage between white and black audiences. White youths turned Newport's streets into a stage where they might act out jazz's identification with instinctual release and plea-sure—that is, where they might "black up" without the blackface. Their en-gagement with jazz was less a new form of interracial solidarity than a strange new form of white privilege—a way that second-generation Ital-ian-Americans, American Jews, Polish-Americans, and WASPs came to-gether in the postwar period as a common group with a common invest-ment in certain fictions of black life. Newport may have been a melting pot of some sort, but the terms of assimilation were forbidding to those who identified with jazz musicians in less grotesque ways.[32] Indeed, while the disturbance was inspired in part by a fiction about black jazz, there is little evidence to suggest that black festivalgoers participated in the rioting or that black musicians condoned in any way the disturbance held on their music's behalf.[33] Contemporary accounts in the black and mainstream press either neglected to mention the racial composition of the rioters or emphasized that "the riots had no racial angles."[34] In addition, black musi-cians were as a group hostile toward the rioters, who threatened their liveli-hood. Max Roach called the riot a "tragedy," "the worst thing that could have happened to the jazz world"; Coleman Hawkins agreed, saying that "it's terrible. Nothing worse could have happened."[35]

The riot was, after all, an unorchestrated event—an expression of incho-ate frustrations rather than a disciplined endeavor anchored to a political philosophy—and so it might be better situated with other youth "status crimes," like the earlier theater riots around the film *The Blackboard Jungle* or the later alcohol-related sprees of white collegians. In retrospect, the dis-turbances around *The Blackboard Jungle* in 1955 were an embryonic ver-sion of 1960 Newport. When teenagers danced in the aisles to Bill Haley's "Rock around the Clock," the first rock 'n' roll number in a movie sound-track, they were mimicking black cultural styles even as the official Negro of the film, Sidney Poitier, steered his classmates away from delinquency. Newport and *The Blackboard Jungle* both offered an official, respectable ethic (black music is to be enjoyed, but not indulged; juvenile delinquents are to be feared, not emulated), and a not-so-hidden transcript (there are new pleasures here for the taking). As at Newport, the crimes around *The Blackboard Jungle* also drove a wedge between teens and adults: teens dis-turbed older patrons "by laughing, throwing 'missiles' from their balcony seats, and competing for the attention of unescorted girls." The teens in the theater were driven to "riot"—ripping up seats and vandalizing candy machines—when theater managers told them to stop dancing or take their feet off the seats. Like the youths at Newport, they were lured to a world where they dominated the audience and hoped to set the rules of ad-mission.[36]

If the Newport riot hearkened back to early rock "delinquency," it also gave a foretaste of a late 1960s youth culture that would redefine civility, not by being assertively polite (the solution of civil rights direct action) but by smashing old codes of etiquette. Alcohol-lubricated sprees were easy to find as the sixties progressed, and the team of Frankie Avalon and Annette Funicello spread the good gospel of Beach Blanket Bingo: there were two, three, many Newports before there were two, three, many Columbias. The same issue of the *New York Herald Tribune* that lambasted the rioters for their "hedonism gone wild" carried a small article about a student "riot" in Colorado, where 200 college students "charged the Grand Lake Fire Department with clubs [and] set fire to gasoline in the street"—all because the town's bars had been shuttered before the customary 8:00 P.M. deadline.[37]

Five years later, a similar indignation at the abridgement of consumer freedom drove a set of beach riots, as the search for "beach, broads, and booze" prompted another series of police actions. At Daytona Beach on Easter weekend in 1965, a crowd of 75,000 maintained a peaceful demeanor until one girl, springing on a blanket, lost her swimsuit in the bargain. Almost 2,000 young people were arrested in the ensuing tumult for public promiscuity and drinking. At Hampton Beach, New Hampshire, over Labor Day weekend, a crowd of 10,000 became unruly in an almost direct parallel with Newport. When youths began flouting the local prohibitions on drinking beer and "bundling" (sleeping co-ed on the beach), the police attacked the crowd with fire hoses, tear gas, and dogs until the National Guard arrived to force the youths across the state line and into Massachusetts. The authorities arrested anyone who refused to leave, and the judge meted out harsh sentences of up to nine months in jail and $1,000 fines. The stiff penalties suggest that, just five years after the jazz festival, the authorities felt more embattled than at Newport, where "rioting" had been something of an innovation and the "hooligans" had been slapped with fines of between $5 and $50. Yet the rhetoric of alarm echoed the warnings sounded by the analysts of Newport: New Hampshire's governor took a page from the earlier pundits when he called the beach riot a "symptom of the moral sickness in American youth." The leisure of Newport—both its hazy promise and its unwieldy reality—was prophetic for a 1960s youth culture that defined itself by its hunger for liberation and its defiance of older standards of civility.[38]

4

THE RIOT IN REVERSE

The Newport Rebels, Langston Hughes, and the Mockery of Freedom

If the history of the civil rights movement were written as a series of cultural skirmishes—disputes over the appropriate forms of art, conflicts over how artists might organize themselves and control the rewards of their profession—then the Newport Jazz Festival might be considered one of the Movement's most revealing 1960 flashpoints, along with the understandably more famous student-led sit-ins. In the unlikely atmosphere of Newport, an older group of black artists tried to translate Martin Luther King's prophetic vision into a working blueprint of their lives, using the "creative extremism" that King invoked as the Movement's spirit. While unruly white crowds threw bottles at cops in the streets and forced the festival's cancellation, a group of musicians led by Charles Mingus and Max Roach held a Newport festival of their own—a "Newport Rebels" festival marked by low budgets, appreciative crowds, and a powerful spirit of musicianly camaraderie. And while the National Guard took control of the region later that weekend, Langston Hughes sat in his room at Newport's Hotel Viking and started composing a poem. The result was *Ask Your Mama: 12 Moods for Jazz*, an experimental poetic sequence that set out to bewilder the rioters and white America generally through well-crafted mockery.[1]

These, then, were the terms of action and reaction. For every festival bloated with pop entertainers and marked by glazed or disruptive crowds, there would be a counterfestival run by the musicians themselves. For every insult like the riot, which impaired the livelihood of jazz musicians by associating the music with unbound license, there would be a generalized insult in return, hurled in the smart and audacious form of verse. These two acts of defiance demonstrated how American culture was being brought to a new reckoning, a new system of bills delivered and accounts paid. Stand-up comedian Dick Gregory, who made his debut at Chicago's Playboy Club in the same year, pointed to this new reckoning when he marveled, "Now I'm getting $5,000 a week—for saying the same things out loud I used to say under my breath." We might consider the counterfestivals of Mingus, Roach, and Hughes as a similar refusal to mask their anger from their antagonists. Mingus and Roach were emboldened to attack the supposed "freedom" within the free market: they fought against their devaluation by corporate entities like the Newport Jazz Festival and held out the promise of a more collaborative venture, a guild owned and operated by artists themselves. Hughes's reckoning entailed a new impudence, a new assertion of black vernacular in content and form: *Ask Your Mama* was subtitled "12 Moods for Jazz" because it played the Dozens with and around its reader, attacking a white interlocutor and pummeling older poetic models from T. S. Eliot to Vachel Lindsay. Both experiments attested to a renewal of bravado and a rejection of the old Uncle Tom and Sambo postures. These artists gained their authority not by leveraging their victimhood but by reaching toward self-sufficiency, advertising their strength, and challenging the laws of their trade. Allies of the civil rights movement, they also spoke to the radical impulses that coalesced in the mid-1960s under the name of Black Power.[2]

Jazz Leaves the Plantation

Held at Cliff Walk Manor only a few blocks away from Freebody Park, the counterfestival represented an early attempt by jazz musicians to protest the corporate logic of the music industry. Brainstormed, staffed, and produced by the musicians themselves, it tried to take back Newport from its new guard and their commercial clutches. Mingus and Roach secured a key backer from Newport's elite: Elaine Lorillard, cofounder of the Newport Festival, who had divorced her husband Louis in 1959 and been ousted from the festival's board of directors. Frustrated that the festival was no longer promoting jazz in a Tanglewood-like ambience and locked in the beginnings of a bitter lawsuit with her ex-husband, she was now willing to help usher a counterfestival through the necessary city channels. The Cliff Walk festival had little Lorillard glitz, though. With its primitively rigged stage, impromptu roster, and small crowds, it was almost willfully under-capitalized: it hoped to deliver on the cult promise of jazz as serious, intimate music that needed no artificial stimulants of a chemical or financial sort. Rather than promote the counterfestival with paid advertising, Mingus simply roared through town in a convertible, standing on the seat and shouting "Come to my festival!" (Someone else drove the car.) To deal with logistics, the musicians seized the means of production with their bare hands: they "constructed a bandstand, decorated it in a brilliant fire-engine red, enclosed the lawn with snow fencing, erected half a dozen tents to sleep in, procured five hundred undertaker's chairs, issued handbills, and, after the weekend was in progress, collected contributions from on-lookers on the wrong side of the fence."[3]

If the Cliff Walk festival protested the general "mastodon ways" of the established festival, more specifically it targeted Newport promoter George Wein's wage scale, which favored mainstream (often white) musicians over cultish (often black) performers. According to critic Nat Hentoff, the Newport festival had developed a "cavalier financial attitude toward jazzmen who lacked mass name appeal but who were recognized by their colleagues as among the most important of current contributors to the music. A Louis Armstrong or a Benny Goodman had the box office appeal and a tough booking office to get top fees from the N.J.F, but the less widely renowned jazzmen were often pressured into coming to Newport for smaller sums than they deserved." The Newport festival assumed that the mainstream audience preferred performers like Armstrong, and so it shunted less obviously ingratiating musicians into afternoon slots where attendance was poor. For Mingus, Roach, and many others who clambered onto the "Newport Rebels" stage at Cliff Walk, this booking policy was an outrage that put the lie to George Wein's high-toned claim that the festival sought to "sponsor the study of our country's only original art form." The civil rights spirit of the counterfestival—its protest against racial business as usual—was not lost on the press corps. The reporter from *Time* magazine argued to his editor that the story of the rump festival "belong[ed] in National Affairs. This is like an extension of the sit-ins. I called it a sit-out."[4]

Even though the counterfestival did not translate into a systematic overhaul of the jazz industry, it remained an important symbolic incarnation of the utopian promise that jazz held for its black musicians. As Nat Hentoff suggested, "It was exhilarating for the musicians involved to realize for once in their careers, they were capable of formulating and sustaining their own ground rules without booking agents, impresarios, and other middlemen."[5] If the Newport Jazz Festival had become a party weekend for the youth it attracted, the counterfestival hoped to function as a kind of workers' playtime—a combination of work and leisure epitomized, in all its vagaries and pointedness, by the jam session. The eventual roster of the counterfestival included prestigious jazzmen and -women across the generational spectrum: swing era titans like Coleman Hawkins, Roy Eldridge, and Jo Jones; beboppers like Max Roach and Kenny Drew; hard boppers like Kenny Dorham, Art Taylor, and Yusef Lateef; and more recent figures like Eric Dolphy, Ornette Coleman, Don Cherry, Charlie Haden, and Abbey Lincoln. Musical observers noted that the cross-generational lineup at Cliff Walk broke much of the usual regimentation of the Newport festival, mixing performers like Coleman, Mingus, Roach, Hawkins, and Dorham in jam sessions on the same stage. To judge from the one album (Candid's *Newport Rebels*) with the rump festival lineup, it would seem that the combination breathed new enthusiasm into old and young. Whitney Balliett, ever the gentleman, studiously avoided any mention of the racial dynamics of the alternative festival, but significantly he praised the event for its "catching bonhomie," its "unfailing smoothness and graciousness." The "yahoos" were nowhere to be found, except for a brief ten-minute interlude at three in the morning, when they "stood beerily about . . . , peacock-colored shirts dripping, pedal-pushers tight and wrinkled." Balliett suggested that Cliff Walk's anticommercialism made it a self-selective affair, a concert that managed to exclude sodden youths while fostering an inclusive, respectful attitude in its audience.[6]

At the same time, the Cliff Walk experience and its aftermath hinted at some of the challenges that the rebels would face. The rough-hewn aspect of the festival may have appealed to the audience, but it had at least one unintentional consequence for the musicians themselves. The profits from the festival were divvied up in the most haphazard manner—with musicians nipping away at the kitty until Kenny Dorham decided to abscond with the full remainder. If these were the economics of jazz utopia, they had a decidedly human face.[7]

The related story of the Jazz Artists' Guild (JAG) was another hopeful but cautionary tale. In an effort to broaden their protest beyond the festival context, the rebels struck again on the highly significant date of July 4, the Monday after the Newport festival. Mingus, Roach, and Jo Jones announced the formation of JAG, a collective with a fighting mission: to keep artistic control in the hands of jazz musicians, to distribute industry profits more equitably, and to stage performances in venues befitting the honor of jazz music itself. The first official effort of the guild was an ostensibly long-term residence at the former Bavarian Music Hall on New York's East Seventy-Fourth Street. No hard liquor would be sold since the music was, according to JAG spokesman Allen Eager, "for people who want to listen to music in an informal atmosphere where musicians and audience both can relax." The concerts began in August with a star-studded lineup reminiscent of the Cliff Walk festival: Eager's quartet with Kenny Drew, Wilbur Ware, and Art Taylor; Max Roach's ensemble with Booker Little; Mingus's Workshop with Eric Dolphy and Ted Curson; and Kenny Dorham and Abbey Lincoln's groups. New York's press enthused about the event. In an article entitled "Jazz Leaves the Plantation," an editorialist wrote, "Whether you care a fig for jazz music or not, if you care about progress you will be pleased to know that the new Jazz Artists' Guild...represents the first clear-cut mass break by Negro jazz-men from their former economic strangleholds." The *Citizen-Call's* Maely Dufty drew a pointed analogy between the civil rights protests in Alabama and the jazz musicians' residence on the Upper East Side. "The difference between that East 74th Street Theater and the province is merely a longitude and latitude of geography. The issue is the same: Liberation."[8]

Yet despite such high-minded intentions, the guild ran aground two weeks into its supposedly month-long residence. Some of its difficulties were as incongruous as they were frightening: it was reported that Max Roach's manager, on his way to conclude a JAG business deal with the owner of the Village Gate, was kidnapped by a group of toughs who drove him to New Jersey, all the while demanding to "know all about the organization incorporated under the name Jazz Artists' Guild." The concerts themselves ran into a much less sensational difficulty—poor attendance. The guild had planned two shows a night, but rarely had to deliver the second one. Mingus and Roach bickered about whether to cut down the residence to five nights a week; Mingus argued for a seven-day week and won, but then bowed out by the middle of the second week. When the guild closed shop shortly thereafter, Mingus returned with another, less costly plan: to establish an agency that would offer a kind of "Good Housekeeping" seal for musicians worthy of discovery by agents and record companies. The Good Housekeeping jazz agency became yet another stillborn Mingus project, for reasons that are not hard to fathom. A jazz editor scribbled this comment on a journalist's rough copy about the proposed agency: "He's got a nerve."[9]

From a different angle, the experience of the Cliff Walk festival and Jazz Artists' Guild suggested another set of lessons about the resurgent visibility of the color line in projects that sought to liberate jazz musicians from a white-controlled industry. After Nat Adderley declined to play at Cliff Walk Manor, Mingus said stingingly that Adderley had "no race pride": playing the counterfestival became a way of proving one's racial bona fides. The absence of major white performers at Cliff Walk—with the notable exceptions of saxophonist Allen Eager, the boyfriend of festival benefactor Peggy Hitchcock; and bassist Charlie Haden, an established member of Coleman's quartet—raises questions as well about the "bonhomie" of the festival. The Gerry Mulligan Big Band, the Dave Brubeck Quartet, and the Herbie Mann Sextet all played at the mainstream festival but not at Cliff Walk. The coalition behind the Newport counterfestival—black performers supported logistically and otherwise by white sophisticates—would become familiar as the jazz community grew more radicalized in the sixties. As musicians turned increasingly toward forms of collective action, white patronage became more visible than interracial onstage collaboration. A check with few strings attached came to seem the most appropriate way to encourage another group's attempt at self-determination.[10]

JAG's greatest historic importance may have been as an inspiration to future artists' collectives and a sketch of their future challenges. It foreshadowed the emergence in the mid- to late 1960s of the Jazz Composers Guild in New York, the Union of God's Musicians and Artists Ascension (UGMAA) in Los Angeles, the Association for the Advancement of Creative Musicians (AACM) in Chicago, and the Black Artists Guild (BAG) in St. Louis—cooperative ventures that protested the rules governing the jazz marketplace, and that not coincidentally revised the rules governing jazz composition, arrangement, and improvisation as well. The rump festival also bridged some of the generational gaps within the jazz community, facilitating one of the more gracious acts of musical and political collaboration: Coleman Hawkins's presence on Max Roach and Oscar Brown, Jr.'s *Freedom Now Suite,* recorded two months after the summer festival.[11]

At the same time, other JAG-inspired lessons were more sobering. The lineup at Cliff Walk suggested how the intensity of protest would put added pressure on the terms of interracial collaboration and activism. The rump festival was, after all, an act of separatism as well as a grassroots protest; it challenged white musicians, who had benefited under the Wein directorship, to weigh their allegiances in a new light. As in later cultural nationalist projects like the AACM, the BAG, and Amiri Baraka's Black Arts Repertory Theater/School—and as in political organizations like the Student Nonviolent Coordinating Committee—antiracist whites faced the dilemma of how to strengthen a community that was relegating them to the sidelines of the struggle.[12] Lastly, the economic difficulties of JAG—the haphazard division of the Cliff Walk gross, the poor attendance at its New York concerts—suggested how artist-run ventures would struggle when they ventured outside the usual contractual and publicity structures of the music industry. A community of musicians needed to develop a sense of its own institutional accountability, and an audience for these new ventures needed to be germinated and cultivated. It was the exceptional musician who was also a gifted entrepreneur, dedicated institution-builder, and expert in community outreach. (Chicago's Muhal Richard Abrams and Los Angeles's Horace Tapscott spring to mind.) Artists' collectives without this sort of extramusical support were usually doomed, like JAG, to a very short life.

Fighting Insult with Insult:
Langston Hughes and Nowport's Black Audience

If the 1960 Newport riot marks the revenge of a white audience against the leisure institution that invited them into being, and if the rump festival marks the protest of black musicians against the employer that devalued them, what of the black audience at the festival, estimated as 10 percent of the total?[13] How did they experience the spectacle of the festival—with pride or shame, relaxation or indignation? The black press, from magazines like *Ebony* to newspapers like the *Amsterdam News* and the *Chicago Defender,* gave regular coverage to the Newport festival, and by and large it affirmed the central journalistic narratives that attached to it, celebrating Newport's status as the "new mecca" for "America's jazz aficionados" and then leavening their festival coverage with criticism of the beer-drinking multitudes.[14]

At the same time, other more fugitive reports pointed to special underlying difficulties for Newport's black audience. Unlike the white audience, who might soak in the glamour of Newport while exulting in the looseness of the festival ambience, the black audience had to confront the Jim Crow contradictions at the festival's heart: that Newport citizens might accept black performers onstage, but were loath to accept blacks in their homes; that the cachet of Newport, built in part on the wealth of the slave trade, had historically been refused black people; that Newport's promise—of decoupling jazz from middle-class anxieties about inner-city poverty, delinquency, and immorality—was endangered by blacks' very presence. In brief: the dream of the inclusive jazz audience collided with the ideology of Northern suburban segregation. The city of Newport and the institution of the jazz festival practiced the sorts of discrimination—legal and illegal, economic and cultural—that persisted in the North even as Jim Crow was formally being dismantled in the South.

From the festival's inception to its takeoff in the late 1950s, black visitors to Newport had difficulty finding accommodations and being served at local establishments. *Ebony*'s seven-page photo spread on the first festival concluded with the information that "pianist Billy Taylor was victim of discrimination in town when he sought service at [the] bar of a hotel." In 1956, the Duke Ellington band was forced to board in a musty barracks above tennis courts, and as late as 1960, Charles Mingus was turned away from a hotel that had accepted his reservation under the assumption that the counterfestival's music director had to be white.[15] Several stories circulated about the Newport elite's refusal to welcome jazz musicians into their homes. In an anecdote related by Elaine Lorillard, a well-placed Newporter asked promoter George Wein to spread the word for a party he hoped to give for festival musicians and panelists, but requested that Wein avoid inviting "Africans." Wein replied, "I'll be careful," then refused to contact any musicians whatsoever—leaving the Newporter stranded that night with his fine silver and linen, and an "army of servants the size of Custer's."[16]

Most stories were not so triumphant, however: they involved the public slights, the incorrigible "misunderstandings," that were customary in a segregated America. In Newport, where private homes offered accommodations to two thousand people but there were only three public hotels, black audience members had no choice but to confront the residential prejudices of the community. A black photographer was turned away from a private home while her white friend was allowed to stay; a black woman from the Bronx wrote to request reservations for herself and two friends, and was instructed that her reservations were for "three white girls" only. When Nat Hentoff publicly raised the issue of lodging discrimination in 1959, the festival's board of directors dithered and parried, saying that they did not practice discrimination themselves, that Newport was no worse than New York, and that the best hotels no longer drew the color line. Neither the municipal government nor the festival's board ever aired a public pronouncement on the persistence of racial prejudice in Newport.[17]

The most articulate and provocative response to the Newport jazz cocktail—equal parts Negro fetish and suburban prejudice—came from poet Langston Hughes, who composed *Ask Your Mama: 12 Moods for Jazz* in direct response to the 1960 riots. Early on, Hughes had breathed in the enthusiasm for the festival, which confirmed for him that black music, with its colloquial rhythms, was a powerful tool for building a more expansive and imaginative audience for the arts. After Duke Ellington's monumental performance at Newport in 1956, where a well-heeled white crowd gyrated to Paul Gonsalves's extended tenor solo, Hughes wrote in the *Chicago Defender* that the "Festival ended with jazz at its jazziest [wailing] its way toward midnight." Hughes biographer Arnold Rampersad speculates that Hughes's enthusiasm for 1956 Newport translated first into his lecture "Jazz as Communication" and, shortly thereafter, into his eagerness to mount *Tambourines to Glory*, a Broadway project grounded in the black gospel tradition.[18] By 1958, Hughes was not only a Newport partisan but an official member of the festival's board of directors—the policy group that included Louis Lorillard, jazz producer John Hammond, Columbia Record's George Avakian, Voice of America DJ Willis Conover, and jazz scholar Marshall Stearns.[19]

In the 1960 tumult, Hughes found himself in a difficult position at Newport, one that included both his enthusiasm for the festival and his growing antipathy for some of its trappings. Signed up to act as emcee for the Sunday "Blues Afternoon," Hughes discovered that he was to be the mop-up act for the festival after it was summarily canceled by the city council in the wake of the Saturday night riot. In response, Hughes wrote the lyrics to the "Goodbye Newport Blues," which pianist Otis Spann then set to a blues in F and performed with Muddy Waters on the Newport stage. Hughes's lyrics examined how the riot affected the musicians at Newport (not the crowds or the festival impresarios), conveying a blues-tinted mix of anguish and perseverance. Hughes asked himself, "What's gonna happen to my music? / What's gonna happen to my song?" then replied with tough-mindedness: "It's a hard, hard world we live in, / And it's been hard so long." In the last verse, he refused "to drown in [his] own tears": "I got to keep on singing / Though I got the Newport blues."[20]

While the "Goodbye Newport Blues" provided good copy for the *Chicago Defender, Time,* and the *New York Amsterdam News* in their coverage of the riots, Hughes composed a much more mordant response to the Newport riots in the form of *Ask Your Mama.* Begun on the stationery of Newport's Hotel Viking during the riot weekend and published in 1961, *Ask Your Mama* is a poetic landmark that infuses the ritual of the Dozens with social protest and jazz rhythms: it represents Hughes's decision to fight the insult of the riot with an ambitious series of poetic insults, keyed to the question "What's gonna happen to my music?" Rather than being a journalistic report on the riot, the poem represents Hughes's struggle with the riot's meaning, his intervention into the fray of racial politics. The poem's "leitmotif"—meant to accompany its recitation at certain key moments—was the "traditional folk melody of the 'Hesitation Blues,'" a blues standard whose chorus might play on a sexual or a political register:

How long must I wait?
Can I get it now—or must I hesitate? (*CP,* p. 475)

The main body of *Ask Your Mama* took the "Hesitation Blues" away from its sexual suggestiveness—the kind of suggestiveness that had, in part, fueled the white riot—and reshaped it into a question of political expectation.[21] To the question "Can't black people just be patient for a little while?" Hughes replied with a defiant, somewhat mocking "Freedom Now." Hughes's sympathies were altogether with the civil rights workers who had begun chanting that slogan at marches and boycotts: in the same year that he published *Ask Your Mama,* he also wrote an authorized history of the NAACP, *Fight for Freedom.* But while Hughes may have shared common goals with civil rights workers, his technique in *Ask Your Mama*—the way he attacked his adversaries, the way he advocated poetically for his people's liberation—was ahead of the cultural curve. Where King preached nonviolence, *Ask Your Mama* preached an insult for an insult. The book made a point of affronting its white audience, and not surprisingly its racial politics and unusual form met with a cool reception in the mainstream press, which had celebrated King as a Ghandian prophet.[22]

In addition, *Ask Your Mama* stood at a critical distance from the prizewinning poets of the late 1950s, whose verse proclaimed its allegiance, often in the most subtly modulated tones of ironic reserve, to a Western literary tradition. While Richard Wilbur and James Merrill were writing homages to the past in ostensibly sturdy forms like the sestina and the sonnet, Hughes was writing an insult to the present in a form borrowed mostly from the barber shop, the street corner, and the neighborhood stoop. Hughes used the streetwise form of the Dozens to give a streetwise analysis of the Newport teenage combustion: the poem was back talk from an inner city that had been deprived of its voice, even as its music had become a new gospel across the land. *Ask Your Mama* unforgivingly addressed the paradox that had struck Charles Mingus and other Newport rebels: while black music had a huge psychological purchase on white America, the black community saw little cultural or economic payoff and remained, in large part, indentured to the minstrel images that white America entertained. Like Mingus, who had claimed musical capital with his rump-festival counterpunch, Hughes claimed poetic capital for the street corner, making the Dozens into a form of performance art, evoking the inner-city voices that the suburban partymaking was supposed to crowd out. In no uncertain terms, *Ask Your Mama* addressed "that gentleman in expensive shoes / made from the hides of blacks," who "tips among the shadows / soaking up the music" (*CP,* p. 519).

Structurally, *Ask Your Mama* ranks as the most elaborate book of Hughes's poetry, with its frank use of several literary and nonliterary traditions at once. Most obviously, the title "Ask Your Mama" and the grouping of twelve poems ("Twelve Moods for Jazz") recall the black ritual of the Dozens, where two antagonists trade dueling insults in a game of one-upmanship.[23] Hughes was especially proud to have taken the ritual—a set piece of ghetto bravado and ghetto deprecation, played out wherever two egos might collide and culminating often in some sexual insult directed toward the antagonist's mother—and reshaped it, against the conventional grain, into a poetic dialogue between writer and reader.[24] Hughes himself had built his entire career since the Harlem Renaissance out of his knowing use of ghetto vernacular, but rarely had he "signified" against a white interlocutor. In the 1930s and 1940s, in poems that dealt more with revolution than the blues, he began directly challenging an implicitly white audience to rethink its racial presumptions ("Open Letter to the South," "White Man," "Note to All Nazis Fascists and Klansmen," "How About It, Dixie") (*CP*, pp. 194, 291, 303). *Ask Your Mama* brought together his ongoing experimentation with vernacular form and this early radical spirit of political challenge, using the Dozens to break the spell of absorption. It presumed to speak directly, defiantly, to its reader.

The new framework also transformed the meaning of the Dozens, which social psychologist John Dollard had theorized in 1939 as "a valve of aggression in a depressed group"—a way for members of a low caste to parry the deprecations of society at large. According to Dollard, the Dozens managed the larger societal insult by redirecting it, in a pointed, half-joking manner, at the repressed anxieties of another black person. Hughes openly marked his debt to Dollard's work, but he also revised Dollard's paradigm of the Dozens in three crucial ways. First, *Ask Your Mama* took Dollard's black-on-black dialogue and shifted it into a black-on-white dialogue, where an urban black voice talked back to the white professional class. Second, it refused Dollard's psychoanalytic model, which relied heavily on the push-pull logic of instinctual repression and release and so scanted the cultural creativity behind the Dozens. Rather than suggesting that black people lashed out because they needed to satisfy their instinctual drives, Hughes pointed to the resourcefulness that lay at the heart of both the Dozens and black music, a resourcefulness grounded in antiphony and improvisation. Third, Hughes added another dramatic context for the phrase "Ask your mama," one that took it out of the sphere of the Dozens and set it in a more poignant family drama. Early drafts of *Ask Your Mama* had an abandoned black child running through it, and the final version ended with "Show Fare, Mama," in which a child asks his mama for money to see a movie because their television is broken. The signature phrase of the Dozens became, in this last context, a form of emotional appeal rather than an act of aggression.[25]

While reconceptualizing the Dozens, the book also converted the ritual into a form of performance poetry, a genre whose modern American roots might be traced back to Vachel Lindsay's "The Congo: A Study of the

Negro Race" (1914). From his beginning days as a poet, Hughes had tied his poetry to music. As early as a 1927 reading in Washington, D.C. arranged by Alain Locke, Hughes was reciting his poetry to the accompaniment of a blues pianist; and more generally, his poetry—especially after his second book, *Fine Clothes to the Jew* (1927)—absorbed such blues elements as an AAB verse and an implicit twelve-bar rhythmic foundation.[26] In the mid-fifties, Hughes discovered new ways to invigorate, and capitalize on, his concern for the interplay of music and poetry. He became an older statesman on the poetry-to-jazz circuit, which he thought would give "poetry a wider following" and jazz "greater respectability," while keeping his distance from the Beat subculture. (He disavowed Kerouac, Ginsberg, et al. with a simple "I don't know the beatniks. They all seem to be down in the Village and I practically never go there. I stay up in Harlem.") Hughes performed in concert halls, at nightclubs like the Village Vanguard, and in open-air bandshells with jazz artists ranging from Earl Hines to Phineas Newborn, Ben Webster, Randy Weston, and Charles Mingus. He recorded an album for Columbia of his poetry set to jazz arrangements by Leonard Feather and Mingus, and collaborated with Weston on the landmark *Uhuru Africa* album. In the summer of 1961, as he exulted to his publisher while making final comments on the *Ask Your Mama* proofs, he was having "the biggest audience in [his] life" (20,000) at a summer Blues Evening on the Boston Common. Like Allen Ginsberg, the great popular poet of the coming decade, Hughes would reach his greatest audience when he tapped into the burgeoning market for mass-music festivals.[27]

Ask Your Mama took Hughes's customary rapport between text and music onto another plane of complexity, featuring a series of musical instructions that could be serviced only by the most catholic of DJ's or the most savvy of jazz outfits. Just as "The Congo" had juxtaposed Vachel Lindsay's evangelizing, emphatic poetry with musical instructions in the margins, so Hughes scrolled a thin column of musical cues to the right of his all-caps poetry—everything from "the rough scraping of a guira" to fragments of German lieder, the "Hesitation Blues," Dixieland jazz, calypso, cha-cha, gospel, bebop and "very modern jazz burning the air eerie like a neon swamp-fire cooled by dry ice." But while Lindsay's modernist fantasy, dedicated to a white missionary who had served in the Congo, had been a virtual sourcebook of primativist clichés ("fat black bucks" chanting "Mumbo-Jumbo will hoo-doo you," "cakewalk princes" strutting in a "Negro fairyland" on a "minstrel river"), Hughes used the music-verse interplay to undercut habitual associations between black music and natural emotional display. Lindsay had imagined a world of primitive ritual that was completely self-absorbed and self-contained, and his musical cues were more on the order of stage directions: a "rolling bass" voice for the voodoo ceremony, a "shrill and high" voice to narrate the dice game. For Hughes, whose central ritual was the Dozens—a dialogue of insult between white and black communities—the music became a fractured series of jump-cuts through a whole world of musical traditions, from Western opera and American hymns through African drums and free jazz. The poem's musical cues advertised the power of the heterogeneous sound ideal that marks so many African-American musical forms: the musics of the world could be absorbed without losing their singularity, laid into a brilliant mosaic of sound.

In general, the haste of *Ask Your Mama*'s music was meant to suggest the quick compositional liberties taken by the late-fifties jazz improviser; it was as ironic and as impassioned as, say, the wide-ranging bass solos of Charles Mingus. The poem's gluttonous use of musical fragments hinted at a central improvisational practice in jazz—the art of jammed quotation, where melodies were plagiarized shrewdly into a new rhythmic structure. Hughes also punctuated his verse with the equivalent of the musical "break" that had made Louis Armstrong, Charlie Parker, and others so famous, but where Armstrong's and Parker's breaks were largely one-time affairs in the space of a song, Hughes used the break as a frequent piece of impudent punctuation. "Where the voice pauses," Hughes instructed his reader, "there is room for spontaneous jazz improvisation" (*CP*, p. 475). The musical instructions, then, not only featured jazz fragments but also were imbued with the improvisatory practices of post-bop jazz at its most volatile. Jazz might be considered the poem's "master discourse," since it was the music most able to swallow, adopt, or quote from other forms. Fittingly, when Hughes was interested in converting *Ask Your Mama* into a multimedia piece involving words, music, and dance, he turned to hard bop pianist-composer Randy Weston for the music (a project that, despite Weston's enthusiastic response, unfortunately seems never to have been realized).[28]

Finally, the structure of *Ask Your Mama* was complicated by the scholarly apparatus at the end—a set of "Liner Notes" that nodded both to T. S. Eliot's footnotes to "The Wasteland" and to the more commercial scribblings of the music industry. These liner notes, originally subtitled "For the racially or poetically unhep," explain the poems aphoristically, through oblique parables about prejudice and its discontents. While Eliot's footnotes draw his modernist fragments into the universal mesh of the fisher king romance, Hughes's notes tie his poems to the contemporary black community through an expansive, riddling idiom. They answer the oral rhythms of the poems with literate puzzles about social coincidence and cultural resistance. The title poem, for instance, is given the following tag: "In spite of shortage of funds for the movies and the frequent rude intrusions of those concerned with hoarding hard metals, collective coins for music-making and grass for dreams to graze on still keep men, mules, donkeys, and black students alive" (*CP*, p. 530). Rather than explain away the enigmas of the main verse—enigmas that emerge from the duel of the Dozens and the cross fire between verse and musical cues—Hughes's liner notes point to the contradictions of his social world. Using tumbling syntax that obscures questions of agency (who are "those concerned with hoarding hard metals"?), Hughes suggests that the rich will grow richer and that the disadvantaged will continue (along with mules and other beasts of burden) to support their own music, their own dreamers, their own poets.

From Dialect to Dialectics:
Struggling through "The Quarter of the Negroes"

In the pages of *Ask Your Mama* drafted at Newport's Hotel Viking, Hughes wrote of moving from "dialect to dialectics"; the wordplay suggested how Hughes hoped to convert the vernacular mode into the open practice of disputation and struggle.[29] Opening up his verse in this way meant adopting a new poetic voice, one that would be based in a vernacular but would take on the larger mandate of representing a community. Hughes in *Ask Your Mama* did not claim to channel the black or proletarian masses, but he did refuse the exceptional, lyrical "I" in favor of a more floating voice, meant to resonate for all who shared a common social predicament. The atmosphere of the poem shifts between several imaginary locales, which are generalized almost to the point of unreal abstraction: the "quarter of the Negroes" in the North and South, the white-dominated suburb, the scene of liberation struggles. Likewise, the stories it tells are generalized too—mass migration, shared experiences of humiliation and joy, shared fantasies of revenge.

The opening of *Ask Your Mama*'s first poem, "Cultural Exchange," takes us far away from the State Department–sponsored tours that exported Louis Armstrong, Dave Brubeck, and Dizzy Gillespie to the Third World. "Cultural exchange" as such is brought home, relocated in the most intensely segregated spaces of America:

IN THE

IN THE QUARTER

IN THE QUARTER OF THE NEGROES

REDEFINING YOUTH CULTURE

WHERE THE DOORS ARE DOORS OF PAPER
DUST OF DINGY ATOMS
BLOWS A SCRATCHY SOUND.
AMORPHOUS JACK-O'-LANTERNS CAPER
AND THE WIND WON'T WAIT FOR MIDNIGHT
FOR FUN TO BLOW DOORS DOWN.

BY THE RIVER AND THE RAILROAD
WITH FLUID FAR-OFF GOING
BOUNDARIES BIND UNBINDING
A WHIRL OF WHISTLES BLOWING
NO TRAINS OR STEAMBOATS GOING—
YET LEONTYNE'S UNPACKING. (*CP*, P. 477)

The "quarter of the Negroes" is the main neighborhood of *Ask Your Mama*. Often serving as a poem's opening tag, the phrase recurs in all of the book's twelve poems. No doubt it appealed to Hughes for both its plantation resonances ("slave quarters") and its reference to current residential segregation North and South. Yet these quarters also mark out a curiously sketchy, indeterminate space. In "Cultural Exchange," Hughes's opening stutter—"in the," "in the quarter"—models an uncertain approach, one that brings us with abrupt but fragmented cuts toward the facades of the ghetto. Language is being broken down and recombined into new molecular structures, along with the landscape. The ostensibly wooden doors of the quarter decompose into mere paper, and then we move into the Cold War gothic suggested by "the dust of dingy atoms"—nuclear dust, perhaps, swirling and making a "scratchy sound" against the quarter's walls or, just as likely, the sound of a scratched record. This dinginess is exploded by a spectral "caper" of "amorphous jack-o'-lanterns," probably a cryptic reference to the torchlight raids of the Ku Klux Klan. Then this scenario—carnivalesque, grotesque—is supplemented by a gate-crashing wind that can't wait "for fun to blow doors down." Are we in the world of the good-time party, as the references to record players, Halloween, and gate-crashers might suggest? Or are we living a racial nightmare, as the references to the thinness of slum walls, nuclear radiation, and the KKK seem to indicate? Hughes's answer seems to be that we are in both places at once. His quarter of the Negroes is neither the dead-end slum of Richard Wright nor the struggling but hopeful Bronzeville of Gwendolyn Brooks. It is a haunted and uncertain world, teeming with ghosts and underpopulated with humanity, where the river and railroad beckon with possibilities of escape but there are "no trains or steamboats going."

The appearance of Leontyne Price—the famous black soprano who debuted at the New York Metropolitan Opera in 1961—may seem like an odd intrusion into this fragile, eerie landscape, with its far-from-operatic "scratchy sound," but *Ask Your Mama* is centrally concerned with the meaning of black celebrity and heroism for the "quarter of the Negroes" and the white world beyond. Martin Luther King, Emmett Till, Kwame Nkrumah, Gamal Nasser, Ralph Ellison, Jimmy Baldwin, Adam Powell, Jackie Robinson, Roy Campanella, Katherine Dunham, Louis Armstrong, and Ornette Coleman—all these (and many more) are interjected into *Ask Your Mama,* less as figures who play a role in the poem's narrative and more as totemic, inspirational presences. As icons patched into this new fragment-laded verse, they bring to the surface familiar stories of subjugation and resistance. Thus "Cultural Exchange" continues, a page later, with:

IN THE SHADOW OF THE NEGROES
    NKRUMAH
IN THE SHADOW OF THE NEGROES
    NASSER NASSER
IN THE SHADOW OF THE NEGROES
    ZIK AZIKIWE
CUBA CASTRO GUINEA TOURÉ
FOR NEED OR PROPAGANDA
    KENYATTA
AND THE TOM DOGS OF THE CABIN

THE COCOA AND THE CANE BRAKE
THE CHAIN GANG AND THE SLAVE BLOCK
TARRED AND FEATHERED NATIONS
SEAGRAM'S AND FOUR ROSES
$5.00 BAGS A DECK OR DAGGA.
FILIBUSTER VERSUS VETO
LIKE A SNAPPING TURTLE—
WON'T LET GO UNTIL IT THUNDERS
WON'T LET GO UNTIL IT THUNDERS
TEARS THE BODY FROM THE SHADOW
WON'T LET GO UNTIL IT THUNDERS
IN THE QUARTER OF THE NEGROES (*CP,* P. 480)

The poem's historical vision stretches from the Middle Passage to the most recent events of the worldwide liberation; its geographical vision throws Africa, the Carribean, and the United States equally "in the shadow of the Negroes." More specifically, Hughes here is puzzling out the relation between the heroes of postcolonial liberation and those Americans who "won't let go until it thunders"—those struggling to create their own breakthrough moment. The roll call of postcolonial heroes from countries as diverse as Cuba, Ghana, Egypt, Nigeria, and Kenya works compositionally much like the intercutting and repetition of phrases like "the quarter of the Negroes": at a certain point, the phrases become more notable for the rhythmic contrasts they create rather than the amount of new meaning they inject into the poem. Yet the names do lead the poem to reveal the trauma of slavery, underscored as a racial trauma with resonances in the present. From "chain gangs" to the "cane brake," Hughes seems to intimate, "cocoa"-colored peoples have become "tarred and feathered nations" within nations. The tar and feathers suggest the weight of shame, and the next lines begin to summon more difficulties—the appeal of Seagram's gin and drug peddling ($5 bags of dagga, or marijuana). From here, we swing into the civil rights scene of Hughes's contemporary moment: the filibuster of the Dixiecrats working against the presidential veto, "snapping turtles" fighting the gospel truth. Notably, at this point in the musical score, Hughes suggests that the "Hesitation Blues" should explode out of the question "Can I get it now—or must I hesitate?" into a thunderous drumroll and a sonorous musical swell. Dramatically, we seem poised for a people's victory: the heroes from abroad have been hailed, the traumatic past has been aired, and the people's will has been proclaimed.

Rather than offering a sincere utopian vision—something like, say, the pluralist paradise of Hughes's "Let America Be America Again" (1936)—*Ask Your Mama* then shifts into the language of insult and parody. While "won't let go until it thunders" sounds like a gospel line, the finale of the poem sounds as if it might be cribbed from a stand-up routine by black comic Dick Gregory—who, as it so happens, was making his landmark appearances in front of white crowds at Chicago's Playboy Club just as *Ask Your Mama* was being published:[30]

AND THEY ASKED ME RIGHT AT CHRISTMAS
IF MY BLACKNESS, WOULD I RUB OFF?
I SAID, ASK YOUR MAMA.

DREAMS AND NIGHTMARES . . .
NIGHTMARES . . . DREAMS! OH!
DREAMING THAT THE NEGROES
OF THE SOUTH HAVE TAKEN OVER—

VOTED ALL THE DIXIECRATS
RIGHT OUT OF POWER—
COMES THE *COLORED HOUR*:
MARTIN LUTHER KING IS GOVERNOR OF GEORGIA,
DR. RUFUS CLEMENT HIS CHIEF ADVISOR,
ZELMA WATSON GEORGE THE HIGH GRAND WORTHY.
IN WHITE PILLARED MANSIONS
SITTING ON THEIR WIDE VERANDAS,
WEALTHY NEGROES HAVE WHITE SERVANTS,
WHITE SHARECROPPERS WORK THE BLACK PLANTATIONS,
AND COLORED CHILDREN HAVE WHITE MAMMIES:

    MAMMY FAUBUS

    MAMMY EASTLAND

    MAMMY PATTERSON.

DEAR, *DEAR* DARLING OLD WHITE MAMMIES—
SOMETIMES EVEN BURIED WITH OUR FAMILY!

    DEAR OLD

    MAMMY FAUBUS!

CULTURE, THEY SAY, *IS A TWO-WAY STREET:*
HAND ME MY MINT JULEP, MAMMY.

    MAKE HASTE!

"Culture is a two-way street": Hughes was taking the principle of cultural reciprocity—that one culture could influence another culture only if it were itself transformed by the exchange—and he was amplifying it into the realm of action, of redistributive justice. What would the appreciation of whites for black minstrels look like if the roles were reversed, if suddenly the blacks might appear in whiteface? With this satiric bait and switch, Hughes undercut the pretense of reciprocity (we love our mammies; they love us; we're one big happy family) by pointing to the condescension within white patronage. When approached by those whites who turn his blackness into a cartoonish menace ("They asked me right at Christmas / If my blackness, Would I rub off?"), Hughes gives them a flip rejoinder that carries a heavy insinuation: "Ask your mama." The phrase summons up, if dismissively, the fantasy and threat of interracial love, the need for contact and the fear of its consequences. As Hughes wrote in his "Liner Notes" to "Cultural Exchange," "What . . . is really happening in the shadow of world events, past and present—and of world problems, old and new—to an America that seems to understand so little about its black citizens? Even so little about itself. Even so little" (*CP,* p. 527). "Ask your mama"—three words that were common currency in ghetto speech—could cut through the customary, enforced congeniality between blacks and whites like a single snip of a circuit wire. They allowed Hughes to break the brotherhood-heavy cheer of Christmas with a piece of backtalk and, by virtue of their very boldness, gave him a segue to a segregationist's worst nightmare.

That worst nightmare was a scenario of political and sexual domination: the fantasy that white patriarchs like Mississippi senator James O. Eastland and Arkansas governor Orval Faubus would be tumbled from the government and become obedient "mammies" for a new black ruling class. The revolution, we should notice, is a peaceable one. The blacks have simply "voted all the Dixiecrats / Right out of power," and the white power elite has been transformed into a stooping, subservient minstrel class. The edge of the satire lies in this very peaceableness: we are to imagine not only that blacks have lifted themselves into power through democratic means, but also that Orval Faubus has had a conversion experience, one that engineers his transformation into "Mammy Faubus." At the same time of course, we are supposed to disbelieve this metamorphosis. It's impossible to imagine a male Dixiecrat willfully exchanging roles with a black female domestic, and a mammy is no mammy if she undertakes her duties in bad faith.

Hughes enlisted our disbelief as a lever for his satire. He meant patently to satirize the paranoia of supremacists, who—more than any school of black politicians—had exploited the imagined threat of a black overlord class. The misrule of Darktown had long been a common set piece of supremacist culture and minstrel shows, with a textbook example occurring early in D. W. Griffith's *Birth of a Nation,* where the blacks who seize the Reconstruction legislature are drunkards incapable of formulating arguments or even wearing shoes. At the same time, the preposterousness of Hughes's reverse hegemony—ruling blacks having secured the consent of hard-bitten whites—struck at the heart of a more popular and venerable story of engineered consent: that blacks were disempowered because they were either incapable of success or felt most fulfilled in the service of whites. Mammy and Sambo were fundamentally figures who preferred proximity to power over power itself.

Hughes's response to that venerable story was an innovative one, and it suggested new possibilities for the bravado of black resistance.[31] Blacks no longer had to protest their caste status through stealthy acts of subversion (wearing the minstrel mask like the grandfather of Ellison's *Invisible Man,* defeating whites with their "yesses"), nor did they have to engage in reasoned debate where they might discuss how to achieve power incrementally through a regime of patience and commitment. Hughes held up the possibility that, at least in poetry, you might speak in ghetto vernacular without adopting the common minstrel roles of dandy, buck, wench, or mammy; you might address white paranoia not through denial but through a peculiar form of insult, where you laughed off your enemy's worst fears. *Ask Your Mama* chose to fight paranoia with a parody written with urgency. Its final line—"Make haste!"—was directed in two ways: first, as an order for Mammy Faubus to scurry with her mint julep; second, as an order for the reader, who had to respond to the speed of the verse, its musical jump cuts, abrupt linebreaks, and shifts of mood. The "Hesitation Blues" might have been the book's leitmotif, its engine of protest, but "Make haste!" was to be accompanied by two joyous choruses of "When the Saints Go Marchin' In"—the music of jubilee crashing the gates.

With this energetic effrontery, *Ask Your Mama* glossed the Newport youth riot in two related ways. First, the book suggested, along with the rebel festival, that the mass audience for jazz was colliding with a smaller black audience that increasingly saw its music aligned with protest politics. Jazz for the rioters was an entitlement offered by a leisure industry (a freedom to unwind, a freedom to consume), but the very destructiveness of this attitude led Hughes, after his 1950s quietude regarding his earlier Communist-affiliated activism, to align his poetry more concretely with the civil rights movement. Jazz poetry became for Hughes a triumphant medium of protest—a means of jabbing at racist presumptions, not by refuting them reasonably or speaking proudly about black achievement, but by giving them a dose of attitude. Second, the poems suggested that the lesson of Newport was a national, and sometimes even a transnational, lesson: Hughes could not explain the insult of the riot without drawing Newport into the meshes of the entire civil rights scene North and South and the liberation struggles of the developing world. The so-called problem of Newport was not simply the story of youth running amok, as jazz critics and editorialists opined, but extended to those mature citizens who barred blacks from voting booths, decent schools, and Northern suburban neighborhoods. Both the riots and the segregationist fervor emerged from a similar dynamic of love and fear—the wonderment about blackness rubbing off, the fear of surrendering to this very contact.

Ask Your Mama occupies a crucial place in black literary and cultural history because it represents the collapse of blackface from melodrama (the loving mammy) into burlesque (the ridiculous mama). Of course, white working-class burlesque had been a crucial component of blackface performance since its antebellum origins, but *Ask Your Mama* signified the moment when African Americans could rub cork on white protagonists and laugh derisively without fear of insulting themselves. It anticipated many of the most forceful poems in Hughes's final collection, *The Panther and the Lash* (1967)—poems like "Northern Liberal," "Dinner Guest: Me," and "The Backlash Blues," which addressed "Mister Backlash" with this blues verse:

> You give me second-class houses,
> Give me second-class schools,
> Second-class houses
> And second-class schools.
> You must think us colored folks
> Are second-class fools. (*CP*, p. 552)

More generally, *Ask Your Mama* anticipated the cultural turn of the late-sixties Black Arts movement, whose achievement poet-critic Stephen Henderson summed up as follows: "for the first time in this nation's history the Black man was putting his oppressors in the *political dozens.*" In the spirit of Dick Gregory's stand-up comedy and the Mingus-Roach counterfestival, *Ask Your Mama* found the performers going on the offensive, talking back and improvising all the way, spiking the impertinence of the Dozens with the method of postbop jazz. A counterfestival in the form of multimedia verse, *Ask Your Mama* was also a thrashing of Sambo and Mammy—two figures who once seemed indestructible features of the American scene, but who now seemed perfect targets for a protest poetry. The white riot of Newport had the ironic consequence of stirring Hughes's indignation and his imagination too, until those grinning icons became perfect material for a more biting laughter.[32]

PART THREE

The Sound of Struggle

5

OUTRAGEOUS FREEDOM

Charles Mingus and
the Invention of the
Jazz Workshop

*M*ingus *Mingus Mingus Mingus Mingus:* the title of the musician's 1963 album had an apt poetry, since Charles Mingus always traded on the joys and dangers of excess. He was a master at amplifying and multiplying himself, his career a series of literal and figurative costume changes. He was street tough and Buddha, Robin Hood and banker, balladeer and screamer, preacher and pornographer, disciplinarian and freedom lover, black militant and dedicated integrationist, performer in the moment and composer for the ages. Among the musicians of the hard bop generation, he was perhaps the most theatrical—he appeared onstage wearing Mexican sombreros and serapes, kimono and headband, African dashikis, Chinese robes, farmer's dungarees—and yet he was also a pioneer of inner expression in jazz, a composer who developed a nuanced musical language for emotions that ran the gamut from extremes of tenderness to extremes of rage. Radical artifice was tied to claims of radical authenticity, as Mingus cycled through his many personas, inflating and deflating them with a sense of drama that was novel to the world of jazz and best described in retrospect as a form of performance art. Mingus was always unpredictable and yet always, inescapably, his own man.[1]

The one principle of continuity, it seems, was the identity Mingus treasured most: as the jazz musician who aimed to be the most tradition-based

Layers upon layers upon layers: Composer-bassist Charles Mingus, here at the piano in a photograph from around 1963, was a master at amplifying and multiplying himself, his career a series of literal and figurative costume changes. (Courtesy of Michael Ochs Archives)

yet experimental of thinkers. Mingus loved to tap into a wide variety of genres—modernist tone poems, Ellingtonia, bebop, mariachi, gospel, cumbia, soul-jazz, free jazz—and pit them against one another in a struggle for mastery. In doing so, he not only negotiated conflict in his music but also threw its challenges back onto his fellow musicians and his audience, who were forced to engage with volatility in real time: his music might be followed, but rarely could it be anticipated. Nor was it intended

THE SOUND OF STRUGGLE

to be appreciated from a place of cerebral detachment. For all his genre blending, Mingus had little use for critical distance, little of the blank-faced irony often associated with postmodern pastiche, and little desire to smooth over the extreme mood swings of his music. In a telling detail that speaks to a much larger matter of principle, Mingus often became infuriated when his pianists inserted diminished chords into their solos, at one point even forcing one unlucky pianist in 1977 to rerecord his solo for committing that harmonic offense. Diminished chords were conventionally used to create a more even transition from one key center to another, to slip via a passing chord from the current tonal framework to the next—in other words, to cushion the force of harmonic rupture. Mingus believed in the integrity of rupture, partly since a music that refused to be seamless could open itself more to the cues of the moment, had a better chance of incorporating radical impulses without flattening them.[2]

This attraction to volatility was perhaps best telegraphed in the phrase "the Jazz Workshop," the name of Mingus's multifaceted rebellion against the pressure of racial stereotype and the forces of musical stasis. Mingus copyrighted the phrase, and the tag became a kind of marketable trademark, attesting to jazz authenticity and Mingus's desire to control his own fortunes. The Jazz Workshop was not only the name of his working band from his first record dates as a leader in the mid-1950s until his death in 1978, but also the name of his music publishing imprint and self-founded record label. No friend to established commercial channels, Mingus hoped his Jazz Workshop operations would help him carve out a self-owned, self-controlled power base in the world of commercial jazz.[3]

At the same time, the name was much more than a convenient legal device. The concept of the Jazz Workshop—the way it publicized the creative interaction between individuals on the bandstand, no matter how ferocious or goading, tender or ecstatic—lies at the heart of Mingus's enterprise as a composer. Thriving on the principle of creative struggle, the Workshop created unruly music, unsuited to a consensus model of liberal politics but perfectly attuned to the incipient dramas of the late 1950s and early 1960s. Mingus's aesthetic implied that jazz composition was an ongoing process, fraught with the high drama of virtuosos contesting one another; it foregrounded what musicologist Robert Walser has called the "signifying" in jazz, rather than the signification of notes as such.[4] Yet this signifying was more than tricksterism, more than witty rebuke. Mingus's music expressed feelings of outrage, jubilation, revolt, swooning passion—states of emotional intensity rather than distraction—and his satire was not indirect but bruising. Moreover, the Workshop emphasized these extreme emotions at a moment when they were breaking into other live arts as well. Its founder acclaimed as the "Lee Strasberg of jazz," Mingus's Jazz Workshop was compared with good reason to the Actors Studio with its inculcation of "the method." Like Strasberg with mid-twentieth-century American drama, Mingus helped establish jazz as music of psychological turbulence—music that probed the soul, stripped away the veneer of conventional decorum, and gave voice to the most knotty, and sometimes least articulate, of emotional states. Mingus became, in critic Gary Giddins's phrase, "jazz's most persistently apocalyptic voice," the man who registered the music's postbop conflicts with greatest sensitivity and at greatest volume.[5]

This chapter and the next follow Mingus and the struggles that swirled around and through him. They track Mingus in his many guises—as a jazz entrepreneur; as an ensemble leader; as a self-dramatist scourging his audience; as an autobiographer; and, lastly and most extensively, as a jazz composer whose music serves as a textbook case of African-American modernism, a roiling synthesis of classical and African-American stylings. Late in his life, an interviewer asked Mingus why he always returned to the Gershwin standard "I Can't Get Started." Mingus replied brusquely but with candor: "'Cause I can't get started." What follows here is that story of "not being started," the story of beleaguered outsiderhood that Mingus channeled into some of the most compelling and spectacularly conflicted music of the twentieth century.[6]

"Once There Was a Holding Company Called Old America"

Throughout his career, Mingus launched guerrilla attacks—high-concept, low-financed, and courageous if short-lived—against nearly every sector of the jazz industry. He was the catalyst behind three record labels and two publishing imprints; the founder of a rebel jazz festival and an early jazz collective; and even, in the mid-1960s, a would-be headmaster for a proposed holistic "School of Art, Music, and Gymnastics." His strategy, over and over, was clear: set up an independent, self-owned capital base, then control the profits that would accumulate and distribute them fairly. Mingus tried to rehabilitate the marketplace relationship by cutting out the middleman and clearing a pathway for the artist to convey himself directly to his audience. He refused to believe that jazz musicians were doomed to small audiences and a life of poverty: "Who told people that artists aren't supposed to feed their families beans and greens? . . . [T]here are some honest ears left out there. If musicians could get some economic power, they could make money and be artists at the same time." If Mingus proposed, in one of his song titles, that "Once There Was a Holding Company

Called Old America," his entrepreneurial work aimed to break up this national monopoly of cultural life.[7]

The upshot of these experiments, however, was not so clear. While they helped publicize Mingus as a jazz maverick, they generally foundered as a result of management difficulties and lack of capital. Sue Mingus described business with her husband as "a blend of theatrical derring-do, frequent time-outs, fits of brilliant imagination, and constant creative trouble." Certainly while Mingus was often the public face of these enterprises, it was his women—Celia Mingus with Debut Records, Sue Mingus with Charles Mingus Enterprises—who did much of the work behind the recording, editing, and distribution of records and allowed them to succeed in their limited way. Visionary enterprises, they remained so. Mingus himself seemed to become more idealistic and more mercenary over time: he repeatedly held out the hope that he might find some way to transcend the law of the bottom line, but he became obsessed with reaping the exact sum of his labors, calling himself a "stone cold capitalist" by the mid-1960s. The spirituality of music and the venality of money became his twin fixations, and even the most creative of business ventures had difficulty reconciling the two.[8]

A large part of the impetus behind Mingus's entrepreneurial activism was his refusal to play by the rules of the major labels. A steady darling of jazz intellectuals like Martin Williams, Whitney Balliett, and Nat Hentoff, he had embattled relationships with record executives, even those sympathetic to his spirit of musical experimentation. In 1957, at age thirty-five, he secured his first major-label stereo effort—*Tijuana Moods* on RCA Victor—only by threatening a lawsuit with the company. RCA proceeded to let *Tijuana Moods* sit on the company's shelf for five years, releasing it only after Mingus had made his name on Columbia. One can imagine his frustration as he watched Miles Davis, with *Kind of Blue* (1959) and *Sketches of Spain* (1960), ride his way to critical acclaim for innovations, such as the use of the "Spanish" scale and modal improvisation, that Mingus had pioneered several years earlier.[9]

With other record labels, Mingus must shoulder some blame for the souring of the relationship. When critic Leonard Feather, in his new job as a musical director for EmArcy Records, asked to record Mingus's quartet, Mingus arrived the next day with twenty-five other musicians so that he might record "Half-Mast Inhibition," a symphonic piece he had composed over a decade earlier. The record *(Pre-Bird)* was Mingus's last for EmArcy and allegedly led to Feather's dismissal from the company. Mingus's association with United Artists was similarly ill-fated. Mingus enlisted the label to produce his October 1962 Town Hall concert, an experience often regarded as a life-changing fiasco for the composer. Mingus hoped to present pieces arranged on an orchestral scale, but he had little arranged for his thirty-one-piece band and even less copied out in parts for the musicians to read. During the concert, a team of copyists scribbled diligently at a table at the front of the stage, supplying parts to the musicians, while the ill-rehearsed orchestra struggled to run through Mingus's complex compositions. Concert promoter Joe Glaser, never known as one to swallow a loss, offered to give the audience its money back; and while the ensuing album featured some impressive music, its production was so muddy that the recording engineer was soon terminated from UA.[10]

Mingus also refused to be bullied by record label accounting practices, adopting his own street theatrics as a countermove. At the end of 1963, Mingus's advance from Impulse Records was supposed to be increased to $15,000, but the label's bookkeeper and producer Bob Thiele agreed that Mingus's sales did not justify the raise. Thiele was made aware of Mingus's displeasure when he arrived at work and found a knife in the back of his chair, impaling a note that read: "Where the fuck is my money? mingus." With Bethlehem Records, Mingus enlisted drummer Dannie Richmond as his confederate in menace. In the middle of contractual negotiations, Richmond pulled out a knife on cue, gave the Bethlehem executive a cool stare, and offhandedly cleaned his nails. In an even more theatrical incident, Mingus dressed up in safari suit, helmet, and shotgun for his visit to the accounting department of Columbia Records. His royalties, Mingus recalled with some satisfaction, were immediately brought up to date.[11]

Behind the theatricality of these gestures was a larger impasse that Mingus declared with the music industry, an impasse that carried a familiar echo of the mass culture debates raging in *Partisan Review* and *Commentary* in the 1950s. Mingus believed that the mass market was closed to expressions of psychological complexity, that Madison Avenue preferred canned emotion to the real, unpredictable thing. As early as May 1953, he protested publicly, saying, "The impresarios bill these circus artists as jazzmen because 'jazz' has become a commodity to sell, like apples or, more accurately, corn." Rejecting what he saw as sentimental convention ("corn"), Mingus testified that he had "no other solution than to write and play my own music in accord with the real emotions of the moment when I am writing and playing." In another interview he attacked the hidden persuaders of the music industry: "Madison Avenue doesn't fool me. If they want to push—pardon me—horse manure; clean it, wash it, sprinkle it, and spray it with perfume, and put it inside a cellophane package with a blue ribbon on it, and say 'This is a new powder, and the best made, and it also has vitamins in for your skin', they will sell it!"[12]

But while Mingus attacked Madison Avenue for its fake drama, he refused to dispense with drama altogether. What exactly, then, was the difference between the sound of "corn" and the sound of intensely felt emotion? His early performance piece "The Clown" (1957) gave one answer. The piece is a dark and absurd allegory about the musical clown, a figure of self-destructive pathos who is trapped within the culture of kitsch. While Mingus elsewhere labeled crowd-pleasing entertainers as Uncle Toms and traitors to the black community, he took their dilemma seriously enough to endow it with sympathetic psychological depth. In a narration set to straight waltz time, the protagonist in "The Clown" discovers that his audience has no appetite for his emotional complexities—"all these greens and all these yellows and all these oranges bubbling around inside him." His act elicits a lukewarm response until he makes an unintentional pratfall on a stage in Dubuque—at which point the crowd roars with laughter, and the performer is as hooked as any junkie. Soon he is descending to the most self-brutalizing physical comedy in order to please his audience. The final twist, worthy of O. Henry, occurs when the performer suffers a fatal accident onstage, which the audience happily, unthinkingly, applauds.

For Mingus, the conflicted emotions of jazz performers—here described in the coloristic language of Abstract Expressionism so appreciated by the New York intellectuals—clashed with the easy pleasures that the music was expected to offer. Few jazz pieces offered such a forthright, even intellectual, analysis of the gap between performer and audience. With its straight Kurt Weill–like waltz time, "The Clown" offered little of one of jazz's basic pleasures, the momentum of swing. Instead, the piece was unmistakable satire: its waltz rhythm was intended as the sort of kitschy effect that, as Dwight Macdonald and Clement Greenberg had argued, contained its own built-in reaction.[13] Similarly, the clown is defeated by the predictability of the audience's response, which the song spins out to its logical, fatal extreme. Like Macdonald's "A Theory of Mass Culture" and a good part of the 1957 anthology *Mass Culture*, "The Clown" argued that the mass appetite for kitsch threatened to crush the singular spirit of the creative artist.[14]

Unlike these other critics, however, Mingus was a working black artist, and he added two race-sensitive observations to the traditional critique of mass-market fakery. First, he said, the music industry asked black artists to sacrifice their integrity for a commercial farce that tapped into stereotypes of black abandon. In one of his earliest public comments, a sly dig at his employer Lionel Hampton, he hoped for a day when "it will no longer be necessary for a musician to jump up and down on a drum or to dance on a bandstand to receive recognition of his talent." (Mingus was eventually fired by Hampton because he wouldn't let the vibist, as part of his crowd-pleasing shtick, use his mallets on Mingus's bass.) Or, as he said in a thinly veiled 1953 attack on R&B honkers and shouters, "Good jazz is when the leader jumps on the piano, waves his arms and yells. Fine jazz is when a tenorman lifts his foot in the air. Great jazz is when he heaves a piercing note for 32 bars and collapses on his hands and knees."[15]

In order to establish a home for a less sensational jazz, Mingus established the Debut label with bebop drummer Max Roach in 1952. He hoped to prove that "jazz can be played just from being read," that it required virtuoso composers but not antic showmen. Following the lead of other artist-led labels like Fantasy (supported by Dave Brubeck in 1950), DeeGee (Dizzy Gillespie in 1951), and Jazz Records (Lennie Tristano in 1951), Debut Records was crucial in establishing the basis for what became known as Third Stream—jazz that married chamber arrangements and compositional innovation, sometimes from a classical foundation, with elements of standard jazz practice such as improvisation and the blues. Ironically, considering how Third Stream efforts would later be derided as feeble "white" versions of jazz, one of the music's pioneers was a label owned by two black artists whose later work would be known for its militancy and passion. Mingus pursued an eclectic range of jazz performance with Debut, as if to say that he refused to be confined by the music's dominant genre conventions. His own work on the label varied from straight-ahead small combos to far-reaching arrangements that borrowed much from contemporary film scorers like Dmitri Tiomkin. A typically idiosyncratic session involved at least thirteen pieces—including French horn, cello, harp, and strings—in an arrangement of "Making Whoopee" led by a Broadway singer. Mingus also used Debut to introduce performers whom he admired but who lacked a corporate outlet: trumpeter Thad Jones of the Jones jazz dynasty, difficult-to-categorize pianist Paul Bley, cabaret pianist Hazel Scott, and singer Jackie Paris. For a few years, Debut became a house organ for the Jazz Composers' Workshop, which Mingus, vibist Teddy Charles, and saxophonists Teo Macero and John LaPorta helped sponsor between 1953 and 1955.[16]

After founding the Jazz Workshop and his increasing turn to a "blacker" aesthetic, Mingus hammered more publicly on a second critique of the music industry: that the business kept the profits, shrunken as they might have been for jazz artists, in the hands of a largely white corporate pool, never distributing them to the black artists who had produced them. He dismissed charges of "Crow Jim"—reverse discrimination by black musicians against white musicians—as an absurdity: "until we start lynching white people, there is no word that can mean the same as Jim Crow means. Until we own Bethlehem Steel and RCA Victor, plus Columbia Records and several other industries, the term Crow Jim has no meaning. . . . Aren't you white men asking too much when you ask me to stop saying this is my music? Especially when you don't give me anything else?" Debut Records was his first extended attempt as an entrepreneur to expropriate from the expropriators. Mingus's mid-fifties pianist Mal Waldron recalled that "Debut was his chance to take the business away from the white man. He felt that the musicians were not controlling their own product, and that the man that was controlling it had nothing to do with music . . . but was interested in making money."[17]

Especially after Debut's collapse, as he achieved his own celebrity as "The Angry Man of Jazz," Mingus sidelined his earlier call for a strictly virtuosic jazz music and began to hammer on this second theme. Just as other intellectuals were turning from a critique of popular taste to a structural critique of power relations, so Mingus in the 1960s began to spotlight the inequities of the jazz industry as a whole.[18] In a 1965 advertisement for his self-owned label, he complained again about "the avarice and corruption existing in the big business of record companies and their cohorts." In print he assailed booking agents who skimmed an extra bit from the nightclub pay of the jazz artists they handled, and he targeted jazz promoters like George Wein for racially biased pay scales. Jazz "liberals" were hauled in for an especially harsh drubbing. In the liner notes to his self-produced *Town Hall Concert* recording (1964), Mingus focused on the sins of John Hammond, "this hamhead organ-mouth liberal tongued beast of high finance." An enthusiast of the Popular Front and the promoter of Billie Holiday and Count Basie, Hammond epitomized the white patronage of jazz as music of emotional vigor, but he became Mingus's nemesis when he deflected Mingus's plan to crack down on bootleg recordings. With friends like these, Mingus suggested, who needed enemies? Combining free association, bombast, and shrewd analysis, he charged Hammond the "hamster" with "genocide" and suggested that Hammond's beloved "people" would "find the Promised Land right under their feet" if only Hammond would stay out of the way. There would even be "no need to picket and fight for it."[19]

Yet John Hammond and his minions *did* exist, and Mingus believed he had to fight for his share of the Promised Land. His alternative to clowning was a heroic refusal that alienated him from the industry, even as it was based in the simple principle of personal integrity. "If you're that strong a man to stick to your guns and believe in music the way you believe in it," he said, "they're *afraid* of you the same as they're afraid of Martin Luther King." Or, as he wrote in an open letter to Miles Davis: "my music isn't meant just for the patting of feet and going down backs. . . . I play or write *me*, the way I feel, through jazz, or whatever. Music is, or was, a language of the emotions. If someone has been escaping reality, I don't expect him to dig my music, and I would begin to worry about my writing if such a person began to really like it." Mingus understood the confessional impulse as a form of anticommercialism; by contrast, any musician who catered to popular taste was courting a creative death sentence. He banked his own musical integrity on his ability to know himself, to understand his own struggles around his racial identity: "My identity is [about] trying to be accepted by my own people as a black man. . . . [W]hat I think good of myself or bad of myself, it's in this one record. So if it's insincere, then I'm not alive, because you can't live and be insincere."[20]

Repeatedly stalling out with the major players in the industry and driven by his own entrepreneurial idealism, Mingus tried to create an independent power base that would handle his recordings and their distribution. He did not want to destroy the commercial qualities of music—and especially had no desire to deprofessionalize the making of music—but he did hope that his own businesses might carve out a sphere apart from entertainment, a space of spiritual insight and fair reward. When he decided in 1963 to expand the Jazz Workshop into an open school for aspiring musicians, he lit upon the idea of a "School of Arts, Music, and Gymnastics." Typically, the school's phone was answered with "Music, Art, and Health, who's calling?"—a holistic catalog of possible self-exploration. Instructors were to include Mingus, Max Roach, and dancer Katherine Dunham, and Mingus even hoped to secure funds from Harlem Youth Opportunities Unlimited (HAR-YOU), an extension of Lyndon Johnson's War on Poverty. Like Amiri Baraka, who brought avant-garde jazz music to the Harlem community through his Black Arts Repertory Theater/School in 1965, Mingus wanted to "play in the parks or on the backs of trucks for kids, old people, anyone."[21]

In the early sixties, Mingus started to lend his recording establishments and general voice to the causes of psychic and social liberation. On Independence Day 1960, after protesting the Newport festival, Mingus joined up with Newport rebels Max Roach, Abbey Lincoln, Roy Eldridge, and Jo Jones to form the Jazz Artists Guild, a collective that sadly lasted only for the duration of one Candid Records session and a few weeks of concerts. (See Chapter 4.) The dream of a jazz co-op persisted, though: it fueled Mingus's next self-produced enterprise, the Jazz Workshop label, founded in a limbo period after he had alienated many of the majors. On the label's first release in 1964, he swore that "this will be the first American company to make a step to give justice to all employed" and ended his liner notes with a rebarbative formula: "With disgust for the American recording industry, I give you, the public this day seven people set to free themselves in music." As late as 1971, Mingus was lending his support to such organizations as the Jazz and People's Movement (JPM), which called for more jazz exposure in the mass media and protested the "racist policies" of the John Simon Guggenheim Memorial Foundation. Astonishingly, the JPM successfully pressured the producers of the *Ed Sullivan Show* to put Mingus on its bandstand, where the JPM ensemble winged through "Haitian Fight Song"—perhaps the only revolutionary anthem to find its way onto the show.[22]

All of Mingus's entrepreneurial enterprises, from his music school to his counterfestival activities and record companies, were short-lived ventures that collectively testify to the difficulty of building jazz institutions without the backing of some sort of institutional capital. Debut Records lasted longest—five years, until the American Federation of Musicians threatened to revoke the label's license over a floating series of debts. By the mid-sixties, Mingus had sold Debut's back catalog to Saul Zaentz's Fantasy Records, and by 1968, Zaentz had taken over the Jazz Workshop mail-order label as well. Neither buyout was particularly lucrative: an attachment to one album featured a revealing plea from Mingus himself, who attested to Zaentz's honesty and asked for contributions from "anyone who cares to alter my deplorable financial condition." Similarly, by the time of George Wein's next Newport festival in 1962, the Jazz Artists Guild was defunct, and Mingus had lifted his boycott and once again become a featured performer. The "School of Arts, Music, and Gymnastics" never enrolled a single student. By November 1964, Mingus had moved out of the large studio on Third Avenue that was set to house the institute, reportedly in response to high licensing charges levied by the police and fire departments. The composer did not assume an institutional role as a jazz educator until 1971, when he took up the Slee Chair in Composition at SUNY–Buffalo.[23]

Still it would be wrong to dismiss these enterprises as failures, even though they were never consistently profitable. As prefigurative ventures they held considerable power, not least in the way that they inspired other artists and prodded the industry to address long-standing inequities. Surely it was more than coincidence that Mingus received his Guggenheim shortly after the Jazz and People's Movement protest there; more than coincidence that the Newport Jazz Festival began to resort its priorities and trumpet a return to jazz for jazz's sake; and more than coincidence that many jazz artists after Mingus (Sun Ra, the Chicago school around the Association for the Advancement of Creative Musicians, Betty Carter, Don Pullen) founded their own labels and arranged their own product distribution. Theorist Jacques Attali has called music a prefigurative art—one whose formal organization often forecasts the structural economic revolutions to come. With Mingus, we can see how several of his economic innovations exerted just such a reverberative effect, if only in the relatively small sphere of jazz production and distribution.[24]

Attali's work suggests other, related issues: how Mingus recast the relations between himself and his fellow musicians, and how he challenged the putative contract between himself and his audience. Mingus may not have "crossed over" as a jazz pedagogue until 1971, but in the meantime he spearheaded a workshop that redefined the protocols of jazz ensemble playing. As "people set to free themselves in music," the Jazz Workshop in turn threw down a gauntlet for the casual jazz audience. Their music— Mingus's compositional book, their execution—was an exercise in antagonistic liberation, one that pitted the musicians in a way against the audience. If this was freedom, it was also apocalypse, the struggle for revelation and the fear of what judgment would bring. If this was the future, it was an uncertain one for musicians and audiences alike. Critic Nat Hentoff observed that onstage the bassist "hover[ed] like a brooding Zeus making up the final score card for eternity."[25]

The Lee Strasberg of Jazz: Mingus and the Workshop Method

Mingus ran his Jazz Workshop with a discipline that was both inexcusable and fiercely productive. The inexcusable side is easy to document, and is perhaps best expressed by the Workshop's sometimes nickname, the "Sweatshop." For all his holistic rhetoric, Mingus became notorious for knuckling his personnel. Trumpeter Ted Curson remarked that "Mingus was the boss. He gave the orders," and even a sympathetic observer like Sue Mingus said of the early 1960s Workshop, "You never knew who was going to be screamed into submission or humiliated." Mingus's fuse was easily lit by employment disputes or perceived shortcomings on the bandstand. When saxophonist Jackie McLean resigned from the Workshop to protest Mingus's frequent reprimands of soloists and the rhythm section, the situation quickly escalated: Mingus tried to punch McLean, who pulled out a knife and nicked Mingus above his heart before he was restrained. Likewise, in 1958, when trumpeter Clarence Shaw was absent from a record date because of the flu, Mingus told him that he would arrange for his murder, mafia-style. (Shaw was physically unharmed, but his resignation was effective immediately.) Pianist and arranger Alonzo Levister, Ellington sideman Juan Tizol, trombonist Jimmy Knepper—all these Mingus associates became his brawling partners as well.[26]

Not everyone preferred to improvise in this supercharged atmosphere.

Saxophonist John Handy said that "Mingus was in the way so much, you couldn't play for it. The man'd stop your solos—he was totally tyrannical." Pianist Jaki Byard sounded more like a man who had been emotionally bruised: "I can do without the dictator approach in music. . . . I like to play a certain thing, but sometimes I don't have that feeling, and when it's forced on me, it becomes another thing entirely." During the Workshop's engagement at New York's Showplace, Mingus would chase trumpeter Ted Curson around West Fourth Street during intermission, the two "shouting about the music as they ran, arguing about whatever had gone wrong during the show." Mingus even humiliated musicians when they were at the top of their game. Curson recalled how, on nights when Eric Dolphy was being cheered by the audience, Mingus would force the saxophonist to perform from the dressing room. And when a woman in the audience made eye contact or seemed to be flirting with one of the Workshoppers, Mingus would take them to the "whipping post"—changing keys in a piece without giving the musician any sort of cue, or forcing the player to solo without accompaniment for several minutes.[27]

Surely it is the most intriguing paradox of the Workshop that Mingus, in the mid-1950s, laid the basis for new forms of jazz freedom even as he constrained his fellow players through the Workshop's febrile instruction. The paradox becomes more understandable, however, when we note that nearly all of Mingus's musical innovations were designed to spark a new kind of emotionalism within jazz playing—in a sense, to uncap the Harmon-mute that Miles Davis had added to his trumpet at the same time. Mingus understood freedom not as freedom from coercion (Isaiah Berlin's classic definition of negative liberty), but as a sphere of musical action governed by the push and pull of the Workshop dynamic. His freedom was collective action with traction: it came about when the community of the Workshop—"these seven men set to free themselves in music"—negotiated the initial rules set up by Mingus the composer. The Workshop thus provided a drama of freedom enacting itself against a set of sometimes rigorous, sometimes loosely drawn, constraints. It worked less as a sheltered sphere of private freedom and more as a musical battleground, where compositional restraint served paradoxically as a kind of emotional provocation. The Workshop was high melodrama as well as high art.[28]

The beginning of the Jazz Workshop, in 1955, was coincident with Mingus's discovery of a new way of teaching his compositions to his sidemen—a new method that, like the Method of Lee Strasberg's Actors Studio, strove to inculcate the compositions within the musicians themselves. Although his compositions were often harmonically adventurous and rhythmically double-jointed, Mingus refused to score them and instruct his musicians through written parts. Instead, as he wrote in the liner notes to *Pithecanthropus Erectus* (1956):

> My whole conception with my present Jazz Workshop group deals with nothing written. I "write" compositions—but only on mental score paper—then I lay out the composition part by part to the musicians. I play them the "framework" on piano so that they are all familiar with my interpretation and feeling and with the scale and chord progressions to be used. Each man's own particular style is taken into consideration, both in ensemble and in solos. . . . In this way, I find it possible to keep my own compositional flavor in the pieces and yet to allow the musicians more individual freedom in the creation of their group lines and solos.[29]

Mingus's Workshop collaborators could never simply be studio men, sight-reading their lines (just as Mingus, despite his instrumental proficiency, did not take session work with other musicians). Like Duke Ellington, Mingus wrote specific parts with specific sidemen in mind (for example, "Profile of Jackie," written for Jackie McLean) and threw upon them the burden of expressing themselves through the forms that he laid down. Jazz composition thus became an interpersonal art, one that tapped the reserves of Mingus's sidemen and tried to "draw them out." As one Mingus Workshopper reminisced, "He would yell at you in the middle of a solo: 'Stop playing licks and get into *yourself!*'" The Workshop was an emotional and musical laboratory—a fusion of the modernist atelier, which stood witness to the ever-changing boundaries of the plastic arts, and Strasberg's Actors Studio, which trained actors to express a wider array of emotions onstage by refusing easy mannerisms and turning inward to their emotional past.[30]

Mingus's pedagogical method was a dramatic alternative to, say, the method of Miles Davis in the same period, although Davis also did not use many written charts and tried to expand the range of musical options that his sidemen might take. On the 1955 Prestige quintet sessions (*Cookin'*, *Workin'*, *Relaxin'*, *Steamin'*), for instance, Davis asked his musicians to work through Tin Pan Alley chestnuts like "My Funny Valentine" and "It Never Entered My Mind" or bebop standards like "Half Nelson." The musicians took daring solo flights but also fed off one another's rhythmic and melodic interjections, so that the music sparkled with the unexpected insistence of soloists like John Coltrane as well as the surprising cross-talk of the rhythm section. By working with an older repertoire, however, the Davis quintet based itself in a musical heritage that they themselves were canonizing with new accents—giving new depths of muted sorrow to "My Funny Valentine," a new nocturne moodiness to "'Round Midnight." The Jazz Workshop, by contrast, worked with Mingus's own compositions, which often departed from the thirty-two-bar Tin Pan Alley formula, incorporating sudden shifts of tempo and using cues instead of bars to signify a transition from one section to another. Davis might teach his music orally because "My Funny Valentine" was part of the commonplace book of the jazz world; Mingus taught his music orally because he wanted his musicians to absorb it until even its irregularities became second nature. This difference was embodied also in two contrasting managerial styles from the bandstand: while Davis put a Harmon-mute on his trumpet and turned his back on the audience when his bandmates soloed, Mingus was given to annunciatory statements on his bass and frequent hollers of enthusiasm, goading encouragement, and furious disaffection.

Given the ambition behind Mingus's project, it took a substantial press offensive for the Workshop to be understood as a fully realized aesthetic. His new jazz forms, which highlighted extreme emotionalism, had to be framed within a workshop setting that placed his experiments alongside modernist tradition and contemporary exercises in other arts. In this light, it is not surprising that Mingus took considerably more control over his liner notes than other artists, preferring a circle of intimates—his girlfriend, Diane Dorr-Dorynek; jazz critic Nat Hentoff; his psychiatrist—and often writing them himself. Of these intimate friends, Hentoff was responsible most for presenting Mingus's Workshop as an avant-garde musical version of the Method. By his lights, the Workshop was an artistic pressure cooker whose heat came from Mingus's glowering self-examination. Mingus had a "relentless drive to excavate his music from the deepest recesses of his feelings and memories," Hentoff wrote, adding with a Yeatsian flourish that Mingus "tries harder than anyone I know to walk naked." This self-excavation, in turn, was a process that Mingus forced on his sidemen through the irregular forms of his compositions: "Mingus expects his men to learn their parts through what their own feelings tell them about the music. . . . [A musician's] technical skills expand because in finding a way to meet Mingus's unconventional standards of self-expression, he has to make his instrument try things he never would have thought possible." Emotional turbulence was thus the motor of technical innovation. In this spirit, Hentoff bestowed what he saw as the highest compliment on Mingus's band: that they had achieved "that level of daring and that power to make their instruments become extensions of themselves."[31]

While the "Sweatshop" nickname suggests that Mingus's Workshop did not always redirect emotions in the most tidy manner, it is important to recall that most of Mingus's discipline was exerted through his musical formulas, not the bluster of his personality. Mingus sorted through his catholic acquaintance with a wide spectrum of musical genres in order to find the right instigatory formulas. He searched through the gospel music he had absorbed at an early age when worshipping with his mother at a neighborhood Pentecostal church; through the example of composers like Wagner and Richard Strauss, whose work he studied with his Los Angeles music teacher; through New Orleans jazz (early on he gigged with Louis Armstrong and Kid Ory); through Duke Ellington's orchestrated swing (he served a brief stint with Ellington in 1953); through the bebop of Parker, Gillespie, Powell, and Roach; through flamenco, mariachi, and other Latin music; through the chamber-jazz experiments of his colleagues in the Jazz Composers Workshop, the predecessor of his own Jazz Workshop; and through the soul-jazz offerings of his contemporaries. As jazz scholar Erkhaard Jost has remarked, "it is doubtful whether any other musician has ever had quite the same amount of direct access to so many different kinds of jazz."[32]

More generally, Mingus turned often to techniques that framed his music as a kind of emotional thermometer. Spontaneity, volatility, immediacy, urgency—all these were qualities that Mingus's technical specifications were meant to dramatize.

Spontaneity: Mingus's "Plastic Form"

The architecture of a Mingus composition was improvised on in the same way that a more typical jazz soloist would improvise on "the changes." The standard thirty-two-bar Tin Pan Alley form implied a regular cycle in jazz performance: the statement of the head, then solos on the chord changes, then the restatement of the head (theme–improvisation–theme). Mingus pursued a more eclectic, and more spontaneous, compositional process that scholar Andrew Homzy has called "plastic form." (Mingus called it "extended form," which does not quite capture the way that his compositions could be stretched in several possible directions.) Sections of a composition would be elongated, compressed, or recombined, their underlying rhythms radically altered through stop-time, background riffs, new bass vamps—and much of this would be signaled as the composition was being enacted. The oral instruction before the gig was followed by a collaborative environment during the gig, where the musicians would cue each other into the next section spontaneously. As Mingus wrote about his piece "Love Chant," "extended form versions are never played the same way

THE SOUND OF STRUGGLE

twice—the mood as well as the length of line on each chord depends on the musician playing. The mood is set by him, and the chord, in this particular composition, is changed only on piano cue by Mal [Waldron] when he feels the development requires it." In a plastic-form composition, musical bars no longer mark the length of a section; there is simply a delineated mode (say, the F-minor blues scale) and the expectation of an improvised "cue" as a segue. If most jazz musicians understood compositions by divvying them up into separate sections of different length (usually, symmetric patterns of eight or twelve bars), Mingus elasticized the separate sections by relying on these spontaneous signals.[33]

These cues could steer a performance in several sudden directions—either by segueing into a new section of a piece at a moment of dramatic buildup or by abruptly augmenting or stripping down the instrumentation as the performers explored a section. Partly as a result of this new plastic form, audiences were instructed to "read" the performance as an unfolding drama whose transitions were signified by the musicians' mood; the composition might be stretched like taffy or dense as metal, depending on that night's take on the piece. The act of dilation is reflected well in musicologist Andrew Homzy's transcription of a 1960 performance of "What Love" (itself a deconstruction of Cole Porter's "What Is This Thing Called Love?"): Homzy dispenses with musical bars and simply writes out a one-measure lead sheet that stretches out over $131\frac{1}{2}$ beats.[34]

The second sort of cues—cues of arrangement—can be heard in live Workshop recordings such as *Mingus at Antibes* (1960), recorded the week after the Newport counterfestival. On pieces like "I'll Remember April" and "Folk Forms," the Workshop churns through its lineup with an arithmetic eye for all the possible instrumental permutations. The full Workshop lineup will suddenly dissolve into a bass-drums-horn trio, which will quickly become a trumpet-alto cutting session; accompanied solos switch off with unaccompanied solos. More generally, the improvisational arrangement keeps changing its scope and focus through an unpredictable sequence of improvised solos, duets, and ensemble playing. Critic Joe Goldberg has made a similar observation about Miles Davis's quintets—that they could seem like duets, trios, or quartets depending on whether or not some members "laid out." Mingus's group heightened the rhythmic instability behind this principle: his players interjected themselves into the mix, through the loud punctuation of horns, the insertion of a bass riff, or the sudden shifting of drumming accents. Davis's group, for example, usually kept "walking time" through a rhythm section of drums and bass, and this walking time gave the foundation for the quintet's improvisations, which famously explored the spaces between the basic groove. In Mingus's group, by contrast, the rhythmic foundation seemed to rest on a San Andreas–sized fault: Dannie Richmond's drums might suddenly cut themselves out; the walking bass might suddenly be swallowed into a hammering vamp; and a last remaining horn would suddenly find itself in dialogue with a lone and maverick bass.[35]

Volatility: The Use of Tempo Changes

Mingus was one of the only hard boppers to exploit tempo changes like sudden decelerandos and accelerandos, where the whole band would be swept up or calmed down with the soloist. While bebop drummers often doubled the tempo in an athletic display of virtuosity ("double-time"), Mingus pursued more fractional adjustments that cut against the axiom that the beat was a pulse laid down from the start by the rhythm section. The accelerando seems to have been Mingus's preferred means of heating up the Workshop's action, of signifying an irresistible and gathering intensity. On a piece like "Tijuana Table Dance," for instance, the ensemble playing takes on momentum over passages that suggest flamenco form: the Workshop shifts between two chromatically neighboring chords with an accelerating seesaw motion. Again, these tempo changes were conceived as on-the-spot alterations of the piece's mood: a small record of this volatility can be seen in a typically noncommittal score of a background part on "Reincarnation of a Lovebird," which suggested that one section would be played "slowly—(or not)." The tempo of a Mingus piece, then, was a way for the audience to gauge the current temperature of the Workshop; it was not necessarily preordained beforehand by the piece itself.[36]

Emotional Immediacy: The Use of Gospel Time Signatures, Timbre, and Affects

Although his early work kept its distance from blues and gospel, Mingus became one of the leaders of the soul-jazz movement, which folded into jazz the kinds of bluesy licks, simple twelve-bar forms, pentatonic chords, and growling enthusiasms that the beboppers (and a younger Mingus) had dismissed as down-home showboating. Just as soul-jazz claimed to recover the roots of jazz in the black church, so Mingus reflected on the emotionalism of his own childhood—his own personal roots. In a typical reminiscence, he tied "Wednesday Night Prayer Meeting" to "a form of music I heard as a kid. My mother used to go to church on Wednesday night. There was always clapping of hands and shouting. Methodist or Holiness Church. Holiness was a little louder in order to stir up the spirits, the dead spirits.

People went into trances. Women shouted and rolled on the floor." Thus did Mingus add the black church to the many environments (atelier, acting studio) that the Workshop was meant to approximate in music.[37]

The Mingus albums *Oh Yeah* and *Blues and Roots* represent this tendency at its greatest flower—albums whose song titles ("Moanin'," "Devil Woman," "Ecclusiastics") pointed to the new churchiness in Mingus's work. Mingus seized on a number of gospel devices. As a composer, he took new pleasure in basic chordal progressions, which seemed to open up for him the possibilities of a more rough-and-ready ensemble playing. On "Wednesday Night Prayer Meeting," for instance, the piece itself is a straight twelve-bar blues, and the melody merely reiterates the blues scale from the flat third on down the octave—a far cry from Mingus's earlier chromatic explorations, which forced his Workshoppers to wing their way through an obstacle course. Mingus also began encouraging instrumental work that jabbed the ensemble rather than being deliberative and self-enclosed. His piano work, on a piece like "Devil Woman," emphasized percussive chords rather than fluent arpeggios, with "comping" taking precedence over more virtuosic solo work. The Workshop's soloists also used more dirty timbres, slurring multiphonics that suggested the variety of the human voice rather than the classical ideal of perfect temperament. For this reason, multi-instrumentalist Roland Kirk, who played many saxophones at once, was a perfect collaborator for the Workshop's jazz-gospel. Lastly, Mingus used his own voice to shape the Workshop into a testifying session unfolding in real time: as a vocalist on "Devil Woman" and other pieces, and as a bassist peppering his bandmates with "Oh yeah!" and "All right!" he took on the office of jazz preacher.

Rhythmically, Mingus was also drawing upon gospel's 6/4 pulse and teaching it how to swing. During the soul-jazz heyday of 1959–60, Mingus worked on three versions of a triple-meter gospel composition ("Wednesday Night Prayer Meeting," "Slop," "Better Get It in Your Soul"); his experiments culminated in "Better Get It in Your Soul," perhaps his most famous composition and a landmark precisely because it represents, in Brian Priestley's estimation, the "first successful jazz use of a 6/4 time-signature." Mingus took the traditional gospel rhythm and, by accelerating the overall tempo, brought out the swinging cross-rhythms that had been hidden in the loping advance of earlier recordings. When his band starts clapping over the 6/4 beat in the middle of the piece—on beats two and five, staggering the straight time by one beat—it is announcing that the scene of jazz has been transformed: the congregation has driven into the dance hall, shouting and honking and accelerating in its passage from heaven to earth.[38]

Individual Urgency: The Bass as Compelling Voice

As an instrumentalist, Mingus heightened the vocal qualities of the bass in a way that made his rhythm section more double-jointed. If most jazz bassists aimed to "play four beats cleanly, even at the fastest tempo," Mingus helped free the bass from its time-keeping, servant role in the rhythm section. Instead of a pure, evenly spaced sound, he tried to expand the annunciatory qualities of his bass; in his hands, the bass became more hornlike, a voice testifying its own gospel. On the level of pitch, Mingus often bent his notes with an aggressive left-hand maneuver that not only stopped the string but also bent it out of true across the fingerboard. The result was an almost yearning quality to the phrase endings on the bass solos that opened pieces like "Haitian Fight Song" or "Better Get It in Your Soul." Likewise, he incorporated arhythmic effects like pizzicato and tremolo, which added suspense by removing an explicit beat. He experimented much with arco work, sometimes reversing traditional roles by bowing a melody line above an arpeggiating tenor sax (on "Meditations") or bowing below the bridge to create squeaky sound effects (on "Bird Calls"). Finally, he perfected the "alternate fingering" technique of saxophonists like Lester Young. In his solos, he would often subtly shade a note by playing it on different strings, with different dynamic emphases and different bendings of pitch. Altogether, rather than aim for a single clean tone, Mingus often preferred approaching a note from a variety of vantage points in order to simulate the burrs and shadings of human speech.[39]

On a structural level, his bass lines drove the ensemble forward not by walking the changes but by offering calisthenic motives that plunged across the bass clef with melodic and rhythmic urgency. On "African Flower," playing with Duke Ellington and Max Roach, Mingus spirals down the bass clef to create a stirring contrapuntal line that evenly balances the stateliness of Ellington's theme. On the more famous "Haitian Fight Song," Mingus elaborates an entire composition on the G-minor scale by building on this kind of innovative bass work. The piece's harmonic shadings are relatively simple, but its plot is thickened by the fundamental bass motive, which pivots on the half-steps above and below the fifth, then leaps an octave down from the fifth. The motive reappears throughout the piece, thus setting the basic parameters for the improvisers (the G-minor chord) while continually unsettling its resolution. Historically, the "Haitian Fight Song" vamp (and several others like it) allowed musicians to work within a more static harmonic framework so that polyrhythms and individual melodic phrasings could be explored at greater length. This lesson was crucial not only to later free jazz musicians, but also to rock and soul musicians, who built extended jams from one-chord bass vamps that gave dancers a clear framework for their footwork. Mingus's bass became the voice of propulsion in the rhythm section, its tempo, accents, and timbre self-consciously volatile.[40]

"You, My Audience, Are All a Bunch of Poppaloppers": The Jazz Workshop and the Consumer Jeremiad

The Mingusian formulas just described could go only so far to define the Jazz Workshop in practice. For his Workshop to succeed in the art of instigation, Mingus needed to model a new consumer, and so his onstage manner combined the jeremiad form so beloved by the Puritans with the loud-mouthed payback of stand-up comics like Lenny Bruce. Mingus was a consistent scold, interrupting his music and upbraiding his audience for their air of distraction; one critic proposed the creation of a Charles Mingus wind-up doll, which would spring into anger upon its release. Mingus's frequent tirades should be understood, however, not simply as a lashing-out against a backsliding congregation of listeners. They were also a tactical response that followed up on the anything-goes ground rules of the night-club, a way of seizing its liberalized atmosphere and taking center stage back from the audience, with as much force as he deemed necessary and in a canny collusion with a stunt-hungry public. Just as his music forced the listener to adjust to sudden interruptions and shifts of mood, so his band-stand demeanor kept the audience from the "distractedness" that he associated with mass culture in general and the jazz nightclub in particular.[41]

Mingus rebuked his audience with much of the same theatrical flair that he brought to the rest of his music. In his most mellow act of civil disobedience, as a protest of the high noise level at the Half Note, he might simply operate a record player onstage while the members of the Workshop played cards or leafed through books. Or he might cut down a Workshop performance to a single twenty-minute drum solo, addressing the audience only to berate those who misunderstood his music. His more famous interventions, though, were combustive outbursts that could not be classified as eccentricity and were often staged for full menacing effect. He flew out of the Five Spot's kitchen with a cleaver in hand and attacked customers at a table near the stage for chatting during his set. In another incident, angered by the audience's disrespect the day before, he came onstage in kimono and headband, took a bullwhip out from a briefcase, and started flicking it around the room, forcing his fellow musicians and the audience at the front tables to duck for cover. In 1964 while being profiled by the *New York Herald Tribune,* he kicked a woman's drink off her table, cussed her out for distracting him from his labors ("If I's a white man, I'd put you in slavery"), then threw his $2,200 bass across the room and stamped it into a splintered wreck.[42]

The same year that Pete Townshend was ritualistically smashing his guitar in London's Marquee Club, and several years before Jimi Hendrix would burn his at the Monterey Pop Festival, Mingus was stomping his bass to smithereens. Why? Was his incendiary behavior akin to theirs—ritualized self-destruction offered as the spectacle's grand finale? Certainly there was some sort of link between Mingus's performance-art jazz and the darker theatrics of the counterculture. The British rock group the Animals, who would share the Monterey stage with Hendrix, were interested enough in Mingus to visit the Five Spot when he played there in 1964, on the very night of his bass-smashing. Yet while Mingus, Townshend, and Hendrix all brought "creative destruction" to life on stage, there were also two great differences between Mingus and the others, one of intention and the other of effect. First, Mingus never said that he meant to explode, and he almost always expressed regrets afterward. The *New York Herald Tribune* profile of Mingus began with the bass-whacking but closed with Mingus apologizing to Iggy Termini, one of the Five Spot's owners, and wondering ruefully if "it's time to end the job. I'm so sick I want people to listen." Mingus's attempts to leash his violence were almost as well reported as his explosions—how he resorted to carrying hot pepper in a Kleenex so that he would "pepper spray" his antagonists rather than punch them (of course the wind scattered it in the wrong direction); how he ran into another room to avoid a brawl with a Southern racist (of course the man tailed Mingus until he was forced to strike). In a typical incident, Mingus physically threw out a football lineman from his audience, propelling him across six tables and eventually toward the exit, and then apologized to the packed house: "I'm sorry, but I'm neurotic. My only defense is that I know it."[43]

Mingus's eruptions were also unlike Townshend's and Hendrix's in that Mingus's broke down the wall between performer and audience with a fierce demolitionism. The nightclub was an exceedingly intimate space—more like a cramped off-Broadway theater than the typically much larger venues of rock concerts. From the few transcriptions we have, it seems that Mingus enlisted the classic techniques of the jeremiad: he would begin by cursing his backsliding audience, would spotlight their sins by scapegoating a particularly noisy offender, then would end by drawing the rest of the audience into his fold with the promise of a more honest and beautiful art. In response to their noise pollution, he dealt back in kind—with an earful of his own improvised, dogged thoughts.

The most extensive transcript comes from Diane Dorr-Dorynek's "condensed" version of a Mingus rant at the Five Spot, a verbal improvisation launched in response to the chatter and clink of the nightclub. He began by asserting that the audience was in the throes of psychological denial:

You, my audience, are all a bunch of poppaloppers. A bunch of tumbling weeds tumbling 'round, running from your subconscious, running from your subconscious unconscious . . . minds. Minds? Minds that won't let you stop to listen to a word of artistic or meaningful truth. You think it all has to be in beauteous colors. Beautiful, like your "lovely" selves. You don't want to see your ugly selves, the untruths, the lies you give to life.

So you come to me, you sit in the front row, as noisy as can be. I listen to your millions of conversations, sometimes pulling them all up and putting them together and writing a symphony. But you never hear that symphony.

Then he criticized his audience's faddish attraction to jazz:

You haven't been told before that you're phonies. You're here because jazz has publicity, jazz is popular, the word jazz, and you like to associate yourself with this sort of thing. But it doesn't make you a connoisseur of the art because you follow it around. You're dilettantes of style. A blind man can go to an exhibition of Picasso and Kline and not even see their works. And comment behind dark glasses, Wow! They're the swingestest painters ever, crazy! Well, so can you. You've got your dark glasses and clogged-up ears. . . .

All of you sit there, digging yourselves and each other, looking around hoping to be seen and observed as hip. *You* become the object you came to see, and you think you're important and digging jazz when all the time all you're doing is digging a blind, deaf scene that has nothing to do with any kind of music at all.[44]

For Mingus the nightclub had failed in its main purpose, which was to consecrate the jazz being created on its bandstand. At the same time, however, Mingus argued that his music didn't originate in some formalistic vacuum where tone-rows collided with rhythmic devices. When Mingus bragged of "writing a symphony" out of the conversations he had eavesdropped on, he was codifying another article of his artistic faith: that his music, though deserving of rapt attention and the utmost respect, explored daily events as they were really lived, in all their ugliness and "untruth."

(Witness his riposte to a less-than-responsive audience: "If you think this [music] is weird, just take a look at yourselves.")[45] Thus Mingus was aiming in two directions at once—on the one hand, presenting his music as high art, to be appreciated only by connoisseurs; on the other hand, asserting that his music was sincere and could appeal to anyone with a heart strong enough to withstand it.

According to the Mingus legend, his audiences heartily swallowed this blend of musical ambition and extramusical honesty. In Dorr-Dorynek's account, "most of the audience [were] yelling, 'Bravo!' 'Tell 'em Charlie!' 'Someone has been needed to say that for years!' 'Most of us want to listen.'" Mingus's speech was calculated to elicit just such a response—to box the audience on the ears, then flatter them with the exceptional possibility that they were among "the few that do want to listen." Janet Coleman wrote in her memoir of Mingus that "audiences loved him for insisting that they share his process, even on the nights he turned on them, lecturing and screaming on how they ought to listen." During a 1962 engagement at New York's Village Gate, Mingus's manager fielded an unusual phone call from co-owner Joe Termini. Termini complained that there had been "no trouble, no telling the customers off. Talk to Mingus, will you? It's bad for business." The Mingus harangue became part of his classic repertoire ("a kind of requirement," in pianist Jaki Byard's words), just as much a badge of his artistic integrity as any composition. In 1964, Mingus himself admitted that he "used to bounce people out of the clubs to get a little more attention, because I used to think that if you didn't get a write-up, you wouldn't attract as many people." Tying "musical soul" to the pursuit of emotional integrity, he redefined his own outrage as his greatest aesthetic selling point.[46]

Of course, not everyone had to swallow Mingus's logic, and you can hear dissenting voices during Mingus's tirade when he focuses on the offending table. Notably, this section of Dorr-Dorynek's account was cobbled together after the fact, "just to give you a more concrete idea of the Bandstand View": it would seem to be Mingus's most deliberate emendation of the event, a finger-pointing set piece. Mingus focused his ire on a woman of the black community, condensing her gossip into a fudgy, surreal picaresque:

You never hear that symphony—that I might dedicate to the mother who brought along a neighbor and talked three sets and two intermissions about the old man across the hall making it with Mrs. Jones' son in the apartment below where the school teacher lives with Cadillac Bill. . . . And how it's difficult to keep the facts of life from her daughter Chi-Chi. The insurance man got fresh with me too . . . giggle giggle. Just a little kiss . . . and oh! how cute he got.[47]

What intriguing chatter! A furtive coupling between an old man and a young boy, a schoolteacher's shacking-up, a daughter trying on her sexuality—all this gossip stirs the imagination, and you can sense Mingus himself enjoying the pleasures of the hyperactive plot. In fact, one might guess that the woman is describing the sort of weird emotional entanglements that Mingus understood as the psychopathology of everyday life in America. And yet this woman is also the villain of Mingus's piece—a flighty talker who can't stop revisiting her life even in the face of the art a few feet away. Mingus's condescension, hidden first by the mass of verbiage, creeps out into the open by the end: "giggle giggle" is a scatterbrain's signature. After Mingus's tirade, the woman contends that she "has to listen to jazz all day long" and "lives on [the stuff]," but she's already lost her argument with Mingus. From the start, he's assumed that she's no music lover, just a loudmouth at an inconvenient table.

Mingus might just as easily have given voice to the high-flown patter of the poseurs he mentioned later, the ones he likens to the blind man who looked at Picasso's works. But they were less threatening: at least they attached cultural prestige to jazz. The gossiping woman, by contrast, insisted that the music was threaded into her daily routine and would remain environmental, prosaic, folksy. She wouldn't put her social life on hold just to pay cultural obeisance to the music. Even more potently, she asserted that the nightclub was not just a shrine to its musicians; it was also a watering hole and gathering place for the community, for the circle of friends who could put a face on Cadillac Bill and Mrs. Jones and Chi-Chi—for the audience, that is, who could understand Mingus's frenzied paraphrase as straight talk.

Here was another vision of the jazz audience: one high on consumer sassiness and low on artistic chauvinism, one keyed to the solidarity of a neighborhood. Note the gender dynamic at work: this woman was focusing on her story, while Mingus labored to drown her out with his own life story in music ("I play or write *me*, the way I feel, through jazz, or whatever").[48] The woman in his audience was defiantly chewing over her community's news of courtship, while Mingus was straining to hypnotize them with his siren song. The fight in the nightclub was a battle over the power of self-revelation—who might circulate their story over the din of someone else's, who might incorporate someone else's story into their own. Thus Mingus held that he could weave the stories of the woman in the audience into a symphony, while she claimed that she could weave his jazz into her own life rhythms. They quarreled over who might speak for whom: Was the jazz symphony as good an instrument of communication as the friend-to-friend chat? What did music do that conversation could not? And behind these more abstract questions was another, simpler one: If Mingus was such a powerful musician of the male-dominated jazz world, why couldn't he control the unruly woman in his audience?

"Save This Sick World, Oh Ye Priceless Whores": The Jazz Workshop and the Cost of Loving

To understand the sexual stakes of this quarrel, we need to turn to a source that is both more brutal and more comic, Mingus's autobiography *Beneath the Underdog: The World as Composed by Mingus.*[49] Despite the musical allusion of the subtitle, the book is almost entirely a sentimental education—the story of Mingus's romantic awakening, sexual exploits, temptation into pimpdom, and final ripening into philosophic maturity. Batted around like a shuttlecock for over a decade, its 370 pages quarried out of a 900-page manuscript, the book offers an object lesson in how the publishing industry shapes a final product to its own needs. First circulating under the titles *Half Yaller Nigger* and *Half Yaller Schitt-Colored Nigger,* the book was shopped around informally with various freelance editors around 1960, then leased to McGraw-Hill, where a "succession of young male editors" tried to cobble it into marketable form and then passed it along. According to Mingus's friend Janet Coleman,

> Whenever there was a possibility for publication, Mingus seemed to balk. Jason Epstein, the big kingpin at Random House, was interested in the manuscript until he heard a few of Mingus's conditions: a white binding with gold letters, a book that could be mistaken for the Bible. Well, fuck him, Jason Epstein said. It is hard to estimate how many people finally worked on the copy, hacks and strangers . . . [B]efore it reached its last editor, Nel King, it had been altered, whitened up beyond repair. *Beneath the Underdog* was published in 1971 by Alfred A. Knopf, without the gold lettering, weak tea indeed.[50]

Perhaps it was weak tea compared to the original brew, but not for those accustomed to blander infusions. *Newsweek* called Mingus "an unusually gifted pornographer, in part because he is an inventive soul, in part because he chases his dreams of tail with astonishing single-mindedness, in part because his sensual vocabulary, the vocabulary of high-rolling black pimps and white whores, is most exotic."[51] "Most exotic" was the kind of arch phrase that separated *Newsweek*'s prose from the "pornography" of Mingus's book; other reviewers took a similar stance.[52] The mainstream press seemed not to notice that the book had been "whitened" over the course of the decade. In fact, it took the opposite position—that the worth of Mingus's book lay in its pitch-perfect evocation of black subculture. The *Times Literary Supplement* remarked that "despite its repetitious copulations and orgies, [*Beneath the Underdog*] is important and should be added to the growing library of worthwhile books by black people about precisely what it feels like to be black." Clive James noted in London's *Observer* that Mingus "has got in what it feels like to be an artist—actually *be* it, in a world that is not only trying to stop you being an artist but has tried to stop you being human in the first place. . . . Mingus builds an *un*stable private world in which [Jim Crow] horrors are compensated for by wild excesses of lust: page after page is alive with tangled bodies writhing in their own juices." *Publishers' Weekly* named the book "one of the most intensely personal, sex-mad, music-crazy, and fame-foolish jazz autobiographies of the current scene . . . steamy, funny, tragic, incredible, but every bit of it ringing true." Rather than being disfigured or confounded by its considerable editing, *Beneath the Underdog* was intensely recognizable. It was plainly the protest story of the black male artist—Charles Mingus Presents Charles Mingus, off-color and candid.[53]

All the reviewers, however, steered clear of the book's tangled explorations into the relationship between prostitution and jazz music—two industries that, as "composed by Mingus," revolve around economies of pleasure and thus challenge a utopian sense of pleasure as innocent self-fulfillment. The antagonistic sexual world of *Beneath the Underdog* is an obvious corollary to the antagonistic musical world of the Jazz Workshop, which drew ecstatic phrases out of the ongoing compositional constraints imposed by Mingus. Put more simply: you might get your kicks in *Beneath the Underdog*, but you'll almost always get your ass kicked in the bargain. Being a jazz artist means that you get to both improvise and sell yourself; being a Mingus lover means that you will be doted upon and suffer for your devotion; sex means that you will alight upon ecstasy and be humiliated for the extravagance of your desires. Clive James notwithstanding, the sex and pimping in *Beneath the Underdog* are not simple compensations for the indignities of Jim Crow in the jazz world—colorful lusts to offset black-and-white deprivations. They are instead concerted efforts to explore around the absent crux of the book, the life of the musician Mingus. Mingus the autobiographer faced the same dilemma, albeit from a different angle, that he had faced as a jazz entrepreneur. As an entrepreneur, he had tried to remain emotionally sincere without clowning or allying himself with an iniquitous music industry. Similarly, as an autobiographer Mingus searched for true love in a world of predatory and commercialized social relations. Honesty and love were the ultimate stakes in a world where the "system" (the music industry, the world at large) was trying to model your very soul in its own despoiled image.

The act of pimping opens onto Mingus's musical identity in three related ways. First, it serves as the occupational alternative to being a jazz musician—the easy route to a life of conspicuous consumption, the American success story of upward mobility. Second, it is the emotional equivalent of musically selling out, literally pandering to the lowest tastes: the prostitute was the clown of the bedroom. Finally, pimping is viewed more instrumentally and less metaphysically—as a necessary, ugly means to financial and therefore creative autonomy. In this light, pimping means playing the gig you don't want in order to get the gig you do. Mingus's autobiography entertains these three possibilities as philosophical options and shows, in practice, the male jazz musician lured and ensnared by all of them.

Through its picaresque plot, *Beneath the Underdog* idealizes love and thrashes it in equal measure. "Life's problems" are always intruding upon pure love in the book, largely because this love is conceived as a mystic, passionate union that binds two individuals together and therefore ranges the rest of society against them (p. 21). Love in this sense works by tapping into the immaterial, the ideal, the expansive: Mingus discovers his first true love at the same time that he finds that he has "mystic powers" that allow him to "contact certain souls in the next room or miles away" (p. 57). At an amalgamated church gathering on Lake Elsinore, outside of Los Angeles, he starts staring at his love Lee-Marie, with whom he creates "a silent oneness that seem[s] endless" (pp. 35–36). Soon after their not-so-mystical petting in a movie theater, Mingus is considering the isolating power of their love, the boomerang effect of their "endless" union: "in the eyes of the world they were only two small children and their passion was against every rule of God and man. 'Man' was the powerful and dangerous adults surrounding them" (pp. 59–60). Even in its most innocent consummation, Mingusian love is the taboo form of sociability.

But if love is originally introduced in the language of mystic communion, it soon takes on an earthier tone as Mingus learns that sexual pleasure is not just mutually reinforcing; it can also be gamy, startlingly competitive at times, even leveraged as a harsh form of social power. Mingus's first lesson in this sort of sexual technique comes from his friend Buddy Collette's father, who sets down some "good rules for fucking" for "those who don't have the natural talent." These "rules" revolve around the art of sexual surprise—how to tease a woman in bed, ambushing her and refusing her with your own thrust and parry, until she "start[s] getting frantic, crying and begging." As Buddy's father instructs Charles, you may wish to give in to her pleadings, but you should keep in mind the value of withholding pleasure. You should plunge into the final rhythms *"when you make your mind to"*—and only then, when you've forced her to recognize that her pleasure will come solely from your consent, that you can marshal your sexual energy, rein it in or release it, with blithe attention to her demands. Buddy's father ends his spiel with this sexual forecast: "Now, Charles, you try that on the next little girl you get. . . . See if she don't tell you these very words: 'Charles, I never had it done to me like that in my life!'" (pp. 72–74). Sure enough, Mingus *does* try out the instructions two chapters later, wrangling with Rita in the surf, and is predictably reassured by her response: "I ought to kill you, Mingus, for leaving me wanting it like this!" (p. 93). Papa Collette has hit his mark.

Of course there is a huge gap between the hypnotic stare that binds two children against the world and the surfy wrangle that keeps its two lovers deadlocked in a sexual tease. But Mingus's energies as an autobiographer are devoted to uniting the two visions of love—as mutual consent and as macho power-grab—within the framework of his own life. With his magnetic powers of sexual attraction, Mingus drifts slowly but surely into the career of the pimp, which he justifies to himself by a painfully absurd compromise that plays upon both idioms of love. His whores are also the women he truly cares for, he reasons, so they offer to sell themselves (because they consent to his love), just as they offer to give their earnings to him (because they recognize that, as a male jazz artist, he needs to pocket their wages). Trapped by his own magnetism, Mingus starts turning them out and storing their earnings beneath his mattress. All the while, though, he curses himself for his own spiritual degradation and refuses to spend the money: "To be a pimp, one would have to lose all feelings, all sensitivity, all love. One would have to die! Kill himself! Kill all feeling for others in order to live with himself. . . . *Mingus* couldn't be this . . . a pimp" (p. 212; italics and second ellipsis in original). Strikingly, the problem with pimping is not that Mingus is abusing his extrasensory powers of sexual control. Rather, the problem is that "Mingus," the great jazz artist to be, cannot associate himself with a business that churns "all feelings, all sensitivity, all love" through a commodity. The act of prostitution, which begins as a sacrifice for the sake of love, quickly becomes its betrayal.

If pimping betrays Mingus's artistic spirit, then why does he continue with it for another hundred pages? Perhaps because, as much as he is revolted by the degradation of sex into an exchange, he is intoxicated by his own fantastic powers—or, more precisely, he is intoxicated by the idea that his pimping career is compelling evidence of such powers. The power of pimping, in its most ideal form, represents for Mingus the power of soft compulsion, the deployment of his supposedly noncoercive sexual charisma in the public arena. In their cruder form, his "mystic powers" can shade into nasty mind games—as when Mingus convinces a woman to sell herself, then tells her he was "just kidding," and she rejoices with a pathetic "Oh Mingus. . . . you've just shown me there's a God" (p. 216). In their more hyperbolic form, Mingus's "mystic powers" involve grotesquely elaborate plots to set the world aright through the practice of mass hypnotism. Shortly before he renounces pimping once and for all, Mingus riffs over the bizarre possibility that he might mobilize all the prostitutes in the world to take political action:

> I wonder if I could hypnotize all the prostitutes of the world so they'd run into the streets nude to rape every man in sight!. . . . Whores, off with the clothes of our leaders! Today! All over the world! If they run[,] cut off where their balls should be. Save this sick world, oh ye priceless whores. (p. 282)

World revolution, spurred forward by one man's sexual magnetism: Mingus's fantasy captures the spirit of black macho at its late 1960s, early 1970s highpoint.

To comprehend the attraction of this oversized rhetoric, we have to understand that Mingus linked his hypnotic powers to his artistic authority. Sexual charisma shaded into musical charisma: both were instances of a willfulness that, instead of demanding consent, could exact it. The passage just quoted, for instance, was introduced by Mingus's statement "I could always hypnotize people. Even when I lost sight of God, I could hypnotize through music—they'd come running and screaming down the aisles and jumping out of bleachers" (p. 281). Here we might recall the gossiping woman and the disdain she piqued in Mingus. Her sins, we can now see clearly, were double and intertwined. First, she resisted Mingus's snake-charming charisma on the bandstand, in a clear rebuke of his hypothetical powers; second, she dared to narrate her own courtship with some cajolery and frivolity—exactly the mundane traits that Mingus excised from his ideal form of love. The outrage this woman provoked in Mingus came from the threat that her "giggle giggle" could drown out the robust labors of the men onstage.

And yet, Mingus's bluster was not so one-sided: if the pimping in *Beneath the Underdog* could be conceived as an extension of his musical powers, it could also signify the lucrative career he renounced for the high road of jazz. By these lights, pimping was another symptom of the Jim Crow economy, the most promising but fatal recourse of the black male capitalist. In the first pages of his autobiography, Mingus searches for an explanation of pimping's allure and settles on its spectacle: the pimps "pose and twirl their watchchains and sport their new Cadillacs and Rollses and expensive tailored clothes. It was like the closest thing to one of our kind becoming president of the U.S.A." (p. 6). Pimps were street entertainers posing as entrepreneurs; their blatant commercialism set them against the artist Mingus hoped to be. In an important (invented) dialogue with trumpeter Fats Navarro, Mingus invokes the promise of jazz as a non-commercial art and is forced to confront the alternative of pimping:

> [Mingus:] "That's what jazz originally was, getting away from the usual tiddy, the hime, the gig."
> [Navarro:] "But Mingus, how about them crumb-crushers of yours when their little stomachs get to poppin' and there ain't nothin' in their jaws but their gums, teeth, and tongue, what you gonna do? Play for money or be a pimp?"
> "I tried being a pimp, Fats. I didn't like it." (p. 191)

The male jazz musician had to face up to his role as family provider: you couldn't feed your "crumb-crushers" on the consolations of art, nor could you accept the money earned by your prostitutes, so you were forced into selling your music.

This turn of logic led to a startling recognition: prostitution, far from being a profession unrelated to the jazz musician's, was in fact its closest analogue. Both prostitute and musician sold what had originally allowed them to escape "from the usual tiddy, the hime, the gig"; both were service workers in a pleasure industry that they did not control. We saw earlier how Mingus defined pimping as a form of emotional deadening—the empathetic sufferings of middle management for the rank and file. It awaits Mingus's cousin Billy Bones, a flamboyant pimp who radiates black macho (he claims he requires a specially lowered toilet bowl), to draw the explicit connection between sexual and musical prostitutes. In an example of the plot twists that drive *Beneath the Underdog*, Billy Bones lambastes Mingus's lover Donna for enjoying sex with a rich and lucrative customer:

> Those people own the backbone and some of everything else in this country—even the chump Mingus's profession, which might be said to make whores out of musicians. . . . By my reckoning a good jazz

musician has got to turn to pimping in order to be free and keep his soul straight. (p. 267)

Billy Bones's logic has one severe hitch, which eventually leads Mingus to renounce pimping once and for all: if jazz musicians are musical whores, then pimps are the equivalent of the industry moguls who plump themselves up by feeding off the jazz musician. The rhetoric of "the whoring musician" has a double edge: on the one hand, it cuts against the music industry and its predations; on the other, it allies the musician with the very women he exploits.

At the end of *Beneath the Underdog* Mingus decides to break with his prostitutes, but that gesture should not be distorted into some upbeat finale. The theme of the book is that money muddles everything, that exploitation and cooperation go hand in hand, that the emancipatory impulses of sex or jazz have to be defined through the economic system they knock against and work through. Within every economy of pleasure, another economy of hard work. For every airy romance, a scrawled pornography. So Mingus renounces the pimping life only to find that his lovers refuse to give up their new career as prostitutes. His sweetheart Lee-Marie proclaims herself a "free lover" as much as Mingus and will not believe that her pleasure is any less sanctified because she takes cash on the pillow. Spurned in his high-mindedness, Mingus is left to strike out for new romantic territory. He soon meets the respectable Judy, a student nurse from White Plains, but the commercial aspects of romance trail him through their lightning courtship, which closes the book. When she asks him, "What would you do . . . if you had your life to live all over again?" Mingus replies with a murky mix of hard-boiled cynicism and heady romance:

"I'd live to enjoy life, not to lecture or preach. I wouldn't believe in any bullschitt like 'love' and I wouldn't get involved with any woman who talked it—any woman in my company would have to admit that what she loved was money. I'd play music as a hobby and only for close friends in the raceless set. I'd study bass for kicks, I wouldn't get involved in commercial competition. . . ."

The girl Judy laughs. She's entertained and amused and she doesn't believe a word of it, otherwise she never would have married him and borne his two youngest children, would she? (p. 354)

This passage exemplifies how Mingus absorbed the contradictions of jazz and romance into the style of his book. While most jazz autobiographies take the form of a testimonial, *Beneath the Underdog* proceeds almost exclusively through dialogue (philosophical musings, romantic smooth talk, business dealings, bandstand camaraderie); we hear Mingus's ideas articulated against their opposite, straining for believability, in a constant search for confirmation. Accordingly, his final speech to Judy strikes some odd, jangly notes. On the one hand, he affirms his long-held belief in a "raceless set" and underscores his dedication to music outside of "commercial competition," music "for kicks." On the other hand, he calls the language of "love" just so much "bullschitt" and says that he'll only target women who think of romance as a species of commercial competition. The resolution of this contradiction lies in the dialogic form itself, in Judy's generous disbelief. Refusing to indulge Mingus as the neglected artist, she humors the possibility that he may be talking trash, working his crowd for as much as they're worth. Without her laughter, Mingus would be doomed "to lecture or preach"—doomed, that is, to the didacticism that shuts out its audience. She dares to laugh, and so dares us to rethink Mingus's machismo as a faltering if binding exercise in collaboration. Most crucially, she teaches us that happy endings are purchased through the workings of skepticism. Mingus is often appreciated best, most generously, when we challenge him back and refuse to take him at his word.

As in the music of the Jazz Workshop, however, this dialogue was a testy affair: Mingus provoked disbelief and confrontation even as his menace often shut them down. While dialogue may be the key form for his autobiography, the dialogues tend to be lopsided; Mingus rarely meets his match in rhetorical overdrive. Judy's sly smile may be her best defense, but it is also a ruse of silence—an act of cunning that draws out Mingus's playfulness but leaves an open space that has to be filled in with further action on her part (marriage and two kids—the final twist of the story: Mingus goes straight). Judging from Mingus's comments on the gossiping woman and his persistent fantasies of sexual control, it's fair to say that as much as he invited a spirit of play into the bedroom and onto the bandstand, he frequently liked his women speaking on his terms. Mingus's bulldozing masculinity is the flip side of his pioneering spirit; and his autobiography's much-fabled raggedness is the persistent flipping of this coin. Mingus the pimp, Mingus the genius; the maligned audience, the beloved audience. Throughout, Mingus plays the improviser who, in the dogged strength of his riffing, risks muffling those who would hear him. Part of an industry that sells the sensation of intimacy, he does not draw a hard-and-fast distinction between his lovers and his clientele. Often, painfully, he ends up scrambling the difference—between those people he loves to need and those people he needs to love.

6

"THIS FREEDOM'S SLAVE CRIES"

Listening to the Jazz Workshop

Charles Mingus loved sparrows. He would sprawl out on a Manhattan rooftop and watch them poke about in the rain gutters, hungry for whatever they could scrounge up. They were an image of himself—scavenger, mongrel, survivor. "Outcasts," Sue Mingus remembers him saying: "They know what to do, though. They're the sharpest of all. When the other birds have split, they'll be around." Another part of Mingus, though, wondered if a mongrel art—an art that was always scavenging and piecing together its own resourceful solutions—would ever find a broader audience. When a jazz writer asked him what he thought of John Coltrane's mid-1960s music, he took the opportunity to riff on the temptation of artistic single-mindedness. "He went back to India, man," Mingus said. "Back to Indian-type pedal point music. He hit a streak." Then he enlarged on his sense of frustration: "Why do guys stylize themselves? Don't they know in the summertime you wear thin clothes and straw hats and then in the wintertime you got a right to play a different tune? You don't have to be stylized. A preacher preaches a different sermon every Sunday. He doesn't preach the same one. You turn to a different page."[1]

The inventiveness of Mingus as a composer cannot be understood outside of his refusal to "hit a streak," his rivalry with those who did, and his sparrowlike ability to pick through the musical archive and assemble what he discovered into his own idiom. More than perhaps any other jazz composer aside from Duke Ellington, Mingus created a repertory of his own.

Driving this spirit of innovation was a constant search for new formulas of sentimentality and sensibility, new ways of making love through music. As in his autobiography, Mingus felt compelled to find a form that was at once lyrical and combative, one that would attest both to love's ethereality and to its sometimes bruising power relations. The sexual contention of the blues, the flirting and sophistication of Tin Pan Alley, the mysticism and heroism expressed in Wagner and Richard Strauss—these were among the diverse "structures of feeling" that he brought together in his art. If Mingus the autobiographer created himself by blending pornography and mysticism in his sentimental education, Mingus the composer created himself by throwing together popular and elite music with an exuberance that could often shade into what he called "creative anger."

In Mingus's art we hear the sound of struggle in something approaching its full, hard-bop variety. We hear a struggle between high and low art, between an elite modernism built on the heroic strivings of genius and a populist modernism built on the creativity of collaborative revolt. We hear a struggle between the classical legacy of German composers like Wagner and Strauss and the jazz-blues legacy in all its catholicity. And we hear a struggle about individual and community in jazz, a struggle between the jazz composer as authoritative fountainhead and the jazz workshop as a site of spontaneous combustion. Moreover, all of these conflicts had a racial dimension, in that the available musical conventions were freighted with certain social presumptions: What would happen, for instance, if the Tin Pan Alley ballad was used for stories of interracial romance? If the modernist overreacher was at once a black musician? If the exalted composer was also a workshopper, a musician's version of the common man?

The four pieces considered in this chapter represent different facets in Mingus's work as a jazz composer. "Eclipse" (1953), one of the many paranormal pop songs that Mingus composed before the consolidation of his Jazz Workshop, synthesized the standard thirty-two-bar pop form with a more chromatic harmonic language in order to recast the Tin Pan Alley swoon as a transcendent, even cosmic, union. In the process, an act of "miscegenation"—to use the inflammatory term in circulation among segregationists—was reimagined as the meeting of two heavenly bodies. The programmatic "Pithecanthropus Erectus" (1956) dramatized the struggle between the first man to stand erect and the masses who revolt against his arrogance. This quasi-Hegelian plot—dialectically split between the modernist master and his ambitious slaves—was manifested in music through Mingus's split allegiance to high modernist German composers and to a jazz tradition that prized collective music-making despite its associations with anarchy and popular insurrection. Tin Pan Alley song form, not coincidentally, was reshaped into an "extended form" with modal episodes; "Pithecanthropus" was one of Mingus's first experiments in more complex, architectonic forms that struck a new balance between composition and improvisation in a small group setting. *The Black Saint and the Sinner Lady* (1962), Mingus's great extended work, was conceived as a drama of sexual antagonism and "soul-fusion." Here Mingus layered together those formulas (chromatic melodies, collective improvisation) that he had earlier kept separate, infusing them with a big-band blues language that borrowed much from Duke Ellington. Meanwhile, the anthropological allegory of "Pithecanthropus Erectus" yielded to the traditional blues allegory of sexual intrigue. Lastly, two recordings of the satiric "Fables of Faubus" (1959, 1960) turned the forces of modernism against Arkansas governor Orval Faubus. Faubus staunchly opposed the integration of schools, and Mingus's Workshop lampooned him through a satiric jazz performance that redefined virtuosity in the interests of collective good humor and political bite. "Fables" demonstrates how Mingus's modernism was more than apocalyptic melodrama. It could also serve as a witty "Southern strategy" that took his musicians' creative antagonism and deployed it like a bomb against his political enemies.

Mingus's Paranormal Pop: The Surreal Drama of Integration

Well before the consolidation of his Jazz Workshop, Mingus had been drawn to Gothic themes that reflected the deepest of emotional states, moods that swelled beneath the crust of routine experience. This paranormalism marked Mingus's earliest work in Los Angeles, such nonimprovisational pieces as "The Chill of Death" and "Half-Mast Inhibition" (unrecorded until 1971 and 1960 respectively). Both pieces focused on the interzone between death and life, and both tried to evoke that spiritual twilight through extended (five- to ten-minute) episodic suites that borrowed much from the film noir underscores of Max Steiner and Dmitri Tiomkin, the latter of whom employed Mingus as a journeyman on the Hollywood film score assembly line. Where their music was used to give atmospheric depth to the psychological struggles of antiheroes like Sam Spade and Mildred Pierce, Mingus deployed such shadings in an autobiographical art. According to Mingus, in 1939, at the ripe age of seventeen, he had experienced a near-death moment while practicing Karma Yoga— a point of total self-control that convinced him that "I could die if I wanted to."

Such paranormal ruminations filtered into the melodramatic recitative of "The Chill of Death," whose protagonist was seduced by Lady Death in an Edgar Allen Poe moment. The piece was an awkward alarm against the charms of materialism: at a crossroads, the narrator follows Death down a "golden and glowing and shining" path and soon finds his road blasted by the fires of Hell. At this early stage, Mingus seems already to have associated materialism with the seductions of women—a point he would drive home through the prostitution in *Beneath the Underdog*. But here, his musical language was self-consciously classical rather than vernacular. Later, he would praise Charlie Parker for bringing "to music a primitive mystic, supra-mind communication that I'd only heard in the late Beethoven quartets and, even more, in Stravinsky"; at this point he preferred to mine these classical sources himself. Entirely precomposed, the music made use of large-scale orchestral instrumentation but did not exploit any of the rhythmic devices commonly associated with African-American music.[2]

Throughout the early 1950s, Mingus experimented with the Tin Pan Alley thirty-two-bar ballad, marrying his interest in the nether worlds of experience with the pop form most associated with romantic balladry. The result was some of the finest pop noir of the fifties, music that gave voice to the painful anxieties behind the hard-boiled attitude. From the beginning of his career, he rearranged Tin Pan Alley standards like "Pennies from Heaven," "All the Things You Are," and "Flamingo" with somber, harmonically dense voicings that suggested a darker side to the American dream of romance. Similarly, his own early compositions—"Portrait," "Weird Nightmare," "Eclipse"—were strange initial stabs at the jazz market, pop songs freighted with spiritual turmoil. "Portrait," a story of God's angst with the world of his creation, was written as background for an Arthur Godfrey variety program; "Eclipse," a cosmological allegory of interracial love, was written for Billie Holiday, who never performed it. In retrospect, the commercial failure of these pieces seems a foregone conclusion: Mingus's desire for a "hook" ran at cross-purposes with the tonal language of his pieces, which featured chromatic melodic movement and highlighted moments of extreme dissonance. The catchiness slammed headlong into the musical vocabulary Mingus associated with emotional distress. "Weird Nightmare," for instance, spiraled chromatically through every key in the book, so that the melodic hook of its title was undercut by a different, dissonant coloration each time it was sung. Such harmonic shadings were apt for a music that aimed for the subtleties of shifting moods—musicologist Andrew Homzy has compared "Weird Nightmare" to Scriabin and postwar Ellington—but they also contributed to the overall effect of Gothic languor, one exacerbated by an instrumental arrangement that cut out the drummer and added a string section. So while the piece followed a standard thirty-two-bar form and took on the conventional theme of sleepless nights (think of Ellington's "Rocks in My Bed" and 1961's "Tossing and Turning"), it also sought musically to evoke a psyche divided against itself, one that interrogated its nightmares with "Why must you torment me?" and "I've been hurt—do you know what that means?"[3]

In "Eclipse," such ethereal explorations were turned to a more social purpose, as Mingus probed the most sensitive segregationist nerve: miscegenation. In this otherworldly Tin Pan Alley ballad, Mingus endowed interracial love with a cosmic blessing—one so cosmic that it is unclear whether any contemporary audience ever picked up on the song's political allegory (its most explicit racial cue was the phrase "dark meets light"). According to Mingus, "I sent Billie Holiday the music. . . . I heard her do Strange Fruit, so I figured she could do this one." Holiday's "Strange Fruit" (1939) was the protest song par excellence of the Popular Front—a graphic antilynching allegory that fused blues intonation and cabaret drama as it pointed to the horrors behind the myth of the South's ever-fertile plantation landscape. The shift in the songs' targets speaks to the shift from New Deal to Cold War milieus: while the Popular Front mobilized a political campaign against antiblack violence, Mingus sought instead to ennoble interracial love as the handiwork of destiny. The lynch mob was recast, in "Eclipse," as the conformist crowd; the bloody black victim, meanwhile, became the esoteric black lover.[4]

Like Sun Ra, who imagined Saturn as a science-fiction theosophical paradise, Mingus constructed a highly allegorical world that transcended the mundane negotiations of social conflict:

Eclipse, when the moon meets the sun,
Eclipse, these bodies become as one.

People go around,
Eyes look up and frown,
For it's a sight they seldom see.

Some look through smoked glasses,
Hiding their eyes,
Others think it's tragic,
Dneering as dark meets light.

But the sun doesn't care
Snd the moon has no fear
Gor destiny's making her choice.

Eclipse, the moon has met the sun.
Eclipse, these bodies have become one.[5]

THE SOUND OF STRUGGLE

"Eclipse" suggests that the 1950s taboo on interracial love was so strong that Mingus—even with control over his own record label and its distribution—preferred to approach the subject through a spiritual allegory, which solved one problem (the sensitivity of imagining black-white sexual relations) but raised still others. On the one hand, Mingus's allegory works to universalize the emotions of interracial love. The moon and sun of "Eclipse" are like any pair of star-crossed lovers who join together at fate's command. They seem to be victims not of racial prejudice (an issue that might demand a race-sensitive solution) but of narrow-minded conformism, a kind of suburban groupthink: the disdainful public sneers and curses the tragedy simply because "it's a sight they seldom see." The price of this allegory, however, was the thinness of its social detail; "Eclipse" is a song so high-minded as to be disembodied. Representing a road usually not taken in Mingus's art, "Eclipse" prefers to escape from social dilemmas rather than explode them from within. Appearing early in Mingus's career, the song's two lovers suggest the young romantics in the beginning of *Beneath the Underdog*—mystified by their love, overwhelmed by the way it carries them out of their bodies and into communion.

Mingus's music deepened this story of love's communion by expertly shifting the tonal center of the piece at pivotal moments in the lyrics. The piece is divided into four sections: a first section of four bars, which announces the harmonic convergence of moon and sun; a second section of eight bars, which announces the sneering response of the crowd; a third section of four bars, which dramatizes the indifference of sun and moon to the crowd's hostility; and a final section of four bars, which recapitulates the first section. In the first section, the mutuality of love is conveyed by the washing chords that accompany the two syllables of "eclipse"—D-flat seventh (#9) and E-flat major seventh (#11/#9)—chords whose underlying complexity is smoothed over by the melody's very basic movement down a whole step. Here the tonal center of the piece is suspended between whole steps as well, as the two chords rock back and forth through these four measures. The swaying mutuality of this first phase segues into the harsh modulations of the second section, which uses dissonant intervals to move from one chord cluster to the next: in these eight measures, the melody pivots on the tritone (the flat fifth) four times and on the flat ninth two times, as the underlying harmonies churn in another universe to the chords of the first section. The crowd is thereby figured as a disordered body with constantly shifting lines of attack, a body askew from the tonal world of the heavens. Here the moments of greatest melodic tension occur on the phrases "smoked glasses" and "it's tragic" (both of which swing from flat ninth to tritone)—exactly the moments when the lyrics suggest social conflict. Strikingly, the third section resolves much of this tension: when destiny makes "her choice," the chordal framework finally achieves a straightforward (ii–V) jazz release. The fourth and final module of the piece—the recapitulation of the two lovers in eclipse—seals this harmonic blessing. It confirms, in a narrative flashback, that the lovers' original promise has withstood the dissonant pressures of their social world.

With such strenuous harmonic navigation, Mingus came closer to the genre of art song than Tin Pan Alley standard. But this was art song complicated by the confessionalism within Mingus's aesthetic: "Eclipse" originally appeared on Debut's sampler entitled *Autobiography in Jazz,* and Celia Mingus Zaentz—Mingus's second (white) wife and Debut Records partner—has remarked that "'Eclipse' was a really important thing for him to do because it was the black-white 'when the moon meets the sun.'" Mingus was thus writing inner confessions as highly veiled allegories—a tortuous practice that had concrete expression in his new ballad form, where the pieces bore the intense imprint of Mingus's unique voicings as a composer-lyricist but required professional singers like Jackie Paris and Janet Thurlow to interpret their sinuous melodies. Mingus became one of the 1950s' more distinctive composers of torch songs, but he never actually carried the torch.[6]

Likewise, there was a noticeable tension between the implicit message in "Eclipse" and its underlying form—a tension that can be traced back to the founding agenda of Mingus's Debut Records. The song's lyrics testified to the unified soul-force that results from black and white coalescence, but its music neglected much of the African-American heritage that Mingus was exploiting in other contemporary recordings. It featured no solo or collective improvisations, no noticeable polyrhythms, no call-and-response work to heighten the spontaneity of the performance itself. Still, contemporary critics understood this sort of work as part of an integrationist aesthetic. Ralph Gleason wrote that Mingus was trying to break down cultural barriers by proving that "there should be no segregation in music between classical and jazz." Mingus himself proposed that jazz could be "mathematically written—every phrase, dynamics, and notations"; and with a few special tricks (for instance, writing out a solo in 12/8 while the ensemble swings in 4/4), the classical musician who had "never even listened to jazz" could "swing the most." A 1952 *Metronome* article likewise suggested that Mingus's work proved that "jazz was maturing to a point where it was ever approaching the complexities of classical music, that the main distinction between the two forms was the rhythmic content of jazz, and that jazz could be so written that a classical musician would swing just by correctly reading the music." There is something ingenious but contradictory about

THE SOUND OF STRUGGLE

Mingus's claims for the art of notation; it is as if he wished to outwit jazz, to create a simulation of improvisation and swing that would not be dependent on the experience of the musicians themselves. If classical music had found its way into the cultural pantheon through its lineage of genius composers (Bach, Beethoven, Brahms), so too would jazz distinguish itself through the genius of its own composers—even if its own lineage posited a much more symbiotic relationship between composition and improvisation, between the writers and the players of music.[7]

"Eclipse" suggests that, for one of jazz's most experimental minds, musical integration in the early 1950s meant using a classical method that aimed for reproducible, reliably scored pieces of music, rather than bebop's loose, open riffing on the harmonic framework of the blues or Tin Pan Alley song form. The sub-rosa lesson of Mingus's early work, then, was that compositional maturity might mean the eclipse of other methods that stressed oral spontaneity—the price of riding the cultural escalator up to the symphony hall. At the same time, as Eric Porter suggests, Mingus was also discovering that an integrationist vision of jazz often excused critics who concentrated their attention on white musicians like Dave Brubeck. After all, it was easier for white musicians to make jazz seem "respectable" and "raceless" since they were not the ones who bore the brunt of postwar assumptions about racial identity.[8] "Eclipse" is an exquisite song, with an achingly beautiful melody and intricate harmonic development—but it would not be the model for much of Mingus's most compelling music. For the rest of his career, post–Debut Records, Mingus tried to figure out how he might arrive at the concert hall without sacrificing the dynamism of R&B, gospel, and earlier jazz.

"Pithecanthropus Erectus": Fanfare for the Uncommon Man

Although he had promoted the idea that he could fool his listeners with the simulation of spontaneity, Mingus switched tacks when he formed his Jazz Workshop, substituting the oral communication of scales for the written notation of swing. By 1956 he was arguing, against his earlier pronouncements, that "jazz, by its very definition, cannot be held down to written parts to be played with a feeling that only goes with blowing free." The cultural stakes behind this transformation are made evident in "Pithecanthropus Erectus," the title piece from his Workshop's major-label debut and the first Mingus piece that forthrightly abjured measure demarcations for oral cues. "Pithecanthropus" is a monumental work of first origins and final endings. Programmatically, it was meant to describe the rise and fall of the first man to stand erect—a major allegory that required a broader musical language of both individual transcendence and social conflict. Within Mingus's career, too, it assumed an apocalyptic significance: not only did it launch his career as a major recording artist, but it was also projected to cap off his career through *Epitaph,* a three-hour opus encapsulating the composer's life, which begins with "Pithecanthropus"'s opening chord sequence, melody, and pumping bass. These first chords (F minor and D-flat major seventh) constitute a kind of autobiographical signature throughout Mingus's work: they appear first in his Gothic compositions "Extrasensory Perception" (1952) and "Eulogy for Rudy Williams" (1954), resurface in "Epitaph," then reappear in "Opus 3" (1974), one of Mingus's last compositions.[9]

"Pithecanthropus" is a musical and political landmark, one that pits two masterplots of avant-garde modernism against each other: the struggle of the heroic genius and the revolt of the masses. In effect, Mingus was contemplating the possibly combative, possibly sympathetic relationship between aesthetic revolution and political revolution. He described his "jazz tone poem" as

> my conception of the modern counterpart of the first man to stand erect—how proud he was, considering himself the "first" to ascend on all fours, pounding his chest and preaching his superiority over the animals still in a prone position. Overcome with self-esteem, he goes out to rule the world, if not the universe, but both his own failure to realize the inevitable emancipation of those he sought to enslave, and his greed in attempting to stand on a false security, deny him not only the right of ever being a man, but finally destroy him completely.[10]

From one angle, Mingus's mass revolt could be understood as a slave rebellion, one motivated by what sociologist Paul Gilroy sees as a central feature of African-American modernism: the "interrogation of the concept of progress from the standpoint of the slave."[11] The crux of "Pithecanthropus"'s larger drama, as in Alexander Kojève's lectures on Hegel and the larger African-American tradition from Frederick Douglass to Ralph Ellison, is the contest between master and slave for mutual recognition. The hunger for "self-esteem" motivates both Mingus's first man, who seeks to "[preach] his superiority" as an end in and of itself, and the masses, who demand their freedom with a Hegelian inevitability. Unlike Kojève, however, Mingus did not see the master-slave confrontation as a contest between individuals but as a struggle between a master and an entire people who seek recognition. He kept the archetypal nature of Kojève's scene but inserted the notion of collective emancipation, in a clear echo of the civil rights and anticolonial liberation movements under way in 1956. As Nat Hentoff remarked in his liner notes, Mingus was consumed by the idea that "we might yet learn—before it's too late to learn anything—how shatteringly destructive the false security of the enslaver can be." In Mingus's mind, the master's security was false precisely because he misunderstood the relationship between authority and freedom, using his own hard-won authority to disable others rather than to empower them.[12]

At the same time, Mingus cast the modernist overreacher, not the typical slaveowner, as the antagonist of collective liberation. In doing so, he made the drama much more morally ambivalent, since he aspired to be the very same messiah that he criticized for his overweening ambition. Mingus's erect man—nonconformist, proud of his heightened consciousness—was a clear figure for the composer himself, who stood above the four-legged conventions of jazz, classical, and pop music. It was Mingus's visionary design, after all, that replaced bars with cues in the B section of the piece, thus rejecting the musical convention that even the most iconoclastic of modernist composers (from Ives to Schoenberg) had left in place. And it was his design that, again in the B section, introduced fantastic, high-register saxophone screams to the world of jazz. The standard expectations of harmony and dissonance, of duration and resolution—all these were reshaped by a compositional imagination that strove to inject elements of rage and dissent that were inaudible in earlier music because they were impermissible. It was no coincidence, then, that the first two chords of "Pithecanthropus" became Mingus's musical signature; the modernist Prometheus was perhaps his favorite alias.

The influence of German composer Richard Strauss on "Pithecanthropus" helps illuminate some of the love-hate tensions that drive this piece. It was in part the example of Strauss that helped bring out the Prometheus in Mingus: the bassist reminisced often about his early love for Strauss's *Death and Transfiguration,* a tone poem depicting an artist who on his deathbed recalls his youthful idealism and achieves a state of spiritual transcendence. As in Strauss's tone poem, Mingus's aim in "Pithecanthropus" was to use the "idea" (the plot of man's evolution and devolution) to inspirit a new musical performance, one whose effects might be incomprehensible within previous musical conventions but were appreciable as expressions of the plot. Like Strauss, Mingus underwrote even his most anarchic exercises in a basic "plot" or musical framework, his compositional agenda authorizing the dissonance to come. And like Strauss again, Mingus used his own tone poem to explore the quasi-religious role assumed by the modern composer, the artist who refused to accept the "realistic" expectations of his own life and the "realist" conventions imposed on his art. Indeed, "Pithecanthropus" would seem to be a wonderful mid-twentieth-century illustration of Strauss's late-nineteenth century motto that "new ideas must search for new forms."[13]

Yet at the same time Mingus added powerful caveats to Strauss's modernist vision: the bassist was divided between his hopes for a forward-thinking art and his doubts about the undertow of "progress." He longed to establish his own mastery but questioned the traditional forms that mastery had taken, haunted by the possibility that every so-called advance was achieved at someone else's expense. In a later interview, Mingus suggested that anyone who "wanted to crown himself the God of music" would indeed "be able to save the world," but then was quick to offer that he had no such ambition: he only aspired to "be the god of [his] own music, not of the whole world's." "Pithecanthropus" shows him dancing on this fine line—imagining a messianic role for music but troubled by the implications of his own adoption of that role. As sociologists like David Riesman speculated about the fate of individual autonomy in America's "outer-directed" society, Mingus reflected on that dilemma from the inside, producing a spectacularly conflicted drama of individual assertion and downfall.[14]

The music of "Pithecanthropus," like its programmatic text, dramatizes both the charisma of the overlord and the power of the masses, translating the struggle between the two into a contest between two types of jazz, the first imbued by sober chromaticism and the second devoted to feverish bursts of collective improvisation. The sobriety marks a first section of sixteen bars, which Mingus described as man's "evolution," while the fever comes through in a second section, a mode of indefinite length meant to dramatize man's "decline" and "destruction."

The "evolution" section balances classical features (a dissonant and slowly ascending melody line, quick crescendos and decrescendos, sudden rests) and jazz features (a swinging 4/4 rhythm section, regular quintet instrumentation). In its lean monumentality, it suggests how Straussian orchestration culturally came to signify primordial ambition: it is a bridge between Strauss's fin-de-siècle work and its famous appropriation by director Stanley Kubrick, who used Strauss's *Also Sprach Zarathrustra* (1895–96) to accompany the first scene in *2001: A Space Odyssey,* where a primitive man takes a tool into his hands. Straussian as it may be, "Pithecanthropus"'s "erect" melody is quite simple—whole notes tied over measures, building up by half steps for the first seven measures, then generally building down by half steps after that. This chromatic melody builds toward a palpable tension over the first eight bars, with the bass exerting a throbbing rhythmic pressure: Mingus simplifies his bass part as he sim-

THE SOUND OF STRUGGLE

plifies the melody, hammering four identical quarter notes on each measure. Refusing to walk his bass, he highlights the unfolding harmonic relationship between the bass part and the unison of the horns. Perhaps most crucially, he signposts moments of greater dissonance with dramatic crescendos that are then broken by abrupt rests. The melody builds to greater tension as we move toward the two crescendos in bars four and eight, with the melody moving from the fifth and major seventh (bars 1 and 2) to the tritone (bars 3, 8) and flat ninth (bars 4, 7). In this way, stark harmonic irresolution is the most dramatic feature of this section's head, whose unhummable melody keeps it at arm's length from the genres of pop and R&B.

The second mode of the piece, meant to dramatize the stirrings of revolt, was at the same time Mingus's first plunge into the idiom that later coalesced under the name of "free jazz." The surge of the masses was programmatically keyed to the simultaneous assertion of several instrumental voices—alto saxophone and tenor sax squealing and riffing on the blues scale while the bass and drums, at their peak, pounded in triplets. This section updated New Orleans principles of collective improvisation by radically simplifying the underlying harmonic framework and radically expanding the range of permissible timbres. While the New Orleans frontline of clarinet, saxophone, and trombone improvised over the chord changes of, say, "Bill Bailey," Mingus's Workshop improvised collectively over a one-chord vamp. This harmonic simplification allowed solo voices (and, in "Pithecanthropus," several solo voices overlapping at once) to pursue their melodic phrases over an indefinite number of bars. At the same time—and this was perhaps the most shocking part of "Pithecanthropus," for all its underlying formal innovation—Jackie McLean played saxophone phrases with a squealing attack, phrases that had little melodic movement but stabbed with great strain at the highest register of the alto sax. His screams were wails of stress, off the map of functional blues harmony, inserted as acts of intentional dissonance. For instance, he repeatedly trilled between two high-register notes but did not seem to follow any pattern of melodic duration (how long the trill lasted), rhythmic placement (where in the measure the trill began or ended), or harmonic shading (where in the F-minor blues mode the trill fits). As a result, McLean's solo work did not model itself after the speaking human voice, but after the shrieking or howling voice—a voice somewhere between a cry of human passion and a baying animal wrath, in that space between the human and animal kingdom where "Pithecanthropus Erectus" happened to fall.

Ultimately, "Pithecanthropus" shows Mingus tipping his hand toward the forces of mass revolt. The Workshop collective is more powerful than any one solo voice, no matter how charismatic. Foreshadowing later free-jazz practice, "Pithecanthropus" demonstrates the absorptive qualities of the jazz idiom—how it might assimilate the most experimental, overreaching techniques of classical music while still plunging ahead into new areas. The first movement's theme is introduced by a unison voicing of alto and tenor, but this unison breaks down quickly as the choruses unfold and the soloists take their turn on the changes. The ominous line that opens "Pithecanthropus" does not shade the reprises of the A mode, where the soloists develop lilting runs on the changes, emphasizing the blues indecision of the third rather than the pure minor triad. In fact, these later reprises, excepting the stylistic singularities of the players, do not sound so different from many other contemporary jazz recordings. The dissonant theme and stop-and-start pacing of the first section is absorbed almost conventionally into the collective contest of the Workshop; the performance, as in so much jazz, takes precedence over the text.

As a larger narrative too, "Pithecanthropus" relates the carnivalesque defeat of the "erect" theme in a battle of musical wills. Mingus did not work toward a Hegelian synthesis (where the first theme might intertwine with the free-jazz practice of the second mode), but forecast the triumph of the second mode entirely. The final minutes of the piece were meant to portray "the final destruction in the manner that a dying organism has one last frantic burst of motion before gasping its last breath"; musically, this plotting meant that the austerity of the first theme was obliterated in a cataclysmic last-minute finale in which bass and drums accelerated their pounding on the triplet rhythm and both horns started interjecting short phrases with clashing tonalities and rhythms. This finale *did* sound entirely different from earlier jazz practice; it suggested that if jazz was to overwhelm the authority of classical music it might do so by enlarging its own ambitions, its own capacity for melodramatic power. Out of the struggle for collective emancipation, new resources would have to be found; out of the contest of musical wills, new kinds of public authority would have to be seized. In the apocalyptic drama of "Pithecanthropus," Mingus suggested that the collective resources of the people—once benighted, here crying loudly—would triumph over the overarching ego of the Great Man. The music also suggested, though, that there would be no prisoners taken, and that the price of such triumph was a turbulent peace. The final moments of "Pithecanthropus"—a whirling saxophone, a trembling bass—were the last heaves of a veiled racial nightmare. Pitted against a master who had assumed the mark of distinction, the Workshop was an avenging public, deforming mastery and taking the laws of musical production into its own very messy hands.

Back in the Bedroom: *The Black Saint and the Sinner Lady*

In his 1963 opus *The Black Saint and the Sinner Lady,* Mingus achieved his most ambitious synthesis of the two musical strains that he had separated and pitted against each other in "Pithecanthropus Erectus." A drama of "soul fusion," *The Black Saint and the Sinner Lady* is remarkable for the richness of its harmonic texture and for the tension that it sustains over a forty-minute series of modal explorations. The chromatic drive in "Pithecanthropus"—expressed by the half-stepping first theme—was taken up throughout the performance by *Black Saint*'s eleven-piece ensemble, which aimed for a complex harmonic blend that invoked the spirit of Duke Ellington. Meanwhile, "Pithecanthropus"'s free explorations around the F-minor mode were extended throughout *Black Saint,* whose every improvisation was built on the Phrygian or Spanish scale. Instead of flipping between chordal and modal improvising for dramatic effect, *Black Saint* sustained modal improvisation throughout but sought to create variety by splicing precomposed themes with a kaleidoscopic range of instrumental backgrounds, textures that the solos spread over and abraded against.

At the same time that Mingus shifted musically, he also shifted in programmatic intent: the cosmic drama of the first man and the masses yielded to a transcendental romance with an explicit liberationist message and racial hue. The title rendered two common blues protagonists into more exalted figures: the do-right man became the black saint; the mistreating lover became the sinner lady. Conceived originally as program music for a collective dance, *The Black Saint and Sinner Lady* was intended to feature dancers in generalized tableaux of communion and conflict, slavery and revolution. A typical woolly cue from Mingus's program notes was the third movement's "(Soul Fusion) Freewoman and Oh, This Freedom's Slave Cries"—a cue that combines the story of love's spiritual journey and the dialectic of emancipation. Love's ethereal dimension was implicit in the "soul fusion," the Mingusian moment of harmonic convergence familiar from *Beneath the Underdog* and "Eclipse." The dialectic of emancipation, meanwhile, came through in "this freedom's slave cries"—a contradictory and poetic phrase that underlines how, for Mingus, it was those deprived of liberty who understood its meaning best. Freedom manifested itself in the struggle against bondage.

The "slave cry of freedom" was a perfect encapsulation of the paradox of the Jazz Workshop, which underwrote the exercise of free expression with the deep constraints of Mingus's compositional frameworks. Moreover, it pointed to how slavery had persisted in the long century after the Emancipation Proclamation: in Mingus's vernacular, "slavery" was a metaphor for the self's limitations as well as a system of overt property relations and noncontractual labor. "We create our own slavery," he said, "but I'm going to get through and find out the kind of man I am—or die." Freedom as a legal status was an empty promise if you were denied freedom of character—or if you denied it to yourself. *The Black Saint*'s final cue—"Of Love, Pain, and Passioned Revolt, then Farewell, My Beloved, 'til It's Freedom Day"—corroborated this balance of rueful pessimism and stoic optimism. Like Duke Ellington's more vaudevillian *My People* (1963) and Martin Luther King's speech at the March on Washington, *The Black Saint* was both a celebration of the centenary of the Emancipation Proclamation and a marker of its unrealized potential.[15]

What made Mingus turn away from first-man apocalypticism and toward emancipatory romancing, and why did he begin grafting modal improvisation onto the less commercially viable form of the big band? The answers lie in part in the shifting context of the music industry at large, which went through a tumultuous process of cultural desegregation between 1956 ("Pithecanthropus") and 1963 *(The Black Saint)*. As historian Brian Ward has noted, whites and blacks in this period began listening to the same artists: rock-and-rollers like Chuck Berry, Elvis Presley, and Fats Domino; vocal groups like the Platters, the Drifters, and the Shirelles; male balladeers like Paul Anka, Sam Cooke, and Brook Benton; and female artists like Leslie Gore and LaVern Baker. The late fifties and early sixties saw unprecedented crossover between white and black music in the new idiom of R&B—a crossover that, Ward argues persuasively, reflected the predominance of the integrationist vision of Martin Luther King, Jr. "In this atmosphere of burgeoning black hopes for meaningful changes in the pattern of racial relations throughout the nation," Ward writes, "integrated airwaves, like integrated charts, integrated concert halls, integrated cinemas, sports facilities, restaurants, stores, universities, and schools, seemed to promise much for a genuinely integrated, egalitarian America." Integration in music, as elsewhere, was a two-way street. Not only did whites thrill (in segregated venues) to the sounds of black artists, but also—a fact seldom noted—black audiences appreciated the softer stirrings of Paul Anka and Connie Francis along with the more impassioned crooning of Sam Cooke.[16]

This integrationist music succeeded, at least in part, by stepping away from the bawdy "plain talk" of the blues and exploring the pink swoon of adolescent romance. Vocal artists like Anka and Cooke "always offered some relief from R&B's dominant vision of opportunistic, predatory, distrustful, and often destructive black sexual politics"; their devotional lyrics "concentrated almost exclusively on evoking a juvenile world of specifically teen trauma and romantic delight." The case of Sam Cooke is a notable example of how the cynicism of earlier blues music was tempered: he took the devotional strains of black church music—so audible in his focus on emotional transport and his melismatic vocal style (the long "you" in "you send me")—and applied them to a newfound, soft-focus "darling." At the same time that Martin Luther King, Jr., was elaborating on the theme of the "beloved community," Sam Cooke and Paul Anka were singing across racial lines about the companionate bond between lovers.[17]

As the mainstream youth market shifted toward this integrationist vision   a kind of vision seen earlier in the Debut Records project of notating jazz rhythms—Mingus headed toward the "blacker" style of soul-jazz. Soul-jazz stressed musical effects identified with African America: emphatic use of open fourths and fifths, rhythmic vamps that shuffled back and forth for extended periods, gospel cries of enthusiasm from the bandstand, melodies that traded the snaky chromatics of bebop for simpler repeated blues statements.[18] Mingus laid claim to being the founder of soul-jazz, the genre's exemplar and hanging judge. He challenged the Cannonball Adderley Quintet's "This Here"—the breakthrough soul-jazz single—as a copy of his own "Better Get It in Your Soul," which had featured rollicking polyrhythms in a gospel 6/4 time. Mingus contrasted Adderley's faddishness with his own lack of irony ("I'm very serious when I do a Gospel piece. When I say 'Amen,' man, I'll be saying 'Amen,' I won't be joking"), and he lambasted "This Here" for its inflexible and inauthentic use of gospel time. "This Here" was "a stiff 3/4, ta-ta-ta, ta-ta-ta!" while "Better Get It in Your Soul" recognized the African principle of "6/4 against 4," polyrhythms evidenced by the way the Workshoppers "clap our hands on the record." Mingus's 1960 critique of Adderley echoed his contemporaneous reproach of the Newport Jazz Festival: that it had confused rock 'n' roll with jazz and that its mass-market success was a sign that the industry manipulated the public to sell fake goods.[19]

Mingus's turn to soul-jazz—broadcast on the albums *Blues and Roots* (1959) and *Oh Yeah* (1961)—brought to the fore a more assertive Mingus, one who joined parables of spiritual ecstasy and sexual warfare and then hitched them to a black identity. Mingus said that *Blues and Roots* came from producer Nesuhi Ertegun's suggestion that "I record an entire blues album in the style of *Haitian Fight Song,* because some people, particularly critics, were saying I didn't swing enough. He wanted to give them a barrage of soul music: churchy, blues, swinging, earthy." This "barrage of soul music" anticipated by several years the vogue of Ray Charles, Stevie Wonder, Martha and the Vandellas, James Brown, and Marvin Gaye: Mingus was creating soul music *avant la lettre,* and his own soul music was eclipsed by the stunning popularity of the later vocalists that fell under the rubric. In many ways, though, Mingus acted as a cultural bridge between earlier R&B and later soul music. His soul-jazz emphasized bare emotional affect and more ambiguously combative sexual relations at a moment when black and white pop centered around earth angels and the harmonious blend of seemingly adolescent voices. For instance, *Oh Yeah*'s "Devil Woman" featured Mingus testifying, in a typically witty blues reversal, "I've gotta get me a devil woman, 'cause angel women don't mean me no good"; meanwhile the music, as Andrew Homzy remarks, drew upon "the rural blues tradition in which vocals, rhythm, and text determine the length of phrases—not simply the pouring of squared-off clichés into a twelve-bar form." Mingus used his Workshop to suggest that love was more struggle and less coziness, and that balladry had to be infused with the plaintive yet teasing language of the blues. With this return to the blues, he thought of himself as reclaiming folk music. He started referring to his new ten-piece edition of the Workshop as "the New Folk Band," and *The Black Saint and the Sinner Lady* album cover proclaimed, in an emendation of Impulse's usual motto, that "The new wave of folk is on Impulse! Ethnic Folk-Dance Music."[20]

The Black Saint and the Sinner Lady stands as Mingus's most extended attempt to revise the blues in two senses, as a narrative of sexual relations and as a musical form. On the level of plot, Mingus reframed the blues through his set of dance cues, which gave a spiritual glow to the struggles of the black saint and sinner lady. Moreover, he psychologized the blues— dressed them up in the trappings of racial alienation and emotional fulfillment—through the set of liner notes that he asked his therapist to write. On the surface, this was a sensational move that capitalized on the confessionalism of Mingus's aesthetic: he had been talking his blues to his therapist, so why not ask the therapist in turn to interpret his musical blues? Clinical psychologist Edmund Pollock responded with a paradigmatic civil rights–era liberal diagnosis, one that emphasized—like the court decision in *Brown v. Board of Education*—the psychological costs of racism. While admitting his lack of musical expertise, Pollock cast the album as one man's struggle for emotional compassion and racial understanding: "[Mingus] feels intensively. He tries to tell people he is in great pain and anguish because he loves. . . . His music is a call for acceptance, respect, love, understanding, fellowship, freedom—a plea to the white man to be aware." In Pollock's view, the blues of "the black saint" were a thin camouflage for Mingus's own existential quest to find love in a world dominated by the color line.[21]

On the level of musical form, Mingus was translating the blues into the context of an expanded, eleven-piece Workshop. He focused on the instrumental timbre of the blues, as familiarized by the Ellington band in their 1920s Cotton Club incarnation and as elaborated through the thirties, forties, and fifties. Like Ellington, Mingus worked with the palette of a large band—an ensemble that included three saxophones, two trumpets, trombone, tuba, piano, guitar, bass, and drums. During the recording session, he set up his reeds in a V formation around a single microphone (baritone and alto close to the mike, tenor at the bottom of the V)—a technique that drew out the overtones in the saxophone blend and thus approximated the full-bodied sound that was a key part of the "Ellington effect."[22] Mingus also recruited individual players to sculpt a more Ellingtonian sound. He enlisted two alums of Ellington's band, trumpeter Rolf Ericson and trombonist Quentin "Butter" Jackson, a striking reversal of his usual preference for younger, up-and-coming musicians in his Workshop. He guided Jackson to play dramatically with a plunger to evoke the intensity of the black pulpit: the score instructs Jackson, for instance, to "rest up butter you preach shortly," and to improvise around a B-flat minor chord with a flatted fifth "and anything elese [sic] you need to preach." Last but not least, Mingus chose Charlie Mariano's alto sax as the leading solo voice in *The Black Saint*. Mariano adopted a liquid, teasing attack that suggested the suavity of Ellington collaborator Johnny Hodges.[23]

While the grit of the blues was identifiably injected into the timbre of the piece, the twelve-bar form of the blues was rejected in favor of an elaborate, forty-minute patchwork of modal exercises that often built around the initial statement of a theme, then crescendoed with the addition of several pieces and a solo voice. Here Mingus was adding to the burgeoning category of jazz experiments with symphony-length form, each of which hung in the shadow of Ellington's *Black, Brown, and Beige* (1941), whose Carnegie Hall premiere had marked jazz's great incursion into the concert hall. By the early 1960s, many postbop artists had followed Ellington's lead in constructing musical suites that were also dramas of racial liberation and struggle: before *The Black Saint*, there was George Russell's *New York, New York* (1959), a hymn to urban possibility that also took a gimlet-eyed view of how the city treated its black artists; Max Roach and Oscar Brown, Jr.'s *Freedom Now Suite* (1960), which traced African-American history from slavery to emancipation; Randy Weston's *Uhuru Africa* (1960), which celebrated African independence movements; and Oliver Nelson's *Afro-American Sketches* (1961), which began by mimicking African drum conversations and then followed African Americans from slavery to the Great Migration north and their "Freedom Dance." The theme of racial liberation—in its grandeur and promise, as well as its underpinnings in violence and struggle—pushed jazz artists toward more ambitious extensions of form; the Tin Pan Alley ballad was incommensurate, even as a palimpsest, with the scale of their aspirations. Mingus upped the ante on these earlier experiments in that he intended *The Black Saint* not as a series of episodes (suite form) but "first of all as a continuous piece." This modernist ambition—the search for an extended form that was an organic, mythic whole—was realized through Mingus's modal directions.[24]

Like Miles Davis in *Kind of Blue* (1959) and John Coltrane in his own quartet work, Mingus embraced modal improvisation, but he made the modal background more volatile and climax-driven: he put its simplicity in the service of excess. For all three artists, modal jazz meant that foreordained chord changes no longer guided improvisation in quick temporal succession. Instead, a mode—or a scale of notes, suggesting many possible chordal combinations—provided an open field for harmonic exploration and rhythmic injection. While Davis emphasized the airy suspension of the mode and Coltrane used the modal impulse to build elaborate harmonic structures over a stripped-down rhythm section, *The Black Saint* emphasized the instability of the improvising in practice. Mingus's modus operandi always laced the mode's repeated elements with harmonic irresolutions and rhythmic surprises (accelerations, displacements of the beat, abrupt endings). His scheme, which intercut precomposed music with lengthy improvised passages, seemed to leave the black saint and the sinner lady in a perpetually tangled power play: they were not hovering in the clouds but tussling on an unstable earth. Like the blues more generally, which specializes in stunning reversals of fortune, Mingus's modal jazz suggested how difficult it was to distinguish between the sinner and the saint, between the earthbound and the transcendent.[25] Each solo voice in *The Black Saint* strained for mastery and authority, but never achieved dominance or resolution. In this context, it is telling that the major solo voice of *The Black Saint*—Charlie Mariano's alto sax—was overdubbed after the fact. Less than soloists in other Mingus works, Mariano's sax does not direct the instrumental background; rather, he seems at the mercy of the Workshop's design, which trades among a repertoire of riffs and has definite preconceived notions, over the course of the forty-minute piece, about when to shift gears in tempo and mood.

One example should suffice to suggest the destabilizing effect of the modal background in *The Black Saint*—how the soloist was made to adapt to Mingus's riffs and orchestrations, which pulled against a more straightforward and "heroic" improvisatory performance. In the last section of the third movement (minutes four to seven), the ensemble builds to a frenzied climax of collective improvisation in *The Black Saint*'s home key of B-flat minor. Partly, this frenzy is a matter of acceleration and heightened volume. Mingus's bass moves first in improvised contrapuntal motives along the minor blues scale, speeds up to walking quarter notes, then ends with a sharp double-time of exploding eighth notes; meanwhile, Dannie Richmond's drums move from a slow-motion military roll to bebop's shimmering high-hat and Elvin Jones–style rolls. The demonic edge to this frenzy is communicated by the background riff that swaps among the saxophones: this four-measure riff repeats for the last three minutes of the piece and is designed to be literally maddening. Rhythmically it could not be simpler (and remember, this riff continues while bass and drums explore polyrhythms galore): the saxes hang on the B-flat for a measure, then move down a half step to A, then swing up to C, then move down a half step to B-natural. The provocation of this riff comes from its marriage of the mechanical and the dissonant. Its mechanical nature is evoked by the holding of each note for the same duration and by the repeated half-step shifts in measures two and four. Its dissonance comes from the two half-step slides out of consonance—in measure two (the major seventh) and measure four (the flat ninth). Sliding around the tonal center of the piece, this demonic riff is inviting and discordant in turn, and utterly, weirdly predictable.

The drama of this section, then, can be understood as the interaction of three characters, who together illustrate the clashing strains within the Workshop: first, the background riff of the brass, which swags up and down mechanically (the demon of preconception); second, the accelerating conspiracy of bass and drums, who push the whole ensemble forward; last, the overdubbed solo of Mariano's alto sax, which throws out repeated hard-boppish blues statements and conveys a sense of individual struggle against preconceived design and execution. Programmatically, this was the section set up as "this freedom's slave cries"; it presented, as well as any passage by the Jazz Workshop, the dynamic of freedom and constraint, impulse and duress.

The last section of the third movement also allows us to see how Mingus's Workshop performed a story of sensuality, how its music recast the drama of the blues into the pursuit of sexual release. In this sense, the music was at odds with Mingus's program notes and his therapist's liner notes, both of which elevated the pursuit of passion into a spiritual quest for soul fusion or a therapeutic quest against the "misunderstanding of self and people."[26] This section carries the unmistakable throb of sensuality: a listener with no concern for the particulars of musicology can hear how these Jazz Workshoppers build toward repeated frenzies of activity (albeit calculated, well-conceived frenzies), then finally climax in a great release.

Here again Ellington seems to have been a key influence: his *Ko-Ko* (1940) also suggested liberation through a climax-driven musical form. Like *The Black Saint, Ko-Ko* was an exposition of how enslaved peoples pursue their freedom through the medium of their bodies—in Ellington's case, by dramatizing the freedom dancers of New Orleans's Congo Square. Musically, *Ko-Ko* has been called a jazz bolero (a reference less to the Spanish bolero than to its most famous appropriation by French composer Maurice Ravel): it hews to a twelve-bar blues form even as it layers on its instruments toward a climax of crashing cymbals and full-throated brass. The climaxing passages in *Black Saint,* as in Ellington's piece, might be understood similarly as jazz boleros: they maintain a fair amount of harmonic stability, via the B-flat-minor scale, even as they gather intensity through the accretion of instruments, the acceleration of tempo, and the raising of volume. Such passages of accumulation dominate *The Black Saint*—in the third through sixth minutes of the second movement, for instance, where a seesaw one-two rhythm speeds up over muted trumpet and trombones; and in the twelfth through seventeenth minutes of the fourth movement, where the Workshop accelerates three times at a breakneck pace away from an original tempo, then throws itself back.[27]

If we follow the therapist's directions and search for instances of "a brooding, moaning intensity about prejudice, hate, and persecution," we will miss how the protest of Mingus's blues—like most blues ever performed—is carried through the romantic story of love's labors. These passages gain their force because they model the Jazz Workshop as a gathering of stormy passion, passion among men, passion that sweeps everyone along with a common velocity and gets them working. Here the Workshop, as a laboratory of the senses, was much more idiosyncratic than *Ko-Ko's* Ellington Orchestra, which maintained a relatively stable tempo and integrated its parts with a kind of New Deal, cooperative camaraderie. Mingus's music, by contrast, seized on errant impulses and made them into central directives. Once *The Black Saint* starts heading into one of its many lengthy *accelerando* passages, for instance, you can be assured that the Workshop will not stop accelerating until it has reached the asymptotic point where acceleration is futile. There is a similar contagiousness to the riffing in *The Black Saint:* the "demonic" riff mentioned earlier is hinted at, played lightly by alto sax, then taken up brazenly by soprano sax and others in an accelerating, unison passage, and it will not stop until it reaches a crisis point of extreme tempo and extreme dissonance. An exemplary Mingus work in this regard, *The Black Saint* consistently understands jazz as the art of extremity, the push toward emotional climax.

Yet Mingus seemed somewhat puzzled about where to go with his

THE SOUND OF STRUGGLE

Workshop once he maxed out with these feverish buildups. Taken as a whole, *The Black Saint* has an air of inconclusive beauty about it: it prizes love's intensity over love's resolution. At the end of the third and fourth movements (roughly halfway through and at the end of the entire piece), after these headstrong climaxes, *The Black Saint* suddenly shifts away from the tonic and into the dominant. Mingus's great sexual summa trails off with dabbling ad lib solos in a suspended key—a kind of refractory period for listener and musicians alike. Mariano's alto sax slashes around in mid-air, out of tempo, alone; without much in the way of grand design, it conventionally opens up the suspense of new possibilities. This is perhaps the final surprise of Mingus's aesthetic of extremity: he consistently deflated the melodramas of his own invention. Rather than closing off his piece with the fervor we come to expect, Mingus ends *The Black Saint* with a wry, open-ended joke. Mariano's solo exploration of the Spanish scale, in a suspended chord, is not only the musical equivalent of a postcoital cigarette; it is also the taste of more music to come, the lone improviser toying with his own suspense.

The Freedom of Ridicule: The Workshop and Political Parody

If Mingus's Workshop could project, with intense melodrama, social conflicts on a transcendent scale ("Pithecanthropus," *The Black Saint*), it could also replace the mask of melodrama with the grinning face of parody. "Original Fables of Faubus" on *Charles Mingus Presents Charles Mingus* (1960) is a shining instance of the sheer lampoonery that could race through Mingus's most obstacle-strewn compositions. An iconic part of Mingus's repertoire, "Fables" demonstrates how he was able to fuse musical and political satire. Like Langston Hughes's *Ask Your Mama* (1961), the piece took on white supremacy not through reasoned debate but through an absurd parody that mimicked, parried, and undercut the irrationality of race hatred. A backhanded tribute to Orval Faubus, the Arkansas governor who had stalled the court-ordered integration of Little Rock schools, Mingus's piece spliced the childhood rituals of the Dozens (modeled through open, mocking warfare among the musicians) with a demanding exercise in chordal and rhythmic improvisation.

The elaborate structure of the piece lands it in the camp of Mingusian extended forms. After an eight-bar opening strut, the first section lasts an asymmetric total of nineteen bars, then is repeated, truncated down to eighteen—at which point we modulate into a sixteen-bar bridge, then swing back into the truncated version of the first section. But the difficulty of the piece is less its unshapeliness than the rhythmic instability of its phrasing. From the introduction, which cross-cuts between two lilting half notes and a roller-coaster run of sixteenth notes, to the chorus, which builds the introductory tumult into a half-stepping series of whole-note end phrases, the piece seems equally poised between tap-dance regularity and jittering bebop. Add to this melodic brew the race-and-stutter accompaniment of Mingus and Richmond on bass and drums, and you begin to sense the utter agility of the piece.[28]

How would this composition cum obstacle course be realized in performance? The answer depended on more than just the inventiveness of the players on a particular day. Mingus's strictures were fed at first through another kind of censorship—the anxieties of a major label record company with distribution in the South. In "Fables"'s initial recording on *Mingus Ah Um* for Columbia in 1959, Mingus was forced to excise the lyrics attacking Faubus, and the finished piece is decorously witty, even wry. The opening blare of the horns is exact in its punctuation, the drums are emphatic but not rattled, and the bass is nimble but not hopping. The tenor of the recording lets you rest assured that the solo horns would never, ever honk. On the bridge of the piece, for instance, John Handy turns the lead melody into a teasing solo—legato and loping, with a tasteful lilt to the edgy ninth. Likewise, you can count on the Mingus-Richmond rhythm section to shift gears without grinding them. Although Mingus and Richmond run a shuffle beat under most of the solos, their stop-start rhythm segues smoothly into their other patterns, whether double time or regular walking. The whole performance is button-down, professional—Mingus playing a society gig, with aplomb but no hilarity.

We might gather much from the performance of the alternative "Original Fables of Faubus" simply by examining the cover of the record on which it first appeared. On the cover of *Charles Mingus Presents Charles Mingus,* the composer-bassist has no buttons to button. He is sitting at a piano, slightly slumped, hands at his side, wearing a pullover top with embroidered stitching. His bass is also slightly slumped, unmanned and laid in soft focus against the wall. Meanwhile, the reams of sheet music on the piano he faces are crumpled on the edges and festooned with notes, worked over. We seem to have eavesdropped on a moment of compositional meditation. Mingus is staring away from the camera, his eyes half shut and his mouth half open, as if caught unawares. Perhaps our man in jazz has not even had time to primp this morning: his close-cropped hair and pencil-thin moustache are set off by a frizzy goatee, which clumps to his neck, exaggerating its thickness. There is an internal tension in the cover that is captivating: it seems to mythologize Mingus as a heroic, one-man industry *(Charles Mingus Presents Charles Mingus)* at the same time that it deflates him into a man of regular fashion, caught off-guard in the humdrum, slightly slouchy act of imagination. The modernist Prometheus is here as earthbound as the rest of us.

In this "Fables of Faubus," the atmosphere has been seeded with hilarity of a peculiarly political sort—nonsensicality that is adamant in conviction. The lyrics have been recovered from major-label oblivion, and they begin with a bite that admits none of their later cartoonishness. "Oh Lord, don't let them shoot us. Oh Lord, don't let them stab us": so Mingus sings in the introductory passage, his voice catching on "stab." Then the shuffle beat kicks in, and we move to a jauntier, less foreboding rhythm. "Name me someone who's ridiculous," says Mingus in a half-singsong lilt, his syllables coinciding with the instrumental signature. Over the repeated signature, Richmond answers "Governor FAWW-bus" with a drawl that can only be called delicious; he is savoring the ridiculousness of the incantation, and—more—he is announcing it to the world, that "Faubus" is a name to stand in high mockery on the airwaves. So Mingus follows up his first question with another, chanted in much the same fashion: "Why is he so sick and ridiculous?" And Richmond answers, "Because he won't permit integrated schools—so he's a fool": just the kind of playground rhyme that Faubus the educational charlatan deserves.

The tenor of the composition has been loosened ineradicably, not only because Mingus and Richmond are trading one-liners with obvious glee, but also because the instrumentation has been stripped to a bare-bones quartet. (In fact, Mingus and Richmond are the only folks shouting because they are the only musicians who *can* shout: saxophonist Eric Dolphy and trumpeter Ted Curson have their lips fastened to their mouthpieces.) In the transition from *Ah Um*'s septet to this arrangement, the harmonic blend has been coarsened and diffused: the buttery horns of the earlier recording are now being spread incredibly thin, and the high register of the tune suddenly seems sparsely populated. The doubled-over horn parts are being played by a single soloist, allowing the rhythm section more weight in the final balance; and, even more striking, Dolphy and Curson are roughening the edges of their notes, so that their blend seems stacked but not quite coincident. When they collaborate on the rattling series of sixteen eighth notes at the end of the bridge, they sound nothing like the famous Parker-Gillespie bebop heads, which are feats of leaping, synchronous melodicism. Instead, at this precious moment of harmonic buildup, they sound slightly staggered, halfway demonic, and thoroughly mechanical, if by "mechanical" we understand that machines are erratically systematic.

The phrase simply pivots between two notes, eight times in a row, on the flatted fifth—a freaky repetition that throws off the song's tonal center with every half beat.

So the mood is delirious and loose, and the political denunciations continue to tumble from the lips of Mingus and Richmond. Curson is blurting out a solo that hitches, stumbles, and shambles forward at breakneck speed, while Mingus and Richmond yell more schoolyard taunts: "Boo! Nazi Fascist Supremists!" (Dolphy smears and cuts out) "Boo! Ku Klux Klan!" (Dolphy snags and weeps). And Mingus and Richmond end with a slogan that could have been copped from a high-school football cheerleading squad, if its reference to indoctrination didn't rankle so: "Two, four, six, eight, they brainwash and teach you hate." Here the two bandmates have taken the chant of the fiercest segregationists—"Two, four, six, eight, we don't want to integrate"—and have hurled it back in the segregationists' faces. The original taunt had been performed in Little Rock during the first tense days of integrating the high school, chanted with vicious enthusiasm by whites while the high school's cheerleading squad, in their prim uniforms, set the rhythm.[29] Just as the segregationists had taken school-yard rhymes and planted them into their political culture, so Mingus was willing to ventriloquize the playground in the musical culture of his workshop. If the segregationists had decided to mine the rhetorical register of the schoolyard—a register of dumb and cruel logic—Mingus would deal back in kind: he would use his music partly as a playground for theatrical idiocy, and he would do so with the knowingness that comes from absorbing the form and switching the message.

In his liberational musings Mingus was eminently capable of high-flown lyricism (witness his poem "Freedom," which yearns for a "day when burning crosses will not be mere child's play, / But a madman in his most incandescent bloom"). He was also capable of speechifying ad infinitum, with a devious fluency that entranced his audiences and flummoxed his interviewers. But "Fables of Faubus" astounds the listener with another characteristic, one that Mingus didn't publicize with nearly the success of his rowdiness: his self-mockery. Like his rowdiness, his self-mockery could be brutalizing, but it wounded the most unexpected targets—in this case, not Mingus himself, but Governor Faubus and his cronies. Mingus understood that a slap and tickle could do as much damage as a knife in the back if it was accompanied by the appropriate soundtrack. Thus would "Fables of Faubus" strike out at the segregationists: not by honoring them with a considered debate, but by refusing to take them seriously; not by blinding them with virtuosity (the solution of bebop), but by stumping them with a professionalism so solid that it knew the virtues of the amateur.

"Fables of Faubus" parodies the formalities of segregation by sacrificing—and so strengthening—its own internal formalities. The rhythm section cuts so much slack, opens up so much space for the other soloists, that we may not notice that Mingus and Richmond, in addition to carrying all the vocal duties, are also ferociously cracking the whip. In this version, their shuffle-step doesn't segue into double-time; it explodes onto the newfound pulse. And on the harmonic pileup that ends the second verse and every subsequent run-through of the verse in the song's form, they act with a kind of mercilessness: suddenly switching from double-time to a stiff series of dotted accents, they stun the beat and pull the sonic carpet out from underneath the horns. What "Faubus" loses in smoothness, it gains in volatility: perhaps this belabors the obvious. But "Faubus" also argues, with a modernist faith in the power of art to model productive acts of rupture, that volatility is not simply the upshot of outrage. It is a virtue born out of the casual certainty that the musical mind can outstrip its audience and force it to keep up, that things are going to change—and fast.

PART FOUR

Freedom's Saint

7

THE SERIOUS SIDE
OF HARD BOP

John Coltrane's Early
Dramas of Deliverance

Here are two small histories of a song becoming something unexpected, stories that suggest how John Coltrane established jazz as music of black awakening:

In 1946, Charlie Parker recorded Dizzy Gillespie's "A Night in Tunisia," a bop landmark whose title referred to the battles in North Africa between the Allies and the Axis during World War II. Fourteen years later, after meeting a group of Liberians at a nightclub performance, Coltrane composed and recorded "Liberia"—a piece of music clearly inspired by Parker's "Tunisia," with its echo of "Tunisia"'s celebrated flat-fifth cadence and virtuoso break. But just as Coltrane moved his country of inspiration down to the western coast of Africa, so did "Liberia" announce a new black aesthetic, one that aimed to convey the intensity of freedom in a world where it was up for grabs. The cultural roots of blackness were ripe for rediscovery, a new world coming into being in the reinvented image of a much older one, and Coltrane's imagination was working excitedly in the service of this project, which also meant reevaluating bebop and its assumptions about musical irony, technical ingenuity, and ensemble interplay. Between Parker's "Tunisia" and Coltrane's "Liberia," bebop traveled to the roots-conscious music of hard bop.[1]

In 1958, Cuban bandleader and percussionist Mongo Santamaría recorded "Afro Blue," a percussive and hypnotic invocation of an African-inspirited blues world. The song sparked countless cover versions that paid tribute to its flexible, almost diagrammatic form. Songster Oscar Brown, Jr. —clever, politically progressive, and bound for a quick if fleeting rise to national celebrity—penned lyrics remaking "Afro Blue" as a praise-song of black-on-black love, which he and Abbey Lincoln recorded in two divergent interpretations. Then in 1963, Coltrane's quartet adopted "Afro Blue" as one of its signature pieces, a vehicle for the dervish-like ruminations of Coltrane's soprano saxophone. In all these versions, "Afro Blue" remained an anthem of a burgeoning blues aesthetic, but in the space of five years it was also transformed—from a Cuban-flavored dance piece to a gentle love song, and then to a commanding and thunderous ritual of spiritual extension.[2]

These two microhistories of how one song became another allow us to explore with some subtlety the innovations of Coltrane and his music. A common theme in writings on Coltrane is that he helped jazz open up into a kind of world music and that this new fusion responded to a global surge of black consciousness and solidarity, the movements of liberation that connected Afro-America to the black communities of Brazil, South Africa, the Congo, and many other nations.[3] The late 1950s and early 1960s were, as historian Robin D. G. Kelley points out, "*the* revolutionary moment . . . the age of nationalist revolt, African independence, the first gathering of non-aligned nations in Bandung, Indonesia, the creation of the Organization of African Unity." Seventeen new African nations entered the United Nations in 1960, the year Coltrane recorded "Liberia." The saxophonist was framing his music as an act of transnational imagination at the moment when other black Americans, as historians Brenda Plummer and Penny von Eschen note, were looking beyond the United States and grappling with the promise of national liberation in a variety of ways. The NAACP, for instance, failed to support the Mau Mau uprising in Kenya or the African National Congress in South Africa; meanwhile, black nationalists viewed Africa and the "Third World" more generally as an example of successful revolutionary practice. Many American blacks, black nationalists or not, saw the "Third World" as an important bargaining chip in the struggle to galvanize the civil rights revolution at home. The United States, it was argued, would never recruit this group of nations to the "Free World" if the South remained an enclave of legal white supremacy and if the North deprived its black citizens of basic economic and social opportunities.[4]

This dialogue with the Third World can be heard in Coltrane's music and is signposted in such Coltrane titles as "Africa," "Dahomey Dance," and "India."[5] But what, exactly, distinguished Coltrane's music from, say,

Humble pilgrim: Saxophonist John Coltrane is shown here around 1964 in a customary pose—locked in a dead heat with his instrument, swept up in a fever of effort. A plaque at his Hamlet, North Carolina, birthplace commemorates him as a "jazz messiah." (Courtesy of Michael Ochs Archives)

the bebop of the World War II period, which was itself tied to a moment of cultural turbulence and racial self-assertion? What musical techniques or materials marked its portrayal of Africa, and what were the principles behind this new transatlantic aesthetic, whose novelty was advertised as a return to basics?

The answer to all these questions begins in Coltrane's refusal of bebop's ironic pose. Amiri Baraka called Coltrane "the heaviest spirit," and it was this heaviness—the intensity and inwardness that Coltrane brewed into a strangely weighty form of spirituality—that distinguishes Coltrane's music.[6] Starting with his famous conversion experience in 1957, Coltrane sought to purify his life of the corrupting influences of drugs and alcohol; he became the jazz scene's most prominent example of the straight life, its most notable convert to the ethics of sincerity under pressure. In a world where "Jazz Is My Religion," as black poet Ted Joans wrote, Coltrane was acclaimed as "the great Pope." Unlike Mingus and almost every other jazz artist of the period, Coltrane achieved his prominence without the usual sorts of celebrity self-promotion: he rarely spoke in detail of his personal life, and almost every friend and acquaintance was struck by the degree of his self-effacement. Yet his music testified loudly to his story of conversion, fueling an aesthetics of honesty in extremis, and in this way he pulled jazz away from the ironic hipsterism that infused bebop and much jazz before 1960. Coltrane discovered and refined a style that he imprinted as his own, a style whose authority seemed purchased through the publicly performed anguish of his concerts and recordings. He pursued freedom not for the hell of it, but for the heaven of it—and he did so by creating settings of musical purgatory that forced him to confront his own limits. His classic quartet thrived by inventing and reinventing a thrashing drama of confusion and self-purification, errancy and ultimate reward.[7]

Redefining Virtuosity: From Tunisia to Liberia

To understand Coltrane's achievement—both how he carried forward the aesthetic of 1940s bebop and how he created a new sound in jazz—we need to take a detour through the world of bebop, and more specifically, through the artistic legacy of Charlie Parker, the saxophonist who served as an icon of the bebop style and who put his unmistakably personal stamp on the underground and commercial cultures of postwar jazz. Their nicknames—Bird and Trane—spoke to the difference between their two styles: Parker's alto darted and flitted with maddening evasiveness and tantalizing grace, while Coltrane's tenor had a straight-ahead, demonic energy that was nearly industrial in strength. You needed a watchful eye to go "Chasin' the Bird," in the words of a postwar Parker piece; but if you hoped to succeed in "Chasin' the Trane," as Coltrane's most famous improvisation was titled in a loving echo, you needed strong legs and perhaps an even stronger heart.

Behind these widely divergent styles was a similarly legendary devotion to craft. Both Parker and Coltrane were famous for feverish acts of woodshedding and for a quasi-religious devotion to their instrument that enabled them to approach escape velocity on up-tempo numbers. Anecdotes suggest the fuller story: Parker supposedly developed the rudiments of his style in the Ozarks during the summer of 1937 when, in the off-hours from his gig playing country resorts, he studied the recorded solos of Lester Young until he could replicate them note for note. He emerged from his mountain summer ready to hold his own in Jay McShann's swing big band—and, eventually, to pioneer his own style.[8] Coltrane, meanwhile, was so self-effacing that much of his friends' reminiscences about his early career center around his intimate relationship to the saxophone. At Granoff Studios in Philadelphia, where he took a full course of music theory and lessons funded by the GI Bill, Coltrane would arrive early in the morning and stay through the evening. As the evening wore on, he would practice but not blow into the instrument so that he could quicken his reflexes without waking his neighbors. Coltrane was renowned not only for practicing endlessly, but also for selecting unorthodox exercises to keep up his musical chops. He went through the familiar bebop practice routines—running blues changes in every key, for instance—but he also learned much from traditional classical exercises, which produced unforeseen difficulties, and unforeseen technical resources, when transposed from piano to saxophone. He borrowed books of Hanon and Czerny exercises from a band pianist, stunning his fellow musicians as he forced his fingers to navigate arpeggios, trills, and wide leaps in melody. Likewise, he absorbed exotic melodies through his harmony teacher at Granoff, who introduced world-music scales and ultrachromatic scales of his own invention. Coltrane, more than almost any other musician, formed his style through his practice regimen. His newly discovered scales were incorporated, much like the formula-driven riffing of the blues in other genres of jazz, into his solos with considerable originality but little guile.[9]

But while Parker and Coltrane were both profoundly devoted to discovering new ways of playing their instruments, their virtuosity found quite different outlets in the culture at large. Parker's version of "A Night in Tunisia" was recorded at the transitional moment when the swing big band yielded to the bebop small group, and it reflects its joint heritage, suggesting both the meticulous togetherness that bebop inherited from swing arrangements and the freedom, eccentricity, and irony that was novel in bebop. The trace of a big band arrangement comes through in the terraced way the different instruments are layered together, where every instrument takes on its own compatible and successive role in the ensemble. Guitar and bass begin with a vamp—a short, repeated phrase—which in this case oscillates between a measure of E-flat and another of D minor; then the alto and tenor saxophones enter with a syncopated but regular riff; then the trumpet comes in with the lead melody. Each instrument has its well-defined place, its own register and rhythmic groove. In this showcase of camaraderie, this machine of seven interlocking parts, Parker seems to be participating in a miniature version of a big band—not surprising, given that "A Night in Tunisia" began as a Dizzy Gillespie full orchestra score, sold to the Earl Hines and Boyd Raeburn bands.[10]

Musical wit reinforces, rather than undermines, the tightness of the interplay. To take merely the opening section: the saxophones play a syncopated figure with a warm attack, one that emphasizes the offbeats against the regularity of the vamp. In a musical effect akin to a sonic illusion, the saxophones actually move up rather than down with the vamp—yet we hear them as highlighting the vamp's harmonic relationship. The vamp, percussively sliding down, and the riff, breathily sliding up, make a persuasive match. We are only a few seconds into the song—we haven't even arrived at the bright trumpet "head," which stitches together triplet and eighth-note figures, flirting with the tritone so that it acts as both an ornamental passing note and an integral pivot for the melody—and yet we feel assured that the performance will balance surprise and single-mindedness, ingenuity and solid craft. And this sense of wit will proceed to infuse the performance that consumes the next three minutes, from such small details as the celebrated flat-fourth figure and Parker's famous four-bar instrumental break to larger elements such as the construction of the solos of Parker (frenetically aloof), trumpeter Miles Davis (suavely brittle), and tenor saxophonist Lucky Thompson (heatedly gonzo).

The land of "Tunisia," as it is expressed in Parker's version, is intriguing yet elusive, inviting yet askew—a foreign musical territory that the musicians prefer to evoke rather than inhabit fully. This sense of exotica is a complicated phenomenon to isolate, but we might notice two distancing effects: first, the sinuous trumpet head, whose intervals suggest a folk scale rarely used in jazz before "Tunisia" and whose accents suggest a nervous explosion of rhythm; and second, Parker's vibratoless tone, which gives his virtuosity a deadpan slyness, an ironic qualification of the emotions behind such a flood of expressivity.

The head evolved out of Gillespie's exploration of new harmonic values, a hallmark of his bebop compositions. Gillespie recalled how "Tunisia" took shape: "I sat down at the piano to improvise some chord changes. Actually, they were thirteenth chords—A-thirteenth resolving to D minor. I looked at the notes of the chords as I played the progression and noticed that they formed a melody." Gillespie's explanation, while it suggests the theoretical energies behind bebop, undersells quite a bit of his composition's magic. First, he downplays the buoyancy of the melody's rhythms. The opening phrase builds from a rushed triplet to a longer held note, then pivots quickly back to a resolution, and this kind of jittering speed—stop-and start but always arriving on schedule—also enlivens the famous cadence that clips off the first section of the piece. Moreover, this buoyancy is given new coloration by the melody's frequent use of the tritone, or flat fifth, both as a passing note and as a key clashing moment of irresolution for the melody in the cadence. Finally, the rhythms of the drums highlight the drama of the head, its cycle of tension and release: the drummer fills in with a propulsive Latin triplet figure as long as the piece stays on its harmonically inconclusive vamp, then telegraphs the cadence with a snare roll and a crash of his cymbals. Rhythm, harmony, accompaniment—all bring into focus Gillespie's act of musical portraiture: Tunisia is a place where complication is handled with ease and considerable verve.[11]

While Gillespie's composition establishes certain qualities of ebullience, drive, and sophistication, Parker toys with these qualities as he teases with the composition itself—affirming the value of virtuosity under duress, but refusing to imbue his playing with straightforward, easily legible emotion. Scott DeVeaux has commented on Parker's irony, comparing the arc and dynamics of his solos—finely but unpredictably terraced, his ghosted notes in dialogue with more loudly articulated phrases—with the much more predictable virtuosity of swing titan Coleman Hawkins, whose solos build from simplicity to complication, levity to intensity, tension to release. Parker is an emotional sphinx—which is not to say that his playing lacks poignancy, just that he refrains from those gestures that made earlier alto players, like Johnny Hodges from Duke Ellington's band, into models of inviting suavity. Hodges typically infused his performances with the quivering warmth of vibrato, which intimated both vulnerability and passion. Parker, by contrast, prefers to speak in different musical languages and emotional registers in quick succession: thus his love of musical quotation—non sequitur made logical—and his amazing ability to pluck a catchy blues riff out of a flurry of more chromatic formulas.[12]

Parker's coolness in "Tunisia" comes through most clearly in the speed of his playing and its lack of vibrato—two effects that are obviously related, since it is impossible to warm into a note if it lasts a mere fraction of

Charlie Parker's four-bar break from "A Night in Tunisia," 1946. (Courtesy of Thomas Owens)

a second before leading into another. His four-bar break, a bebop touchstone, is a perfect instance of this kind of virtuosity, a winning admixture of nonchalance and deadpan wit (see figure). During the recording session, the rhythmic ingenuity of this break so confounded Parker's fellow musicians that the timekeeping of the ensemble fell apart several times, but now we hear a musician marvelously in sync with his own double-jointed sense of time. Without taking a breath, Parker runs through a phrase composed mostly of sixteenth notes, with two extra-quick triplets at pivotal moments when the melody reverses direction (measures 2 and 4). Parker never clinches a run when it might have been predictable—for example, at the end of a bar—and we can hear why, at the recording session, Miles Davis eventually had to agree to count the bars and conduct. Parker's melody seems to suspend the usual rules of time, the tacit metronome marking each measure, in favor of an unpredictably individual sense of the moment.[13]

As in "Tunisia" more generally, this rhythmic fluidity is enlivened with a sense of harmonic exploration. The turnaround is a break in F major, but Parker turns to many notes outside the blues scale, teasing with accidentals that always manage to resolve to more stable tones. Even when Parker seems to skirt this rule at the very end of his break, resolving on the interval of the seventh, we quickly see that he has outwitted us with an ironic punch: the seventh of the break's F chord is an E-flat—the harmonic center of "Tunisia" and the beginning note of its opening vamp. We arrive, marvelously, full circle. Yet the deeper marvel of Parker's playing is that it is both flag-waving and evasive at the same time, supremely intelligent yet strangely dispossessed: his vibratoless timbre gives his fluidity a brittle, almost inhuman tone, what novelist Ralph Ellison called "a sound of amateurish ineffectuality." We can almost forget that there is a human breath behind this flurry of notes because it is so disguised, the fact of breath rather than the gesture of breathiness. While most listeners can agree that the force of Parker's break comes through its acrobatic virtuosity, its emotional content remains impenetrable, or at least masked by calculation and artifice. Having opted out of swing music's conventional means of seduction, its vocabulary of smooth phrases sung in inviting tones, Parker aims to intrigue rather than to charm.[14]

The compelling qualities of Parker's "Tunisia"—its well-managed teamwork, its crafty exotica, its pursuit of virtuosity without self-disclosure—are thrown in relief by John Coltrane's "Liberia," which uses "Tunisia" as its blueprint but radically recasts it. Democratic teamwork is replaced by the rule of friction and amplification: "Liberia"'s musicians rub, strike, and hammer together, rather than keep to their well-defined place. If "Tunisia" suggests an exotic locale where the boppers could divert themselves, "Liberia" is a purgatory that the Coltrane quartet is made to inhabit. And the irony of "Tunisia"—irony expressed in the arrangement's sly interplay, as well as in the evasiveness of Parker's playing—is foreign to "Liberia." Instead, Coltrane creates a blues drama of self-expression and self-questioning, a sermon of hollers, cries, and screeches that also engages the rest of his quartet in a project of spiritual outreach.

Coltrane recorded "Liberia" in October 1960 at a moment of creative efflorescence when he had graduated from being an anonymous, then a prominent sideman, and could front his own band. He had scuffled for nine years (1946–1955) in various bands big and small—in the blues-heavy band of Eddie "Cleanhead" Vinson; in the version of Dizzy Gillespie's big band (1949–1950) that struggled to keep afloat by highlighting the danceability of its complex music; in the band of R&B star Earl Bostic, whose flamboyant saxophone style probably tipped Coltrane to explore the technique of circular breathing and to push his instrument's high range; and in many more short-lived gigs too, with blues impresarios Bullmoose Jackson and King Kolax, show band Daisy Mae and the Hep Cats, Ellington altoist Johnny Hodges, and organ superstar-to-be Jimmy Smith.[15]

After those years of scuffling and obscurity, he had risen quickly as a tenor soloist, soaking up the influence of Thelonius Monk in a celebrated 1957 engagement at the Five Spot and, most crucially, collaborating in one of jazz's most famous bands, the Miles Davis quintets of 1955–1960. Much of postwar jazz history has been written, with good reason, through the shifting sound of these Davis bands. The 1955 quintet was key in pioneering the hard bop style: favoring straight-ahead blowing sessions over complicated arrangements or experiments in contrapuntal harmony; returning to the stark economy of the blues but invigorating these roots through a more aggressive rhythm section; preferring darker settings in a minor mode; and developing new kinds of tension between rhythm section and soloist—destabilizing, for instance, the upbeat in up-tempo numbers by seeming to perform solos too slow (Davis) or too fast (Coltrane).

In 1959, the Davis band again set a new trend for jazz groups of its generation, bringing the term "modal jazz" firmly into the critical lexicon. Just as Coltrane was emerging as a recording session leader with his *Giant Steps,* the Davis outfit was hitting a new stride with *Kind of Blue,* a blowing session that reduced traces of sonic clutter in pursuit of streamlined introspection and open-ended interplay. Much could be said (and has been) about the innovations of *Kind of Blue,* and its influence on jazz has been incalculable. Davis developed a new sort of blues, a more abstract-sounding blues that did not force its musicians to meet the usual deadlines for chordal improvising. Instead of following the conventional "story" of the twelve-bar blues stanza (I–IV–V), the improvisers were told simply to improvise on a scale—and this static form gave the feeling of a harmonic force field, more meditative and open to individual exploration. Jazz musicians had always been improvising, explicitly or not, on a set of scales, but modal jazz radically slowed down the pace at which these scales shifted, with the net result that improvisers were suspended above a more stable harmonic background. Critic Francis Davis, noting the Zen-like balance between collective space and individual grooving on *Kind of Blue's* "So What," has memorably called the piece "the sound of one finger snapping."[16]

Coltrane toured with Davis for a year after *Kind of Blue,* but in the spring of 1960, he left the Davis band to lead his own group for the first time. By the fall, after a long-standing gig at the Jazz Gallery and an abbreviated national tour, Coltrane's new sound had coalesced around two new collaborators: pianist McCoy Tyner and drummer Elvin Jones, cornerstone members of what became his "classic" quartet. Intensely productive as a composer now that he was on his own, Coltrane introduced a host of new pieces and reinvented standard tunes so that they bore the imprint of his new style, which, like the Davis band in "So What," eschewed quick chord changes in favor of bass-piano vamps that gave new room to the soloist. When Coltrane finally entered the recording studio with this new group in October 1960, he was ready to give birth to a new sound, and the recorded output for that single week of studio work is staggering: the albums *My Favorite Things,* featuring Coltrane's hit version of the title piece, as well as "Summertime"; *Coltrane Plays the Blues,* featuring "Mr. Syms" and "Blues to You"; and *Coltrane's Sound,* unreleased until 1964, but featuring the famous compositions "Central Park West" and "Equinox," as well as his modal arrangement of that chestnut of harmonic complication, "Body and

Soul." He found his new sound in part by rewriting the anthems of bebop: Tadd Dameron's "Hot House" was recast as Coltrane's "Fifth House," Charlie Parker's "Confirmation" as "26–2," "How High the Moon" as "Satellite," and "A Night in Tunisia" as "Liberia."[17]

"Liberia" is far from the most famous of Coltrane's 1960 recordings, but it suggests how he sought to reinvent the jazz tradition, appropriating older materials in a way that departed from the ground rules of bebop. Beboppers "signified" with great cleverness on their material, stealing the harmonic blueprint of Tin Pan Alley standards while ingeniously hiding their source material through radically altered melodies and intense rhythmic flexibility. In bop, the older Tin Pan Alley chord patterns serve as the basic framework for a new head, which opens and closes the piece, and for a souped-up improvisation, which ranges in between. To take three famous cases from a repertoire of hundreds: Parker's "Ornithology" reworks "How High the Moon," his "Bird of Paradise" takes on the changes of "All the Things You Are," and his "Ko Ko" accelerates the pace of "Cherokee" while keeping its underlying chords intact.

The bebop head, which became the signature of the genre, fulfilled the modernist imperative of defamiliarization: it announced that the music to come was going to keep the listener from lapsing into comfort and routine. As Scott DeVeaux explains, "The effect of the bebop head does not lie in ingenuity of orchestration. It is simply a melody played in bare octaves or unison by available melody instruments. . . . The bebop head differs from the Swing Era riff in its unpredictability. Within its brief confines, bop musicians concentrated all that was most novel and disorienting in their musical language. By placing it *first*—before the listener could situate the improvisation within some recognizable context—the beboppers made it impossible to hear their music as a version, a 'jazzing,' of some other repertory."[18]

Coltrane did not want to out-bebop bebop: his "Liberia" does not try to destabilize, or render unrecognizable, its "Night in Tunisia" blueprint. While bebop heads were unpredictable, shooting off at odd angles, Coltrane's "Liberia" takes "Tunisia" and radically simplifies its melodic scaffolding. The exotic trumpet melody is replaced, in Coltrane's version, by the most elemental of blues riffs, the tracing of the minor third. The famous "Tunisia" cadence, whose flatted fifths were shorthand for bebop's complex vocabulary of harmonic innovation, is pared down to a single distinguishing feature. "Tunisia" pivots on the flatted fifth in two successive chords; Coltrane keeps only the first flatted fifth in his cadence, so that it sounds closer to a single blue note than a broader principle of melodic inclusion. Coltrane's urge to simplify extends beyond the rewriting of the lead melody and toward the harmonic scheme of the whole piece. In contrast to the beboppers, who often added chromatic passing chords to simpler harmonic frameworks, enriching Tin Pan Alley's tonal palette, Coltrane takes "Tunisia" and eliminates much of its harmonic movement. For instance, whereas the earlier opening vamp pivots between E-flat and D minor, "Liberia" settles in a static minor mode; and whereas the bass suggests shifting keys in "Tunisia"'s coda, "Liberia"'s bass hammers repeatedly on a single note in the parallel section. More generally, "Tunisia"'s ensemble dances together through its chord changes; "Liberia," built on pedal points, prefers a much more harmonically static bass line, a stable center of gravity that every instrument pulls toward and away from.

These acts of simplification give us another clue why this kind of hard bop can be heard, quite fairly, as "roots music"—and why Coltrane seemed to exemplify a new globally aware jazz. When beboppers stripped a Tin Pan Alley composition down to its harmonic outline, they proceeded to make it unrecognizable, a ghost visible only to the musically initiate. When Coltrane, meanwhile, reduced "Tunisia" to its basics, he did so not to claim a higher originality but to reveal an even more direct and powerful drama of energy within the original piece, a charismatic drama that had been hidden by its earlier scaffold of sophistication. Coltrane dug into "Tunisia" to rewrite it as a song of spiritual declamation, the preaching of a particularly bracing sermon. In this way, he seemed to have unearthed old roots even as he built his own new forms: "Liberia" was one of Coltrane's first explicit experiments in writing world music of his own, music that transformed pop song form into the basis of ritual. Before "Liberia," he had interpreted several compositions of his contemporaries—"Dial Africa," "Oomba," "Gold Coast," "Tanganyika Strut," "Dakar," and "Bakai"—that invoke Africa through ornamental tone colors and rhythms. But "Liberia" marked the beginning of a new interest on Coltrane's part to create a music of global spiritual renewal, where his more static modal forms might stretch a sense of time just as religious rituals follow the workings of the spirit and aim to escape the worldly tickings of a clock. The modular "Liberia" would lead, in the next few years, to more ample dramas of spiritual extension, many of which fill up an entire side of an album: the ominous flamenco of "Olé," the joyous "Dahomey Dance," the brass extravaganza of "Africa," the vamp-driven "India," the soprano-sax ecstasy of "Afro Blue," and many more.[19]

How does Coltrane create such a sense of spiritual drama in the performance itself? His first move is to install himself at the head of the pulpit. "Liberia," unlike "Tunisia," is not centrally about teamwork, even though Coltrane's rhythm section must count as one of the most telepathic in the history of jazz. It begins with Coltrane announcing his favorite interval, the minor third, in a free and declamatory manner. The riff is so basic, so elemental a part of the public domain, that it could be repeated in another context and would not be considered a quotation. (In fact, Coltrane begins "Equinox," from the same session as "Liberia," and *Giant Steps*'s "Cousin Mary" with a version of the same minor riff.) But although the riff is unexceptional, it is also daringly out front: while "Tunisia" begins with a terraced introduction of the different ensemble parts, "Liberia" is dominated by the voice of Coltrane, who seems to instigate everything that follows. The piano, bass, and drums are recessed, and there are no melodies juxtaposed contrapuntally with Coltrane's. McCoy Tyner is comping as usual with abstract quartal chords, filling in the middle register but without much in the way of predictable voice-leading; Elvin Jones is rolling on his snare and crashing on his cymbals in free time, lending an air of high drama to the proceedings. Above all, we are hearing a recitative: Coltrane melodically above his fellow musicians—and louder too—rapt in the workings of his own logic, articulating the call in a dialogue of call and response.

Out of this opening moment, "Liberia" develops into a piece energetic yet deeply serious, as if Coltrane and his quartet were working with redoubled effort to strip away all traces of lightheartedness from "Tunisia"'s genre of exotic portraiture. Partly this seriousness comes from the dramatic arc of the composition, which relies on pedal points in the bass to create an almost unbearable tension, a tension resolved in paradoxical fashion—by moving onto another taut pedal point. In these tense passages, Coltrane seems to have ingeniously stretched the "Tunisia" cadence—a quick one-measure turnaround on the standard ii–V–i changes—to tremendous length, until it occupies the remainder of the song's form. After the opening recitative in D minor, he transposes his minor blues cry into the upper register of his saxophone, hanging on the dissonant flat ninth of a C-seventh chord. The bass, however, hangs on the third as Coltrane states his blues riff four times and as Elvin Jones propels the quartet forward with Latin triplet rhythms.

Snapping out of this pedal point, the quartet moves back to the original D minor blues, but the bass, surprisingly, does not return to the home key. Instead, it hangs on the pedal point of the fifth as Jones's Latin rhythms continue to charge forward. In the coda that follows, the pedal-point tension only ratchets up further. The bassist remains on the fifth as Coltrane pounds—thirty-three successive times—on the minor third. Meanwhile Tyner colors in the midrange with increasingly complex chords that unsettle the simplicity of Coltrane's blues statement. When the coda finally col-

John Coltrane's four-bar break from "Liberia," 1960. (Courtesy of Peter Curtis)

lapses after twelve bars, it is only Coltrane who is left standing: we've arrived at his version of Parker's solo break, with great relief. In "Liberia" as a whole, the quartet seems to race forward until it hits a harmonic wall, which it proceeds to ram, bruisingly, until it can burst forward—at which point it hits yet another wall. Coltrane's break is a merciful moment when the landscape seems to have been cleared, and a lone individual is free to roam.

Ironically, however, Coltrane seems implacably squeezed, trapped in this solo moment (see figure). Parker's break gave us virtuosity without self-disclosure; Coltrane's break gives us self-disclosure pushed to the point where it defeats virtuosity, where awkward truths are preferred to elegant nonchalance. In the space of his four measures, Coltrane plays a string of eighth notes without swinging them at all, and without much in the way of narrative accent. His clunky phrase has little of Parker's blinding speed, which assimilated sixteenth notes in one surprisingly smooth swoop up and down the treble clef, alternating ghosted and accented tones. Coltrane seems to be locked in struggle with his instrument—not surprising, considering that he is manipulating its keys to create a highly chromatic and unpredictably circuitous melody, one that suggests a series of clashing tonalities (G minor; E-flat minor; A major; B major) within its highly confined, single-octave range. Taken in tandem with Coltrane's rhythmic regularity, this harmonic irregularity keeps us from fastening onto any one moment in the break for a sense of orientation. Like Coltrane, we are made to grapple with the freedom that arrives unexpectedly when a long-familiar barrier vanishes.

Crucially, Coltrane wages this struggle—to act freely while his environment convulses around him—not by holding his emotions at an ironic distance but by exploiting and channeling them in defiance of previous convention. Parker sometimes sounds "amateurish," in Ralph Ellison's words, because he withholds so much, because his vibratoless tone gives us few signals about his interiority; Coltrane, by contrast, sounds amateurish because he is willing to try anything—screeches, ungainly blurts, meandering runs—that might add to his powers of testimony. For this reason, his playing connects us to the roots of language and sound, the untempered extremities of the human voice. His saxophone tone is all too human: instead

FREEDOM'S SAINT

of aiming for vibrato, the device of the sensitive man, he gives us the full range of blues expression, from his straight-ahead attack in the middle register to his keening ascents in the upper reaches of his saxophone. As detailed in the next chapter, this impulse to "scream" when necessary became Coltrane's most magnetic quality for Black Arts poets in the late 1960s; here we need only note that Coltrane's virtuosity, which puts the quest for self-expression above the demands of professional competence, allows for—and perhaps even rewards—awkwardness. No note is a wrong note if it gets us from here to there; no noise is unredeemable if it carries the breath of spiritual effort.

The world of Coltrane's "Liberia," then, prizes intensity of statement over finesse; prefers to ratchet up levels of tension rather than obey more predictable patterns of dissonance and resolution; and suggests that, even when all external restraints are removed (the moment of the break), we are left to struggle with the compelling contradictions that we keep within ourselves. The music seems not only to mirror the turbulence of a community seeking liberation, but also to articulate the values of committed seriousness and anguished self-knowledge—the tragic as well as the heroic facets of the quest for freedom. Similar generalizations could be applied to many of Coltrane's mid- and up-tempo numbers from the period between 1960 and 1964, celebrated pieces like "Africa," "Impressions," "Chasin' the Trane," and "India."

In fact, when he next entered the recording session as a leader, Coltrane extended many of "Liberia"'s innovations through "Africa," the ambitious sixteen-minute centerpiece of his Impulse album *Africa/Brass*. Here Coltrane's spiritual heft was realized through a jazz wall of sound. The fifteen-piece ensemble was given darker coloration through an eight-piece brass section that included four French horns, euphonium, and tuba; the bottom of the sound was deepened by the presence of two bassists, one of whom played a steady vamp that Coltrane said was inspired by an African field recording, the other of whom improvised in the spaces of the vamp. Instead of the call-and-response section playing that structures most swing arrangements, here brass and reeds collaborated on massive block chord riffs, themselves derived from pianist McCoy Tyner's favorite voicings and rhythms. Throughout, one gets the sense of instruments being pushed to their limits—as when the French horns produce whoops and shouts, or when Coltrane reaches for the upper partials on his saxophone, mimicking the nasal sound of Asian and North African reed instruments.[20]

Not only did "Africa" have a larger, more populous sound than "Liberia," but also it simplified the modular structure of "Liberia," reducing the series of pedal points to a single bass vamp that runs beneath the entire piece.

Here we can hear most clearly how the turn to modal jazz changed the voyage that musicians and listeners took, as well as their relation to the soundscape being invoked. Despite the transatlantic distance between Coltrane's New Jersey recording studio and the continent of Africa, his music did not set itself apart from the land it hoped to translate into music. "Liberia" and "Africa," unlike Parker's "Tunisia," are not so much like spaces for musicians to travel through; they are places to inhabit. In the solos of "Africa," for instance, Coltrane and Tyner do not have to run a Tin Pan Alley obstacle course. Rather, they are made to grapple with the harmonic force field established by the bass's ongoing vamp and the rhythmic pressure of Jones's hard Afro-Cuban swing, each of which sets out an improvisational challenge that will not go away. Inescapable and pressing, the world of "Africa" is a spur to self-creation: sixteen minutes of dire promise.

Coltrane and the New Jazz Criticism

In his liner notes for Coltrane's *Live at Birdland* (1963), which led off with a commanding treatment of "Afro Blue," Amiri Baraka breathlessly praised the beauty of Coltrane's playing, its ability to annihilate the world as it was. He came to Coltrane, crumpled and overwhelmed, and was delivered into clarity:

> [A]fter riding a subway through New York's bowels, and that subway full of all the things any man should expect to find in some thing's bowels, and then coming up stairs, to the street, and walking slowly, head down, through the traffic and failure that does shape the area, and then entering "The Jazz Corner Of The World" (a temple erected in praise of what God?), and then finally amidst that noise and glare to hear a man destroy all of it, completely, like Sodom, with just the first few notes from his horn, your "critical" sense can be erased completely, and that experience can place you somewhere a long way off from anything ugly.[21]

It's not too much to say that Baraka's guided tour, taking us through hell and up to paradise in the space of one deliciously agrammatical sentence, marked a new ripeness in the genre of liner notes. Here the jazz critic promised not that his product would entertain, but that it would strip away the "noise and glare" that shell-shock us urban denizens; that it would undo our presumption of critical distance; and finally that it would transport us, against all odds, into the realm of the beautiful. After a journey through purgatory we would arrive at that most unlikely and delightful temple, the jazz shrine. There, we would "think of a lot of weird and wonderful things" and—in a final punch—"might even become one of them."[22]

And yet this sort of overwriting was newly convincing, newly apt, since Coltrane *was* trying to do so much. His music confronted jazz critics with a considerable dilemma, one that electrified jazz magazines like *Down Beat* and *Metronome* in the early to mid-1960s, as critics fought over labels like "anti-jazz," "free jazz," "action jazz," "the new thing," and several others. The crux of the dilemma was this: could Coltrane's music be appreciated in terms inherited from earlier genres (matching the elegance of swing, the virtuosity of bebop, the grit of the blues), or did it demand to be measured by a new set of aspirations, in which case jazz critics would have to broaden their vocabulary of judgment and praise, and perhaps even jettison the critical attitude itself?

After several years of sharp in-fighting—which shook up the masthead of *Down Beat* and eventually led to the founding of left-wing publications like Pauline Rivelli's *Jazz and Pop* and Amiri Baraka's *The Cricket*—Coltrane emerged as a clear victor of the critical consensus. His emergence as a jazz hero was twinned with the arrival of a new generation of jazz critics, most prominently LeRoi Jones / Amiri Baraka, who concentrated on the radical energies of the music and on its roots in history, from the religious rituals of Africa to the African-American experience of slavery, Jim Crow, and civil rights struggles. To praise Coltrane was to articulate a black aesthetic, to recover a tradition obscured by the white monopoly of the music industry's record labels, magazines, and radio channels. In *Blues People* (1963), a founding text of this new wave of black cultural criticism, Baraka wrote that "Negro music is *always* radical in the context of formal American culture." For Baraka this radicalism was a matter of attitude, a deeply embedded philosophical difference that he traced back to the religious worldview of the African men and women who became American slaves and then, many generations later, American citizens.

Coltrane's music seemed to exemplify this roots culture at its most contemporary. It was best understood as a ritual to be experienced in real time, not as an artifact to be contemplated in retrospect; it was focused on the achievement of spiritual wholeness, rather than on entertainment and commercial gain; and finally, it seemed to bridge the archaic and the avant-garde, deploying the past in order to project a novel future. Baraka wrote that this rediscovery of "roots" was "perhaps the profoundest change within the Negro consciousness since the early part of the century." In this context, Coltrane came to figure as a latter-day conjure man, working his roots to defeat a seemingly more powerful adversary—the intertwining worlds of musical and social convention. He embodied the modernist urge for revolutionary "creative destruction," the imagination of a new world out of the ashes of the old, at the same time that he grounded his appeal in that time-honored populist gesture, the cry of the blues.[23]

Since we still live very much with the "Saint Coltrane" elegized by the Black Arts movement in the late 1960s, it can be surprising to discover just how embattled Coltrane was in the early 1960s—how, almost immediately after fronting his own group in 1960, he found himself at the center of critical feuds that tore through the jazz community. Baraka's was, in many ways, the minority point of view. Coltrane seemed to push the limit in expressing new kinds of emotions in jazz: he was understood as the modernist in tortured pursuit of his own authenticity, and critics argued over whether such anguish ennobled or enfeebled the music.

The "anti-jazz" gauntlet was thrown down by *Down Beat* editor John Tynan in November 1961, when he objected to "the musical nonsense currently being peddled in the name of jazz by John Coltrane and his acolyte, Eric Dolphy." Earlier, Tynan had criticized Coltrane's role in Davis's ensemble, arguing that Coltrane's "onrush of surrealism and disconnected musical thought" were signs of his "neurotic compulsion" and "contempt for an audience." The anti-jazz column spun out this logic in a review of a recent Hollywood appearance by Coltrane's own group, the same group whose album *Live at the Village Vanguard* later shocked jazz critics with its apparent inconclusiveness and musical abandon. Tynan applied the tag "anti-jazz" because he felt that Coltrane and Dolphy were "intent on deliberately destroying" the essence of jazz, the "discernible rapport and working unity between soloist and rhythm section" that created "that elusive element, swing." Tynan mocked Coltrane's aspirations to take jazz beyond the realm of swing and entertainment: such spiritual communication, he wrote, "must have been elevated to an astral plane beyond my consciousness." Such comments were in keeping with Tynan's critical allegiance to principles of intelligibility, modesty, and grace—and with his aversion to dramas of psychological alienation. A year earlier, he had similarly damned Jack Gelber's play *The Connection,* a production incubated by the avant-garde Living Theater that set its jazz-adoring heroin addicts in a Beckettian world of darkly absurdist routine. Tynan wrote that "one cannot describe it as theater. . . . It lacks the essential of dramaturgy—creation of dramatic conflict and consequent resolution. No questions are asked and, consequently, none can be answered."[24]

The term "anti-jazz," then, was a form of slander, but it also hinted at an insight: Coltrane's artistic revolution was in skewed alignment with other postwar rejections of traditional modes of psychological representation, the "anti-theater" of Beckett and Pirandello as well as the "anti-painting" of Abstract Expressionism and Pop Art. Critic Leonard Feather developed the analogy, but ultimately allied himself with Tynan as he considered the worrisome implications of a jazz divorced from "the mathematical rules that control all music." The visual arts, he wrote, might not depend on continuity, but "all music has been inextricably related to the number of cycles per second represented by each sound." Coltrane affronted these laws with his brand of "anti-jazz nihilism" by constructing solos "bound by no restrictions of time or space and by no pervasive obligation to the beat. . . . Repudiating the time factor, Coltrane sometimes continues for half an hour playing variations on a theme that may consist of a twelve- or thirty-two-bar trifle, whose harmonic course must therefore be repeated endlessly by the accompanists nailed to this treadmill."

In his animosity, Feather lit upon Coltrane's most sensational "anti-jazz" move—his radical approach to the duration of jazz music. There had been some precedent for Coltrane's extended solos in the grooving blues of organist Jimmy Smith and other soul-jazz musicians in the late 1950s, but Coltrane raised more red flags in pushing jazz away from its long tradition as music of celebration. Coltrane's music was unapologetically difficult; it could seem like a treadmill since he refused to dress up its elemental dramaturgy, which presented the soloist in fierce dialogue with himself, sometimes stuck in exasperation, often running through unusual scales in hopes that their comprehensiveness would lead someplace unexpected. Coltrane himself explained that the solos were "long because all the soloists try to explore all the avenues that the tune offers. They try to use all their resources in their solos." In these dramas of exhaustive exploration, Coltrane drew the listener's focus to the soloist's act of concentrated self-engagement: by reducing the harmonic complication of the accompaniment, his group allowed concentration to redouble on itself, meditatively. Yet for Feather and others, this rumination was unbearably solipsistic. Feather had harsh words for the usual defenses of Coltrane's art—that its anguish was a humane response to a dehumanizing age, and that it carried the unimpeachable value of "sincerity and passionate dedication." "Hitler was sincere," he wrote witheringly. The "anti-jazz" trend was merely the "timeproof story of the emperor's clothes."[25]

With the release of *Live at the Village Vanguard* (1961), the larger jazz community reflected on these changes in Coltrane's sound, which had been camouflaged by the popularity of *My Favorite Things* and his other Atlantic albums. The album stirred critical passions to such a degree that *Down Beat,* in a rare but increasingly necessary move, assigned two reviewers to the album. Neither gave Coltrane a strong endorsement. Ira Gitler, an early partisan of Coltrane who had memorably praised his "sheets of sound," took a hard line against the eighty blues choruses of "Chasin' the Trane": Coltrane "may be searching for new avenues of expression," he wrote, "but if it is going to take this form of yawps, squawks, and countless repetitive runs, then it should be confined to the woodshed. Whether or not it is 'far out' is not the question. Whatever it is, it is monotonous, a treadmill to the Kingdom of Boredom." In the same issue, Pete Welding did not fault Coltrane, but "the task he has set himself": "Chasin'," he said, "seems more properly a piece of musical exorcism than anything else, a frenzied sort of soul-baring." Yet while it was a "remarkable human document," "one of the noblest failures on record," it represented the pitfalls of autobiography in music, a piece of "disjointed, inconclusive meanderings" and "sputtering inconclusiveness." Artistry, Welding implied, was based in detachment, not self-absorption.[26]

Tynan, Feather, Gitler, and Welding were rebuffed most forcibly by black critics Amiri Baraka and A. B. Spellman, who assailed the basic principle that the power of art was best harnessed and appreciated through ironic or critical detachment. Spellman, who became a key poet and arts activist, began his review of a 1961 Coltrane appearance at the Village Gate with an elliptical, startlingly palpable appraisal of the concert:

> [I]f music is the action, if jazz is the music, there is something like a bridge but not at all a bridge between mouth and ear that puts ear inside mouth or mouth inside ear and makes experience mutual.
>
> Here is a group consisting of three ogres, their priest, and his altarboys. Often they assault innocent little tunes, ripping their flesh apart while the renegade priest points the way to new violence with the bones of the victim.[27]

Here Spellman struck the two keynotes of the Coltrane legend as it would later develop in the Black Arts movement. First, he described a telepathic connection between Coltrane and his audience, a charismatic identification that made every Coltrane concert a "mutual" experience, and an intimate one at that ("mouth inside ear" suggests a mystical soul kiss or love nibble). Second—and this element was in tension with the first—he drew glowing attention to the violent magic of the music itself, a violence here so extreme as to be unreal, and all the more powerful for it. Writing in 1961, Spellman anticipated the militarization of protest rhetoric that filtered into, and sometimes dominated, the far left in the late 1960s.[28]

These two ideas were amplified in the pages of *Kulchur,* the Greenwich Village magazine that tracked the experimental arts and whose editors in-

FREEDOM'S SAINT

cluded Gil Sorrentino (poetry), Frank O'Hara (arts), and LeRoi Jones / Amiri Baraka (music). Reviewing both *Live at the Village Vanguard* and the *Down Beat* pan of the record, Spellman wrote, "The present Coltrane is inseparable from his audience. You let yourself get involved in what he's doing & he tears your reason down. You stay aloof & look for what works & what fails & the solos get long & repetitive." The critic was less a judge than a fellow bandmate, ready to participate in the "mind scraping" of "Chasin' the Trane." "Catharsis is personal, & it's a drag to justify it against the kind of empty & reactionary charges the *DB* people made," he added, segueing to his famous put-down of the white critical establishment: "What does anti-jazz mean & who are these ofays who've appointed themselves guardians of last year's blues?"[29]

Spellman's comments were seconded by Amiri Baraka, who heard revolutionary energies in Coltrane's sound and who perhaps did the most to situate his work within an emergent black avant-garde. Considering *Live at the Village Vanguard* alongside the work of free jazzers Cecil Taylor and Ornette Coleman, Baraka suggested that all three were reclaiming the "blues shout" in "a jazz anarchic"—meaning that they had held onto blues rhythms and blues tonalities, the blues cry, while dispensing with the conventional harmonic narrative of the blues. Like Spellman, Baraka saw Coltrane killing off the weaker music of the past: "Coltrane's salvation," he wrote, "will only come as a murderer, an anarchist, whose anarchy seems so radical because references to the 'old music' still remain."[30] By 1965, after barely touching on Coltrane in his 1961 *Metronome* article "The Jazz Avant-Garde," Baraka took Coltrane as the exemplar of a black aesthetic, its great educator. In his liner notes to *New Wave in Jazz,* the album that commemorated a pivotal benefit concert for Baraka's Black Arts Repertory Theatre/School, he wrote that Coltrane "showed us how to murder the popular song. To do away with weak Western forms. He is a beautiful philosopher." This passage is classic Jones/Baraka—first, in its assertion that formal innovation was a type of "murder," a far-reaching analogy that collapsed the boundary between aggression in art and aggression on the streets; and second, in its hardened conviction that this murder was a thing of beauty, a philosophical principle of self-reliance and strength. Coltrane was an avatar of a black vernacular modernism, a hero who confronted older forms in order to dispose of them—and, in the process, made himself unrecognizable to his previous selves. As Baraka wrote aphoristically, "New Black Music is this: Find the self, then kill it."[31]

Where critics like Feather and Tynan heard aimless anxiety, Baraka heard something earthshaking: a black consciousness so in touch with itself that it could begin to transcend its past. As literary critic Werner

Sollors has remarked, this process of rebirth through self-murder was a key theme animating Baraka's broader work as a poet, playwright, and activist. Baraka hoped to discover, and emulate, the "visionary, descended from cosmic sun-rays," who would raze "old Western conceptions in order to raise new race-conscious ones" (thus the title of his 1971 essay collection *Raise Race Rays Raze*). Baraka's first poetry collection, in 1961, had been titled *Preface to a Twenty Volume Suicide Note;* 1964's *The Dead Lecturer* found him again confronting his imminent death, but this time he saw the larger world in a state of collapse, ready for a "Black Dada Nihilismus" who would terrorize Damballah's "lost white children." In this context, he was prepared to leave behind his "stewed black skull, / an empty cage of failure," because he could imagine himself severed from that old self:

When they say, "It is Roi
who is dead?" I wonder
who will they mean?[32]

"Find the self, then kill it": such was Baraka's prescription for a more vibrant black music and a more vital black community, and he began with himself. His *Blues People* was an unprecedented work of cultural criticism that told the history of black America through its musical forms, but it was also a personal act of re-making—an attack on the white jazz critics who had given Baraka a platform for his own writing, and a critique of the black middle-class world that he had grown up in, as the child of a postal supervisor and a social worker and as a student at Rutgers and Howard University. The basic thrust of *Blues People* was to reclaim the blues as a way of looking at the world, not just a music: "each phase of the Negro's music," he wrote, "issued directly from the dictates of his social and psychological environment." Baraka attacked white critics for pretending that all music was equal, that it could be evaluated in isolation from the cultural needs of the community that created it. "The catalysts and necessity of Coltrane's music must be understood as they exist even before they are expressed as music," he wrote. The question for the critic was less "What do I think of Coltrane's scream?" and more "Why does this man—and so many like him—feel compelled to scream in the first place?" The goal of jazz criticism was understanding, not appreciation.[33]

Understanding contemporary black music for Baraka meant locating it as part of a long and complicated struggle, one between the dominant forces of Western modernity and a black countertradition that had often been derided and suppressed. This struggle was grounded in separate worldviews, separate systems of ethics and aesthetics. While the "'enlightened' concepts of the Renaissance," he wrote, "created a schism between what was art and what was life," black music refused to separate art from living ritual. While American culture was geared to rationalization, compartmentalization, and "economic-mindedness," black music filtered mystery, tragedy, and joy into a compelling form of consolation and resistance. Baraka used this overarching theoretical framework to understand the cultural work of specific musical genres, from work songs, shouts, and spirituals to the blues and jazz in all its forms. At its most incisive, *Blues People* told the history of jazz as the history of a hybrid music, the sound of creative social antagonism. One of *Blues People*'s most powerful passages, for instance, describes how early New Orleans musicians were riven by the contradictory desire both to connect with the black community and to "make it" in white and Creole society, and then links this inner conflict between "freedman" and "citizen" identities to the music's synthesis of blues timbre and brass-band orchestration.[34]

More problematically, Baraka devoted much space in *Blues People* to a bruising attack on the black middle class, which he saw in thrall to a "Puritan ethos," the love of acquisition that had motivated the practice of slavery in the first place. Baraka made the repudiation of black music—and the values he ascribed to it—into the hallmark of black middle-class identity. Here he followed his Howard University teacher E. Franklin Frazier, whose *Black Bourgeoisie* was a well-known indictment of the black middle class as a self-hating group, a wedge between the black working class and the much larger dominant culture. The "moral-religious tradition of the black middle-class," Baraka wrote, "is a weird mixture of cultural opportunism and fear. It is a tradition that is capable of reducing any human conceit or natural dignity to the barest form of social outrage." Baraka claimed that, of all the arts, black music prospered most in America because, ironically, the black middle class had scorned it as coarse and illegitimate.[35]

Baraka's argument was probably at its most brittle when he claimed that jazz musicians and the black middle class were axiomatically at odds—that "a middle-class blues singer" was "a contradiction in terms" and that black music was only "authentic" if it was radically nonconformist and anti-commercial. There is little room in Baraka's analysis, for instance, for those musicians like Oscar Brown, Jr., who tried to imagine a solidarity between the black working- and middle class. For their part, contemporary jazz historians have devoted much energy to understanding how jazz musicians tried to succeed both as artists and as workers who needed to make a living through their music—which is to say, as professionals. The work of Burton Peretti and Scott DeVeaux, for instance, has suggested how jazz artists from the Chicago school of the 1920s and 1930s through New York's bebop musicians used their identity as professionals to navigate the middle class, flout the canons of white America, and establish more stable economic foundations for their livelihood all at the same time. Jazz and the blues have often given black musicians creative ways of "making it" in the teeth of middle-class presumptions about how that might be done. Or, as Ralph Ellison pointed out from another angle, the distinction between jazz as protest and jazz as tepid commerce is difficult to maintain when the full contexts for music-making are considered. The blues might be understood both as folklore and as entertainment, depending on the context; commercial and noncommercial types of music are difficult to disentangle, when the same song might be performed on a stage for money or sung to children for love.[36]

In retrospect, we can see that while Baraka may have overstated the distance separating the black middle class and black music, his animus toward the black middle class did mark a contemporary crisis in that class—an upheaval reflected by new energies and rifts in the civil rights movement. After the wave of sit-ins in 1960, black students became leading players in the Movement, and their organization, the Student Nonviolent Coordinating Committee (SNCC), increasingly defined itself against Martin Luther King, Jr.'s Southern Christian Leadership Conference (SCLC), both in its more instrumental use of nonviolence and in its stated preference for grassroots, rather than charismatic, leadership. This split was pronounced even at the 1963 March on Washington, where SNCC chairman John Lewis hoped openly to criticize the Kennedy administration and threaten a "nonviolent revolution," "a source of power, outside of any national structure, that could and would assure us victory"—but then was pressured by King and more moderate civil rights leaders to revise his text. Baraka's *Blues People* was part of this shift among young, well-educated blacks, part of a growing repudiation of "middle-class" values of patience and decorum. More and more "Negroes" were turning away from the promise of a unified national culture, trying to unmask the ideology of assimilation, and deciding (in Baraka's words) that "a society whose only strength lies in its ability to destroy itself and the rest of the world has small claim toward defining or appreciating intelligence or beauty." In the October 1963 issue of *Liberator*, future Black Arts writer Askia Muhammad Touré announced the emergence of "a generation of militant young people" "suspended between [the Nation of] Islam and the civil rights organizations," nationalists who were ready to ally themselves with African liberation movements. The same year, James Baldwin posed his famous question in *The Fire Next Time:* "Do I really *want* to be integrated into a burning house?" Young blacks—and not a few young whites too—were yearning to be counted as blues people, and artists like Baraka were showing how it might be done: by disdaining the complacency of affluence, reclaiming a heritage of political and cultural struggle, and shedding the parts of oneself that were a betrayal of that legacy.[37]

For a younger jazz generation, many of whom identified with the radical wing of the Movement, Coltrane was a perfect goad and role model. Listening to him at the Five Spot, Baraka wrote, "we heard our own search and travails, our own reaching for definition. Trane was our flag." Only a few years later, after Coltrane himself had embarked on a looser form of playing and his classic quartet had dissolved, this group of younger jazz players and partisans would have the critical mass of a movement in their own right—a movement that flew the banner of free jazz at the very moment that the more militant civil rights workers began adopting the philosophy of Black Power. In the early sixties, however, these new aesthetic and political movements were only in incubation. Free jazz was taken up by a group of performers who seemed sui generis, idiosyncratic geniuses at home in the future, waiting for their time to come (Cecil Taylor, Sun Ra, Ornette Coleman). Likewise, although the militancy of Black Power was latent in much early civil rights protest (even Martin Luther King, Jr., had begun the Montgomery bus boycott with a stockpile of guns for self-protection), it had only a few high-profile exponents in the early sixties: the Nation of Islam, whose chief mouthpiece was Malcolm X; and Robert F. Williams, the NAACP leader who advocated armed self-defense for the black citizens of Monroe, North Carolina, then started broadcasting Radio Free Dixie from Cuba after fleeing false charges of kidnapping and assault. The roots of free jazz and Black Power were taking hold, however, and the story of John Coltrane's ascension as an icon was also the story of these parallel movements in black music and politics.[38]

Charismatic Freedom and the Black Aesthetic:
The Journey of "Afro Blue"

In the heated debate over Coltrane's art, the saxophonist himself seemed a bystander beside a fuming pile-up. Tynan and Feather condemned him for refusing intelligibility, assaulting and boring the listener, and departing from jazz's traditional strengths; Spellman and Baraka defended his unintelligibility as the highest power of art—its ability to estrange us from who we thought we were, to attack the false trappings of a culture that we had unthinkingly internalized. Meanwhile Coltrane in his public comments was so peaceable as to seem almost impervious to this language of anger, violence, and self-torture. In a magazine symposium on the "jazz anarchy," he declined "to answer the controversy about 'anti-jazz'" and said simply, "I'll continue to look for truth in music as I see it, and I'll draw on all the sources I can." When he defended his work in a 1962 *Down Beat* interview, he spoke in similarly positive and spiritual terms: "the main thing a musician would like to do is to give a picture to the listener of the many wonderful things he knows of and senses in the universe. That's what music is to me—it's just another way of saying this is a big, beautiful universe we live in, that's been given to us, and here's an example of just how magnificent and encompassing it is." Coltrane asked his critics to contact him in person so that they could come to some mutual understanding about the aims of his art, then was disappointed when none did.[39]

How are we to understand this puzzle—the generosity and tranquility of the man, set against the violence of the rhetoric used both to vilify and to exalt him? Were Baraka and his critical opponents at *Down Beat* merely locked in a delusional struggle, happy to have one another as enemies and co-conspirators? Certainly it is true that, unlike other artists in the jazz orbit, Coltrane kept his anger on a metaphorical level. He did not assault his fellow musicians (as did, say, Charles Mingus), or participate in urban insurrections (as did, say, Amiri Baraka), or even speak harshly against the predatory economic practices of the music industry (as did Max Roach, Archie Shepp, and many others by the mid-1960s). After his conversion experience in 1957, his most destructive habit may have been his addiction to sweet foods, which rotted his teeth and kept him from smiling in most public photos. So when, in a typical instance, Baraka praised Coltrane as one of his "generation's private assassins," he was referring solely to his practice of "murdering" other musical forms and rules. His "violence" was a formal one—an attack on the conventions of chordal improvising and on the emotional range of his Tin Pan Alley material.

Yet listening to the mid-sixties Coltrane quartet, we can understand equally why Baraka felt the need to inflate his rhetoric and why Coltrane himself spoke in willfully mellow terms: his music was both aggressive and peaceable at once. Infused with a militant spirituality, it seemed to reconcile opposites in a needful synthesis—and thus mimicked a broader movement in American cultures of dissent, which both critiqued the violence of American society (as manifested in the Vietnam war, police brutality, and so on) and appealed to the need for forceful retribution. More and more Americans were anticipating H. Rap Brown's argument that "violence was as American as cherry pie" and were considering fighting fire with fire. Coltrane was a powerful force in this cultural current, which focused both on the reality of violence and the need for peace. His music carried the larger hope that the artistic work of "creative destruction" might stand in for acts of physical violence and offer a nonviolent means to existential power. Both aggression and meditativeness came through in his reworkings of popular song: as A. B. Spellman declared, Coltrane seemed to "assault innocent little tunes," but the ultimate result was a trancelike ritual of soul-possession and redemption.

Coltrane's version of "Afro Blue" is a fertile case in point. He remade the original version—a hybrid of Afro-Cuban textures and blues form—into a much more commanding synthesis that favored ritual over romance, the abstraction of commitment over the familiar pop dream of true love. In its original version, Mongo Santamaría's "Afro Blue" is an engaging performance of Afro-Cuban atmospherics in 3/4 time, enlivened by a polyrhythmic percussion section and tasteful solos on flute, vibes, and congas. Part of the generation that followed the dance bands of Tito Puente, Perez Prado, and Mario Bauza, Santamaría worked with Prado and Puente but then pioneered a more stark Afro-Cuban sound: he put percussive interplay, not suave melodies or rich horn arrangements, in the foreground, and he invited vocalists to chant in a unison style that suggested religious ritual more than pop crooning. "Afro Blue"'s instrumentation telegraphs its basis in an Afro-Cuban aesthetic that prefers rhythmic suppleness to harmonic embellishment: the most heavily miked instruments are the congas, and several instruments that might possibly be melodic (bass and vibes) play in fixed rhythmic patterns, layered in the ensemble. A lonely flute carries the melody in a high-end space with little air traffic. As in "A Night in Tunisia," the listener is introduced to the complexity of the piece through a terraced, step-by-step introduction of each instrument: first congas, which drive propulsively in the two-measure unit, on the last beat before the turnaround and on the first beat that comes afterward; then bass with a three-to-the-bar ostinato in F minor; then shekere, which evenly stitches three eighth-note triplets in the two-bar space; then vibes with a simple ostinato; and finally, the flute with the melody. As in "Tunisia" too, the instruments interlock in a knowing, predetermined rhythmic formula.

The form of "Afro Blue" was strikingly simple, a blueprint that many jazz musicians would elaborate on in the coming years. Its pentatonic melody is rudimentary and folkloric, limited to seven notes (D-flat–E-flat–F–G–A-flat–B-flat–C) and utterly symmetrical. It is divided into four phrases, each of which take up four bars of the piece's sixteen-bar head. One phrase is announced, then repeated over the same chords; then a second phrase is announced and repeated. In the third measure of each phrase, the underlying chords plane upward and downward with the melody's movement, solidifying a sense of unity; and in the first, second, and third melodic phrases, we return again and again to the F-minor home chord, crystallizing a sense of stasis.

Interestingly, though, the solos themselves—the meat of the Santamaría performance—do not keep to this abstract chordal framework, which relies on planing resolutions (from A-flat down to F minor, and from D-flat up to F minor). In Santamaría's original version, and in a celebrated Monterey performance with Cal Tjader's group a year later, flute and vibes solo over more standard chord changes—a minor blues (i–iv–i–V–i) in twenty-four, not sixteen, bars. This decision seems to have been Santamaría's and Tjader's way of incorporating Latin rhythms without overly boxing in the soloist and without making the full turn to a more modal framework. Tjader, one of the stars of Latin jazz, remarked in 1957 that "Latin has its definite limitations, especially from the standpoint of improvisation. It's like a hypnotic groove. First you set the rhythmic pattern, then the melodic formulae follow—until pretty soon you realize there's not much real music invention happening." In its original conception, then, Santamaría's "Afro Blue" effected a compromise between its "Afro" and its blues: it kept an Afro-Cuban flavor throughout the performance with its prominent congas, shekere, and vibe ostinato, but it also utilized more conventional jazz-blues patterns underneath its solos to create a sense of momentum within the cycle of its form.[40]

In 1959, "Afro Blue" was picked up by the politically minded Oscar Brown, Jr., and Abbey Lincoln, both of whom collaborated a year later with Max Roach on his *Freedom Now Suite.* Brown penned lyrics that turned "Afro Blue" into a song of dreamlike racial homecoming, a three-stage journey to the "land my soul is from." The journey begins when the singer hears "a hand stroke on a drum" and loses himself in a purposefully unreal dream state. This fantasy is savored repeatedly in the refrain, which recalls "shades of delight, cocoa hue, rich as the night, afro blue" and evokes a landscape of abstract, dark pleasure: shady and rich as evening, tasty as cocoa, sensuous as the texture of the blues. Soon, Brown places two attractive black figures in this exotic landscape—figures familiar from Harlem Renaissance poetry, which often tried to convey a black aesthetic through descriptions of cabaret life. In Brown's case, the two figures are an "elegant boy" and a "beautiful girl" who dance and whirl together, then repair to a "secluded place" where they exchange "passionate pleas" and "tender cries." Finally, the singer bursts out of this dream with the happy realization that the two lovers are none other than himself and his beloved. He is actually *living* the "afro blue" dream, yet only now has he awakened to it.

Brown's lyrics were realized quite differently in Abbey Lincoln's "Afro

Blue" (1959) and in Brown's own version (1960). Brown closed his album *Sin and Soul* with the piece, which serves as a kind of lullaby. The instrumental setting is spare to the point of nakedness; Brown's singing is accompanied only by the playing of a conga drum. His vocal style, rich and ingratiating, allies him with the likes of Harry Belafonte and Nat King Cole. He articulates every word with a dignified exactitude, expressing a deep formality that matches the register of the lyrics, which have none of the jive irony of Brown's "Signifyin' Monkey" or "But I Was Cool."

On *Abbey Is Blue,* meanwhile, "Afro Blue" was both more poplike and more strident. The pop quality comes through in drummer Max Roach's arrangement, which dispenses with Afro-Cuban percussion and foregrounds instead the dialogue between Lincoln's vocals and the three-horn section of trumpet, trombone, and tenor sax (Tommy Turrentine, Julian Priester, and Stanley Turrentine, who filled out Roach's working group). Lincoln's "Afro Blue" inverts the dynamics of Mongo Santamaría's version, where melodic instruments assume the function of percussion. Instead it focuses attention on the harsh singing of Lincoln herself, who was in the middle phase of her transition from the sexually vulnerable chanteuse of her early career to the mature queen of her 1990s' comeback.[41]

Lincoln's "Afro Blue" marked her turn from glamour girl to woman warrior, from the sepia sex symbol who performed in the *Gentlemen Prefer Blondes* dress of Marilyn Monroe to the assertive songwriter who held the banner of black nationalism in the early 1960s jazz world. She was born Anna Marie Wooldridge in Chicago in 1930, and began performing as the supper club singer Gaby Wooldridge. In the mid-fifties she changed her stage name to Abbey Lincoln, gratified by her manager's joke that "Abe Lincoln didn't really free the slaves, but maybe you will." Like Coltrane's own celebrated "conversion" away from drugs and alcohol, her conversion into a jazz singer began in 1957 and reflected a toughened sense of self-purpose. "It was the early days of the civil rights movement," she recalled, "and we were all asking the same questions. But they were questions that glamour girls weren't supposed to ask. As I toured the country, I noticed that black people everywhere were living in slums, in abject poverty. I wanted to know why." In June 1957, *Ebony* was still able to run a five-page photo spread that matched Lincoln with Marilyn Monroe pose for pose and in the same low-cut gowns and bathing suits. By the end of the year, however, after Lincoln had read a copy of *The Negro in America* and begun associating with jazz musicians like her future husband Max Roach, she decided to stop exploiting her sex appeal in the terms thrust upon her by the industry—refusing to drink with nightclub patrons during intermission, raising her necklines and lowering her hemlines, and developing a repertoire that mixed tough-minded love songs and social commentary. In a tacitly feminist move, she stopped singing about unrequited love and "no-good men who didn't know how to treat women. I discovered you *become* what you sing."[42]

"Afro Blue" was part of Lincoln's third album for the jazz label Riverside, and its material reflected her new seriousness. There were two plangent songs cowritten by Kurt Weill (Langston Hughes's "Lonely House" and Maxwell Anderson's "Lost in the Stars"); three race-conscious numbers by Oscar Brown, Jr. ("Afro Blue," "Brother, Where Are You?" and "Long As You're Living"); Duke Ellington's spiritual "Come Sunday"; and her own "Let Up," which asked with clear-eyed skepticism when her troubles would end. "Afro Blue" was the only optimistic love song on the record—a result, perhaps, of its explicit focus on a black-on-black love. Yet Lincoln's style as a jazz singer shaves much of the optimism from the lyrics. While Brown's singing aims to soothe with its round tones, Lincoln's has an almost metallic timbre: when she sings in the refrain about "shades of delight, cocoa hue," the luscious language is undercut by her deliberately flat, declamatory phrasing. Brown invites his listeners to join him in his glimmering Afro Blue dream, and when he awakes from the dream, we still feel as though our reality has been enchanted. Lincoln conjures up the same dream state, but the harshness and distance of her voice intimates that it may not be so easy to collapse the boundary between the reality and the dream, that "the two young lovers face to face" may not, in fact, see eye to eye.

When Coltrane began performing "Afro Blue" in the early sixties, then, he was remaking a song that had already spanned quite a bit of the jazz-pop bandwidth—as a smooth but percussive groove in Santamaría's original version, as an innocent hymn to romance in Oscar Brown's cover, and as an ambivalent praise-song, chafed with militancy, in Abbey Lincoln's version. Earlier in this chapter, I remarked on Coltrane's lack of irony, his refusal to ventriloquize other styles unless he could commit to them completely as his own—in which case he was no longer ventriloquizing. Unsurprisingly, then, Coltrane's version of "Afro Blue" bears no great resemblance to any of these previous versions: as a modal piece in 3/4, it echoes much more clearly his own 1960 recording of "My Favorite Things," the Rodgers and Hammerstein tune that Coltrane converted into a hypnotic piece for soprano saxophone and a jazz hit single. Coltrane's "Afro Blue" is thrashing where the Santamaría version is politely polyrhythmic, wrenching where the Brown version is mild, and expansive where the Lincoln version is pinched. If critics like A. B. Spellman and Amiri Baraka praised Coltrane's zest for "assaulting innocent little tunes," for murdering older kinds of songs and the selves that produced them, the case of "Afro Blue" suggests that Coltrane did not limit himself to putatively "whiter" forms like Tin Pan Alley and Broadway show tunes; songs proclaiming a black aesthetic were also up for grabs. Yet "Afro Blue" also suggests that Coltrane's revisions—his acts of "signifying"—were not as parodic or hostile as the language of murder might suggest. Coltrane deepened the dream of "Afro Blue," its fantasy of homecoming, by modeling a trancelike state of possession where the easy compatibility of Brown's two lovers—their "delicate whirl" and "undulating grace"—yielded to the tense interplay of Coltrane's quartet. He conveyed an emotion more extreme and richer with ambiguity than Brown's cocoa-hued "shade of delight"—the struggle for rapture that he later called a "love supreme."

As much as any Coltrane piece from the mid-sixties, "Afro Blue" captures the sound of searching: it suspends a larger sense of harmonic progression while swinging furiously, trapping the soloist in a momentum that is irresistible but does not seem to lead anywhere. Anywhere, that is, but within: while there may be no movement out of "Afro Blue"'s larger F-minor groove, there is often a sense of microprogression, as Coltrane and McCoy Tyner begin with small motives, then develop them until they explode with complication and intensity. They model an impassioned, self-critical act of discovery, one that allows for digression as much as it welcomes clarity of thought. It is this self-critical aspect of Coltrane that leavens his charismatic power and makes his preacherly saxophone playing seem excruciatingly human: Coltrane heaps his energy with a kind of desperation, always performing as if he is on the brink of failure or spiritual exhaustion. He voices his own struggle with the resources of his instrument: publicizing every move he makes, every squawk and every flight away from stable harmonic ground, he seems to be searching for a new way out. A melodic dead-end might become in a moment the seed of a new idea; a meandering exercise in abstraction might transform itself into a recognizable blues shout. Coltrane's saxophone is the sound of an individual challenging the world's weightiness, its unbudgeability—beginning with the difficult task of moving oneself.

To understand how Coltrane conveys this sense of spiritual ritual over the eleven minutes of "Afro Blue," we can consider three different facets of the piece: the way he stretches the form of the song, dilating its sense of time; the general rules that govern the interaction of the quartet and create its propulsive rhythm; and Tyner and Coltrane's solos, which tend toward acts of militant expressiveness, gestures of imposition.

Formally, Coltrane's "Afro Blue" is dominated not by its arrangement but by its improvisations, which set the piece in the static mode that Santamaría's "Afro Blue" refuses. Santamaría's four-minute recording sparkles with explicit variety, in the layering of its instruments, in its succession of solos, and in its choice of the minor blues changes under the solos. The members of Coltrane's quartet, by contrast, all join the musical action within a few seconds of "Afro Blue"'s opening saxophone cry; and their tussling extends, with few new variables put into play, for the next ten minutes of the piece. Coltrane's solo, which is a bit shorter than McCoy Tyner's, lasts over 220 bars, or the equivalent of fourteen choruses. Moreover, the accompaniment generally remains in a single mode, a single chordal backdrop—a more extreme constraint than that employed in early modal Coltrane exercises like "My Favorite Things," which swings between minor and major modes, or "Impressions," which pitches up a half step in its bridge. The interest lies in the use Coltrane makes of this stripped-down form. Just as he reduced "Night in Tunisia" to its bare outline in "Liberia," so in "Afro Blue" he directs a rudimentary drama free of explicit Afro-Cuban atmospherics: there are no congas, no shekere, no ostinatos—just the four members of the quartet with their standard jazz instrumentation.

Yet what a sound comes from this "standard" group! Coltrane leads with his soprano saxophone, the instrument he reclaimed from jazz pioneer Sidney Bechet by emphasizing its more dervishlike aspects. Rather than swinging lightly and consistently, he seems to move among quite different voices. At the end of the head, for instance, after two straight-ahead statements of the theme, he playfully titters on an alternate melody, using staccato almost in mockery of its repetitiveness; then he ends with three off-beat triplet slurs that suggest spiritual possession, as if he had suddenly lost control of even this simple melody. Against Coltrane's soprano saxophone, the other members of the quartet establish an interlocking groove. Coltrane praised drummer Elvin Jones, with good reason, for his "ability to be in three places at the same time," and in "Afro Blue" Jones is Coltrane's leading partner in the stretching of musical time. Just by listening to his ride cymbal, which he plays with astonishing variety of accent and timbre, we are quickly liberated from the regularity of waltz rhythm, the metronome tick of the downbeat every measure. The rhythms of Jones seem to burst across the bar line—an effect that poet and drummer Clark Coolidge has called "momentum as seduction, in which the 'one' of that ever first beat tends very soon to lose its 'e.'" Yet at the same time, Jones is an incredibly emphatic drummer, his snare rolls and cymbal crashes announcing key moments in Coltrane's statement of the melody. The net effect of this pairing of momentum and emphasis: the quartet seems both extremely on the move and extremely together. Critic Brian Priestley, not given to overstatement, has described a similar Coltrane-Jones dialogue as "the sermon of a two-headed angel of vengeance."[43]

Pianist McCoy Tyner, meanwhile, subtilizes this rhythmic groove and establishes the harmonic range of "Afro Blue," its abstract yet bluesy character. His opening move—banging a low octave on the "one" with his left hand, then hitting a suspended blues chord on the "two-and" with his right—is perfectly apt. Tyner is the master of a percussive style that, like Jones's drumming, generates excitement with oversized but complicated gestures; his thunderous attack, as one writer has quipped, seems destined to leave permanent dents in the keys.[44] In the piano improvisation that comes between statements of the head, he creates a powerful churning rhythm through another call-and-response passage between left and right hands. While his left hand dances through a series of quartal chords—chords based in the interval of the fourth, which seem "abstract" since they do not feature a major or minor third—he parries each unresolved chord by spinning out fragments of an expanding blues lick in his right hand. In doing so, he suggests in microcosm how Coltrane's "Afro Blue" places its blues within a larger ritual of spiritual extension: the blues riffs seem as though they could be linked together endlessly, first because Tyner is such an inventive conjugator of blues melodies, but also because his chordings never resolve into a straightforward F-minor chord.

Critics sometimes heard this dilation of time as a "treadmill to the Kingdom of Boredom," but *Live at Birdland*'s "Afro Blue" succeeds more brilliantly than many Coltrane pieces because its soloists are supercharged with an introspective energy that spills in furious crescendos through the rest of the quartet. Take McCoy Tyner's five-minute solo, which is largely a dialogue between Tyner's piano and Jones's drums. It begins with Tyner playing clustered chords with locked hands, chords that divide the six beats of a two-measure unit into four parts. The technique puts a 4/4 wrench into "Afro Blue"'s presumptive 3/4, ratcheting up the musical tension. Over three different sequences of a minute or so, Tyner follows these offbeat clustered chords with an ingenious variety of technique—with emphatic pentatonic riffs, with gospel-laden chords, with half-step shifts up to an F-sharp key center, with elaborate and multimeasure single-note runs in his right hand—yet he always returns to these unresolved block chords. And each time he returns, he seems galvanized by Jones's increasingly dramatic drumming, with its rising number of snare accents and sweeping cymbal crashes. The two musicians find ways to build and build, ways that they might be in synch and in tension at once. At the end of Tyner's solo, it is not just the pianist's hands that are locked together, but Jones's hands too: they hammer together in the 4/4 off-rhythm. Jones's cymbal is in a permanent state of shimmer, usually at high volume; he also closes the chorus with a thunderous drum fill that extends over several bars. The intensity is a rush, palpably new, but it also follows the expressive logic of Tyner's solo, which spirals outward only to return back to the same point on a grander scale.

His entrance announced by the drum fill, Coltrane arrives with a sustained peal on the high C of his soprano saxophone, exploiting the extreme end of that extreme instrument, hanging on the high note and its neighbors for the first eight bars. The solo that follows is a model of musical self-examination: it has an easy-to-grasp narrative quality, with Coltrane often suggesting a figure, elaborating on it for a few more passes, digressing for a bit, then returning to the original figure, perhaps transposed into a different register or key. For instance, in measure 33 of his solo, Coltrane plays a four-note figure that traces the F-minor chord, then lands on the fourth. He then conjugates this figure, adding three notes in the middle of the phrase. Then he seems to digress, running from middle C up two octaves, playing a small variation on the F-minor scale. The endpoint of Coltrane's digression, however, is a hidden return: he gives us back the original motive in the higher register that his scale has led up to. This time, though, it does not peak on the fourth but instead strains up to the high E-flat, the very limit of Coltrane's soprano range. This kind of improvisational development suggests why self-reflexiveness—the recursive pursuit of melody launched by a rhythmically simple motive—is the hallmark of Coltrane's style. When we listen to him, we are not so much following a soloist running through a musical form as following a soloist in hot pursuit of himself.

Coltrane's solo in "Afro Blue" continues, in this unpredictable but fascinating vein, for another 170 or so bars. In an echo of Tyner's solo, he toys with the superimposition of a harsh 4/4 on the dominant swinging 3/4, abetted by crashing clusters on the piano and crashing cymbals from the drumkit. Sometimes he seems to slip entirely out of the F-minor mode—for instance, around measure 121 of his solo—but always he comes back to the pentatonic elements that structure "Afro Blue"'s melody. Finally he clinches his solo; but when we return to the head, the flavor of the piece has been enriched, intensified. After the head is stated once, Coltrane returns as a soloist, filling over the F-minor vamp—but whereas Tyner began the piece with a mere sixteen-bar fill, Coltrane here takes sixty-four measures, much of which he spends in a flurry of sixteenth notes and a busy series of eighth-note chromatic runs.

With the return of the head, we soon make a startling discovery: Coltrane is readying a further extension of "Afro Blue," one that will lead to a splitting of his own voice. While beboppers practiced the art of double-time, Coltrane here slows the head down to a kind of quarter-time so that it occupies sixty-four, not sixteen, bars. Yet this stretching does not mean that the quartet's energy lessens, just that it dilates. The tempo remains constant, but each note in the melody carries four times its previous value. In a crucial gesture, Coltrane uses long, sustained trills—some as extended as seven bars—as a way to stretch the final statement of "Afro Blue"'s melody to its new, quadrupled bar length. One can easily be forgiven for hearing something spiritual, or perhaps uncanny, in these trills: oscillating between two tones, Coltrane seems to aspire to have a larger voice, a wider affect, than is humanly possible. The form of "Afro Blue" has been dilated, and now the individuals within that form are spreading out too. When, at the very end, Coltrane starts trilling on his soprano's open fingering, he exacerbates this sense of self-loss: oscillating not between neighboring tones, as is customary in a trill, but between notes separated by the interval of a fourth, he seems to model an out-of-body experience or an act of possession, some sort of spiritual quaking or quickening. Like many of Coltrane's most powerful musical moments, it suggests simultaneously a kind of self-emptying and an intense act of will, an unstable compound of ecstasy, loss, and concentration. The modern Russian composer Scriabin, himself a mystic, spoke of his tenth sonata, which relied on a series of trills, as "a sonata of insects." Coltrane, a convert to pan-spirituality, did not label "Afro Blue," but the piece seems to share Scriabin's faith that musicians might, in the act of playing something new, become something else.

8

LOVING *A LOVE SUPREME*

Coltrane, Malcolm, and the Revolution of the Psyche

When Elvin Jones left the Coltrane quartet in March 1966, frustrated by Coltrane's turn away from the furious partnership in swing that they had developed in tandem, he said sardonically about the saxophonist's latest music, "Only poets can understand it." His comment was meant as a not-so-subtle dig, but it was somewhat prophetic too. In the late 1960s, a critical mass of Black Arts intellectuals deemed John Coltrane the great artistic liberator—and they celebrated his scream, not his lyrical side or rhythmic force, as his signal accomplishment. A subgenre of Black Arts poems, for instance, began with trembling invocations of Coltrane, then exploded with performative acts meant to approximate the peal of Coltrane at fever pitch:

> trane playing in my guts and it's me and my
> ears forgetting how to listen and just feeling oh
> yeah me i am screammmmmming into the box and the box
> is screammmmmming back
> —Carolyn Rodgers, "Me, In Kulu Se & Karma"

> SCREEECCCHHHHH SCREEEEEEECHHHHHHH
> SCREEEEEECHHHHHHHHH SCREEEECCCCHHHH
> SCREEEEEEEECCCHHHHHHHHHHH
>   a lovesupremealoversupremealovesupreme for our blk
>   people
> —Sonia Sanchez, "a/coltrane/poem"

the blues exhibited illusions of manhood.
destroyed by you. Ascension into:

scream-eeeeeeeeeeeeeeing	sing
SCREAM-EEEeeeeeeeeeeeing	loud &
SCREAM-EEEEEEEEEEEEEEE-ING	long with feeling

—Don L. Lee, "Don't Cry, Scream"[1]

Starting especially in the mid-1960s, Coltrane's scream was held up as exemplary behavior by black militants, who were themselves faced with inner-city explosions and the splintering of the civil rights coalition. Lindsay Barrett, a Jamaican-born journalist, novelist, and playwright, explained how Coltrane's music was the black population's secret weapon in its struggle to recover its true strength. "If a black man could grasp a Coltrane solo in its entirety as a club, and wield it with the force that first created it," he wrote in the seminal Black Arts collection *Black Fire* (1968), then he would not only recover his cultural patrimony but also vanquish his oppressor. The screams in jazz were not just musical notes, he said, but "the screams of a thousand lost and living voices whose existence has begun to demand the release of the soul's existence"—in other words, the screams of history urging a fair accounting, a liberation from pain. Barrett counseled black people to recover their own cultural language, and his essay at one point raised itself to a kind of prose poetry as it envisioned a world where the recovery of this language would decisively break the racial deadlock. "Like wielding a Coltrane solo as a club. Like seeing all white as red," he wrote in a section called "Wade in the Water." "Like breaking heads with words. Like this language wasn't mine and is mine now. The river runs in the head."[2]

Barrett's surreal, mixed metaphors—which converted Coltrane's music into a weapon, whiteness into the color of blood, and his own head into a baptismal river washing away all sin—signaled both the pressure of his logic and the burden of his hope. Coltrane's art allowed critics like Barrett to consider violence as a necessary ingredient in struggle, to wrestle with the possibility of a nonviolent act of aggression and then to come out of that imaginative act with a sense of rebirth and even exaltation. It was a sign of the times that Coltrane's scream was seized upon as a vehicle of hope: a new world, a world without ghettos, seemed impossible to imagine without a disfiguring act like that scream, and without a willful turn away from reasoned argumentation, patient analysis, and the whole regime of nonviolent direct action. His scream was a last resort, in certain respects, but it was also the beginning of a new cultural politics that, partly arising out of the crucible of hard bop, sought to redeem hard bop's promise of a community that liberates itself through struggle.

In a fascinating short story, "The Screamers" (1967), Amiri Baraka used a Coltrane-like figure to unravel this relationship between aesthetic and political liberation, giving a blueprint for community empowerment that was a black nationalist version of the hipster general strike suggested earlier by David McReynolds (see Chapter 2). In Baraka's story, a nightclub audience is transfigured by the performance of a blues honker who, with the utmost charisma, carries his crowd into the streets screaming along with him. Unlike the hipster strike, though, the spontaneous uprising around saxophonist Lynn Hope is an all-black phenomenon, and it is less a carnival of possibilities than a violent ritual of rebirth. Hope's scream is an infectious call to authenticity—one that inspires first his fellow musicians to join in unison, and then the whole audience to scream "at the clear image of ourselves as we should always be." Like the Black Arts poetry just quoted, Baraka's story suggests that the best response to a scream is *more screaming,* this time en masse.[3]

Hope is not quite a Coltrane stand-in—in fact, Coltrane had mixed feelings about his stint in R&B bands, and left a gig in embarrassment after his friend Benny Golson caught him "walking the bar" to please the customers. Baraka was probably recalling a real-life Lynn Hope, a Philadelphia tenor man who shared Coltrane's jazz scene in the 1950s and who, having converted to Islam along with his pianist sister and drummer brother, wore a turban onstage and spoke of taking the pilgrimage to Mecca. Still, Baraka's description of the honk sounded much like his and other appraisals of Coltrane's sound:

> The repeated rhythmic figure, a screamed riff, pushed in its insistence past music. It was hatred and frustration, secrecy and despair. It spurted out of the diphthong culture, and reinforced the black cults of emotion. There was no compromise, no dreary sophistication, only the elegance of something that is too ugly to be described, and is diluted only at the agent's peril.

Hope satisfies his audience's appetite for an expression that is neither decorative nor imitative, but somehow real: a sound "past music," free of compromise and sophistication, which finds a new purity and elegance in an ugliness that beggars the powers of conventional language. By this logic, the very shock of the musical language—its incomprehensibility as anything but noise—is the strongest testament to its incorruptibility, to the directness of its expression. Baraka and the Black Arts poets write about the scream as a naked cry of power, astonished in part at its own nakedness. And they find that empowering scream in R&B as well as avant-garde jazz, a "changing same" that carries across the broad spectrum of black musical expression.[4]

"The Screamers" imagined the black community mobilized not by a concrete political program, and not even by a political speech, but by the appeal of a common cultural denominator at the limits of speech. In this sense, Hope's scream is a great equalizer not unlike the slogan "Black Power," which evoked an assumed sense of cultural solidarity as the basis for collective political action. Baraka's story is built on the hope that a cultural revolution might coincide with a political revolution—that in fact they would be one and the same, since both would be backed by a single revolution in popular consciousness, what was known at the time as the "Negro-to-black conversion process" or the "revolution of the psyche." Screaming at the ideal image of themselves, Hope's audience becomes "ecstatic, completed, involved in a secret communal expression": they have discovered a buried, religious sense of connection, a consciousness that is anything but double.[5]

This dream of cultural solidarity—a community knit together by black art and galvanized to action by that art—gathered undeniable momentum in the late 1960s. It drove the Black Arts movement more generally, although it was often expressed as an axiom of cultural life rather than as an utopian ideal—for instance, when critic Larry Neal in his aptly titled "The Cultural Front" (1965) began with "The political liberation of the Black Man is directly tied to his cultural liberation," or when Harold Cruse argued that "the Negro question in America is essentially a cultural question" and propagandized for black-owned and -operated cultural enterprises that would in turn lead to revolutions in "commodity production, political organization, or racial democratization." And although this vision did not succeed in unifying the black population as a whole, it did inspire black artists to found community arts organizations across the country, such as the Black Arts Repertory Theater/School and the New Lafayette Theater in Harlem, Spirit House in Newark, the Organization of Black American Culture and the African Commune of Bad Relevant Artists (AFRI-COBRA) in Chicago, the Broadside Press and the Concept East Theater in Detroit, the Black Arts Cultural Center in Pittsburgh, Black House in Oakland, and the Watts Writers' Workshop in Los Angeles. Within the field of jazz alone, it was the vision behind the Underground Musicians and Artists Association in Los Angeles, the Black Artists Group in Saint Louis, the Association for the Advancement of Creative Musicians in Chicago, and Strata in Detroit.[6]

By looking at the twin evolution of Coltrane as an icon and an artist we can begin to see why militant black artists were drawn to his music as the soundtrack, and the tool, of cultural liberation. *The Autobiography of Malcolm X* and Coltrane's *A Love Supreme* were perhaps the most resonant conversion narratives of the 1960s, stories in words and music about the pursuit of spiritual perfection, each testifying in its own way to the rewards of a straight life and to a global vision of black culture and liberation. It is one of the fascinating ironies of this period that a man so quiet and good-natured—so far, that is, from the sensational qualities that are the usual stuff of celebrity and so removed from the in-your-face gestures that marked the 1960s culture of dissent—should have become a "jazz messiah," as a plaque at his Hamlet, North Carolina, birthplace declares. Compounding this sense of irony is another: that while Coltrane was loath to attach his music to a specific political ideology, preferring a language of universal spirituality, he became posthumously an icon of a uniquely black epistemology. This chapter tries to make historical and aesthetic sense of these ironies, which were themselves a large part of Coltrane's insistent magnetism.

Jazz as a Religion of Work: Roy DeCarava's Coltrane

Shortly after Coltrane formed his classic quartet in 1960, he began to count among his most dedicated fans photographer Roy DeCarava. Thus was born one of the more remarkable collaborations between sound and image in the history of jazz. Part of a slightly older generation, DeCarava had apprenticed in the more radical culture of the New Deal—frequenting the Harlem Community Art Center along with Paul Robeson and Langston Hughes, working in the poster division of the WPA's New York project, contributing to black-themed publications like *Crisis* and *Opportunity*—and he brought to his photographs of Coltrane a preoccupation with the labor of jazz. "I don't think of musicians as *musicians*," DeCarava said of his extensive series of jazz photographs, later exhibited as *The Sound I Saw*, "but as people—and as workers." DeCarava was attracted to jazz, and to Coltrane in particular, because he thought that jazz musicians fulfilled the promise of an older phrase like "the dignity of labor" as they imbued their work with a fierce sense of spiritual purpose. Speaking of one of his jazz images, DeCarava took pleasure in how his musician practiced "a true religion . . . a religion of commitment, the religion of work and the religion of selflessness; of giving oneself to what one does completely."[7]

Religion and commitment, generosity and selflessness—these were terms commonly applied to Coltrane as he spiritualized the function of jazz, steering it away from entertainment and toward moral uplift and clearing a path for a younger generation of free jazz players. DeCarava provided perhaps the most compelling images of this new spirituality literally at work. He contrived to evoke the ingenuousness and absorption of Coltrane—qualities he summed up in the remark "He didn't try to be noble, but he was noble because he never gave up." His more recognizable Coltrane photographs capture the saxophonist in a self-induced fever of effort: a hard-working man in a dead heat with himself, wrestling the dark with great duress and yet with confidence, too. For instance, in image number thirty-two of his Coltrane series we're posed breathtakingly close to Coltrane—so close, in fact, that the bell of his saxophone seems ready to nudge us in the stomach. DeCarava conveys how Coltrane's music depends on an almost spiritual form of intimacy, on the desire to narrow the gap between the making of music and its apprehension. Coltrane is at a slight angle and tilting backward, so that we seem to stand at the point where he would be standing if he were upright; and the fingers of his left hand, by some optical illusion favored by their blurring in action, reach for us even as they handle his saxophone. DeCarava, who followed the Coltrane quartet up and down the East Coast, from New York to Washington, D.C., places himself not at a fan's remove, but on the bandstand itself.[8]

At the same time that we're being pulled into the music, however, we're also swathed in the atmospheric obscurity that is DeCarava's signature. DeCarava believed strongly in using only the available light, and as a result his photographs often have a surface like black marble, reflecting detail in their darkest corners. ("Most of my images that seem black are not black at all," he said; "they are a very dark grey.") This choice to limit his light source derived in large part from DeCarava's distaste for camera work that was either overly intrusive or overly distanced; he hoped to dwell in his locales, to avoid the trap of becoming a tourist drawn to picturesque detail, or a muckraking sociologist drawn to signs of squalor. He refused to "rig" the milieu of performance because he feared tampering with the spontaneity of motion and action—and because this respect for his surroundings forced him to refine his artistry. To put it another way: the same drive for sympathy that places DeCarava on the bandstand also keeps him from shedding artificial light on it. In the case of the aforementioned image, Coltrane's face is swallowed by the dimness of the nightclub and is lit, barely, by its own sweat. The available light is concentrated, spectacularly, in the glimmering of the saxophone—in pools that form at the lip of its bell and at the slant of the horn. This is what DeCarava has telegraphed to us, winkingly, by way of metaphor, and it is a message borne out in many of his nightclub photos: illumination may be hard to come by in jazz venues, but it can be glimpsed in the sweat of effort, the struggle of musicians with their instruments.[9]

DeCarava was here engaged in a nimble balancing act: he was conveying both intimacy and unknowability—the intimacy that comes with closeness and the unknowability that comes with the recognition that no matter how close you get you can never see with absolute clarity. DeCarava conveys an intimacy that has little in the way of romantic connection, little even in the way of eye contact. In this balance between intimacy and unknowability, the photographer was aided, perhaps unconsciously, by the symmetry between Coltrane's aesthetic and his own. Both were connoisseurs of the dark, artists drawn to its variable intensities: DeCarava's shadowy palette was a visual equivalent of the minor blues so beloved by the saxophonist, which married a sense of play to a seriousness of purpose. Moreover, the photographer's small-camera "candid" approach built on many of same premises as Coltrane's music. Both attuned themselves to the opportunities of a fleeting moment, and both clutched these improvisatory opportunities out of remarkable constraints—the static modal forms in the music, the dark palette that came with photographing a nightclub. Just as Coltrane turned to more abstract melodies in his modal improvisations, turning away from quotation and catchy hooks, so did DeCarava often deal with his tonal constraints by favoring abstraction over clearly framed portraiture.

In the subtle "Coltrane and Elvin," for instance, shot at the beginning of the quartet's collaboration, we can detect this novel, improvisatory abstraction at work. The saxophone's metal is brought into clear focus, while the face of Coltrane peers out of the gray on the right and Jones emerges as a spectral figure on the left, no more than a black head daubed above a shroud of a shirt. We can see DeCarava steering a course between social documentary, which downplayed the artistry and sympathy of the photographer, and pure abstraction, which downplayed the poignancy of his subjects and community. There is an amazing symmetry to the composition, in how the curve of the saxophone bridges the curving profile of Coltrane and the arched body of Jones; and this symmetry unites Coltrane and Jones even as the photograph's vantage point, with Coltrane so close that Jones becomes a faraway blur, suggests their distance from each other. In this instance, while DeCarava's abstraction leads him to focus on the object

FREEDOM'S SAINT

of the saxophone rather than his ostensible human subjects, the abstraction also works against the grain to intensify the human drama of the photograph, its suggestion simultaneously of teamwork and privacy.

A partner with Coltrane in his technique, DeCarava was able to suggest the saxophonist's charisma without resorting to hero worship. He framed Coltrane's art as a "religion of work"—with the intensity of belief, the clarity of purpose, that one associates with religion, and with the humble day-in, day-out labor that constitutes the working life. DeCarava was not entrapped by what saxophonist-composer Anthony Braxton calls the myth of "the sweating brow"—that "there is only one level of 'involvement' by black people" and it can measured by the quantity of sweat produced in the heat of performance. Attentive to the private Coltrane, DeCarava appreciated the work the saxophonist performed off the bandstand too, when he was no longer an icon of feverish spirituality. Considering this, Geoff Dyer wittily cites poet Wallace Stevens's question, whether we prefer "the beauty of inflections / Or the beauty of innuendoes / The blackbird whistling / Or just after." DeCarava gives us Coltrane whistling, as it were, in intense close-up, ablur in the action of improvising, and he gives us Coltrane at mid-distance—with his back to us at the Half Note, with his head bowed in listening, or, as in "Coltrane Alone," with his body encircled by the checkered tabletops of an empty club. Or he places Coltrane in the larger jazz community—for instance, hugging fellow saxophonist Ben Webster in a moment of levity. The message of DeCarava's series is that we don't have to choose one Coltrane over the other—indeed that we shouldn't, since the tranquillity of the latter images needfully balances the urgency of the former. DeCarava opens up his jazz series to Coltrane's livelihood in its totality. In feverish close-up, Coltrane appears larger than life, an icon who "overblows" his humanity. At a distance, quite another Coltrane emerges: the quotidian musician who studies, rests, abides.[10]

DeCarava's love of understatement, captured both in the way his images emerge from a play of darkness and in his attraction to these off-time moments, marks almost every photograph in his series. As a genre, the photo essay allowed DeCarava to reside with Coltrane, to view him prismatically as a spiritualist of the bandstand, a worker studying his craft, and a member of a jazz community who bridged generations and styles of performance. A similar devotion to the power of the commonplace marked DeCarava's aesthetic more generally: for instance, in his 1952 Guggenheim Fellowship application, he declared his focus on the "strength, the wisdom, the dignity of the Negro people. Not the famous and the well-known, but the unknown and the unnamed, thus revealing the roots from which spring the greatness of all human beings." It is interesting to consider the latent politics behind this understated portrayal of Coltrane, because DeCarava clearly shared a faith in "the unknown and the unnamed" with the Black Arts movement, and yet the keynotes of his Coltrane series—its tenderness and quiet power—seem to clash with prevailing assumptions about the Black Arts aesthetic, its supposedly confrontational spirit and unblinking acceptance of violence as a necessary part of struggle.[11]

DeCarava lived up to this commitment to the unknown and unnamed in his professional life through a long personal history of arts activism. Beginning as a visual artist at the Harlem Community Art Center and the WPA, he applied principles of collective action and community organizing throughout his career. He was part of the often-overlooked wave of grass-roots union activism that followed World War II, in the period before corporations and labor came to the truce that marked the 1950s and 1960s (better wages and benefits in return for a more peaceable and manageable workforce). He organized a union at the advertising agency where he worked in the late 1940s, assuming the leadership in the drive after the original organizer left the firm. Shortly thereafter, he began participating in the Committee for the Negro in the Arts, which aimed to invigorate Harlem's cultural life and promote the careers of black artists. In the early 1950s, DeCarava served as the head of the committee's Art Chapter.[12]

Later, when DeCarava was immersed in Coltrane and the jazz culture at large, he launched a new activist project. In 1963 he became the founding chairman of the Kamoinge Workshop, a black photographers' organization that opened a gallery on 125th Street in Harlem with the explicit goal of uniting the community and its artists. The Kikuyu word "Kamoinge" translates as "group effort," and the Kamoinge group worked to bring together artists with one another and with their buyers. The workshop ran a regular schedule of group meetings so that members could discuss each other's work, and sold group portfolios from their 125th Street gallery. Like the group Spiral, which Romare Bearden, Norman Lewis, and other visual artists also founded in 1963 in a spirit of civil rights empowerment, the Kamoinge Workshop testified to how an older generation of artists—not the baby boomers of the Black Arts movement and not their parents either, but the generation who had come of age during the New Deal—took up the challenge of community arts organizing, creating new venues, working more collaboratively, and forcing the arts establishment to be more accountable for the images it presented of black life. DeCarava, at least, extended his activism into the late 1960s. When the Museum of Modern Art opened its controversial *Harlem on My Mind* exhibition in 1969, DeCarava could be found on the picket lines outside the show as part of the Ad Hoc

Emergency Cultural Coalition, protesting both the museum's emphasis on documentary, rather than artistic, representations of the black community and its attempt to mount a show about the Harlem community without involving the community itself.[13]

DeCarava, then, represents a fascinating link between the radical aesthetic of the 1930s and the Black Arts movement—a link made more intriguing by the Black Arts movement's well-known tirades against other possible pioneers of the black aesthetic (one thinks of Eldridge Cleaver's attack on James Baldwin for being homosexual, and the various repudiations of Ellison's *Invisible Man*). Reviewing a 1969 DeCarava exhibition at the Studio Museum in Harlem, Larry Neal praised his "consistent commitment to social change" as well as his sympathetic portrayal of "people who struggle daily to make their lives more meaningful." And the younger photographer James Hinton celebrated DeCarava as "the first to devote serious attention to the black esthetic as it relates to photography and the black experience in America." Their warm reception of DeCarava confirms historian William Van Deburg's argument that the Black Power movement was centrally about reclaiming an African-American cultural legacy, and then building from self-definition to self-determination. DeCarava did not have to be confrontational to capture the younger activist generation's allegiance; he simply had to seem like an artist who emerged from, and gave back to, the black community.[14]

DeCarava may have pioneered a black aesthetic, but he also stood at some distance from some of the other, younger exemplars of that term—refusing, for instance, to magnify Coltrane's aura or convert him into an object of worship. His appreciation for the saxophonist drew him to Coltrane's routine qualities: the way he sweated, as many workers must sweat, for the sake of achievement; the way he relaxed, as committed artists often relax, by concentrating on his work. DeCarava's Coltrane does not seem to be driving his world to riot, as Baraka's Lynn Hope would do; he is restoring its hidden grace, often by exploring (strange twist!) its hidden torments. Black Arts poets were later drawn to Coltrane's scream for its suggestion of rupture and radical transformation. DeCarava meanwhile preferred to capture how Coltrane gave back to his community in less spectacular ways—through teamwork ("Coltrane and Elvin"), offhand joy ("Coltrane and Ben Webster"), and most of all, through perseverance. His Coltrane is the 1930s common man, with a modern adjustment: his pain and his effort to convey it, his alienation and his working life, are indistinguishable from each other. In DeCarava's eyes the intensity that many heard as demonic sincerity, as an exorcism of feelings, was transfigured humbly into the blessing of good work.

A Love Supreme: Enter the Recording Angel

Coltrane forthrightly dramatized that blessing with *A Love Supreme,* his most famous album and a legacy of his 1957 "spiritual awakening," which led him to reorient himself and give up the drugs and alcohol that had marked his life since the early 1950s. The album is an extended suite devised as a tribute to God, a pilgrim's progress that tracks Coltrane's acknowledgment, pursuit, and discovery of the holy spirit. Recorded in December 1964 and released the following year, it achieved a popularity that was almost magical, given the way that Coltrane's music had previously riven the jazz community. Critics applauded and the public responded also, buying half a million copies by 1970; *Down Beat* and *Jazz* named it album of the year, and *Down Beat* readers delivered to Coltrane a triple crown—"Jazzman of the Year," best tenor saxophonist, and induction into the magazine's Hall of Fame. All told, *A Love Supreme's* success was evidence of a deeper cultural reversal: jazz had gone from being seen as the "devil's music"—music whose appeal lay in its supposed release of unrestrained passions—to a resonant expression of spiritual uplift and gratitude. Like Duke Ellington, who staged his first Sacred Concert with a jazz liturgy in 1965, Coltrane affirmed that jazz could express the deepest of religious longings and even, in Coltrane's case, the most oracular of prophecies. This new ambition led, in turn, to the discovery of a new form. *A Love Supreme* is one of jazz's great concept albums, a forty-minute suite that links together four different pieces into a larger, circular narrative of spiritual and self-discovery. Its success encouraged Coltrane to pursue the suite form in the more ambitious works of his final years: the clamorous eleven-piece *Ascension,* the underappreciated *Meditations* (recorded by quartet and sextet), and the series of six spectral duets he recorded with drummer Rashied Ali, released under the title *Interstellar Space.*[15]

More than Coltrane's earlier music, *A Love Supreme* presented explicit clues about the nature of the faith behind it and gave listeners a larger musical scaffolding, an album-length narrative, to explore. Coltrane included a poem in the album's packaging, one whose generalized, liturgical language captures the music's elemental drama of submission and empowerment, its faith in the act of surrender and the simultaneous revelation of a supreme force. "I have seen ungodly—none can be greater—none can compare to God," Coltrane wrote. "Thank you God. He will remake us. . . He always has and he always will." Humility and empowerment, pursuance and constancy: these were the opposites seemingly united, or at least given mutual expression, in Coltrane's suite. He strove to exemplify how "God breathes through us so completely . . . so gently we hardly feel it" in his own breathing through his saxophone. And so he was driven to a daunting act of simultaneous impersonation—to be both the pilgrim who surrenders himself to God and the vehicle through which God speaks in his most commanding voice. The poem conveys this sense of self-denying devotion by telling us almost nothing about Coltrane other than his will to serve God ("I will do all I can to be worthy of Thee") and praising God in language that is plain-spoken and stripped of metaphor ("God is. He always was. . . . No matter what . . . it is God"). The voice of Coltrane's poem is so self-abnegating that readers might be tempted to consider it artless; yet the poem succeeds largely, like Coltrane's music, by fusing abstraction and a sense of human vulnerability. Its ending—"elation—elegance—exaltation—All from God. Thank you God. Amen."—reads like the destruction of the individual ego in the creation of collective strength, transcendence expressed through gratitude.

I will explain later how Coltrane developed this sound of empowered vulnerability, or vulnerable strength, but first we should consider the structure of A Love Supreme. The suite's structure is what makes it uniquely satisfying among Coltrane's work—or, more precisely, the structure is what gives this piece a greater sense of self-fulfillment, of spiritual resolution, than most of Coltrane's other music, which by contrast conveys the restlessness of transition. A Love Supreme takes the sense of destiny that informed Coltrane's faith—the sense that God "always has and . . . always will" remake us—and translates it into a musical drama of turbulent resolution, where the act of remaking is suggested through the volatile energies of improvisation, while the sense of resolution is suggested in the suite's larger movement into stasis. We move through four parts: "Acknowledgment," an open-ended prelude built on a bass ostinato that later folds into the chanting of the words "a love supreme"; "Resolution," an up-tempo cooker that raises the intensity of the suite; "Pursuance," an even more frenetic piece, which begins with an extended Elvin Jones drum solo and seems bursting with improvisatory energy as it strays far from its (small amount of) precomposed thematic material; and "Psalm," a free-form but static saxophone chant where Coltrane "sings," with a note for every syllable, his praise poem "A Love Supreme." Altogether, the album marvelously balances freedom of form and complexity, looseness and intensity. "Acknowledgment" and "Psalm" frame the piece with double-jointed interplay built around remarkable harmonic constraint (a bass ostinato in the first, a drone on the piano in the second), while "Pursuance" and "Resolution" offer the more familiar Coltrane pleasure of the quartet running through song cycles of twenty-four and twelve bars, respectively.[16]

Let's begin with "Acknowledgment," which guides the listener from humble beginnings to one of jazz's most famous moments of synchronicity. As Lewis Porter has expertly shown, "Acknowledgment" is built around very simple harmonic material, the three notes of F, A-flat, and B-flat. Introduced in a repeated bass figure that propels much of the piece, these three notes form a melodic "cell" that is so adaptable—so easily recoded rhythmically and transposed into different keys—that they serve both as the basis for the bass ostinato and as the building block of Coltrane's 149-bar improvisation. Crucially, they are also the notes that Coltrane, with his love for the abstract sound of fourths and the pentatonic scale, favored more generally: he used them, for instance, at the beginning of "Afro Blue" and (in a different key) "Liberia," "Cousin Mary," and "Equinox." And so while these notes are rudimentary in conception, at this point in Coltrane's career they unmistakably serve as his musical signature too—the crux of the identity that, as a pilgrim, he places before his God. Just as Coltrane seemed to strip himself of personality—abstaining not only from alcohol and drugs but also from any gesture that might draw attention to the act of self-presentation (for instance, Charles Mingus's embattled assertion of his genius as a composer, Duke Ellington's love-you-madly bonhomie)—so his musical identity in A Love Supreme is stripped down to the humblest of materials, a mere three notes. Coltrane was an unlikely cousin of Gertrude Stein, who quipped that compositions must be simple, but simple through complication. He built elaborate structures, with the same unstoppable energy that Stein brought to her voluminous writings, out of purposefully rudimentary beginnings. And, like Stein again, he did so through acts of repetition that were more like conjugations in that they suggested different ways of performing the same action.

Through this kind of repetition-based harmonic development, "Acknowledgment" portrays the religious action of spiritual dilation, where the self admits its insignificance so that the spirit can fill the vacuum with its plenitude. Out of its core three notes emerge a whole world of melodic exploration; a minimalist sense of origins dovetails with a maximalist sense of possibility. As Porter explains, Coltrane conjugates the melodic cell in three ways over his 149-bar solo: first, by intensifying its rhythm, jamming it into a contracted amount of musical space and inserting it around the downbeat; second, by playing it on the full range of his saxophone, climaxing with purposeful strain on ascents into the altissimo register (up to a fifth above the usual top f″); and third, by transposing it into keys other than its home key of F minor—in fact, into keys quite dissonantly related to F minor. In the first 120 measures of his solo Coltrane employs all three methods, playing ingenious, rhythmically jammed, harmonically flipped variations on the melodic cell. Often he strings together consecutive

FREEDOM'S SAINT

versions of the cell (for instance in measures 33 to 43, with the two groups C–E-flat–F and F–A-flat–B-flat) and plays with a doubled, six-note motif that completes a pentatonic scale.

These acts of melodic addition and manipulation prepare the way for a conclusion that is stunning, by contrast, in its transparency of technique. At measure 121 Coltrane begins playing the bass ostinato on his saxophone. Then he modulates it intact through a series of keys—up a step to G, down to D, up to A-flat, and so on—until he has cycled through every key possible. Finally, after twenty-six of these modulations, he returns to the home key of F and then, putting down his saxophone, begins chanting the four-syllable phrase "a love supreme" over the four-note ostinato, with an added voice adding heft. The voices continue chanting for forty seconds over Jones's Afro-Latin accents and Tyner's punctuating quartal chords.[17]

In *A Love Supreme*'s drama of spiritual perfection, this moment of chanting feels especially perfect—and although it's easy to speculate why, it's more difficult to capture the sensation. Partly it is the appeal of voices in unison: Coltrane's quartet usually operates through loosely interlocking grooves, so it is a small wonder to hear bass and voices singing together. The excess in Coltrane's sound has been pared away, the need for heightened drama has disappeared, and we feel clarity, relief. But this relief is infused by the strangeness of hearing Coltrane's actual voice, the strangeness of him chanting in a register that is close to the relaxed tones of everyday speech. We are accustomed to hearing his voice through his instrument, and locked in extreme struggle with it, squawking, honking, screeching—doing everything, that is, *except* talking serenely. At least for this brief moment of chanting, he seems to have surpassed the resources of his instrument and found a new, calm voice. Ironically, he becomes God's explicit vehicle by dropping his saxophone, the instrument that has brought him to this point of transcendence but now seems a mere accessory.

Perhaps most crucially, though, the power of this moment comes from our sense that a preordained design has just been revealed to us. Coltrane's solo had been tending toward the four-note, four-syllable mantra the entire course of his solo *and we had not realized it*. For this reason, the ending of "Acknowledgment" satisfies the listener in unusual ways. Unlike most jazz arrangements, which cycle after the solos back to a restatement of the head, "Acknowledgment" cycles to a revelation of the head: the central melody precipitates out of the solo. Moreover, Coltrane has seeded this unison moment of revelation with a series of gestures that seem to make a systematic point. By playing the ostinato in every key and register immediately before the chant, he works to illustrate his poem's central proposition: "In You [God] all things are possible." He seems to be willfully testing the boundaries of dissonance, suggesting that "a love supreme" can bless even the most dissonant notes with the ability to sound as though they have their place. He conjures a universe where noise and harmony can merge, where every individual, no matter how errant, can succeed in the fulfillment of some larger design. The small melodic cell may begin as Coltrane's private signature, but its infinite transformation suggests that it might just be ours too.

Just as "Acknowledgment" moves from peaceful simplicity to tense energy and then back to an act of restful recapitulation, the whole of *A Love Supreme* moves in a larger arc from relaxation to intensity and then to peace. Coltrane follows "Acknowledgment" with "Resolution" and "Pursuance," both of which ratchet up the energy of the quartet. The tempo accelerates, the quartet's interplay becomes more dense, and Coltrane's playing in particular becomes more digressive and chromatic, recalling the sweat-soaked 1961 Village Vanguard performance of "Chasin' the Trane." The oddly titled "Resolution" is the movement that departs most dramatically from "Acknowledgment"'s central melodic cell and the pentatonic scale. It has a keening eight-bar melody, repeated three times with slight variations at its end, which descends inventively down an octave. Beginning on a high E-flat, it climbs down to rest on the dissonant flat fifth (A), then segues through the harmonic minor (G-flat) to the lower E-flat. The flat fifth and harmonic minor foreshadow the direction of Coltrane's subsequent improvisation, which twists through a distinctly chromatic solo.

"Pursuance," meanwhile, reintroduces "Acknowledgment"'s melodic cell, but in a disguised form. As Porter explains, Coltrane shrewdly plays the cell in "Pursuance's" theme but transposes it to the scale of C, even as the rest of the quartet uses B-flat as its tonal center. Thus does Coltrane recall *A Love Supreme*'s original motive while placing it out of joint; and remarkably, his improvisation remains on this raised path, his explorations of the pentatonic C scale set against the B-flat ruminations of Tyner and Garrison. It's as if Coltrane were operating in a universe parallel to Tyner and Garrison—one that allows him to mimic them but keeps him from a richer identification. Here Coltrane uses the suite form to test the limits of unity—both the unity that joins past and present (the first and third movements, joined by the three-note cell), and the unity that joins self and other (Coltrane and his bandmates, joined by the improvising in the pentatonic scale).

What is the point of this grand performance, spun out of the most rudimentary materials? "Psalm," the final installment of *A Love Supreme*, underscores that the larger logic of the piece is one of self-sacrifice: Coltrane is trying to dramatize the integrity, ubiquity, and power of God through a paradoxically empowering act of self-limitation and self-purification. As in a black church service, the ritual of the chant—the preaching of the word and the gestures of call and response between preacher (Coltrane) and congregation (the rest of the quartet)—create a vacuum that the Holy Spirit then floods with energy. After "Resolution," which strays far from the three-note cell, and after "Pursuance," which reintroduces the three-note cell but does it askew, Coltrane ends with a harmonically static saxophone chanting of his praise poem. It is a performance whose beauty emerges out of a controlling set of compositional restraints. As we noted earlier, Coltrane follows his own praise poem note for syllable, with each poetic phrase joined to a musical phrase.[18] The repeated phrase "Thank you God," for instance, corresponds with a three-note figure that varies slightly and returns us emphatically to the tonic. All the musicians perform in a C-minor force field with a strong gravitational pull: Tyner rocks on G–C–G in his left hand, Garrison sticks largely to the signposts of C minor, and even Coltrane the perennial wanderer does not deviate from the minor pentatonic scale. "Psalm" extends the recitative texture of the opening moments of "Liberia" over its entirety. For seven minutes, Coltrane sings rubato over Jones's splashing cymbals and rolling timpani. Because "Psalm"'s static harmonies limit the eventfulness of the piece, we are especially attuned to its larger dynamic, the drama of a saxophone preaching to its congregation. In this case, of course, Coltrane has literalized the metaphor of his saxophone as the voice of a preacher, with his poem "A Love Supreme" serving as his sermon.

We can appreciate "Psalm"'s ritualized beauty—how Coltrane's phrases, for instance, approximate the rise and fall of a preacher's cadences in the black church—but still wonder whether "Psalm" succeeds as the exemplary piece it was meant to be. Can we assimilate its journey of spiritual inwardness and self-purification? The musical evidence suggests that "Psalm" defies literal emulation: few jazz musicians have performed "Psalm" since its 1964 recording—a telling sign, given that many free-jazz ensembles from the mid- to late sixties *did* try to simulate the free form of Coltrane's less popular later suites like *Ascension,* while almost any contemporary jazz pick-up group can wing through early Coltrane standards like "Blue Train" or "Equinox." *A Love Supreme* seems like such an intensely personal religious statement that to cover it would require the kind of chutzpah that does not shrink from the accusation of sacrilege. But perhaps more forbiddingly, "Psalm" is an oddly terminal performance, one that brings us to a limit of stillness that is difficult to aspire to. Its static harmonies and static rhythms convey the integrity of an ensemble that, remarkably, has freed itself from the pressure to be original; yet they also settle the musicians into a sort of entrapment, a condition of purity that forces them to give up so much. The one voice on "Psalm" allowed substantial room for exploration is Coltrane's—and even here his notes are tied to the rhythms and meaning of his precomposed poem.

Coltrane's saxophone playing even seems to admit this difficulty, that the pursuit of integrity—if taken to its logical extreme—is hard to sustain and pressures the self into brittleness. It's fascinating to consider that, at moments of greatest supposed musical resolution, Coltrane resorted to effects that split his voice in two or otherwise doubled it. At the end of "Afro Blue" he trilled until he seemed to be singing two divergent notes at once. At the culmination of "Acknowledgment," he dubbed a second voice over his mantra. And at the end of "Psalm," in the last moments of *A Love Supreme,* he (or an unidentified saxophonist—it remains a mystery) over-dubbed a high C that rode above its final flourish, the breath after its "Amen." In the context of Coltrane's entire body of work, these moments may seem trivial, yet they point to a productive tension in his aesthetic. While Coltrane largely created a style of jazz that argued for single-mindedness and against the ambivalence of double consciousness, at these moments he seemed to suggest something quite different: that the splitting of one's self was the final frontier of a self in extremis, a kind of rebirth. In a less mystical vein, we might say that these moments of voice-splitting and voice-doubling signaled that Coltrane's integrity was not an end in itself, but a means to fresh discovery. The split tones were his way of ending his musical journeys by pointing to another fork in the road. Thus Coltrane's refusal to stand pat with the innovative form of *A Love Supreme* or, before it, with the harmonic experiment of "Giant Steps," the modal jazz of "My Favorite Things," and so forth. The pilgrim moved on.

Working-Class Heroes: Coltrane and Malcolm

To understand the impact of *A Love Supreme*—how and why Coltrane was raised as an icon—we need to step out of the world of music and consider the cultural tensions of the mid-sixties through the other great spiritual autobiography of 1965, *The Autobiography of Malcolm X.* Although Coltrane and Malcolm X may seem to be opposite figures in disparate universes—the first apolitical and seemingly disconnected from the actual groundswell of the freedom movement, the second firebreathing in his politics and seemingly disconnected from the world of the arts—they did share a broad cultural connection. Both became icons of integrity, figures of an uncompromising and uncolonized black selfhood. So it was that the same black poets who lauded Coltrane in the late 1960s took up Malcolm

FREEDOM'S SAINT

in other moments—with Carolyn Rodgers, for instance, asking her audience to be a "Black Nationhood Poem / for/ El Hajj Malik El Shabazz" because Malcolm's authenticity demanded a matching perfection from his people. Or the two icons could become one, as when Amiri Baraka later praised Coltrane as "Malcolm X in Super Bop Fire." The "Malcolm poem" was the counterpart of the "Coltrane poem" in the Black Arts movement, with both figures called upon posthumously to unite blacks who *knew* they were black with those (usually identified with the middle class, or with the student population) who repressed such self-knowledge. As Black Arts poet-critic Stephen Henderson wrote in 1969, "What Coltrane signifies for black people because of the breadth of his vision and the incredible energy behind his spiritual quest, Malcolm X signifies in another way—not as musician, but simply and profoundly as black man, as Black Experience, and that experience in the process of discovering itself, of celebrating itself."[19]

Henderson's joint praise for Coltrane and Malcolm begs some very basic questions: *which* "Black Experience" was deemed to stand in for all the others? And which black identities were deemed inauthentic or transitional, better left in the dustbin of history? Coltrane and Malcolm's lives taught a similar lesson: they both gave up the hipster's life of irony and darting transgression, the life that defied the law and middle-class mores, in favor of a straightforward vanguardism that was a kind of working-class righteousness. In so doing, they were held up by critics like Henderson as antidotes to double consciousness, men who had dissolved the supposed conflict of interest between being American and being black. They suggested, explicitly and by force of their example, that black culture did not need to be appreciated through the lenses of white society but might be appreciated on its own terms; and in so doing they put incredible pressure on the question of what these terms would be.

Coltrane and Malcolm's most compelling works took the form of autobiographical conversion narratives: *A Love Supreme* and *The Autobiography of Malcolm X* are both stories of individual tribulation and ascent. Coltrane and Malcolm raised a fresh, if not unprecedented, question in the tradition of American autobiography: what would it mean if the autobiographer was a working-class black man, and if he chose to lift up his community rather than climb out of it? *A Love Supreme* was designed as an inclusive ritual of ascension (although one with hermetic secrets); Malcolm's autobiography, which diagnosed with laser precision and lethal seriousness his experience of American racism, was written as an invitation for black readers to join his movement for justice. In this way, Coltrane and Malcolm both tried to affirm their own personal quest for truth without dividing themselves from the black community that had nurtured that questing spirit—to affirm the pursuit of individuality without supporting an ethic of individualism.[20]

While Coltrane's *A Love Supreme* marked the new position of the jazz musician as spiritual avatar, Malcolm X's autobiography crystallized parallel trends: the movement of street-corner intellectuals to the center of American cultural life and the emergence of Black Power as a dominant impulse in the Movement. Malcolm remains at the head of the "Class of 1965," as cultural historian Carlo Rotella has named the fleet of urban intellectuals who came forward to explain to mainstream America why its black citizens were taking up arms, why Martin Luther King's dream of a beloved community had begun to sour, and—to make the question concrete—why Watts was burning five days after the August 6 passage of the 1965 Voting Rights Act, a legislative victory for the Movement signaling that the federal government would protect blacks' access to the ballot box. Malcolm's autobiography took its place alongside Claude Brown's *Manchild in the Promised Land* and Kenneth Clark's *Dark Ghetto* as touchstone reflections on the embattled state of black manhood in the inner city, written from the authenticating point of view of the black man himself. Malcolm's autobiography, like Brown's and Clark's work, spoke to the traps and temptations of ghetto life—especially the lure of drugs, gangs, and petty crime—but it also countered with a tale of hope and uplift, the story of an individual who, by "making it," exemplified how the community as a whole might pass through its trials and come out ahead. As Ossie Davis proclaimed in a famous eulogy, Malcolm was "our shining black prince" and "living, black manhood"—which is to say, he gathered much of his power from the way he brought together militancy, masculinity, and black pride.[21]

Malcolm's defense of black manhood was part of a much larger controversy about black family life and sexual values, a firestorm touched off by the now infamous 1965 Moynihan report on the black family. Through years of sit-ins, boycotts, marches, and other forms of community organizing, the Movement had won the passage of a federal civil rights statute; and the question that has chased everyone since—what next?—was suddenly on the table of Movement leaders and government policy makers. Labor Undersecretary Daniel Patrick Moynihan leapt into the fray with his report *The Negro Family: The Case for National Action*. Moynihan argued that the legacy of slavery and job discrimination had trapped many black families in a "tangle of pathology" that would keep them from profiting from the legal and political gains of the Movement. "The essence of the male animal, from the bantam rooster to the four-star general," Moynihan wrote, "is to strut"; and black men, in slavery and now in the urban ghetto, were the equivalent of walking wounded. The crux of the "pathology," as many critics of Moynihan have since remarked, was the poor black family's inability to replicate the middle-class white family. Since there were too many black men deserting their families, Moynihan argued, there were too many black women heading households in their absence (one-fourth), and too many black children born out of wedlock (again, one-fourth) and growing up on government relief.

The Moynihan report had an explosive reception, partly because its logic suggested that the federal government should stop spending money on the poor and instead focus on improving their moral character, and partly also because it touched on larger issues of sexual control and freedom—issues that young white people were testing too—while deflecting them onto black men and women. Although it now stands, in journalist Nicholas Lemann's words, as "probably the most refuted document in American history," at the time of its publication it found a sympathetic reception in the liberal white press, who popularized its findings in the aftermath of the Watts rebellion. By October 1965, however, it became clear that Moynihan, who supported jobs programs for the poor, had miscalculated. Conservative commentators enthused that "self-help" was now going to replace government handouts as the answer to black disempowerment and deprivation. Black leaders across the political spectrum denounced how the report seemed to blame the values of the disadvantaged rather than attack the root causes of entrenched inequality, such as discrimination in banking, housing, and the criminal justice system. In fact, the now-familiar phrase "blaming the victim" was coined in response to the report by William Ryan, a white psychologist and civil rights activist in Boston. Meanwhile black and white radicals would come to question the patriarchal assumptions of the report—that women-centered households were dysfunctional, that men were born to rule the roost, and that working-class black families with two wage earners needed to cast themselves in the increasingly anachronistic image of the white middle-class family run by the breadwinning male.[22]

It is in this context that Coltrane's *A Love Supreme* and Malcolm's autobiography achieved their magnetic popularity, offering counterimages of the working-class black man in his vulnerability and his strength. As icons, they contested the Moynihan Report's presumption that black working-class culture was deficient to the point of pathology and answered its call for a restored sense of black manhood. In Coltrane's music, this quality of authenticity meant refusing bebop's irony and projecting instead a religious ritual of self-discovery, in a voice that did not shirk from the most intense of personal expressions. If the black church has historically been one of the black community's most independent institutions, Coltrane's ritual-istic music aspired to a similar state of independence. It was no coinci-dence, for instance, that he did not quote Tin Pan Alley melodies in his so-los—for what would it mean if you quoted someone else in your expression of spiritual ache? Nor did he engage in the usual team play of the bebop combo, where the soloist "trades fours" with parts of the rhythm section—for what would it mean if you had to tailor how the spirit moved you? His recursive and additive solo lines seem self-generated, the result of a personal logic; and it is fitting that his concert repertoire increasingly be-came self-defined, almost hermetic—more and more versions of the so-prano-led "My Favorite Things" and the tenor-led "Impressions." While Coltrane did not stand outside of commercial channels—he profited from his association with Impulse records, where he was canny enough to record a wide spectrum of his music, and he relied on the jazz concert and club circuit for his livelihood—he did craft music that seemed autotelic, driven by its own sense of purpose. "My music is the spiritual expression of what I am—my faith, my knowledge, my being," he said in a late interview. "I'd like to point out to people the divine in a musical language that transcends words. I want to speak to their souls."[23]

For Malcolm, the quest for authenticity entailed what critic Cornel West has termed "psychic conversion": "the decolonization of the mind, body, and soul that strips white supremacist lies of their authority, legitimacy, and efficacy," a process that "begins with a bold and defiant rejection of Black degradation" and "often ends with early death owing to both white contempt for such a subversive sensibility and, among those captive to Black self-contempt and self-doubt, a Black disbelief." Malcolm held that black people did not need to be hybrids, existentially balanced between the demands of white and black America. He rejected the pluralist vision of, say, Ralph Ellison, who argued that American culture was inextricably var-ied and that the wonder of cultural forms like jazz came in part from their resourceful blending of white and black idioms past the point where the two might be separated. By contrast, Malcolm unequivocally condemned blacks who seemed to have struck a truce with mainstream America and the powers that ruled it. In his famous distinction between "house ne-groes" who protect their white masters and "field negroes" who resist them, Malcolm made clear his allegiance to the path of unyielding resistance and uncompromised selfhood. As historian Robin Kelley points out, Malcolm assailed the black bourgeoisie for "their station in the Big House and their unwillingness to walk out"; and although he entertained a certain ambiva-lence about how black nationalism could succeed in the light of these class

FREEDOM'S SAINT

differences, he never backed away from his claim of representing "the masses of Black people who really suffer the brunt of brutality."[24]

Coltrane and Malcolm shared even more than their projection of a new black authenticity, though. Born less than two years apart, they passed through similar generational and class experiences, which gave depth to the mid-sixties testaments of *A Love Supreme* and *The Autobiography of Malcolm X*. Both were products of the 1930s' and 1940s' migration of the black working class from agricultural areas to Northern cities—Coltrane moving with his cousin Mary from High Point, North Carolina, to Philadelphia in 1943, Malcolm moving with his family from Omaha to Michigan and then, more independently, to Boston and New York in the early 1940s. After a wartime stint working as a laborer in a Philadelphia sugar-refinery, Coltrane spent much of the late 1940s and 1950s gigging around the city, moving between R&B groups like Bullmoose Jackson's and bebop big bands like Dizzy Gillespie's, and becoming increasingly dependent on alcohol and drugs. Malcolm meanwhile partook of an earlier hipster subculture. Going "wherever Negroes played music" and "selling reefers with the bands as they traveled," Malcolm claimed that he "was known to almost every popular Negro musician around New York in 1944–1945." At Boston's Roseland and Harlem's Savoy Ballroom, he plunged with his zoot suit into a dance world that, with its group choreography, individual styling, and emphasis on pleasure for its own sake, offered an alternative to the values of the black middle class. As a Roxbury soda jerk, Malcolm had to serve the "penny-ante squares" with "millionaires' airs," but he escaped them in these nights on the town.[25]

While both Coltrane and Malcolm eventually turned away from this hipster's life—Coltrane converting to an ascetic pan-spirituality, Malcolm converting to the Nation of Islam and then to orthodox Islam—they retained their connections to black working-class culture. In contrast to Charles Mingus, who thrived in interracial settings like San Francisco's Beat scene and Greenwich Village's café circuit, Coltrane did not actively reach out to the countercultural audience that welcomed him; and although he had an on-and-off affair over three years with a white woman in the early 1960s, his two marriages were to women with roots in the black religious community, Muslim Naima (formerly Juanita) Austin and pianist Alice MacLeod, who began her career playing churches in Detroit. Likewise, in a career marked by huge changes in compositional style and improvisational format, Coltrane held onto a voice and style of phrasing that emerged from his apprenticeship in R&B bands. His music always relied for much of its power on his saxophone's vocal qualities—the honk that might turn into a scream—and on the way he returned, after displacing the beat for several measures, to that sturdy groove known as "the one." *A Love Supreme* is a typical Coltrane piece in this respect, both in the attention it focuses on the timbre of Coltrane's saxophone (the key to the drama of "Psalm") and in the way his saxophone returns, after much harmonic digression and rhythmic displacement, to a simple and emphatic phrase (the key to the drama of "Acknowledgment").[26]

Malcolm's tie to working-class blacks was less abstract: as a spokesperson and grassroots organizer for the Nation of Islam, he recruited among disciplined and frugal ghetto folk who did not identify with middle-class strivers. The Nation of Islam practiced a complicated attack on the value system of the middle class, claiming for black working people the virtues traditionally associated with the bourgeoisie (cleanliness, abstention from alcohol and drugs, respectability) while building independent strength within the black community. Malcolm censured middle-class blacks with the same vigor he used in his attack on white Americans, because he saw the two groups in perverse collusion. As Robin Kelley points out, Malcolm's critique of the black middle class focused not on their income or occupation but their allegiance to the values and power structure of the dominant culture: "Uncle Tom wears a top hat. He's sharp. He dresses just like you [college students] do. He speaks the same phraseology, the same language." Members of the black bourgeoisie—including civil rights leaders who, Malcolm alleged, were handpicked by the white establishment—were "ashamed of black, and don't want to be identified with black or as being black." For this reason, they favored the ideal of integration over the promise of black empowerment, and desegregation over land, money, and freedom. Malcolm was an outspoken critic of these "professional beggars," attacking America's systematic racism and instilling black pride in a way that still resonates with black youth in the postindustrial city.[27]

Finally, in assessing Coltrane and Malcolm's appeal as icons of black integrity, we must note a remarkable complexity in their construction of "integral" selves: both figures were famous for the protean quality of their identities, the way they maneuvered and responded to the temper of the times. If they were working-class heroes, they conveyed the sense that the working class was on the move. As Adolph Reed writes of Malcolm, his "appeal grew largely from the way he counterpunched in very concrete terms against the changing elements of that reality—for example, in his responses to the Birmingham church bombing, the sanctimony surrounding the Kennedys, the Civil Rights movement's strategic reliance on the stereotype of the patient-suffering-slow-to-anger Negro . . . [H]e energized us by playing the dozens on the official narratives of race and power under which we strained." Working in a more humble vein, Coltrane may not have counterpunched political figures, but he did interrogate himself: "Most of what's happened these past few years has been questions," he said, typically, of his most popular music. "Someday we'll find the answers."[28]

Both Coltrane and Malcolm seemed to progress through stages, each of which suggested a new problem that in turn begged a new solution. Coltrane moved from hard bop and modal jazz to the suite form of *A Love Supreme* and then to freer combinations that dropped the musical pulse entirely. Malcolm famously moved from hipster and thief to Nation of Islam spokesman and, after his 1964 trip to Mecca, combatant of all forms of racial supremacy. The greatest evidence of Coltrane's and Malcolm's integrity, it seems, lay in their openness to confront the contradictions raised by their own choices and in their complete commitment to the solutions that they discovered, even as they readied themselves for new contradictions and new solutions. They were absorptive personalities, always willing to remake themselves in an act of discovery—Coltrane in his musical digestion of everything from bebop to Indian ragas, Buddhist temple music, slave spirituals, Stravinsky, and the harp playing of Harpo Marx; Malcolm in his virtuosity as hipster, convert, scourge of the "white devils," and adherent of an orthodox, nonracialist Islam. For this reason, their legacy was a whole repertoire of responses to the demands of art or politics. As A. B. Spellman wrote of Malcolm shortly after his assassination, "We must accept Brother Malcolm's political life as being valid for every one of his thirteen political years."[29]

This openness to self-transformation also gives us another avenue to explore Coltrane's and Malcolm's relationship to the cultural controversy around the Moynihan Report, which attacked the black family as it affirmed the virtues of a patriarchal order. What sorts of masculinities did Coltrane and Malcolm embody? The jazz music of the 1950s and 1960s has been characterized, rightly, as a fraternal order, but Coltrane's music suggested that jazz brothers might share their fragility as well as their strength; jazz became an unconventional but more powerful route to dignity. *A Love Supreme* placed the submission of the self at the heart of its drama, beginning with the "acknowledgment" of one's vulnerability, then moving on to a vision of God that stressed generosity and, of course, an all-powerful love. It is strange, but probably right, to consider *A Love Supreme* one of the 1960s' most compelling love songs, since it recast the dimensions of what love might be; Coltrane wanted to express a love humble enough for anyone and large enough for the whole world to share. He was writing a love song for the Almighty and, partly as a result, when he turned to the ballad form with "Psalm," he turned to a new kind of ballad playing, shorn of the romantic qualities (the harmonic embellishments, the breathy mode of address) that he had used, if sparingly, in his ballad playing elsewhere. His work on "Psalm" is closest perhaps to his playing on "Alabama," written to commemorate the four children killed in the 1963 Birmingham church bombing: both pieces are prayers for supreme love that come out of the recognition of supreme vulnerability.

By contrast Malcolm, for all his changes, presented a less flexible image of manhood and a baldly inequitable view of gender relations. "All women, by their nature, are fragile and weak," he wrote in his *Autobiography;* "they are attracted to the male in whom they see strength." His version of Islam instructed that "while a man must at all times respect his woman, at the same time he needs to understand that he must control her if he expects to get her respect." Malcolm's black nationalism put the struggle of the black man at its center while narrowing the meaning of manhood: for instance, Malcolm attacked the civil rights movement's nonviolent tactics by arguing that "anybody can sit. An old woman can sit. A coward can sit. . . . It takes a man to stand." And while there sometimes were cracks in this heroization of the black man at the expense of the black woman—in a 1964 interview he offered that "in every country you go to, usually the degree of progress can never be separated from the woman" and went on to praise the education of women—in general, Malcolm did not connect racial oppression to gender oppression.[30]

In the end, the great appeal of Coltrane and Malcolm may lie in how they admitted the difficulty of being "out there"—marginal and militant—while seeming to convert this difficulty into the challenge of a fresh commitment. They balanced their marginality with an outlook so avid and expansive that they repositioned themselves as the centers of a new, more comprehensive aesthetic and a new comprehensive politics. Their firm grasp of the local allowed them to reach for the global: Coltrane built on the foundation of the blues until he had created a form of world, and even interstellar, music; Malcolm enlarged upon his analysis of the challenges facing Northern blacks until he could envision the global liberation of the racially oppressed. Shedding earlier personalities in the pursuit of perfection, widening their circle of followers as they found a new voice and a new community, Coltrane and Malcolm gave credence to the prophecy that the last would be first, that even the underdog would have his day. Their shattering, untimely deaths—Malcolm at the age of thirty-nine, Coltrane two years later at the age of forty—left the freedom movement with a sense of promise cut grievously short, but promise nonetheless. Their emergence as posthumous icons points to an understudied but powerful strain in the Black Arts movement: its scouring search for hope.

PART FIVE

In and Out of the Whirlwind

9

"LOVE, LIKE JAZZ, IS A FOUR LETTER WORD"

Jazz and the Counterculture

Now that we live in the aftermath of the rock revolution, it's easy to think that rock was destined to supplant jazz as the music of white rebellion and protest and that the two idioms represented irreconcilable cultural stances. Jazz was cerebral, acoustic, and human-scale, while rock was guttural, electric, and spectacular. Jazz was the noirish shades of Blue Note album covers, while rock was the saturated colors of the psychedelic light show. Jazz was heroin, its inwardness and suspended sense of time, while rock was the hallucinatory cocktail of speed, grass, and LSD. Jazz was driven by the creativity of black musicians, while rock was driven by the love affair of white musicians (British and American, working-class and art-schooled) with black music. Behind all these contrasts was the difference in how the two types of music addressed their audience: postwar jazz was hip, an insider's music, while rock was participatory, a music meant to please—and generate—a crowd. Playwright Sam Shepard, whose early 1960s' work grew out of his contact with the jazz world, testified to the magnetic pull of rock in the late 1960s: "rock and roll made movies theatre books painting and art go out of the window none of it stands a chance against The Who The Stones and the old Yardbirds Credence Traffic The Velvet Underground Janis and Jimi and on and on." Shepard was one of many breathless observers who believed that rock was the only game in town; no other cultural form seemed to offer the double experience of aesthetic intensity and cultural solidarity, the feeling of a new youth culture discovering itself. And the bottom-line figures seemed to support this sense of rock triumphalism. In 1970 the music industry's sales of records and tapes ($2 billion) exceeded the sales generated by movies and all sports events ($1.6 billion and $600 million respectively), and by the early 1970s nearly 80 percent of recorded music fell into the category of rock.[1]

Yet like so much history conveyed in shorthand, the story of this shift from jazz to rock conceals as much as it reveals. The lines between the two idioms did not begin as cultural givens but were made so through a complex set of negotiations between artists, the culture industries, and their audiences, all of whom were reinventing themselves, unaware of how the story would end. In the mid-1960s, for instance—before *Sgt. Pepper,* before Black Power—jazz observers on the left could still imagine a healthy and reciprocal relationship between the budding New Left, the civil rights movement, and jazz music, and could speculate on how to transfuse the Movement ethic of "participatory democracy" into the jazz industry.[2] Jazz artists stood in a complicated relationship to the growing popularity of rock and soul. Sometimes they defended the terrain of jazz against rock's encroachment or, on the other end of the spectrum, made obvious attempts to cross over (recording, for instance, covers of Beatles tunes or the music of *Hair*). But many musicians took up the challenge of fashioning a form of jazz that would match the appeal of rock or soul music and build bridges to a younger audience. "Fusion" and new forms of soul-jazz emerged alongside the audiences for rock and soul proper, while free jazz was taken up by a group of Black Arts musician-intellectuals who understood the music as an ally of the black community's surging "soul force."

While the next chapter looks at how jazz musicians responded to the promise of soul, this chapter charts how jazz both contributed to the largely white counterculture and ceded its place in the radical imagination. It begins by tracing how the jazz festival gave birth to the rock festival, which embodied to many observers the innovative appeal and force of the counterculture. Then it matches this institutional history with the stories of two individuals, playwright Sam Shepard and poet-activist John Sinclair. Shepard emerged as one of America's leading experimental playwrights as he moved from a kind of jazz expressionism to a rock-influenced postmodernism: he began the 1960s in an aesthetic collaboration with Mingus's son; he began the next decade in a similarly intense partnership with proto-punk singer-songwriter Patti Smith. Meanwhile, Sinclair began his career writing under the sign of John Coltrane but transferred his allegiance to the hardest forms of white rock, becoming in the late 1960s the chairman of the White Panther party and manager-propagandist for the MC5, a high-decibel forerunner of punk music and the only band to perform at the Yippie-sponsored "Festival of Life" at the Chicago Democratic Convention in 1968. The stories of Shepard and Sinclair illuminate something of the impact of Mingus and Coltrane, respectively, even as they reveal how figures of the counterculture distanced themselves from their early apprenticeship under the jazz aesthetic. This chapter tries to account for this shift in cultural energy and focus—to understand what was lost, gained, or rechanneled, often in surprising form, as the freedom movement in jazz was joined to, and overshadowed by, the cause of rock liberation.

"All Quiet on Newport Jazz Front"

Despite the many threats to the 1960 Newport Jazz Festival—the violent youth riot, the mood of insurgency expressed by the Mingus-Roach counterfestival and Langston Hughes's *Ask Your Mama*—the festival managed to recover and even flourish financially in the coming decade. Newport and the legions of jazz festivals that it directly or indirectly spawned—in Chicago, Las Vegas, Monterey, and other cities across the country—reconfigured themselves and their audiences throughout the 1960s. They attracted larger and larger crowds, recruiting an older pop-jazz crossover audience through established figures like Louis Armstrong, Frank Sinatra, Duke Ellington, and Dizzy Gillespie, and they managed these crowds with beefed-up security in larger arenas that were built to capitalize on their success. At the same time, they paved the way for the great festivals of the counterculture, which were anchored in the music and spirit of a younger generation. The idea for the Monterey International Pop Festival, generally regarded as the first rock festival, came to rock promoter Alan Parisier after he attended the Monterey Jazz Festival in 1966; Monterey Pop eventually borrowed its site and format from the jazz festival. From Monterey, the rock festival lunged toward its mammoth 1969 incarnations—the 150,000-person Newport '69 (a three-day rock festival actually held in California's San Fernando Valley), the 400,000-person Woodstock, and the 300,000-person, tragedy-marked Altamont.[3]

The jazz festival—formerly a flashpoint for young people's leisure—thus increasingly took on the dilemmas of a successful cultural parent. It lured a few rock performers, while distancing itself from the trappings of rock's decadence; it advertised interracial harmony, but drew a vague line where harmony might ratchet up into action; it sought the youthful audience, but shied away from the near-religious fervor whipped up in rock performance. Generally, it became more capitalized on an economic level and less topical as a cultural innovation, gaining its notoriety only inasmuch as it "crossed over" to the counterculture. While Monterey and Woodstock aimed to consolidate a new youth culture, jazz festivals were content to turn a healthy profit.

The Newport Jazz Festival led the way in making a corporate truce between jazz entrepreneurs, concerned city officials, and the jazz audience. In 1960, the festival had seemed a terminally ill patient, a victim of competing legal actions, unpaid debts, and riot-wary Newport denizens.[4] Cofounder Elaine Lorillard brought a suit against the festival's board of directors for ousting her—and soon her ex-husband, Louis, resigned from the board, dispirited by the lack of support he received in the lawsuit. His letter of resignation paved the way for the festival's reorientation, most strikingly signified by the installation of entrepreneur George Wein as its producer-director. From its inception Wein had been the dynamo behind the festival, responsible for the booking arrangements with musicians and handling much of its publicity and accounting. More changes were made after 1961: the Newport Jazz Festival changed its tax status and officially became a for-profit corporation; and the board of directors, which had formerly served an advisory role to the festival's programming, was dissolved. Wein spoke of his ascendancy as the return of pure jazz to Newport: "I'll try to make [the festival] as much of a purist festival as possible this year. . . . There'll be no more haphazard presentation of too many groups in too short a time."[5]

One of Wein's first moves was to broker a truce with the city of Newport, which still worried about riot protection. The year after the riot, the city had turned away from the Newport Jazz Festival corporation and licensed a competing organization to produce "Music at Newport," a festival that tried to attract an older audience through pop entertainers such as Bob Hope and Judy Garland. To enhance its image, Music at Newport had contracted a large regiment of security officers to patrol the city—all 77 Newport police, 300 volunteers from outside communities, and 50 Pinkertons were posted outside the entrances, where the 1960 riot had gestated. The show of force was not lost on observers: *Variety* headlined its coverage with "All Quiet on Newport Jazz Front as Regiment of Cops Squelch Punks."[6] When Wein took back the festival from its 1961 backers, he shifted his bookings away from figures like Judy Garland but maintained the emphasis on security. In the coming years, side streets were closed off and grassy areas were ringed with snow fencing. Police officers were instructed to be courteous but firm: at the first sign of trouble, they were to clap the malefactors into custody. To supplement the seventy members of the Newport police, Wein availed himself of the Navy's shore patrol, off-duty state prison guards, and a hundred policemen from surrounding areas. In 1965, the city formally banned festivalgoers from sleeping on the beach.[7]

In a step that spoke volumes about the relationship between the city and the festival, the festival in 1965 also moved its grounds out of the centrally located Freebody Park. After irate town residents had filed a Superior Court injunction against the Newport Jazz Festival, the city council in 1964 banned future festivals from the site. Unfazed, Wein negotiated a deal on property at the edge of the town limits, near the sewage plant and the town dump, a thirty-five-acre area that became known as Festival Field. Where Freebody Park had a carnivalesque, impromptu atmosphere (the musicians dressed in tents; sound quality was often dicey), Festival Field promised the well-oiled excitement of a theme park. The stage was a massive fifty-five-by-sixty-foot affair, backed by a forty-five-ton scaffolding of steel girders. A nearby building served as the site of festival administration; another served as musician dressing rooms, connected to the stage via a fifty-foot ramp. Most important, Festival Field could accommodate ever larger crowds that would not spill over into the town center. When riots came back to Newport (as they did in 1969 and 1971), they would no longer threaten the property of the town, only the physical well-being of the festivalgoers and the financial welfare of George Wein.[8]

The Newport Jazz Festival served as both proto- and antitype for jazz festivals across the country, which mushroomed in number through the late 1950s and early 1960s. Starting in 1958, Wein expanded his Newport operations to include popular satellite festivals in French Lick, Indiana; Toronto; Boston; Detroit; and Buffalo. Other promoters soon jumped on the festival bandwagon. In 1959, *Playboy* began hosting a Chicago festival, which attracted up to 70,000 customers over its three days of programming. The Annual Festival on Randall's Island, New York, begun in 1956, offered summer jazz to more interracial audiences just outside of Manhattan. Wein was hardly squeezed by his institutional competition: in the early 1960s, he launched jazz festivals in Cincinnati, Chicago, Pittsburgh (co-sponsored by the Catholic Youth Organization!), Detroit, Atlanta, New Orleans, and Hampton, Virginia.[9]

Jazz festivals soon surged into the most established of venues, having made peace with such parties as musicians' unions, corporate entertainment, and even the federal government. In 1962, Las Vegas began hosting its own festival in its sparkling new Convention Center, marking a newly sealed partnership between jazz and the tourist trade. The Las Vegas festival also marked the first time that an affiliate of the American Federation of Musicians had organized a jazz festival as a union-related benefit concert. In the same year, the President's Music Committee sponsored Washington, D.C.'s first International Jazz Festival, a five-day affair that spread events across Howard University, Constitution Hall, the Smithsonian Institution, the National Gallery of Art, and the National Guard Armory. All proceeds were to benefit the People-to-People Program, an arm of Cold War cultural outreach. Jazz—for years a prize export of the U.S. Information Agency to the nonaligned nations of Africa, India, and the Middle East—was finally being welcomed by the federal government on its own turf. It had become part of Kennedy's Camelot portfolio, another exemplary and exceptional American art form, one that won over hearts and minds by evangelizing for freedom without seeming to embody a coarse American nationalism.[10]

From Monterey Jazz to Monterey Pop

Although Wein's festivals and the festivals he inspired continued to draw large crowds, the festivals remained ambivalent about the countercultural audience that flowered in the mid-sixties. Newport, for instance, was roiled by more riots—sporadic disorder in 1967, full-fledged stampedes in 1969 and 1971—each of which was followed by a "purist" festival that highlighted jazz and employed more police. The link between the jazz festivals of the 1950s and the Woodstocks of the late 1960s was forged most strongly on the West Coast through the Monterey Jazz Festival, the most powerful challenger to Newport in terms of its vision, popularity, and cultural legacy. Launched publicly in 1958, the Monterey festival was supposedly for love and art, not for profit; it welcomed an interracial audience, while Newport tiptoed around one; it dramatized the sensuous pleasures of youth, while Newport tried to frame its pleasures as healthy, pedagogical, and orderly; and finally, it imagined its audience communing with its musicians, while Newport had always been fractionalized between critics, musicians, knowledgeable and unknowledgeable publics. San Francisco music writer Ralph Gleason, later a key figure behind *Rolling Stone* magazine, spoke of the 1966 Monterey festival as an experiment in free love:

> The festival is for the musicians and the festival is for the patrons— both. Each one digs the other and they both dig the digging. A festival is to have fun, to be festive, to give and receive love. And love, like jazz, is a four letter word and surrounded these days with inhibitions and taboos. But at Monterey, for this one weekend, we are all free to love and jazz is free to be our music.[11]

Gleason was speaking here with the accents of the late 1960s (digging, taboos, freedom, love), but his ideas were grounded in the Statement of Principles that the Monterey festival had issued in 1960, its third year of operation, as a clear counterthrust to the canons of Newport. The festival vowed to place its programming "in the hands a professional musician . . . , not a booker or promoter": just as Charles Mingus supervised the programming of the Newport rebel festival, so John Lewis of the Modern Jazz Quartet supervised the roster of Monterey for twenty-five years. Also, the festival promised never to allow "flashbulbs, rowdyism, and similar disturbances" to "interfere with the enjoyment of guests." In this spirit of healthy pleasure, the festival promised to donate all profits to Monterey Peninsula College for music scholarships, under the guiding principle that profits should be invested back into the surrounding community. Unlike Wein's Newport, Monterey had no ambition to mushroom into a national network of jazz festivals.

The Statement of Principles also promised "a true *festival,* not merely an unrelated series of concerts." Even before the holistic surge of the late sixties, Monterey was offering a unified experience of jazz rather than a string of box-office draws. As Gene Lees exulted in *Down Beat* about the 1959 Monterey festival, "Nothing, in point of fact, ever has demonstrated the growing maturity of jazz as much as this year's Monterey event. . . . Monterey this year made previous jazz festivals look like grabbags, musical potpourris that do not compare with the smoothly purposeful and thought-provoking Monterey festival."[12] Lees's 1959 Monterey was a far cry from Gleason's 1966 festival—analytical where the other was love-heavy, purposeful where the other was frivolous. But both shared a faith in the cumulative experience of the festival, in the feedback loop it established between art and life. In 1961 Jimmy Lyons, the founder of the festival, reasoned similarly that "Monterey compares to Newport as a small budget 'art' film compares to a super extravaganza like 'Ben Hur.' Perhaps the low budget is a blessing in disguise. In many ways it forces us to concentrate on the unusual and original, rather than merely to fling a lot of expensive talent on the stage."[13]

Compared to the 400 officers who trolled the 25,000-capacity Newport festival and its environs, the 7,000-seat Monterey festival was a liberalized and informal zone—a fact that also may have contributed to its growing appeal to a black audience. Monterey began as a predominantly white affair, but by the mid-1960s its audience was split evenly between black and white. By the mid-1970s, it was 60 to 70 percent black. The festival's informality, it seems, also resulted in more countercultural programming. Although Jimmy Lyons was less rock oriented than his friend Ralph Gleason, he nonetheless extended a friendly hand to the burgeoning Fillmore scene. In 1966, the Jefferson Airplane and the Paul Butterfield Blues Band were added to the Saturday afternoon roster. In 1967, the Saturday afternoon show featured future Woodstock stars Richie Havens and Big Brother and the Holding Company, who, according to Gleason, ended one number with an "amplifier-hugging, guitar-smashing finale."[14]

The rapport between Monterey and the San Francisco scene was somewhat reciprocal—a warm if uneven exchange between cultural parent and burgeoning offspring. Even before Miles Davis began spreading the gospel of jazz-fusion through appearances at the Fillmore and his landmark album *Bitches' Brew* (1969), jazz greats were sprinkled in counterculture fests. In January 1967, at Golden Gate Park's Human Be-In, also known as "A Gathering of the Tribes," Monterey stalwart Dizzy Gillespie shared the stage with the Grateful Dead, the Jefferson Airplane, Timothy Leary, and Allen Ginsberg. Ginsberg intoned Hindu mantras; Yippie Jerry Rubin celebrated his release from a Berkeley jail cell and passed around a hat to raise legal funds; and the Diggers, a radical community group, distributed free fruit, free vegetable stew, and free tabs of acid. Over 20,000 spectators (including Charles Mingus) crowded into the polo grounds for the four-hour concert. Generally regarded as the first rock festival and advertised at the time as "a love feast" joining "Berkeley's political activists" with "San Francisco's hippies," the Be-In now seems almost too countercultural to be believed—a sign that its events, while scandalous enough to earn the headline "Hippies Run Wild" in the *San Francisco Chronicle,* have been absorbed into familiar narratives of 1960s culture.[15] Yet the presence of Gillespie—a political stuntman who announced a mock "Dizzy for President" campaign in 1963, complete with the support of the "John Birks Society" and plans to revoke the citizenship of George Wallace and deport him to Vietnam—suggests a less publicized, subterranean link between bebop showmanship and countercultural pranksterism.[16]

When the First International Monterey Pop Festival emerged in 1967 as the virtual embodiment of the Summer of Love, it did so by distancing itself from the "square and unaware" jazz audience while inheriting the lofty ambitions of the Monterey Jazz Festival. Like the jazz festival, Monterey Pop was strictly a nonprofit enterprise, one that wanted to keep its distance from grubby commercialism. When Ben Shapiro, a booking agent for Miles Davis and Bob Dylan, launched the festival by starting a for-profit corporation, he encountered firm resistance from the musicians he approached. Paul Simon and John Phillips of The Mamas and the Papas suggested instead that the festival become a nonprofit operation, "a kind of enormous weekend party and idea session," which would lure top performers through its freewheeling charm. Simon and Phillips prevailed. A board of governors—a countercultural dream team that included Paul McCartney, Mick Jagger, Brian Wilson, and Donovan—was installed as the presiding body of the festival, and Shapiro soon sold out his $50,000 investment. The board was more of a symbolic entity—its members never met at one time—yet its composition suggested a departure from the board of directors of Newport in its nonprofit days, which had included jazz critics and impresarios rather than jazz musicians, under the rationale that jazz musicians would practice favoritism. Suspicions of favoritism were replaced by the enthusiasm for a family affair. Monterey Pop was designed—like Mingus's counterfestival and the Monterey Jazz Festival—to put supervisory power in the hands of the musicians. Ultimately, its protocol most resembled the Monterey Jazz model of having a single musician direct the programming. With Paul McCartney, Mick Jagger, and Donovan on one continent and Brian Wilson on another, the daily decision-making devolved upon promoter Lou Adler and musician John Phillips.[17]

But while the Monterey Pop festival was inspired in part by Monterey Jazz, the transition from jazz to pop stripped Monterey of most of its black audience—a phenomenon that speaks volumes about the relation between the San Francisco music scene, itself heavily steeped in blues and jazz, and the black residents of the area. To judge from D. A. Pennebaker's scrupulous filming of the Monterey Pop crowd, it would seem that African Americans made up around 5 percent of the audience, or around one-tenth of the jazz festival's audience. Some observers called Monterey Pop "whitey's festival," noticing that black performers had been pushed to the margins: with the sole exception of Otis Redding, no R&B black performer headlined the event. Smokey Robinson was nominally on the board of directors, but neither his group, the Miracles, nor any other Motown artists played the festival. Chuck Berry was one of perhaps many black artists who refused to perform for free; the Impressions and Dionne Warwick agreed to perform, then backed out. In the final roll call, nightclub singer Lou Rawls and South African-born trumpeter Hugh Masekela (booed during his performance, like Laura Nyro) were simply curiosities that pointed to the preponderance of white blues and psychedelia at Monterey.[18]

Critic Robert Christgau explained the vexsome relationship between these white San Francisco bands—most of whom felt deep affinities with jazz and the blues—and more mainstream black musicians:

The San Francisco bands try for a soulful sound, but they are more interested in urban blues (Muddy Waters, B. B. King) than in the more popular and commercial Negro music. . . . [T]hey hone their lyrics and experiment with their instruments and come to regard artists like Martha and the Vandellas, say, as some wondrous breed of porpoise, very talented, but somehow . . . different. And their audience concurs. This attitude is anything but condescending (in fact, it is almost always reverent), but the Negro performer, who prefers his music to any other, is understandably disinclined to regard himself as a cultural oddity.[19]

The unease of white performers with soul culture led to a strange convulsion at the end of the story of Monterey Pop. Before the concert itself, rumors had circulated that its profits would filter to the Diggers, the radical community group that handed out free food daily in Golden Gate Park and whose stunt-activism clashed with the sensibilities of New Left political organizations like SDS. However, under pressure from the good burghers of Monterey, John Phillips denied that any money would "go to a hippie underground organization." Instead, a substantial slice of the $200,000 in profits, generated largely by the white counterculture at "whitey's festival," was directed to the New York City Youth Board for guitar lessons in the ghetto and to Atlantic Records's Sam Cooke Memorial scholarship program for black music students. It was a clear tribute from white musicians who couldn't play black, exactly, but who recognized the depth of their music's debt.[20]

Monterey Pop marked more than the emergence of a new music, derived from jazz and blues but apart from contemporary black pop. As an event held in the shadow of the Be-In, and as the precursor of the 1969 festivals that would dwarf Newport jazz, Monterey Pop suggested a new social formation as well: a counterculture that embraced its own massiveness and hoped to render obsolete many of the worries over "mass culture" that circulated in postwar intellectual circles. D. A. Pennebaker's *Monterey Pop*—a cinema-verité documentary of the event—conveyed this newborn enthusiasm for the flower-bearing mass audience. Where the Newport-based *Jazz on a Summer's Day* had largely concentrated on quirky vignettes of jitterbugging couples and tailgate bands, *Monterey Pop* moved at crucial moments to envision the full scale of its audience. Where Bert Stern's film had focused on idiosyncrasy, Pennebaker's suggested that, beyond the iconoclasm of individual hippies, there might be an equally noteworthy shared experience. For this reason film historian William Rothman has called *Monterey Pop* "an American answer to Leni Riefenstahl's *Triumph of the Will*"—an attempt to depict a utopian democratic festival in the same way that Riefenstahl's work proposes a utopian fascism through a Nuremberg rally for Hitler.[21]

Although it diverged ultimately from Stern's formula, *Monterey Pop* was indebted to the earlier film's basic premise and techniques. Like Stern, Pennebaker was creating an ethnography of the event, one that implicitly claimed that the experience of the festival was its meaning. And like Stern, Pennebaker tried to imagine the point of view of the crowd—fully absorbed in the action onstage while remaining on the surface of that action. Much of the camera work in both films appears hand-held and idiosyncratic, although both try to find an equivalent for the music's rhythms through well-timed cuts (in Pennebaker's case, always to the beat). Pennebaker's opening hand-drawn titles over a swirling light show and the cranked-up music of Big Brother and the Holding Company—and his recurrent use of the light show on the scrim behind the stage suggested yet another link to Stern's film: like Newport jazz, countercultural rock was the foundation for exercises in surreal visual abstraction. Where Stern offered the glint and ripple of the Newport harbor (the water viewed either so far or so close that it became less legible as part of an ocean), Pennebaker used a psychedelic light show that eddied and surged with purposefully unnatural colors—hot yellows, bright reds, deep blues. The "trip" of Monterey was sensory overload: its abstractions resembled hyperkinetic brain waves more than the smooth wavelets of Newport.

Perhaps the best way to explain the difference between *Monterey Pop* and *Jazz on a Summer's Day* is to say that *Monterey Pop* turns the concert documentary into a more profound exercise: it raises the emotional and philosophical stakes out of the realm of light entertainment. It traffics in anguish and annihilation where Stern's film relies on Dixieland jamboree; it ends with transcendent, orgiastic spirituality where Stern's film ends with gospel-driven joy. Unlike Stern's film, which has only infrequent bouts with solemnity, Pennebaker's film revolves around the paradox that his peaceable audience is enthralled by music that advertises its destructive power. On the surface, the film's motto might be a line from a song performed by The Mamas and the Papas: "California dreamin' is becoming a reality." Monterey couples flounce in loose shifts and medieval-looking tunics, holding hands, distributing flowers, blowing bubbles. A cop banters with a bearded hippie—the lion lying with the lamb. As one woman asks the camera invitingly, "Have you ever been to a love-in? It's going to be like Easter and Christmas and New Year's and your birthday all rolled into one."

The drama of the film, however, comes from the break between the love-in and the explosions of anger onstage. Singing "Paint It Black," Eric Burdon spits out "I see the girls walk by dressed in their summer clothes," at which point the camera cuts to couples walking underneath umbrellas—as if to imply that Burdon's black mood has literally rained on their parade. Later Pennebaker films a colony of young people camping with pup tents and sleeping bags scattered on the grass—at which point a piercing scream by Country Joe and the Fish suggests a rape in Arcadia. When the Who smash their instruments and Jimi Hendrix annihilates his guitar near the end, they are merely exploding a tension that runs through the entire film, one that threatens the festival's air of charitable good feeling and perhaps its very existence as well. As Pete Townshend lunges to stab the amplifiers with the sharp stick that is the remnant of his guitar, the tech crew rushes onstage and starts gathering up the detritus of the Who's performance. And after Jimi Hendrix torches his guitar, Pennebaker captures the roadie who, after applauding briefly, makes a motion to clean up the stage. The rituals of destruction are trailed by the workaday efforts toward damage control. All told, the film gives credence to historian George Lipsitz's insight that the counterculture's "apocalyptic strain" was "even more powerful" than its utopian love ethic, with its "popular songs routinely project[ing] fatalism and dread about political crises."[22]

In *Monterey Pop*'s finale, however, Pennebaker tries to shift his film's balance toward its utopianism, toward the suggestion that the festival can move through these acts of "creative destruction" and emerge into another realm entirely. Pennebaker ends with the performance of Indian raga master Ravi Shankar—a significant choice, given that Shankar's concert did not close the festival and that it was the one concert that had not sold out in advance. Like Stern, who closed his film with a gospel performance by Mahalia Jackson, Pennebaker opted to close his film with a religious idiom that stood apart from the categories of art music and pop music. Both films, after documenting the joyfulness of their crowds, moved toward a form of music that was loose but also beyond suspicion, music that aimed for feelings of shared spiritual transport. When Shankar's raga begins with the solo sitar, Pennebaker delivers what film scholar William Rothman calls "a veritable National Portrait Gallery of hippies, flower children, and bikers; of weird hairstyles, outlandish costumes, and tattoos; of 'normally' coiffed, dressed and un-made-up people of every race, ethnic group, and class." As the raga builds toward the dazzling interplay between Shankar on sitar and his tabla player, the camera switches to the performers onstage: it becomes absorbed with their self-absorption, with their informal yet knowing signals to each other, their spirited licks and switchbacks. Then, when the raga culminates in a rush of sitar runs and tabla thrums, the camera suddenly pans outward from the stage with the ovation—and we suddenly see that the National Portrait Gallery of diverse individuals has been transformed by Shankar's music. Seen from a bird's-eye view, the audience is knit together into a jubilant mass of applause.[23]

Pennebaker extends his scene of applause for so long that it might be counted as the final number of his Monterey Pop festival—the crowd finally producing its own music in unison. Cutting from the bird's-eye view, he tracks for nearly two minutes alongside row after row of the audience, all of whom are on their feet and applauding with enthusiasm. Pennebaker's Monterey Pop festival celebrates the power of the mass audience, while Stern's Newport festival preferred individual idiosyncrasy and the quirkiness of youthful cliques, Stern's film, we might recall, ends with the young Dixielanders, crashed out in their roadster as they exit Newport, their festival spirit exhausted. By contrast, Pennebaker ends his film euphorically, placing his camera near hand level so that we see the motions of the applause as well as the faces behind it, the instruments of this unison as well as its individual makers. This camera angle is a curious choice that works to confirm our identification with the crowd—who wouldn't want to be part of this spiritual euphoria, so winningly shared?—even as it reminds us of the film's artifice by lowering the camera beneath eye level. We are made to *know* that we are being included. More utopian than any other sequence in the film, this final tracking shot intimates that the music need never die as long as the crowd renews itself—and it puts the question to us, as viewers in another sort of crowd, whether we too are ready for the challenge.

Sam Shepard and the Fate of the Jazz Impulse

Remembering his first work as a playwright in the early 1960s, Sam Shepard spoke of the deep influence of Charles Mingus:

> [I] was stunned by his sense of polyrhythm—rhythm on top of rhythm on top of rhythm. I was fascinated by the idea of merging that with writing, seeing if there was a way of evoking the same kind of collage in the writing of plays.
>
> I started thinking about the kind of structure jazz has, the kind of life it implies, and I decided to see if I could be a playwright myself with what I'd learned from [jazz musicians].[24]

Himself a drummer of considerable skill, Shepard was one of the artists who most intensely listened to jazz in the 1960s and most successfully translated its aesthetic principles into another medium. In one-act plays like *The Rock Garden* (1964), *Cowboys* (1964), *4-H Club* (1964), and *Cowboys #2* (1967), all written not long after his arrival in New York at age twenty, Shepard helped create a theatrical form that had "the kind of structure jazz has"—or more specifically, the kind of structure that the most apocalyptic of postwar jazz has.[25] Like much of Mingus's work, these early one-acts were dramas of inflation and deflation, built on the different rhythms of the different players and marked by sudden rhythmic shifts that fundamentally altered the terms of dialogue. They owe a great debt to Mingus's aesthetic—in their love of excess and incongruity, their quick, confusing shifts between playfulness and violence, and their ambiguous attraction to radical artifice and ideals of authenticity. In fact, the aspects of Shepard's art that were immediately acclaimed in the New York theater world—his rhythmic handling of conflict and his inclusion of elliptical "arias," or surreal monologues that seemed to voice the improvisatory thoughts of his characters—are difficult to appreciate fully outside the context of the jazz aesthetic. Drummer-composer Max Roach, who scored music for a series of Shepard performances at La Mama in 1984, not only spoke of "the profundity of the man," but also offered a possibly deeper tribute: "He thinks like a drummer."

Shepard's early collaborator was none other than Charles Mingus III, the bassist-composer's son and a high school friend from Duarte, California. The two lived together in a cheap loft in Greenwich Village, at one point rooming with Jazz Workshop drummer Dannie Richmond as well, and spent much time at jazz clubs like the Village Gate (where Shepard worked) and the Five Spot (where Mingus's Workshop often performed). So when Shepard spoke of "the kind of life [jazz] implies," he often meant the hand-to-mouth improvisational existence he pursued in Greenwich Village with the younger Mingus, playing games and feuding as they grappled with the difficulties and possibilities of this new urban life. His jazz-inflected dramas of the early 1960s usually revolve around trickster types, young men inventing identities and discarding them with a reckless energy—experimental theater versions of the jazz hipster. Set on a minimalist set with a flashing traffic barrier, *Cowboys* has its two male leads (originally played by Mingus and Shepard) trying on a series of nonurban fantasy roles: a father and son practicing baseball, two matinee cowboys on the lookout for Indians, boyish pranksters splashing in the mud of a cloudburst. Likewise, *4-H Club* has its three male characters stuck in the kitchen of a frowsy apartment and riffing on a series of scenarios, each of which springs out of their living situation—and gives them an imaginative way of escaping it.[26]

By the late 1960s, however, Shepard had distanced himself from the jazz music that grounded his early writing, leaving behind much of the expressionist improvisation that he associated with the music. Incorporating live rock music into his plays and sometimes drumming or playing guitar in the shows himself, Shepard no longer identified with jazz and its "kind of sophistication." "I started reacting against that, the whole jazz influence," he said. "So I began to think rock and roll music represented another kind of back to a raw gut kind of American shitkicker thing." Shepard's use of rock was purposefully abrasive, with high-voltage sounds blasting through the tiny spaces of underground theaters like New York's La Mama. The characters that wandered through this rock soundscape, meanwhile, were much more cartoonish than his earlier tricksters: prototypes of postmodern pastiche, they often performed the most intense actions with little affect and even less motive. Partly Shepard was reacting here to what he saw as the changes that the rise of the counterculture brought to New York's urban scene: "When this sudden influx of essentially white middle-class kids hit the streets, the indigenous people—the Puerto Ricans, the blacks, the street junkies, and all the people who were really a part of the scene—felt this great animosity toward these flip-outs running around the Lower East Side in beads and hair down to their asses. There was this upsurge in violence and weirdness . . . in New York it got very scary."[27]

Jazz, it seems, was the perfect soundtrack for the carnivalesque underground community of the early sixties, but rock—in its electricity, coarseness, and impersonality—was the medium for this rougher age. The story of "Shepard's sixties" is, then, at least three stories at once: the story of the counterculture's emergence from an underground subculture to a broader cultural movement; the story of the connection between early 1960s experimental theater and experimental jazz; and the story of jazz's declining relevance for some of its most observant young listeners.

Shepard was indebted to the jazz world literally for his introduction to the Off-Off-Broadway movement. A busboy at the jazz club the Village Gate, he worked alongside head waiter Ralph Cook, who had recently become "minister to the arts" for St. Mark's Church, a hub of the underground performance scene then taking root in the basements, lofts, and coffeehouses of Lower Manhattan. Cook had founded Theatre Genesis at St. Mark's, a project dedicated "to the new playwright," but had no one yet lined up to fit the bill—until Shepard, armed with only a few notebook scribblings, offered himself. *The Rock Garden* and *Cowboys* were staged as Theatre Genesis's second production in 1964, the first of many Shepard-Genesis collaborations over the next seven years (*Chicago, Forensic and the Navigators,* and *Mad Dog Blues* were also Genesis productions). Shepard used St. Mark's as his home base—he slept and took meals there, socializing with other artists affiliated with the church—and became a key exponent of what might be called the St. Mark's aesthetic. Like much of Off-Off-Broadway performance, his plays were staged on minimal budgets and with the barest of sets: Shepard and Mingus, for instance, lugged their own bathtub from their apartment to Theatre Genesis for the staging of *Chicago,* in which it was the central prop. Yet the plays found ways to make a theatrical impression without the resources of conventional, set-based realism. Narrative logic was often suspended or undermined through rapid jump cuts between scenes; characters often shared the same stage but seemed to exist in different universes; actors were frequently instructed to give intensely physical, rather than well-modulated, performances; and the dialogue had an unpredictable dynamic, either too quiet (as seen in long stretches of silence) or too loud (as when characters started screaming).[28]

Jazz music helped catalyze these theatrical innovations, although jazz itself never made it into Shepard's early work. Until he turned back to this music in the mid-1970s, Shepard did not use jazz accompaniment nor did he feature jazz musicians as characters. Rather, jazz was a medium that gave him a more abstract form of inspiration. It put Shepard in contact with a theory of character that emphasized the instability of mood and the improvisation of self; it gave him a polyrhythmic sense of how voices could operate with different cycles and on different frequencies; and it may have introduced him to an ethical way of evaluating these improvised selves, an understanding that the pursuit of freedom is diminished when it is not part of a collaborative effort. Shepard shared with an earlier generation of white artists—for instance, Beats Jack Kerouac and Allen Ginsberg—a sense that jazz represented the pursuit of Dionysian freedom, the uncensored expression of the soul's impulses. But he avoided some of the racial pitfalls of Beat writing, in part through simple evasion. Unlike Kerouac, who repeatedly saw black life as a reverse image of his own discontent, Shepard rarely dealt explicitly with issues of contemporary race relations. His cooperative productions with Charles Mingus III, for instance, turn to the frontier mythology of cowboys and Indians, but avoid the line of questioning that drives social-problem films about interracial friendship like *The Defiant Ones.* When Shepard did put a group of black radicals on stage with *Operation Sidewinder,* his treatment of their plight was so stereotypical that black students at Yale, where it was to be premiered, blocked its production in December 1968, and the play was moved to Lincoln Center with its black roles significantly revised. So in some sense, we may be grateful that Shepard's early work is jazz drama—extensions of the music's sense of play and sense of time—rather than drama *about* jazz. Shepard uses jazz as a way of understanding the improvisation and tension within

American urban life, but does not force black characters to pay the price for white freedom.[29]

The one-act *4-H Club* is a good example of how jazz principles were translated into the flesh-and-blood interactions of characters on stage. The action of the play is set in the small kitchen of an all-male abode (apparently loosely based on the living situation of Shepard and the younger Mingus); the room is positioned extreme upstage left. In this corner of the stage are clear signs of squalor: the kitchen's floor is littered with paper, cans, and trash, its walls are dirty, and its three male inhabitants are dressed in torn and grimy clothes. Immediately, though, the audience is made aware that we are far from the world of kitchen-sink drama (and not just because the set design is so minimal that there is a hot plate in this kitchen but no sink). Stage space and real space are made to overlap: as Shepard instructs in his stage directions, "the lighting should be equal for the whole stage with no attempt to focus light on the kitchen." Shepard captures, then, an extreme sort of onstage grittiness *and* draws attention to the theatrical imagination that creates that grit—a fitting decision for a play that revolves around the role of fantasy in the life of young bohemians.[30]

Despite its wholesome title, *4-H Club* is in fact full of anguish, the successive venting of fantasies that give some escape but no relief from life's pressures. For a drama about slackers, there is surprisingly little sense of slack in the play itself. From its opening moment, when one character is kneeling at the hot plate and the two other characters are laughing so hysterically that they fall on the floor, the play establishes a sense of disparate realities lived out in disjunctive rhythms. Bob and Joe, the two jokers, deal with the serious John in cruel but unpredictable ways—cursing him for eating an apple, mocking him for his attempts at domesticity, blatantly misinterpreting him, and in the end, ignoring him as he rhapsodizes eerily about man-eating mandrills and the inviting landscape they inhabit. When not badgering John, they are drawn into their own riffs of hyperbolic and spontaneous violence, developing scenarios with an associative and often surreal logic. For instance, in quick order Bob and Joe imagine themselves throwing their garbage can out the window, smashing an old woman in the head, drawing a confused crowd, launching a volley of deadly apples at this crowd from their window, and then instigating a riot complete with armored tanks charging up the street and police shooting apples out of the sky.[31]

Bob and Joe's riffs may recall a kind of collective jazz improvisation, but they are not a vehicle for celebration or for earnest self-expression. Instead we get a strong taste, as we do in Mingus's Jazz Workshop, of the disjunctions of improvisational logic and the apocalyptic possibilities opened up by such logic. Beneath the surface of everyday life, there is, if not an abyss, then at least a very deep rabbit hole. The desire to clean up an apartment can, in a flash, become a frenzied desire to seek out pests and exterminate them; a pang of hunger can lead to an almost murderous sympathy with the killers of this world. Moreover, we as the audience are made to partake in this sensation of unpredictability, this burden of living in the moment. *4-H Club* operates by a logic of emotional excess—feelings build until they explode—but it places this excess in a barren setting and refuses to allow its emotions to add up to a shared feeling or resolution. This feeling of disconnection is perhaps at its most intense in the play's final moment, when Bob and Joe scream at each other about whether they should be silent to lure the apartment's mice out of their hiding places, and John drifts off into his rhapsody about the merciless mandrills and the beauty of their habitat. There are obvious associative links between Bob and Joe's argument and John's rumination: both deal with predators and victims (Bob and Joe and their mice, the mandrills and their prey), and both are inspired by a fantasy of control and escape (through the extermination of the mice, and through the journey to a place where "you just float and stare at the sky"). Yet the audience is left with these connections hanging in midair, the kitchen as grimy as ever, and Joe banging on the coffee pot "in a steady beat." The chaotic polyrhythms of the play are resolved through a militant, off-putting, and seemingly futile gesture of control.[32]

It is odd to think of a play like *4-H Club* as optimistic, but in the context of Shepard's later rock-inflected work, it seems a fair call. At the least, the surreal and jazz-inflected sources of energy in Shepard's early plays—the dreamy monologues, the fits of expressionist action—tend to disappear in his late-sixties work, as if rendered irrelevant as strategies of resistance. He shifted his focus from trickster figures who flirt with successive identities to failed heroes, would-be rock stars, ineffectual revolutionaries—in critic Stephen Bottoms's words, "helplessly plastic people" in search of "a depth and a stable reality which the superficiality of the plays denies them." The source of hope in these plays, such as it exists, is often located in pastiche versions of Native American spirituality—for instance, the Mayan witch-doctor rituals of *La Turista* or the UFO-meets-Hopi-snake-dance visitation of *Operation Sidewinder*. Ironically, Shepard's pessimism deepened as his own star rose and as the larger theater world opened itself up to the counterculture he helped seed. By the end of the decade, he had received a succession of arts foundation grants and was premiering his work in venues as established as Lincoln Center. Meanwhile even Broadway was sponsoring countercultural plays like Kenneth Tynan's *Oh Calcutta* (1967), a revue about sexual liberation that featured a scene from Shepard's first play, *The*

Rock Garden; and the musical *Hair* (1968), directed by La Mama's Tom O'Horgan, who also directed Shepard premieres in 1967 and 1969. Shepard increasingly took on a role as one of the counterculture's most interesting internal critics. Like musician Frank Zappa, he created a body of work that articulated the movement's ideals (the refusal of sexual and social limits, the discovery of an authentic self outside the trappings of civilization, the democratic sense that "everybody is a star") even as it punctured them with a savage skepticism.[33]

Shepard's turn to rock music in his plays was linked to a new, willfully flatter treatment of character and a heightened interest in establishing a larger social backdrop for the action of his plays. When he revised 1964's *Cowboys* into 1967's *Cowboys #2,* he made a number of telling revisions to this drama of two young men improvising a series of identities as a kind of serious sport. Most crucially, he added two other roles, the blankly named "Man #1" and "Man #2," who were coat-and-tie look-alikes of Stu and Chet, the improvising pair. The earlier play's expression of spontaneity is seriously compromised by the way that these two new characters frame the action. They begin the play as offstage voices that prompt the first idea for an improvisation and then whistle at Stu and Chet like dogs, suggesting that even the most entropic-seeming acts of improvisation are the result of social compulsion. In the last section of the play, as Stu and Chet wrap up their playacting, this bland pair emerges more clearly as the alter egos of the "cowboys." First heard offstage in a mundane discussion about how to live cheaply in the city, they come onstage for the first time and then, strikingly, read from the beginning of the play's script in monotone, recapitulating the improvisation at the play's center but divesting it of its emotional, in-the-moment urgency. The desire to escape from social roles, to improvise new ones out of thin air, is apparently just another preprogrammed desire—and worst of all, it seems to be in collusion with the most deadening aspects of the culture, everything signified by a pair of young men in suits who call all the shots without any sign of emotional life.[34]

Some of the complexities of Shepard's use of rock—his attraction to its message of liberation as well as his skepticism about its claims—emerge in 1967's *The Melodrama Play,* the first of many Shepard works that center around the dilemmas of rock stardom. The fulcrum for the play's action is a hit song with the chorus "Oh prisoners, get up out a' your homemade beds." Duke Durgens, who has ridden the song up the charts, is struggling to come up with another hit; a series of melodramatic reversals occurs around the song, as a thug arrives to coerce Duke into being creative and his brother injects himself into the action as the song's true composer. The bulk of the play thus shows us the machinery behind the pop song, the sketchy network behind its dream of liberation—but this fact does not keep the song from articulating the play's central concern (how to escape self-created prisons), nor does it keep the song itself from having an odd force. Just as Shepard hoped that the larger play might move "from the mechanism of melodrama to something more sincere," so the song begins with a lighthearted vignette of someone deciding to go back to bed rather than get up for the day and ends with a moment of wakefulness: "You'll walk right outside without no name, / You'll walk right outside from where you came." Inasmuch as there is any promise of freedom in the play, it is expressed in this casual but riddling couplet, with its sense of nameless and wandering self-discovery.[35]

By and large, *The Melodrama Play*'s use of rock music hints at a much darker theme: that it is nearly impossible to maintain a sense of individuality in a world where dreams of rebellion are the hottest item on the market and where claims of originality mask a creeping conformity. Acts of failed impersonation drive the story forward; we see individuals repeatedly unmasked as fakers and posers, but this unmasking does not give us a sense of who they really are. It is almost impossible to see into the inner life of the characters, partly because the play shifts its focus frenetically—Duke disappears halfway through and the thuggish Peter becomes the center of the rest of the action—and partly for the simple reason that everyone in the play wears dark glasses that deflect any attempt at discovering who they are. Eyelessness—something worse than blindness, just as a failed impersonation is worse than a failed bid at authenticity—is a central motif. Duke appears on stage between huge photographs of Bob Dylan and Robert Goulet, both with their eyes cut out. Caught between an icon of rock and an icon of schlock, Duke not only seems to be unsure of whom he should emulate but also seems to be trapped by the superficiality of the icons themselves. Later the eyelessness of Dylan and Goulet has an echo in the long, surreal story that Peter relates, in which he is followed by a crawling, coughing man who tails him even when he runs at a furious clip: "his face had no eyes. Mind you, they weren't eyes that had gone bad and closed up or white eyes that were glazed over or eyes like a blind man has. There weren't any eyes there at all." Here, then, in one of those psychedelic compressions that Shepard favors, we get the shades-wearing Duke following the eyeless Dylan and Goulet, and then the shades-wearing Peter being followed by an eyeless man.[36]

The Melodrama Play suggests something more troubling than the usual irony of the blind leading the blind, since there is little promise of sight or insight anywhere to be found. Characters never arrive at any epiphanies and are generally so flat as to seem incapable of them. When the dead bodies that litter the stage rub their heads and wake into life at the end of the play, there is no sense of spiritual uplift or even relief, simply a confirmation of the shallowness of the theatrical illusion. What has happened to the utopian possibilities of self-exploration that Shepard previously associated with jazz? One answer is that the rock plays are aware, sometimes to the point of paranoia, of the social pressures that influence self-expression. Authority asserts itself much more forcibly in these dramas, whether in the form of a record company boss and his thug *(The Melodrama Play)*, gas gun-wielding Exterminators *(Forensic and the Navigators)*, or a plotting network of scientists and military men *(Operation Sidewinder)*. And while these evil figures are often revealed as confused bumblers, the disclosure of their weakness does not allow for the return of jazz-inflected spontaneity. They may be debunked as individuals, but a system of authority will remain, as ubiquitous as the "unseen hand" in Shepard's play of the same name, which presses down on anyone who has a rebellious thought.[37]

The difficulty of uttering a spontaneous thought comes through in *The Melodrama Play* in a dialogue between Peter and Drake, Duke's brother. Introduced as a thug in police costume, Peter is revealed as someone who desperately longs to understand how others see him. Battering and badgering Drake, he becomes a surprising partisan of the jazz impulse, asking over and over for Drake to give him an improvisatory appraisal of himself:

Peter: And then you say whatever just comes into your head in that split second. Whatever happens to be sitting there in your memory of the second before and it just spiels out trippingly off the tongue. It just gushes out in its most accurate way. Word for word, without a moment's hesitation to calculate where it's going or how or why. It just falls out into the air and disappears as soon as it's heard. That's what I want to hear! That's what I want you to say to me. Right now, before it's too late!
Drake: Just let me sing a song, Peter. Please. Let me make up a song for Floyd.

A number of ironies attach themselves to this moment of dialogue. The obvious one is that Drake is being beaten into a performance of spontaneity—a familiar predicament in Shepard's rock plays, where individuals are so trapped in a system that they cannot imagine what they would be like, and what they would express, outside of it. A secondary irony is that, in the act of imploring for spontaneity from Drake, Peter seems to achieve a limited kind of spontaneity himself. Inasmuch as spontaneity survives into Shepard's rock plays, it often takes the form of fixation, obsession, the desire for that fleeting thought that "falls out into the air and disappears as soon as it's heard." While spontaneity itself is as elusive as a will-o'-the-wisp, the hunger for spontaneity is expressed everywhere—even by the system's emissaries.[38]

Jazz may have disappeared from Shepard's late-1960s plays, but the desire for what it represented did not. In the mid-1970s, he came to jazz as never before, fashioning a series of plays *(Inacoma, Savage/Love, Angel City, Suicide in B Flat)* that openly used the music and acknowledged his debt to its model of creative expression. In a note that Shepard attached to *Angel City*, he suggested that the actors needed to rethink the idea of character along the lines of jazz: "Instead of the idea of a 'whole character' with logical motives behind his behavior which the actor submerges himself into, he should consider instead a fractured whole with bits and pieces of character flying off the central theme. In other words, more in terms of collage construction or jazz improvisation." As Shepard's language suggests, with its hint of shrapnel "flying off," these plays are extremely disorienting, sometimes coming at the viewer as a stream of discontinuities. After passing through his conflicted romance with rock, Shepard returned to jazz with a twist: the self conveyed through jazz-inflected improvisation no longer claimed to be "authentic," but it did represent the promise of a self under active construction, struggling to piece together a world out of the bits and pieces that flew its way. This may not have been the fulfillment of the ideals of the counterculture, which Shepard continued to treat skeptically, but it was at least an alternative to an act of capitulation, a refusal to take the path of least resistance.[39]

John Sinclair and the Embrace of "Total Freedom"

While Sam Shepard kept his distance from organized political movements, poet-activist John Sinclair tried to fuse cultural and political radicalism, first through jazz and then through rock, all the while rethinking the meaning of "freedom." In December 1971, Sinclair was the focus of a 15,000-person "Free John Sinclair" concert-rally in Ann Arbor, headlined by John Lennon and Yoko Ono, with supporting performances by Archie Shepp, Phil Ochs, Allen Ginsberg, and Stevie Wonder. The concert protested Sinclair's ten-year jail sentence for selling marijuana, and it worked like an activist's dream. Fifty-five hours after John and Yoko left the stage, Sinclair was set free, his imprisonment having been revealed as a glaring violation of Michigan's revised drug law. The concert was also the result of rarely seen cooperation between the New Left's media activists—in this case, Yippies Jerry Rubin and Abbie Hoffman—and its community organizers, who favored sustained grassroots mobilization over flamboyant stunts like the Yippies' throwing dollar bills into the Stock Exchange. After pursuing conflicting agendas and strategies at 1968's Chicago protests, for a brief moment the two sides of the New Left found common cause. Jerry Rubin announced during the concert, "What we are doing here is uniting music and revolutionary politics to build a revolution around the country!" and later called the Sinclair rally a "political Woodstock." On the other side of the spectrum, pacifist and grassroots-oriented David Dellinger named it a "people's convention." Allen Ginsberg described it as "the great breakthrough that everybody had been waiting for. . . . To redo Chicago '68, but in a much wiser way—as a real festival of life, instead of an aggressive contest. I thought that an enormously important social and political and artistic union was taking place."[40]

It's fair to say that Sinclair himself, who helped organize the "Free John Sinclair" campaign from his jail cell, had been building to this moment for the prior decade. His life gathered momentum in volatile mid-1960s Detroit, where he acted as a catalyst of that city's radical arts community and its avant-garde jazz scene in particular. He helped sustain the Detroit Artists' Workshop, an umbrella organization that sponsored a wide variety of other ventures: spin-off arts organizations like the Wayne State University Artists' Society; a series of poetry readings and jazz concerts spotlighting Detroit artists; new musical ensembles, including the Detroit Contemporary 4, the Workshop Arts Quartet, and the Workshop Music Ensemble, which performed Sinclair's compositions; and even a self-education program at the Artists' Workshop Free University of Detroit, for which Sinclair taught courses on jazz and contemporary poetry. Detroit had been one of the major crucibles of hard bop, nurturing saxophonists Yusef Lateef, Charles McPherson, and Pepper Adams, trombonists Curtis Fuller and Kiane Zawadi (Bernard McKinney), trumpeters Donald Byrd and Thad Jones, vocalist Betty Carter, vibist Terry Pollard, pianists Tommy Flanagan, Barry Harris, and Hank Jones, and drummer Elvin Jones. With Sinclair's help, the Motor City also became a breeding ground for the avant-garde explorations of free jazz.[41]

Sinclair also poured much of his energy into writing—more specifically, into the underground press that coalesced in the mid-1960s around experimental art and politics. While serving as *Down Beat*'s Detroit correspondent, he founded the Artists' Workshop Press and used the press to edit and publish a series of iconoclastic magazines: the poetry-based *Work*

(1965–1967), the "avant-jazz" *Change* (1965–1966), and the counter-cultural *Whe're* (1966). Sinclair's ventures were part of a much larger wave of independent, radical publishing operations, from the Liberation News Service to Dudley Randall's Broadside Press, founded in 1966 in another part of Detroit and one of the first black publishing houses in the country. Just as Randall hoped that his inexpensive pamphlets would be so widely disseminated that they would be posted on refrigerators as part of the news of the day, Sinclair hoped that his avant-garde operations would find and create a wider audience.[42]

Sinclair's largest source of inspiration in the mid-1960s was the jazz avant-garde, a point reflected in the titles of his own chapbooks of poetry: the Ornette Coleman–inspired *This Is Our Music* (1965), the Archie Shepp–inspired *Fire Music: A Record* (1966), and *Meditations: A Suite for John Coltrane* (1967). Sinclair may have written more poetic tributes to jazz musicians than any other writer of the mid-1960s. Over the course of his three volumes, he paid homage not only to Coleman, Shepp, and Coltrane, but also to Sonny Rollins, Elvin Jones, Miles Davis, Freddie Hubbard, Marion Brown, Andrew Hill, Cecil Taylor, Eric Dolphy, Albert Ayler, and several less recognized local musicians. His poems often took the form of fervid album reviews that either tried to capture the experience of listening or took on the major controversies of the jazz world. Meanwhile his actual album reviews, written for jazz magazines like *Sounds and Fury, Jazz,* and his own *Change,* themselves blended prose and poetry in a white-hot mixture of rant, rave, and insight.[43]

What drew Sinclair to the aesthetic of free jazz? Most important, there was the music's seriousness of purpose, its refusal to be taken as escapism or entertainment. In his mind, free jazz not only insisted that art imitated life but, even more, forced you to measure yourself by the utopian standards of the music, to reconsider who you might be. Reviewing Shepp's *Fire Music,* for example, he wrote:

> The music, it *fires* me, to make me try to emulate its strength & beauty, in my own art (my own life).
> These men take music (as I do) as their *life-term,* it is no casual thing, to be bought or sold, to be played *with.* No, to be played out, or should I say, *worked* out, as men work out their lives, if they care for them.[44]

Taking on this challenge to "work out" his life, Sinclair rejected what he saw as the compromises of the affluent society, its anesthetic of material comfort. *This Is Our Music* opened with an epigraph from Black Mountain poet Charles Olson:

> In the land of plenty, have
> nothing to do with it
> $\qquad\qquad$ take the way of
> the lowest,
> including
> your legs, go
> contrary, go
>
> sing[45]

Going the "way of the lowest," for Sinclair, meant forging alliances with black musicians—a point illustrated by the cover of *This Is Our Music*, which shows Sinclair rapping on a street corner with cornetist Charles Moore. It was also a message implicit in the chutzpah of his adoption of Ornette Coleman's title. Sinclair was at home claiming the black avant-garde as his own usable tradition, much as three years later he founded the White Panther party, moving onto the radical ground staked out by Bobby Seale, Eldridge Cleaver, and Huey Newton.

Casting about for role models, Sinclair identified most intensely, like many cultural radicals, with the figure of John Coltrane. His early 1965 poem for Coltrane, one of the first poems written about the saxophonist, echoed Ossie Davis's admiration of Malcolm X as the ideal image of masculinity, praising Coltrane for "teach[ing] us to stand / like men / in the face of the most devas- / tating insensi- / tivity." His 1967 chapbook *Mediations* was devised as a poetic improvisation, equal parts meditation and love chant, written in tandem with seven Coltrane pieces from the albums *Meditations* and *Kulu Se Mama*. Strikingly, *Meditations* was dedicated not only to a host of free jazz players—Coltrane, Pharoah Sanders, Rashied Ali, Cecil Taylor, Sun Ra, and Marion Brown—but also to princes of psychedelic rock like Donovan, the Jefferson Airplane, and Love. By 1967, Sinclair was delving into the experiments in music, lifestyle, and politics that came to be identified with the counterculture, dropping acid regularly, founding *Guerrilla: A Newspaper of Cultural Revolution*, and involving himself with Detroit's rock venue the Grande Ballroom. The same month that he composed the bulk of *Meditations*, which is thick with Beatlesque incantations like "the word is Love / and the song has no end / and the song is Love," he also helped to organize in Detroit a "total cooper-

Cover image of John Sinclair, *This Is Our Music* (1965): Poet-activist John Sinclair, who perhaps wrote more tributes to jazz musicians than any other poet of the 1960s, was at home claiming the black avant-garde as his own usable past. In 1968, he founded the White Panther party, hoping it would be "the voice of the lumpen hippie, just like the Black Panther party was the voice of the lumpen proletariat." (Courtesy of Leni Sinclair)

ative tribal living and working commune" known as Trans-Love Energies Unlimited. Sinclair was not just talking love; he was hoping to produce it, share it, unleash it, live it.[46]

Sinclair's *Meditations,* then, is one of those cultural signposts that points backward and forward at once. It's not surprising that it was the last of his jazz-inspired chapbooks, since it offers perhaps more tribute to LSD than it does to Coltrane:

> I told my brother and my wife once,
> the first time we all took acid, sitting out in the car
> in front of 4825, and before we took the trip by car
> all the way to Chicago to hear Trane

still full of the acid, that we would see the day
after the post-Western revolution
when the language would work again
strictly as a function of the body, its
glow & gesture . . .

         that the language would be stripped
of all negative force, and the new poetry
would burn itself down
to just one word. . . .

           and the word is LOVE

While Sinclair's earlier jazz poetry had tended toward combativeness, frag-mentation, and inconclusiveness, *Meditations* was written as an affirmative incantation; its cadences suggested Ginsberg and Whitman as much as Olson or Baraka. It embraced a politics of affect, valuing body over mind, anticipating the day when the "post-Western revolution" would return language back to the realm of "glow & gesture," feelings tactile and luminous. Its last poem, "Welcome," ended with twenty-two "Yes"'s streaming down the page, and its motto seemed perfect for the door of the Trans-Love Energies Unlimited commune: "It is time / for all to come."[47]

Sinclair was turning from avant-garde jazz to rock 'n' roll at the same moment that the more stolid guardians of jazz were also recognizing that they had to reckon with rock. In the June 29, 1967, issue of *Down Beat*, edi-tor Dan Morgenstern announced that the magazine would "expand its edi-torial perspective to include the musically valid aspects of the rock scene." By and large, the earlier tone set by *Down Beat*'s critics had been a kind of aesthetic schadenfreude, with critics relishing the supposed inanities of rock. Leonard Feather wrote typically (in a 1957 issue of *Playboy*) that rock was "esthetically impoverished," "a bastardized, commercialized, debased version" of jazz. "Rock 'n' roll shares a common beginning with jazz," he concluded, "but it has evolved no further than the primitive, gibbering ape." When a *Down Beat* reader insisted in 1960 that rock was not "junk music" but added, in a tone of conciliation, that "rock and roll might be pushed out tomorrow," the editors quipped, "Tomorrow and tomorrow and tomorrow—all we ever get is promises." By 1967, however, *Down Beat*'s editors were prepared to recognize the music as a "medium for cre-ative expression." They began commissioning articles that sought to assess rock as art music, distinguishing themselves from the likes of *Crawdaddy* and *Rolling Stone*, magazines targeted solely for a rock audience and which explained the music as the voice of a new generation.[48]

Over the course of 1967, Sinclair plunged himself into Detroit's rock scene, as he began seeing the revolutionary energies of free jazz incarnated in the hardest forms of white rock and roll. Trans-Love Energies Unlimited, like the Detroit Artists' Workshop, soon served as an all-purpose clearinghouse for local artists and scenesters: it produced dance concerts; orchestrated light shows; printed books, pamphlets, posters, and an alternative newspaper; and organized a cooperative booking agency for rock groups like the MC5 and Iggy Pop's the Stooges. Yet the transition was not without its awkward moments. The "avant-rock" MC5 had some difficulty courting Sinclair, whom they regarded as Detroit's "chief hippie." When they tried to play a 1966 party celebrating Sinclair's release from jail—the "cultural event of the summer," according to lead guitarist Wayne Kramer, and a foretaste of the 1971 benefit—they were prematurely unplugged by Sinclair's wife in the middle of their 4:00 A.M. set. Sinclair even attacked them in the local underground press as "jive rock & rollers" and asked them "to pay attention to real music like Sun Ra and John Coltrane." Kramer promptly headed over to Sinclair's home, informed Sinclair that in fact the MC5 knew Coltrane's music, and—in one of those acts of effrontery that double as ingratiation—asked to use the Artists' Workshop rehearsal space.[49]

Eventually Sinclair became the band's manager and invited the MC5 to live in Trans-Love Energies Unlimited, inaugurating a partnership that led to the formation of the White Panther party and some of the most extreme propaganda about the liberating value of hard rock. Soon Sinclair was not only participating in a manager's day-to-day tasks—arranging the MC5's booking schedule, organizing their equipment—but also developing the high-energy concept of the band. As music historian John Szwed explains, "Under Sinclair's musical and political tutelage, the MC5 took rock and roll in directions it had only teased at before. They came on stage carrying rifles and guitars, their amps emblazoned with inverted American flags. They played thirty-minute songs, planned an album to be called *Live on Saturn* [Sun Ra's home planet], created versions of Archie Shepp's, Pharaoh Sanders's, and John Coltrane's compositions, and recorded [the Sun Ra-based] 'Starship' on their 1969 *Kick Out the Jams* Elektra album." Perhaps most crucially, the MC5 took the free jazz emphasis on energy and electrified that energy through their amps and their guitars, with hopes of shaking the senses of their listeners. Sinclair theorized that the MC5 stage show "was a beautiful demonstration of the principles of high-energy performance: as the performer puts out more the energy level of the audience is raised and they give back more energy to the performers, who are moved onto a higher energy level which is transmitted to the audience and sent back, etc., until everything is totally frenzied. This process makes changes in the people's bodies that are molecular and cellular and which transform them irrevocably just as LSD or any other strong high-energy agents do." For Sinclair this feedback loop of bodily pleasure was not just an end in itself; it also aimed to destroy the enemies enumerated in his verse—the deadening life of affluence, the grind of white power.[50]

As the MC5's music turned toward the aesthetics of noise, their overt politics took a more radical turn. In August 1968 the band was the only group to play the Yippie-sponsored "Festival of Life" outside the Chicago Democratic Convention. (When their performance was cut short by the arrival of police helicopters overhead, the band quickly rushed its gear into their van and stormed across the park to escape the ensuing riot.) Two months later, Sinclair converted "The MC5's Social and Athletic Club," the band's fan club, into the White Panther party. Again Sinclair was gesturing to the black vanguard while following his own path: if the Black Panther party was brainstormed in a West Oakland community center subsidized by Lyndon Johnson's Great Society, the White Panthers took root in the Trans-Love Energies Unlimited commune, which heavily salted its message of liberation with an enthusiasm for mind-altering music, drugs, and sex. Sinclair hoped the White Panthers would be "the voice of the lumpen hippie, just like the Black Panther party was the voice of the lumpen proletariat—which means working class without jobs."[51]

While Sinclair founded the White Panther party partly out of genuine political conviction, he also did it as an innovative way to promote the MC5's high-voltage music and communal lifestyle. He shared an ideological affinity with Yippies Jerry Rubin and Abbie Hoffman, who saw the mass media as a tool to be used in the struggle for liberation, not an establishment machine that would compromise any radical utterance. In Sinclair the Yippies found their most enthusiastic proponent of the thesis that rock and roll, *as* a mass medium, was an agent of revolution; *Rolling Stone* writer Stu Werbin noted, "The White Panthers considered the MC5 their strongest weapon." Just as he had praised free jazz as music that respected the law of the gut, Sinclair saw revolutionary rock and roll as an escape from the banality of the bad trip, a way to "have a better time than just sitting around smoking bogus dope, dropping bogus speed-filled acid, shooting smack, and listening to brainwash low-energy jams." Even better, promoting rock music was a way to play the system and subvert it at once. Plugging the MC5's album *Kick Out the Jams,* Sinclair wrote, "With our music and our economic genius we plunder the unsuspecting straight world for money and the means to revolutionize its children at the same time."[52]

The most programmatic statement of White Panther ideology came in the party platform, which Sinclair expanded from three earlier points ("dope, rock & roll, and fucking in the streets") into a manifesto-like "Statement for the White Panther Arm of the Youth International Party." The keyword in the manifesto was "freedom"—"it is all one message, and the message is freedom"; "We demand total freedom for everybody!"—but it was a sort of freedom that shared little with the philosophical vision of Martin Luther King, Jr., the aesthetic principles of 1960s jazz, or even the freedom demanded in the first paragraph of the Black Panther party's own 1966 platform, which tied freedom to collective power and self-determination for the black community. While King defined freedom as the realization of man's autonomy in a world governed by higher laws, and while jazz musicians like Sun Ra and Charles Mingus always insisted that collective discipline enabled collective freedom, the White Panther party manifesto returned freedom to the realm of commodities and individual freedom of choice. It demanded "free exchange of energy and materials . . . the end of money"; "Free food, clothes, housing, dope, music, bodies, medical care—everything free for everybody"; "Free access to information media—free the technology from the greed creeps"; even, with self-conscious absurdity, "Free time and space for all humans." Then it called for various sorts of liberation, all defined as the freedom from authority: "Free all schools and structures from corporate rule"; "Free all prisoners everywhere"; "Free all soldiers at once"; and lastly, "Free the people from their 'leaders.'"[53]

It was a mark partly of Sinclair's willingness to work through the market, to exploit the commodity world and fashions of youth culture, that his concept of "freedom"—an individual choosing things without any constraints on his or her ability to purchase them—now seems more intuitive than the "freedom" of King or Mingus, who tied freedom to citizenship, power, and self-discipline. Sinclair rejected acquisitive individualism—that was why he wanted everything to be free—but he did reinforce an expressive individualism that often operated at cross-purposes with his hopes for building a movement. Yippies like Sinclair were willing to bargain that they would have an easier time revolutionizing the system if they played by its preference for shock over substance, for the glitter of celebrity over the anonymity of grassroots protest. They abided with the media's fondness for individual iconoclasm, betting that a different kind of celebrity—one who promoted the liberation of mind and body—could revolutionize the system from within.

Even though Sinclair seemed to broadcast a single-minded notion of freedom, however, in his life he could not escape dealing with the complex difficulties of reconciling individual freedom with community liberation. He saw the Trans-Love Energies Unlimited commune as "the life-form of the future," but in practice his dream of communal liberation often was purchased at the expense of the women who stepped up to it: as former Elektra Records executive Danny Fields recalled, "On the one hand you had the politics of revolution and equality and liberation and on the other hand you had silent women in long dresses, gathered in the kitchen, preparing great meals of meat, which were brought out and served to the men—who ate alone." Such practices would not long escape the scrutiny of the women's liberation movement. Meanwhile, Sinclair was sharply disappointed by the MC5 when the band dropped him as their manager, signed a $50,000 contract with Atlantic Records, and poured their money into payments on new cars. In retaliation, he purged them from the White Panther party—with the quip that "You guys wanted to be bigger than the Beatles, but I wanted you to be bigger than Chairman Mao." From his jail cell, Sinclair was made to wrestle this challenge to Yippie ideology: how "jamming the system" was seemingly only a hairpin turn away from selling out.[54]

In the late 1960s, Sinclair's greatest debt to the jazz world may have been how he applied jazz's insistence on self-improvisation to the life of the activist, reinventing himself like his heroes Malcolm and Coltrane, reacting to every twist of the radical screw and every slap of the backlash. He lived a jazz-inflected life even as he propagandized for slash-and-burn rock and roll and pursued an idea of freedom that would have frustrated jazz disciplinarians like Mingus and Sun Ra. His sense that the activist was an improviser came through in "Spectrum," a 1966 poem dedicated to pianist and Black Arts Repertory Theater/School musical director Andrew Hill. The poem asked how activists motivate themselves in the face of daily setbacks and ended with this analogy between the jazz musician's archive and the activist's tool kit:

> That *all* of it is just
> material, all of it
> can be put to work, the choice is only
> among the materials in
> front of you, what you will
> use, what has the biggest
> utility, the measure
>
> & the spectrum
> of our own possibilities[55]

10

THE ROAD TO "SOUL POWER"

The Many Ends of Hard Bop

August 1965, Watts. It's a few days after the passage of the Voting Rights Act, the legislative climax of the civil rights movement, and the streets are painfully alive. Groceries and liquor stores have been looted and burn unchecked along Avalon Boulevard. Some 2,000 national guardsmen and 9,000 armed police enforce a state of martial law and an eight o'clock curfew. The catchphrase of a local DJ—"Burn, baby, burn!"—takes hold among Watts residents: between 31,000 and 35,000 adults will take part in the disturbance at some point, and about double that number will be involved as close spectators. Inside a local community arts center, jazz musician Horace Tapscott is rehearsing his Pan Afrikan Peoples Arkestra. The police enter the center, guns at the ready, and order Tapscott to stop playing. Tapscott refuses. The officer in charge pulls back the hammer of his gun and screams, "I said stop the goddamn music!" Tapscott notices that the police are lining up a group of women, probably taken from one of the center's workshops; he motions for the band to stop. The officer lowers his gun, and the rest of the policemen begin to head out—at which point one of the Arkestra's bassists, looking straight at the departing police, plays a familiar motif and the band starts up again. They launch into "The Dark Tree," a Tapscott piece with an insistent pulse and a deep allegorical undertow. Driven by an Afro-Cuban rhythm taken from Desi Arnaz's "Babalú," the piece is a parable about the resilience of black culture, the story of a tree of life that survives even though it is always "passed over and left in the dark."[1]

Most jazz musicians in the mid- to late 1960s did not have to improvise at gunpoint while their communities literally burned to the ground, but they might be forgiven for feeling that way. Especially after the Watts riot, there was a palpable sense of urgency and desperation in the air, as the civil rights movement hit new walls and as black Americans struggled with the cumulative effects of deindustrialization, discriminatory housing-loan policies, the demolition of central-city neighborhoods for highway construction, and the relocation of the residents of these neighborhoods into public housing high-rises. The riots that spread from Watts to Chicago, Detroit, and forty other U.S. cities spoke to the need for remedies greater than the desegregation of public facilities or the guarantee of access to a voting booth: the underlying causes of black inequality, not just its most infuriating symbols, called out to be addressed. Meanwhile the white backlash against the riots suggested the intense resistance that would meet any proposals beyond the formal declaration of legal and political equality. Seeing the need for remedies that would not be forthcoming without a pitched battle, many black Americans turned to the ideas of self-determination and self-defense that coalesced in the rallying cry of "Black Power." Leading the way, two key organizations of the civil rights movement—the Student Nonviolent Coordinating Committee (SNCC) and the Congress on Racial Equality—opted to follow what Stokely Carmichael and Charles V. Hamilton called "the fundamental premise" of Black Power: "*Before a group can enter the open society, it must first close ranks.*" By 1966, both were formally black-led, rather than interracial, organizations.[2]

Black jazz musicians responded to this volatile political climate with all the diversity of their generational cohort, but they also suffered greatly in this period, whipsawed by the deteriorating infrastructure of urban America and the declining sales of jazz relative to soul and rock. It took courage and resourcefulness to survive as a jazz musician through the late sixties— not least the courage of redefining the meaning of jazz and the role of the jazz musician in the community. As the suburbs expanded, fewer people were venturing downtown for entertainment, and even fewer were going to hear jazz. By the early 1970s, many of the New York clubs that had sponsored bop and hard bop had either closed their doors (the Hickory House, Slugs) or shifted their programming to rock and fusion (Birdland, the Five Spot). In San Francisco, a large number of clubs—Basin Street West, the Blackhawk, the Both/And, the Coffee Gallery, the Half Note, the Hungry i, the Jazz Cellar, and El Matador—were shuttered after enjoying some success in the fifties and early sixties.[3]

Forced to look for sources of livelihood outside of concert circuits and recording contracts, jazz musicians entered pit bands, classrooms, community centers, Hollywood studios—or left America for Europe or other parts of the world. Energies were scattered. Max Roach and Abbey Lincoln turned to stage productions and recorded little; Charles Mingus was evicted from his studio and dropped out of the performance circuit; Benny Golson and Oliver Nelson focused on writing television and film music; Randy Weston settled in Rabat, Morocco, and ran a nightclub; Ornette Coleman composed much, but in private; singer Betty Carter took a hiatus to raise her two children; and Sonny Rollins abandoned music altogether for several years. Some took advantage of the opportunities opened up through student-led demands for black studies or jazz-related curricula: Archie Shepp taught at SUNY-Buffalo, Horace Tapscott at UC Riverside, his Arkestra colleague Bobby Bradford at Cal State-Dominguez Hills, and Cecil Taylor at Antioch and the University of Wisconsin (where he was let go for flunking too many students). Through it all, musicians wrestled with what their dislocation meant. One measure of the stress on the profession was the number of health-threatening breakdowns suffered by jazz's most creative artists—from Mingus and Rollins to Lincoln and pianist Mal Waldron.[4]

Yet jazz artists did not only suffer setbacks in the late 1960s. They joined jazz to a "soul" aesthetic in a way that was willfully open-minded, eclectic in its reclamation and reinvention of jazz history—a kind of fusion of postmodernism's playful skepticism with the Black Arts imperative to give the community a liberating image of itself. In response to the disintegration of music education networks in the inner city and the discouraging preferences of the music industry, they created jazz collectives that schooled a generation of younger players and offered grassroots performance alternatives. And they explored how the music of jazz might be a more explicit ally of a politics of racial empowerment and liberation, forming alliances with groups from the Black Panthers to Jesse Jackson's Operation Breadbasket. These turns in the music, sometimes on parallel tracks and sometimes in tension, had all the complexity and turbulence of late 1960s American political life and might fill up a separate book in their own right. This chapter merely hints at the repertoire of responses that jazz musicians made to these twin crises—in the market for their music and in the communities that they hoped to help rebuild.[5]

From Grits to the Banana Peel

The impulse that Stokely Carmichael and Charles Hamilton defined as the root of Black Power—to close ranks and work more programmatically toward a sense of racial solidarity—was taken up by many in the jazz world, although the results might surprise those who slight the Black Power movement, and its cultural affiliate the Black Arts movement, for making reductive appeals to the essence of blackness. The desire to put African-American audiences in touch with a newly rediscovered tradition, combined with a keenly felt sense of social upheaval, led to a wide variety of new musical practices. Soul-jazz had another vogue, and a fresh crop of Hammond B-3 organists like Charles Earland and Lonnie Liston Smith brought a lighter, more pop-oriented groove to albums with names like *Black and Proud, Everything I Play Is Funky,* and *Black Talk.* Pianist Herbie Hancock adopted the Swahili name Mwandishi at the end of the sixties and experimented with a bracing fusion of jazz and funk, a musical formula explored by his mentor Miles Davis as well. Tenor saxophonist Joe Henderson mixed electronic sounds, world-music settings, and more traditional hard-bop improvisation on a series of albums whose titles—*Power to the People, If You're Not Part of the Solution You're Part of the Problem, In Pursuit of Blackness*—announced (without necessarily explaining) their cultural ambition. In the interesting case of a white player reclaiming his own radical tradition, bassist Charlie Haden founded the Liberation Music Orchestra, a pan-ethnic outfit that put the music of the Spanish Civil War at the center of its ecumenical, Popular Front–inspired vision. One example of the expansiveness of Black Arts–affiliated jazz in this period was the 1970 "Black Festival," organized by arranger-composer Cal Massey as a benefit for the legal defense of the New York "Panther 21," the Black Panther leadership who had been charged with numerous counts of conspiracy by the New York District Attorney. (They were eventually acquitted of all charges.) Between 5:00 P.M. and 5:00 A.M. at a Brooklyn community center, listeners enjoyed a wide spectrum of hard bop and experimental jazz, including the lyrical Wynton Kelly; Blue Note stablemates Cedar Walton, Jackie McLean, Freddie Hubbard, and Grachan Moncur III; earlier Coltrane collaborators McCoy Tyner and Elvin Jones; later Coltrane collaborators Pharaoh Sanders and Alice Coltrane; free jazz poet-musician Archie Shepp; and even a group from the Chicago-based Association for the Advancement of Creative Musicians (AACM) that included Anthony Braxton, Leroy Jenkins, Steve McCall, and Leo Wadada Smith.[6]

In much of the most experimental jazz, the desire to define a black tradition worked hand in hand with a more open sense of the jazz archive. Avant-garde performers, such as the Art Ensemble of Chicago and Anthony Braxton, as well as more "inside" performers, such as saxophonist Roland Kirk and pianist Jaki Byard, specialized in sampling disparate musical practices and assembling music with an eye for incongruity, theatricality, and humor as well as more traditional hard bop qualities like groove and intensity. Constructing the blackness in "Great Black Music" (the motto of the AACM), these performers were often happy to let the scaffolding show. They could set a steady groove, or they could just as easily enter into out-of-tempo explorations. They could draw on the energy aesthetic that emerged out of John Coltrane's late work, where every breath into a saxophone was seen as the working of the spirit, Pentecostal flames coming out of the bell of the horn, or they could find inspiration in more unorthodox sources (for example, Scott Joplin) and more unorthodox instruments (pennywhistles, zithers, Chinese pipas, children's toys, even amplified shovels). While some of these performers were more "postmodern" than others and only a handful were directly affiliated with the Black Power movement—Tapscott, for one, arranged music for Black Panther Elaine Brown—all of them participated in the project of cultural reclamation that swept through black communities under the influence of the Black Power movement.[7]

To trace how this project of cultural reclamation shifted over the course of the 1960s, we might compare two pieces that both aimed to define the essence of the black community: Betty Carter's "Jazz (Ain't Nothin' But Soul)," a 1960 midtempo swinger that capitalized and riffed on the soul-jazz vogue; and alto saxophonist Jackie McLean's "Soul," a 1967 collaboration with trombonist Grachan Moncur and poet Barbara Simmons that fused poetry, gospel, and experimental jazz and also hoped to define the meaning of soul in the act of performing it. The songs sounded nothing alike even as they purported to do the same thing—a sign of the distance jazz and American culture traveled in the interval between the rallying cries of "Freedom Now" and "Black Power."

Carter's 1960 performance of Norman Mapp's "Jazz (Ain't Nothin' But Soul)" stands at the beginning point of jazz's celebration of soul pride. It is frankly exultant, a declaration of strength free of embattlement, two minutes of distilled jazz-pop pleasure. Recorded for ABC's *The Modern Sound of Betty Carter,* the song was a relatively early effort for the thirty-year-old singer. She had apprenticed in the early 1950s with Lionel Hampton's big band; still to come was her ascension as a postbop diva. In a striking sort of jazz feminism, Carter founded her own Bet-Car record label in the 1970s, schooled a series of brilliant pianists from Don Pullen and John Hicks to Mulgrew Miller and Cyrus Chestnut, and earned her "rediscovery" at age fifty-eight by Verve Records, which led many to appreciate her voice as one of the most remarkable instruments in postwar jazz. More than even such celebrated scat singers as Sarah Vaughn and Ella Fitzgerald, Carter toyed with phrase endings and dissonant intervals, decomposing the given melody with a fearlessly abstract intelligence. In her hands, a melody might be compressed into a tight space or elongated over a vamping rhythm section, yet always the volatility of her technique was balanced by the lightness and joyful energy of her voice. Perhaps most striking was Carter's savvy, well-armed sensuousness. Although she purred around notes in her lower register, she could never be mistaken for a sex kitten, since she always laced her songs of vulnerability and desire with a shrewd virtuosity. Her own compositions—such as "We Tried," which described how she and her lover had tried, and utterly failed, to conceal their affection for each other—had the bite of sarcasm if little of its pessimism.[8]

"Jazz (Ain't Nothin' But Soul)" captures the upbeat Carter in a particularly celebratory mood. The song allies jazz with down-home virtues: jazz is "makin' do with taters and grits / standing up each time you get hit"; it is "livin' high off nickels and dimes / tellin' folks 'bout what's on your mind." The music's keynotes are resourcefulness, resilience, and straight talk. Jazz is a way of life posing as music, with its "trumpets cussing saxophones" and its "rhythm making love." If there could be any doubt that this is a specifically black expressive culture, Carter banishes it with the line that jazz is "the voice of my people." The music, however, is not straight soul-jazz à la Cannonball Adderley or Horace Silver: there are no funky riffs played by trumpet and sax, no shuffle rhythms. Its soulfulness is marked instead by a limber approach to rhythm, one that can make asymmetry swing. Every time Carter returns to the refrain "Jazz ain't nothin' but soul," the band slams on the word "jazz," even though Carter has just (one beat earlier) finished the verse's rhyming couplet; then, just after stunning the beat, the band rolls on without blinking. Similar asymmetric accents from the band give an extra punch to the triplet rhythm that Carter uses when she rewrites the verse's melody. Jazz's soul is expressed, then, in flamboyant yet seemingly effortless touches—as, for example, when Carter stretches "saxophones" into a six-syllable word, and follows it up by doubling the syllable count of the rhyming phrase too.

Seven years later, Jackie McLean, Grachan Moncur, Barbara Simmons, and four other members of McLean's band collaborated on the poetry-jazz experiment "Soul," which spotlighted the questions raised but buried in Carter's act of affirmation: Why, in the midst of the affluent society, did black folks have to live high off of nickels and dimes, or make do with taters and grits? If jazz was "standing up each time you get hit," who was trying to knock you to the floor? This new spirit of challenge fed off the insurgent tone of the Black Power movement. Perhaps most important for the theatricality of jazz as an idiom, Black Power channeled a new set of extreme emotions into the political theater of protest. Open anger and scathing mockery often replaced the stoic, dignified aspect of much nonviolent direct action; "respectability" became a possible sign of collusion with a corrupt system, and rebellion took on startling new forms. The wave of urban riots in the mid-sixties were the most glaring sign of this collapse of traditional protest politics. More than explosions of impatience with police brutality, rat-infested housing, and the lack of meaningful work, they were also seen as part of a new political vocabulary of insurrection and uprising—expressions of a collective will to protest the state's unjust exercise of power. Jazz musicians like McLean took note of this new mood of suspicion, these new questions asked, and this new attempt to explore the meaning of violence rather than condemn it in toto.[9]

A hard bopper who perennially hovered on the brink of stardom, McLean had long been exploring the space where roots music met experimental music, as if on a personal quest to make soul and the avant-garde into friendly neighbors. His "out" playing on Mingus's "Pithecanthropus Erectus" arguably set the mold for the extreme emotionalism of free-jazz saxophonists; his albums of the late fifties, like the aptly titled *New Soil*, married harmonic exploration and gutbucket feeling; and his mid-sixties efforts with Moncur, vibist Bobby Hutcherson, and trumpeter Lee Morgan were noted for bringing together the main ingredients of that low-ceilinged, high-pressure music known as the "Blue Note sound"—aggressive and taut compositions, minor-key atmospherics, a rhythm section with enough drive to be called compulsive, and solo lines that were both stabbing and funky. With compositions like "Vertigo," "Minor Apprehension," "Lost," and "Esoteric," McLean willfully trafficked in disorientation, an impulse no doubt encouraged by his experience as an actor in the Living Theater's anomie-ridden *The Connection*. Yet McLean's dark intensity was matched by an interest in community education and uplift, an interest that allied him with critics like Amiri Baraka and performers like Charles Mingus, Sun Ra, Horace Tapscott, and Andrew Hill. In 1966 he worked in the jazz division of HARYOU-ACT, the federally sponsored antipoverty program designed for black youth. He even tried to expand the jazz division into a full-fledged music department with a curriculum covering composition, voice training, steel band performance, and the like, and was tentatively offered the position of music director until a bureaucratic upheaval led to the scrapping of the Arts and Culture program altogether—a common tale of the government's fleeting commitment to community arts.[10]

Both McLean's darkness and his fondness for uplift leave their mark on "Soul," which disrupts the joyful celebration of Carter's song even as it hopes to emulate it. The piece begins with Barbara Simmons asking "Tell me about Soul / Do you know? Have I got it? / Do you have it? Can you touch mine?" When the poet does hazard a definition, it comes in the form of a joke with a surreal punch line, an image of accident, possibility, and disorder:

> Soul is an elastic man
> who lives in an invisible shell
> and drifts to heaven or to hell
> when you get shot or trip or slip
> on a banana peel left living in the street.

Oh, for the days when soul was red beans and rice, cornbread and collard greens! In Simmons's Alice-in-Wonderland world, elasticity prevails, shells are deceptively invisible, people go to heaven or hell based on the drift of entropy, and the proverbial banana peel has a life of its own. Simmons's poem pivots very quickly between good humor and thinly veiled satire; it's torn between the impulse to define soul and to mock those who would try to pin down the black aesthetic or sample it from a distance.[11]

Meanwhile the music both appeals to the bedrock certainty of black authenticity and exults in the breakdown of that certainty: McLean's group plays both "inside" and "outside" jazz. The main theme of "Soul" is a blues melody that is strikingly genre-based, almost to the point of formula. Over a slow gospel-tinged 3/4 beat, the band transposes a simple riff through blues changes with no variation. This gospel section, however, is set up to be disrupted: just after Simmons mentions her banana peel, she switches to the idea that "Soul's a trumpet playin'"—and the music segues abruptly up a half step, the horns drop out, Lamont Johnson starts comping with dissonant clusters on the piano, and Rashied Ali (fresh from his collaboration with John Coltrane) plays coloristic raps on his cymbals. The rollicking "soulful" beat has vanished, along with the expectation that the band will follow the path of the traditional blues. Thirty seconds later, Simmons describes her trumpet player coming to the idea that "there's gonna be / gotta be / an explosion," and the band suddenly takes over the recording, becoming for a minute a stormy free-jazz unit. McLean attacks the G-minor blues scale, while Ali roams over his drum kit, dissolving the pulse intimated by McLean's feverish riffing. Taken as a whole, the performance of "Soul" honors the values of diversity and spontaneity. The song pitches a big tent covering churchy gospel, moody piano interludes, quartet-style free jazz, and out-of-tempo blues rambling while respecting the right of performers to switch between genres as the spirit moves them. Rather than fusing all its elements into a single recognizable soundscape—one of the accomplishments of, say, Coltrane's classic quartet—McLean's ranges hungrily among alternatives without committing to any in particular.[12]

Instead of simply affirming black pride, then, "Soul" teases out a set of tensions: soul is the foundation of the black aesthetic and just the beginning of individual "signifying"; it is sublime and ridiculous, a source of spiritual power and a reservoir of absurd humor; and it is easy to point to and impossible to track down. As Simmons says, in a passage that recalls the "Black is and black ain't" prologue of Ellison's *Invisible Man,* "You can't touch it or see it / but you touch it and see it / it moves ya when you feel it, / and you feel it when it moves ya." Soul's evasiveness is in fact an invitation to the imagination. "You can't go round spillin / out pat definitions / on Soul," she says near the end of the ten-minute piece—but that, of course, is only more reason to come up with officious, absurd, or estranging definitions of soul:

Soul is the titular head of your emotional household

[Soul is] a rose with a gutter smell

Soul is a heart cut out of watermelon rind
screamin, "I wanta VOTE!"

The rose that smells like the gutter, the heart in the watermelon rind: these are images meant to shock, just as the scream "I wanta VOTE" is meant to unsettle the system of American apartheid. Simmons is taking the stock images of black life—the association of watermelons with smiling darkies and the gutter with grinding poverty—and making them more difficult to read. Is the "rose with a gutter smell" funky in a good or bad sense? Has the heart been cut out in symbolic anger, or as an ambivalent kind of self-mutilation? These are questions that the poem prefers to raise rather than answer.[13]

By contrast, Simmons is more transparent when she turns to the villains of her piece: Mr. and Mrs. Westerveal Duddly Hammington, vacationing at a South Seas Hilton and in love with the exotic locale. Simmons signifies on the couple by treating them with a dignity beyond what they deserve. Relaxing near "the whistle of the waves," "Mr. Duddly" and "Mrs. Duddly" take a dip at the hotel pool and drink from ceramic coconut shells; they love soul but think they can buy it, restrain it, keep it at a distance. Their vacation dream is disrupted by "drums beatin" "in the distance," a native celebration that carries the message that "this ain't art / It's Real / Movin!" In the light of this "real" and dynamic performance, Simmons has no trouble dismissing the feeble dance of Mrs. Duddly in her "corseted moo moo" with the summary judgment, "Nooo soul." In a similar spirit, Simmons ends "Soul" by attacking those who have listened to her and failed to profit from the experience: "for those who don't understand / Soul, there is this word, / you never will." There is condemnation here, but also a certain defensiveness, as if Simmons were registering how her poem has given us a booby-trapped definition of soul, one that prides itself on its inability to be co-opted and bought by the likes of Mr. and Mrs. Duddly.[14]

Here we arrive at a key distinction: while "Soul" wants to appeal to a sense of militancy—thus its invocation of the scream, whether it be the scream for a vote or the scream of McLean's saxophone—it prefers to define the enemies of soul rather than its practitioners. The Hammingtons of the world are in clear focus as soul fakers, and in "Soul"'s satire of them we can hear the murmur of a skeptical realpolitik that regards wealthy white liberals with a jaundiced eye. But the weight of the performance leans toward the affirmative aspect of the Black Power movement, its reclamation of black culture and its simultaneous attempt to expand the meaning of that culture. In music and words, "Soul" intimates that black culture is what people make of it and that the materials at hand are so various as to boggle the mind—gospel, blues, bebop, free jazz, the expressive culture of the church and subway and nightclub, even the stalest of minstrel clichés.

Just as the Black Power movement tried to redeem ways for black people to express their anger and love, so does "Soul" try to balance its aggressive critique of the here and now with a utopian vision of life as it might be. In its moments where free jazz explodes out of calm, we're cued to hear a fiery testimonial that's long been silenced, and whose immediacy is a sign of protest and breakthrough. More globally, in its playful spirit of musical and poetic digression, we can hear the drive to discover an aesthetic that is at its best on the run, tripping over itself and finding new company. Simmons begins her recitation in that riffing spirit of exploration, calling out her audience as a scale of notes and ending with a playful pun that suggests a collective free fall:

YO SOUL / MY SOUL / HE SOUL /
FA SOUL / LA SOUL

WHEEEE
SOUL[15]

Fighting the Exploitation Blues

Another way of understanding McLean's omnivorous approach to soul is within the context of a music industry where jazz was rapidly becoming an ever smaller player, dwarfed by the bullish sales of rock and soul music proper. The arrival of soul music in particular posed a considerable dilemma to jazz partisans, who felt that jazz captured the spirit of civil rights agitation but also recognized that the music was losing its foothold, especially within the black community. What would happen if the vanguard led the way, but no one took notice of its banner? Some critics, like Amiri Baraka, began to rethink their hostility to commercial art and found ways to celebrate a broad continuum of music under the rubric of black nationalism. Meanwhile, many artists, especially those allied with free jazz, responded to the commercial squeeze by founding their own musicians' collectives and community arts organizations. Their answer to the failure of the market was to create new markets—black capitalism for a black audience or, alternatively, artist-run enterprises for communities that wouldn't just buy art but would educate themselves and live through it, too.

The journal *Liberator* provides a good index of the evolving rapport between jazz and the cultures of political agitation and artistic entrepreneurialism and of the way that black artists reflected on their marginal place in the black community. *Liberator* began in 1961 as the slim newsletter of the Liberation Committee for Africa, whose chairman, Daniel Watts, doubled as editor-in-chief. Its early motto, borrowed from Frederick Douglass, was "Who would be free themselves must strike the blow." By 1964 it had evolved into a thirty-page monthly with the enlarged ambition of sponsoring the liberation of African America as well. Black Arts theorists Larry Neal and Rolland Snellings (later Askia Muhammad Touré) served as editors, and its contributors ranged from Harold Cruse, who debuted an early version of *The Crisis of the Negro Intellectual* in its pages, to cultural essayists James Baldwin, A. B. Spellman, Addison Gayle and Houston Baker, writers Langston Hughes and Ishmael Reed, and jazz musicians Max Roach, Abbey Lincoln, Nadi Qamar, Milford Graves, Don Pullen, and Jon Hendricks.

By and large, *Liberator* presented avant-garde jazz as the true music of black America. The cues were often implicit, the silences unremarked. The magazine reviewed jazz albums but no soul releases, and it covered rock music only to pillory white musicians like Janis Joplin. A 1966 Ray Gibson photo essay entitled "Spiritual Voices of Black America" called its musicians "the repositories of the spirit of freedom and expression imbedded in the social history of black people," then presented somber portraits of experimental jazzers Sun Ra, Marion Brown, and Grachan Moncur. Two years later another Gibson essay on the "black musician" featured Betty Carter and free-jazz drummer Sunny Murray—and no musicians identified with soul. Harold Cruse's four-part essay on the need for a cultural revolution in black America was also illustrated with images of a passionately blowing saxophonist and a sax-drums duo. Jazz artists were the only group spared the blade of the stiletto-wielding Cruse: while most of his essay's energy was spent attacking the civil rights establishment, would-be cultural nationalists, and the banality of American culture at large, he did digress a few times to suggest that jazz musicians were alone among black artists in developing a "specifically 'Negro school' of aesthetics."[16]

Cruse's hypothesis that jazz musicians were uniquely self-conscious—and uniquely separatist—filtered strongly into *Liberator*'s actual jazz coverage, whether in profiles of John Coltrane, Ornette Coleman, Cecil Taylor, and Archie Shepp or the writings of jazz musicians like Milford Graves and Don Pullen. As Marc Brasz, *Liberator*'s most polemical jazz writer, commented, "Jazz is the imposition of Black American feeling upon an Aryan culture. . . . The ineluctability of black." Musician Nadi Qamar extended this logic by identifying jazz as a product of Africa and therefore "the only music capable of lifting Black minds . . . from the depths of self-depreciatory phantasies." In the minds of Qamar, Brasz, and *Liberator*'s other cultural nationalists, jazz was music that refuted the logic of the melting pot, music of unalloyed black conception.[17]

Askia Muhammad Touré's "Keep on Pushin' (Rhythm & Blues as a Weapon)" might have been expected to provide a different slant, but it did so only to confirm the verities of *Liberator*'s jazz coverage. Touré argued that bebop had "gone away" "to make the cash registers clang and sing . . . in the air-conditioned nightmares of the West" and that the R&B of Fats Domino, Ray Charles, and Dinah Washington had filled the vacuum by serving as "OUR voice, OUR ritual, OUR understanding of those things far too complicated to put into words." R&B, then, was the ritual that mainstream jazz was too entangled in white commerce to be. Touré took heart, however, in the ritualistic turn of artists like Coltrane, who seemed to channel the traumas of the black past—"the bloody Whiplash moans and screams of our greatgrandfathers and grandmothers bending low"—into a new assault-prone music. The essay ended with the prophecy that avant-garde jazz would fuse with R&B and the most far-reaching revolutionary politics:

the "Keep on Pushin'" in song, in Rhythm and Blues is merging with the Revolutionary Dynamism of coltrane of eric dolphy of brother malcolm of young black guerrillas striking deep into the heartland of the western empire. The Fire is spreading, the Fire is spreading, the

Fire made from the merging of dynamic Black Music (Rhythm and Blues, Jazz) with politics (guerrilla warfare) is spreading like black oil flaming in Atlantic shipwrecks spreading like Black Fire.

Touré imagined that black music would inflict a retaliatory trauma on the West, shipwreck fires that were payback for the Middle Passage and its legacies.[18]

Yet if many *Liberator* articles had this same endpoint—the proclamation of jazz's righteous blackness—they were also driven to probe the riddle of experimental jazz's reception in the black community. This surely was the question that kept artists like Cecil Taylor and Archie Shepp awake at night: if their hard-edged jazz was the true expression of black America, then why were their audiences small and salt-and-pepper at best, even frequently dominated by whites? Whereas mainstream *Down Beat* critics like Ira Gitler lit into free jazzers for failing to attract a sizable audience, the pages of *Liberator* make clear that avant-garde musicians were painfully familiar with this difficulty. They were aware, in Cecil Taylor's words, that "jazz has been separated from the audience it is most responsive to." The dilemma was akin to that faced by Movement organizers, who often believed that they represented a Rousseauian general will but had always to bring bodies together in practice, not in theory, or face the discrediting of their leadership. The issue had a geographical dimension too, since so many of the musicians and critics who aspired to community leadership—Archie Shepp, Sunny Murray, Marion Brown, A. B. Spellman, and Amiri Baraka—had settled in the early 1960s around New York's Cooper Square near the Five Spot, not in Harlem.[19]

Liberator's contributors approached the puzzle of why avant-garde jazz was not more popular among blacks from a variety of angles. An article entitled "Has Jazz Lost Its Roots?" answered—yes and no. On the one hand, jazz had lost its roots because the music was "a long way, both physically and emotionally, from its original source" in communities like Harlem; on the other, it had kept its relevance because jazz expressed "certain truths about Negro life in America" that blacks were repressing at their own peril. Larry Neal placed the blame for jazz's small black audience with Western capitalism, which churned the music through the commodity form, and with bourgeois avant-gardism, which presumed that artists had to be alienated from their community. The "popcorn society," in Neal's words, forced black musicians to entertain their audience rather than offer them "spiritual content and conviction." Meanwhile white middle-class audiences, who claimed to be seeking spiritual elevation through art, were in fact collecting jazz music as part of their stash of cultural capital. Shepp speculated in a related vein, "I think it will be a long time before the Black artist and the Black community can really stand next to each other because so much has been done by power to separate them; and, for pure economic reasons, many have moved away from Harlem. . . . I think it would be very difficult for Cecil and Ornette or myself to just go up to Harlem and expect to be accepted right away." Altogether, musicians were drawn to the theory that their professional struggle was a function of the unpleasant truths they were expressing and of the spiritual vision that they were offering to an audience accustomed to lighter fare. They speculated, that is, that they were either too alienated or too spiritually centered for the black audience, or perhaps both—too alienated from the white culture that black folk had internalized to their detriment.[20]

Whatever the diagnosis, however, the prescription for recovery was the same in the cultural nationalist pages of *Liberator, The Cricket,* and *Change:* musicians needed to return to their community, take control of their own industry, and educate those they wished to enlist as their audience. Drummer Milford Graves and pianist Don Pullen explained that "the chief mistake the Afro-American musician and artist makes is the exclusion of himself from the production aspect of music and art." The two tried to rectify the injustice by founding their own label, SRP Records, and releasing an album of free-jazz duets on it. (The initials SRP stood for "self-reliance program.") Amiri Baraka's *The Cricket,* published from Newark after the 1967 unrest, gave a related lesson in political economy in the form of a late-sixties back-cover cartoon called "Exploitation Blues!" A black saxophonist stood on a street corner, "blackmusic" floating in a bubble out of his sax. His coat and pants were threadbare and heavily patched, though his goatee, sunglasses, and rolled turtleneck suggested that it was not for lack of a sense of style. A chain ran from a manacle on his leg to the cup of a gangster in trench coat and fedora, a shrunken white man smoking a fat cigar. Dollar bills poured from the sky into the gangster's cup. "How'm I doin', Norm?" asked the musician—to which Norm responded, "The public's not ready for you yet—we're not makin' a dime! Keep playin'!"[21]

The cartoon was heavy-handed, but it made its point: jazz artists deserved a fair return on their talent, and it was impossible for them to be sure they weren't being fleeced if they did not control their own booking, record labels, or publishing companies. In the mid-sixties, clusters of musicians across the United States banded together in community arts organizations, some of which lasted only a few months, others of which have lasted as long as forty years (and counting), taking on different colorations and ambitions depending on the political and musical scenes that nourished them. Cities that were crucibles of hard bop gave birth to collectives like Los Angeles's Union of God's Musicians and Artists Ascension (UGMAA), Pittsburgh's Black Arts Cultural Center, Detroit's Strata, St. Louis's Black Artists Group, Chicago's AACM, and New York's Jazz Composers Guild, Black Arts Repertory Theater/School (BARTS), and Collective Black Artists.[22]

The first (and perhaps most underappreciated) of these organizations was Horace Tapscott's UGMAA, founded in the early 1960s and still active as of this writing despite the death of its founder. Like Charles Mingus, Tapscott had felt frustrated by his experience with Lionel Hampton's band—in his case, because he questioned whether he could meaningfully give back to his community if he worked with a touring band. Tapscott built his collective, which was originally known as the Underground Musicians Association (UGMA), around the large working group he called the Pan Afrikan Peoples Arkestra: "Pan Afrikan" because the Arkestra aimed to embrace the music of the entire African diaspora; "Arkestra" because it hoped to serve as a "cultural safe house," a jazz-inflected version of Noah's ark. While the Arkestra welcomed younger players and performed in the parks of South Central L.A., the umbrella organization of UGMA sponsored a wide variety of other forms of community outreach: classes in basic reading, writing, and arithmetic for children; classes in acting and dance; and even a short-lived program called Medimusic that took music to the elderly and the mentally ill. From the start, UGMA was interested in giving young people in South Central a sense of heritage and a sense of possibility, and its relative anonymity may partly have been a result of the openness of its proceedings: the primary goal of the Arkestra was community action and uplift, and the collective put little energy into "making it" by the traditional routes of record contracts and tours on the concert circuit. The first Peoples Arkestra recordings were made in 1978—almost two decades after its founding, and after jazz titans like Arthur Blythe, Sonny Criss, Charles Lloyd, Butch Morris, and David Murray had passed through its ranks.[23]

In the mid-sixties, at the breakaway moment when the civil rights movement began shifting much of its energy to urban areas outside the South, there was much new community-based organizing in the jazz community too: Greenwich Village's Jazz Composers Guild, Harlem's BARTS, and Chicago's AACM all emerged in 1964 and 1965. Experimental composer Bill Dixon launched the Jazz Composers Guild after the success of his 1964 "October Revolution in Jazz," six nights of packed concerts at the Cellar Café on New York's West Side. By its own admission, the guild was more of a worker's collective, primed with talent, than a community arts forum. Its handpicked and interracial membership included Sun Ra, Paul and Carla Bley, Michael Mantler, Archie Shepp, Roswell Rudd, and Cecil Taylor.

Members hoped to pool their talent, withhold their labor from low-paying gigs, collectively negotiate contracts for nightclub and concert work, and verify the fairness of record company royalties—the stuff of a workers' guild specially outfitted for the jazz industry. The Jazz Composers Guild had its successes—its orchestra held regular concerts, aptly, in a loft two floors above the Village Vanguard—but it soon fell victim to the allied forces of economics, misogyny, and entropy. Archie Shepp started negotiating a contract with Impulse Records without notifying the other members, exactly the sort of star promotion that the guild protested. Morale dropped, and members began attacking one another. At one point, Sun Ra prophesized that the guild was like a ship that would sink unless it threw its woman overboard (the obvious target being Carla Bley). Even Dixon dropped out of the guild, reflecting that "the Guild was organized as an alternative to the conditions of exploitation, but the nature of some of our conflicts . . . has served to clarify what and how bad the conditions really are and the insanities they have caused." The organization disbanded shortly thereafter.[24]

While the Jazz Composers Guild reflected the hopes and tensions of the avant-garde Village scene, Amiri Baraka's Black Arts center brought together jazz musicians like Sun Ra and Andrew Hill with Harlem's full spectrum of leftists and black nationalists—people from the Nation of Islam, the Yoruba Temple, *Liberator* magazine, the African Jazz Arts Society (a neo-Garveyite group), the Revolutionary Action Movement, and the Progressive Labor Party—as well as many "gangsters and hoodlums and people in 'the life.'" Baraka reflected on the messiness of this coalition, as well as its basis in a shared language of sincerity and experience: "The Black Arts itself was a pastiche of so many things, so many styles and ideologies. We had no stated ideology except 'black,' and that meant many things to many people, much of it useful, much of it not. . . . Our sincerity was our real ideology, a gestalt of our experience, an eclectic mixture of what we thought we knew and understood."

Funded as part of the federal government's Operation Bootstrap, a stop-the-riots program in the summer of 1965, BARTS used its budget to bring painting, drama, and music into the streets, playgrounds, parks, and housing projects of Harlem. Like the civil rights movement, it reclaimed public spaces to stage dramas of exuberance and social tension—the former, for instance, in a spangled parade up 125th Street led by Sun Ra's Arkestra to announce BARTS's grand opening, the latter in the guerrilla performances of agitprop plays like Baraka's *Black Ice*, which began with a black man brandishing a pistol and apparently chasing a white man through the streets. BARTS survived the tumultuous summer of 1965, but not long after Watts exploded and Harlem was convulsed in a citywide blackout, the arts group unraveled in a round of violent infighting. Baraka moved back to Newark, his friend Larry Neal was shot in the leg, and eventually the police raided the Black Arts building, seized its firearms, and arrested six of those left in the building. Still, by 1973, there were 150 black community arts groups across the country—many of them tracing themselves back to the performance activism of BARTS.[25]

Chicago's AACM combined the music-focused guild structure of Dixon's organization and the community arts orientation of BARTS. In an astonishing testament to group solidarity, discipline, and invention, the AACM has managed to last into the twenty-first century—this despite the eclectic and challenging music it has sponsored through offshoots like the Art Ensemble of Chicago, which combines chance operations and broad blues gestures, "out" solos, and a nonrealist dramaturgy of costume. Much of its success may be traced to pianist and composer Muhal Richard Abrams, the AACM's president at its launch in 1965, whose wide-ranging style and sense of moral responsibility steered the AACM to its original fusion of experiment and uplift. Abrams put the idea of self-respect at the center of the AACM's organizing efforts, and his air of moral discipline pervaded the AACM's programming, which involved regular concerts, radio shows, open rehearsals, and other forms of community education.

One might say that the AACM had a Midwestern kind of anti-hipness, a focus on human potential that refused the idea of one-upmanship. Instead of being one step ahead of the crowd, the AACM aspired in its 1971 manifesto to convert that crowd into a community:

> Our curriculum is so designed as to elicit maximum development of potential within the context of a training program that exposes youngsters to constructive relationships with artistic adults. Superimposed over our training framework is our keen desire to develop within our students the ability to value *self*, the ability to value *others* and the ability to utilize the opportunities they find in society. . . . [S]uch values should be based on the cultural and spiritual heritage of the people involved.

That last sentence testified to the remarkable balance struck by the AACM as the country became increasingly polarized between Black Power and the white backlash in the late 1960s. The AACM inventively rediscovered the roots of a black aesthetic even as its focus on "creative" music suggested that jazz was music beyond category, the ongoing discovery of an open form. It was no coincidence that one of the pioneering albums by AACM leader Roscoe Mitchell was called simply *Sound* (1966): the usual exploration of harmony, melody, and rhythm was subsumed in a larger quest to explore the nature of sound, including all its nonscalar and possibly serrated edges. Like Coltrane and Duke Ellington at the end of their careers, the artists affiliated with the AACM understood their music as a spiritual vocation—ambition vaulting to the heavens and ennobled by duty. Yet in their wedding of constancy and experiment, they also infused jazz with what Ted Gioia calls "the first stirrings of postmodernism" as "music theory was superseded by a quasi-primitive celebration of unmediated and undiluted sound" and as earlier musical styles and traditions were unpredictably blended. Like Jackie McLean's "Soul," the AACM's music was inside and outside jazz at the same time, a form of uplift that took the listener to uncharted territories.[26]

Meanwhile, through the late 1960s and beyond, Horace Tapscott's UGMA expanded its sense of mission. The "underground" musicians' association was renamed, in a symbolic move that spoke to its emphasis on spiritual unity and its refusal to lurk under the radar of the community, as the "Union of God's Musicians and Artists Ascension." As Tapscott reflected, "In the beginning, it was more like breaking the old mold, the old routines; just take a bulldozer and run it down. Then, we had to think about how to build it up to what we were talking about." In practice, this community building meant that the Arkestra would perform for any group that the members of the Arkestra thought would bring respect to the neighborhood—an ecumenical standard that led them to play for black politicians trying to make inroads into the political system, including soon-to-be L.A. mayor Tom Bradley, Ron Karenga's cultural nationalist U.S. organization, the local Black Muslims, and the Black Panthers. The Arkestra's support for Black Power groups was not without serious consequences. According to Tapscott, Arkestra members were tailed by FBI agents "in Hawaiian shirts and dark sunglasses," and Tapscott himself avoided his house at one point so that he would not be caught in a FBI roundup of suspected black revolutionaries. The FBI even raided the Arkestra headquarters in the late 1960s because its second story had become a gathering place for revolutionary nationalists like H. Rap Brown and Stokely Carmichael, who discussed strategy while the Arkestra rehearsed below.[27]

As the word "ascension" suggests, Tapscott's UGMAA represents a powerful way that the spirit of John Coltrane lived on in the jazz world. Perhaps more than any other jazz collective, UGMAA led the way for a jazz that aspired to be singularly community-minded and that would respond to the crisis in the jazz market by declaring independence from its pressures and trading the usual professional ambitions for others. Artistry and spirituality were indivisible in this idiom of the music. The ritual-like music of Coltrane was echoed in Arkestra performances like "The Dark Tree" and "The Giant Is Awakened," pieces that testified to cycles of suffering and redemption, lived out both on an individual scale and on the scale of an entire people. And, like Coltrane again, the Arkestra was magnetic in part because its musicians floated above the rifts that fractured their community into warring factions. Tapscott recalled, "People were always asking us what we were":

"Are you guys Muslims?"
"No, we're not Muslims."
"Are you Black Panthers?"
"No, we're not."
"Are you U.S. Organization people?"
"No."
"Well, what are you?"
"We're black Americans, and want to live in the American way."
You dig?

Tapscott's answer about simply wanting to live in the American way was not disingenuous, although it did have a defiant ring to it: this was one "Pan Afrikan" group that refused to be locked out of the American promise. The Arkestra's music was inclusive, the sounds of shared dreams and shared freedom, part of the struggle to find common ground with the world and protest its wrongs at the same time.[28]

Mingus in the Bunker

It is one of this period's saddest historical ironies that Charles Mingus, the jazz figure who had been among the music's most insightful social critics and most innovative composers, entered into a severe depression—half a decade of paranoia, insomnia, and musical inertia—just at the moment when his social and aesthetic prophecies seemed to be coming true. Mingus had urged jazz musicians to pool their resources and create their own guilds, and now they were doing so in cities across the country. He had blasted the music industry and American culture for being systematically unfair, not just psychologically "prejudiced," and now even the mainstream civil rights movement was focusing less on appeals to individual conscience and more on the structures of disadvantage that constituted racism (a word that took hold in the late 1960s). He had injected jazz with a dynamic dose of soul—equal parts virtuosity and gospel fire—and now young listeners were taking up the music of Aretha Franklin, James Brown, and Stevie Wonder, much of which was propelled by Mingus-like bass riffs. Lastly, with his abiding interest in mysticism and charismatic power, Mingus had brought a new range of apocalyptic moods to jazz, and now the white members of the counterculture were thinking apocalyptically as a matter of principle, testing the foundations of their world through explorations in music and drugs and through their involvement in the politics of the New Left. Intimations of apocalypse were, in the late sixties, considered to be accurate analyses of the situation at hand, and yet the apocalyptically minded Mingus fell out of step with the culture around him, dropping out of the jazz world and settling into an atypical period of silence.

When Mingus sank, he sank quite low—into something more tortured than oblivion. He lived in a Lower East Side neighborhood so down on its luck that even the local outlet of the Con Ed power company was missing two of the five letters of its neon sign. He ate constantly and gained weight, all the while experimenting with various combinations of speed and vitamin shots, benzedrine and demerol, cocaine and wine. A few years later, he admitted, "I thought I was finished. Sometimes I couldn't even get out of bed. I wasn't asleep; I just lay there." His suspicion of the world ballooned into theatrical forms of paranoia that isolated him from friends, lovers, and fellow musicians. He hollowed out his copy of Edmund Shaftesbury's *Cultivation of Personal Magnetism in Seven Steps* so that he could stash a handgun there; he rigged his doorknob so that it gave an electric shock to the unwary and his doorway so that a rifle could fire at anyone breaking in. One year around Christmastime, his answering machine picked up with "No one gives a damn about me. The lights on my tree are out. And all you motherfuckers out there who are threatening my life, I know who you are! You can take this as a warning: I've got a surprise in store for all of you!" Mingus suspected that the authorities were monitoring his bodily fluids, so he refused to use his own toilet and filled a stash of Tropicana juice bottles with his urine. (One insane irony among many: Mingus had toilet-trained his cat, so the cat used the toilet even though he didn't.) At perhaps the lowest point in this cycle, Mingus had a breakdown while with his children Carolyn and Eric at a small playground in Central Park. He started gasping about a witch pricking him with a needle, took off his pants, and scattered hundred-dollar bills to the wind. Eric ran to his mother, Judy, who worked as a nurse at Mt. Sinai Hospital across the street; she arrived but could not calm Mingus. He was taken to Mt. Sinai, where he spent a month under

Beneath the underdog: Throughout his life, composer Charles Mingus identified with outcasts who were nonetheless survivors. In the late 1960s he entered into a severe depression—half a decade of paranoia, insomnia, and musical inertia—just as his social and aesthetic prophecies seemed to be coming true. (Courtesy of Michael Ochs Archives)

observation and medication. For the next few years, Mingus was on mellaril, a thorazine-like antipsychotic drug that dampens moods and can cause disorientation and restlessness.[29]

Unsurprisingly, Mingus grew distant from the jazz community during this period. He stopped practicing his bass and lost the calluses that he had taken such pride in developing. He did not release any new music of his own between 1965 and 1970, nor did he enter a recording studio. The Jazz Workshop performed rarely and then often with a thrown-together roster, and by 1970, for the first time since the early 1950s, its musicians were largely playing from written charts—not for any aesthetic reason, but simply because the new players were unfamiliar with the music. One critic observed that Mingus's "records were a rumor." The man himself spent much time at a bar catty-corner from his apartment on East Fifth Street and Avenue A, a place called Chic Choc, where he was one of the regulars, simply "Charlie," not a jazz musician who aspired to revolutionize the music. His friends there were a diverse crew with a sense of hard-bitten fellowship. Mingus described them as "Ukrainians, blacks, Puerto Ricans—a house painter, a tailor, a woman who owns a bar, her bartender, a maintenance man who says, 'I'll walk you home tonight if you get drunk. And if I get drunk, you walk me home.'" Chic Choc was, in some sense, the end of the line, but it was also one of the few communities left for Mingus, who drifted in this period outside of jazz and outside of an anchoring romantic relationship. During his comeback in the early 1970s, he gave heartfelt thanks to the bar's regulars: "I don't know if I could have come out of the graveyard had it not been for them."[30]

While it may be impossible to determine exactly why Mingus's life and career unraveled in the late 1960s, it's fair to say that Mingus's social isolation was exacerbated by his conflicted relationship to two cultural movements that swept through his life in these years—the counterculture and Black Power—and by his inability to enter into a lasting romantic relationship (itself, as we shall see, a historical as well as personal problem). Mingus was attuned to the appeal of the counterculture and Black Power movements but could not take them up as his own—could not find a new home in the communities they were creating. He kept his distance not out of ignorance or simple distaste: living in the Lower East Side from 1966 to 1973 he found himself at the epicenter of cultural change, drifting into antiwar rallies while walking down the street, meeting Black Panther activists at his nightclub performances, even at one point sharing the bill at a Fillmore East benefit with Peter Yarrow (of Peter, Paul, and Mary) and the freewheeling garage band the Fugs. As his final wife, Sue Mingus, wrote in her unsparing but loving memoir, "Charles knew everyone and joined no one."[31]

Although he balked at its libertarian extremes, Mingus was intrigued enough by the promises of the counterculture to taste its pleasures, experiment offhandedly with its aesthetic, and befriend some of its most luminous figures. He had a casual but consistent interest in its activities—attending the first Human Be-In at Golden Gate Park in 1967, where he wandered unrecognized in the crowd; working for a short while as a photographer for the Off-Off-Broadway La Mama group (around the time that it was premiering Sam Shepard's rock plays); and, after he had recovered some of his spark in the early 1970s, cohosting regular dinner parties for the staff of *Changes,* the New York–based arts magazine that his wife-to-be, Sue, helped edit. While many observers condemned wholesale the counterculture's spirit of transgression, this was not Mingus's point of view. He was sympathetic to the idea that art might willfully violate boundaries between high and low, sacred and profane, and that it might involve theatrical acts of imposition. At one point, in an attempt to win back Sue in the mid-sixties, he even set up a psychedelic light show in his own apartment, creating a "fierce and incandescent" display that "splattered bright, rude and incessant through the dark," complete with images of "shining crosses" and "ejaculating phalluses."[32]

Mingus did reject, however, what he saw as the anarchic playfulness of the counterculture, its desire to affirm chaos and chance as much as the rules of order and form; in his aesthetic, transgression was meaningful only in the context of a framework of order that it violated. There is much evidence, albeit anecdotal, of Mingus's "old-school" attitudes on this score. When he attended an experimental Stan Brakhage film in 1964 that played with the flicker of subliminal images, he was so infuriated by its aleatory structure that he stood up and screamed "Fraud! Fraud!" at the screen. His relationships with Allen Ginsberg and Timothy Leary are also illustrative. Mingus counted Ginsberg as a friend from their first heady conversations in the Beat subculture of mid-1950s San Francisco. As Mingus biographer Gene Santoro points out, they shared "the artistic egoists' ability to see themselves reflected everywhere, and everything refracted through themselves." Ginsberg even delivered, at Mingus's request, an impromptu wedding ceremony for the bassist and Sue at a friend's prenuptial party: without skipping a beat, the poet launched into an impassioned meditation exercise, a chant accompanied by two small Indian cymbals that he held inside his palms. Yet Mingus did not consider Ginsberg enough of a kindred spirit to accept an offer of collaboration. Though his career was at a low ebb, the bassist refused the poet's invitation to record William Blake's *Songs of Innocence and Experience*—a great loss to the recorded archive. Ginsberg became one of the counterculture's great tribunes of liberation, its all-accepting Buddhist sage and intellectual jester; but Mingus did not follow suit. Anything but Zen, he always retained the prerogative to bristle at his experience before he swallowed it whole.[33]

A similar rift colored Mingus's relationship to Timothy Leary, the counterculture's most famous propagandist for the benefits of mind-altering substances. On several occasions, Mingus retreated to his friend Peggy Hitchcock's sumptuous estate in Millbrook, New York, where Leary held court among—in Sue Mingus's words—"artists, poets, musicians, the beautiful, the spaced out and the very rich." The bassist participated in the estate's communal dinners and improvisatory arts projects, but he held back enthusiasm for Leary's undertakings. He declined Leary's offer to become an in-house guru and refused to drop acid, explaining at one point that "I don't want to go crazy. I don't enjoy not knowing reality," and offering on another occasion that he had no desire to transform his approach to the bass or to music in general. Leary believed that individuals needed to empty themselves completely, to let go of their history and cultural imprint so that they could rise to a new, higher consciousness. Mingus, by contrast, held tenaciously onto the identity that he had constructed for himself in his decades of scuffling and struggle. At Millbrook, he deflated Leary's high-flown theories on a regular basis—loudly spraying insect repellent and smacking himself when Leary was giving a religious speech; telling him, "You've got nothing for Harlem, man. . . . Nothing for the workers, the people who go to their jobs, the people who get up at six"; and cutting down Leary's free-form dramatic improvisations with the line "You can't improvise on nothing."[34]

Certainly the Black Power movement made a much greater effort to appeal to Harlem, and just as certainly, with its emphasis on community togetherness (sometimes expressed as an authoritarian impulse to dictate what the community wanted and should do), it offered an alternative to the creative anarchism that drove Leary's side of the counterculture. Yet despite his deep sympathies with Black Power's critique of the status quo and his affinities with its street machismo, Mingus always felt ambivalent about its rhetoric of black separatism and resisted openly affiliating himself with the movement. The Black Panthers' minister of information regularly came to hear Mingus perform at the Village Gate, but Mingus could not be bothered to listen to his rap. In December 1971, he attended a Black Panther benefit at a gutted Brooklyn warehouse and was largely unmoved—except when black women at the party shot disapproving glances at him for being in the company of Sue, a strawberry blonde.[35]

Some of the complexities of Mingus's relationship to Black Power ideology can be gleaned from Tom Reichman's *Mingus,* a 1966 documentary filmed largely on the eve of Mingus's eviction from his downtown studio. The film offers some of the most indelible images of Mingus's militancy as he kills time in his studio. He sings his own version of "America (My Country 'Tis of Thee)," changing the second line of its couplet to "sweet land of slavery." He takes out a theatrical trick rope and stages his own mock lynching, drawing the noose around his neck and asking his tiny daughter Keki to pull the rope until it breaks. (She laughs, disturbingly, when it does.) He loads his shotgun and shoots it at the ceiling in a somewhat chaotic show of self-defense. Asked by a reporter what he feels at the moment of his eviction, he replies, Cold War be damned, "I hope the Communists blow you people up." And in one of the film's most inspired moments, he offers his own barbed tribute to American ideals in the form of a self-styled pledge of allegiance:

I pledge allegiance to the flag, the white flag. I pledge allegiance to the flag of America. When they say black or Negro it means you're not an American. I pledge allegiance to your flag—not that I want to, but for the hell of it. . . . Yeah, I pledge allegiance to the United States of America. I pledge allegiance to seeing that someday they will live up to their own promises to the victims that they call citizens. Not just the black ghettos, but the white ghettos, the Japanese ghettos, the Chinese ghettos, all the ghettos in the world. Oh, I pledge allegiance. I could pledge a whole lot of allegiance.

With its surprising turn toward solidarity beyond the color line, the rewritten pledge gives us Mingus the improviser fashioning his own sense of commitment. He ends by proclaiming that he isn't "jiving": this pledge is, after all, "an 'ism' that I have to die for."[36]

Yet while Mingus may not have been jiving, he *was* playing in a more serious sense. Throughout his career, he put considerable energy into acts of violence that were theatrical and symbolic rather than life-endangering—stopping short of where some Black Power advocates were prepared to go. Just after the ceiling crumbles from the impact of the shotgun blast, Mingus turns to the camera and says, winkingly, "We're just acting, right?" He was extremely ambivalent about his own shows of force, deflating them with apologies, caveats, explanations; theatricality allowed Mingus to give voice to the possibility of violence without committing fully to it. The theatrical impulse gave him liberty to try on seemingly fake identities and to expand what it meant to live as a black man in America. He sang his parody of "America (My Country 'Tis of Thee)" while wearing an oversized sombrero, as if to suggest that the mongrel art of satire was one with a mongrel sort of citizenship. You could make up your own pledge of allegiance, imagine a national identity that was based in the solidarity of outsiders locked out of the American promise, and try to make this kind of citizenship stick by performing it in ways that were comic, tragic, or both at once. For their part, the Black Panthers may have put their faith in a similar cross-ethnic alliance of the disempowered—their manifestos repeatedly argued that there would be an uprising of working people led by a black vanguard—but the Panthers had a seriousness, sometimes hardening into dogmatism, that did not gel with Mingus's penchant for the theatrical and the absurd. As historian Brian Ward suggests, with a bit of understatement, "the Panthers tended to underestimate the politics of pleasure."[37]

A more powerful factor in Mingus's depression—more powerful than his ambivalent relationship to Black Power and the counterculture, if more difficult to submit to historical analysis—was his acute sense of romantic isolation. Mingus's mental health could be graphed as a function of his romantic life: the beginnings of his breakdown coincided with the disintegration of his marriage to his third wife, Judy; it worsened during his separation from his wife-to-be, Sue; and it went into definitive remission upon the return of Sue, who not only gave him emotional support but also took up the management of the reconstituted Jazz Workshop. As Gene Santoro's biography has meticulously documented, Mingus's manly bluster coincided with his utter dependence on the women in his life. White women were his most consistent benefactors and musical enablers, as well as his most sympathetic sounding boards: Celia Mingus Zaentz, his second wife, helped found Debut Records with her mother's money and did much of the creative and day-to-day work behind the running of the label (when she pulled out, the operation ground to a halt); Peggy Hitchcock, a member of the Mellon family, helped sponsor Mingus's Newport counterfestival and later invited him to her Millbrook estate; Diane Dorr-Dorynek, his girlfriend from the late 1950s and early 1960s, acted as the assistant to the Jazz Workshop in one of its most productive periods; and Kate Mulholland, an old friend, let Mingus stay in her sprawling Berkeley villa in the late 1960s. These sorts of arrangements were not uncommon in the jazz world at the time, and they suggest some of the cultural complexities that underlay jazz's emphasis on the achievement of black manhood. In the case of Mingus, he both drew attention to his dependency on women (what else is *Beneath the Underdog* if not an attempt to reconcile his ostensible charisma with his lack of power?) and rendered it obscure with denials, digressions, and heated rhetoric about infidelity in love and disloyalty in business.[38]

In the late 1960s, Mingus felt this dependency as a crushing burden. These were his years in the romantic wilderness, the years when *Beneath the Underdog* was finally cobbled together into publishable form (with the assistance of a white female editor). Strikingly, these were also the years when second-wave feminism took hold. Inspired by the grassroots power of the civil rights movement and the New Left, which many of them had been part of, and also by the indifferent or even mocking reception that their ideas about sexual equality had met in these circles, women activists spearheaded a movement to challenge sexism in economic, political, and social life. The standard-bearer for liberal feminism, the National Organization for Women, was founded in 1966, and a host of more self-consciously radical groups, including New York's The Feminists—which went beyond arguments for gender equity to the issue of patriarchy as a system of oppression—emerged in the late sixties and early seventies. Spurred by these movements, more and more American women questioned why they were expected to work for less pay than men, to give up careers for the sake of child rearing, or to play a lesser, "helping" role in marriage. Many felt, in historian Alice Echols's words, "that the contradiction between the realities of paid work and higher education on the one hand and the still pervasive ideology of domesticity on the other had become irreconcilable."[39]

Sue Graham Ungaro (later Mingus) was one of these women who were trying to reconstruct their life and find a new balance in the world. While her memoir does not claim feminism as a source of inspiration (she remembers that "the first feminist poster I ever saw was in [Mingus's] studio—a defiant housewife with a broken broom"), it also testifies powerfully to her interest in maintaining her independence and sense of wholeness in the context of her relationship with Mingus. This was no small task: Mingus was given to jealous rages with little provocation, constructing, in her words, "moral tests, dares, or obstacles that were alternately demonic or pathetic." She recalls, for instance, the time at a Tijuana strip club when Mingus suddenly decided that she had been lusting after a nearby college student, and—more—that the student had been planted at the club by coconspirators.[40]

Throughout the early years of their courtship, Mingus insisted that their love needed to "have an address"—to have all the permanency of a shared home—while Sue wrestled with her twin desires: "wanting to connect; wanting to be allowed a life apart." A Smith graduate with a long-standing interest in the arts, she had already been married once and had borne two children. Now was an opportune time to strike out in new directions: in the late 1960s, in the interval before she committed fully to Mingus (much of which time she spent apart from him), she became copublisher of the *New York Free Press* and moved to Tompkins Square in the Lower East Side, locating herself in the counterculture's nerve center. The question of the fullness of her commitment to Mingus was "the source of every fight" until the couple took up a shared address in 1973, nine years after they had met at the Five Spot. They came to an ambivalent, if familiar, accommodation on the question of Sue's career. Mingus never quite supported her work in publishing, but their worlds did overlap: he contributed some of his own writing to her publications, and her editorial colleagues and writer friends were frequent guests at the couple's apartment.[41]

With much help from Sue, Mingus pieced back together his life and his career in the early 1970s—and, as a figure who had become a celebrated part of jazz history, finally began to reap some of the rewards of his earlier efforts. The Jazz and People's Movement, led in part by former Mingus sideman Roland Kirk, won more airtime for jazz and gave Mingus a spot on Ed Sullivan's stage; the group lobbied the Guggenheim Foundation to recognize the idiom, and a month later Mingus received a grant as a composer. He had weathered his season in hell and had emerged as a living legend, one who thought more and more about the Mingus repertory and his legacy as a composer. *Beneath the Underdog* appeared shortly thereafter, with the notable subtitle "the world as composed by Mingus." The man who, a few years earlier, had almost been lost to the world was soon celebrated in publications from *Newsweek* to the *Times Literary Supplement* as the heartbeat of Black America, its spirit of survival. There was considerable irony in this—the persona in *Beneath the Underdog* was much easier to love in print than in person, as Mingus's experiences of the late 1960s suggest—but the bassist-composer was in a position to savor that irony, not condemn it.[42]

In the years before his 1979 death, Mingus continued to write for the ages. His 1977 piece "Cumbia & Jazz Fusion" is one of the most complicated and wide-ranging of his extended forms, a rattling and episodic half-hour journey that starts with the musique concrète sounds of a jungle and takes diverse tours through Columbian-inflected clave, harmonically exquisite balladry, and gutbucket blues. The gutbucket, it turns out, is a good place for settling old scores—here the pickaninny-themed song "Shortnin' Bread" is given a comic dressing-down. Over a rollicking beat and in a guttural, gargantuan voice, Mingus growls, "Who said Mama's little baby liked shortnin' bread?" then answers, "That's some lie some white man up and said. . . . Mama's little baby likes truffles, Mama's little baby likes caviar, Mama's little baby likes all the finer things of life." Mingus himself was quite a sophisticate. Having given American culture a blueprint for the sixties and then having watched the sixties pass him by, he turned his imagination to music that was less timely, less tied to contemporary social dramas, but still fired by his long-standing refusal to play by the script he was given.[43]

Cannonball in the Breadbasket

Unlike Mingus, saxophonist Cannonball Adderley figured out how to ride the whirlwind of the late 1960s—a talent that is powerfully documented by a recording of an Adderley performance at Jesse Jackson's Operation Breadbasket in 1969. Jackson is pumping the crowd with a call-and-response exercise familiar to all Movement veterans. "We shall." "We shall." "Overcome." "Overcome." The crowd is responding with conviction but not much fervor. After Jackson gets through the refrain, he switches to a fresher and more assertive slogan: "soul power." The chant rings through

Saint Francis church, and the crowd thunders back with ear-popping enthusiasm—"soul power!" Saint Francis seems to have suddenly experienced a change in air pressure or a surge in its amplifiers, but what is happening is less occult and more far-reaching: an audience prompted to, and thrilled by, the act of self-discovery.[44]

Looking back over thirty years later, we can see that this chant was a fleeting moment of crystallization, one given sharp detail by the magic of Adderley's soul-jazz and the surprising momentum of Operation Breadbasket, the Jackson-led project in community organizing. "We shall overcome" was a slogan with a dignified history, but "soul power" was a slogan for the now, one that honored the Breadbasket community's experience of collective empowerment and underlined its cultural dimension. Like all such slogans, it was intended to mobilize a specific community—in this case, the two thousand or more people who gathered each week on Chicago's South Side, brought together by Breadbasket's Saturday morning services. The Adderley concert was an inspirational event in a long line of inspirational events: every Saturday, Breadbasket visitors would wend their way through sidewalks thick with vendors of black literature, African handicrafts, and copies of *Muhammad Speaks;* they would find their seats with the assistance of dashiki-clad ushers; and then for three hours they would participate in the morning service, described by one congregant as "a combined town meeting and revival." For Breadbasket's audience, then, "soul power" was not just a slogan, but the basis of action and commitment, a way of being in the world. As Jackson defined the aims of Breadbasket, "If I thought we were just developing some more black capitalists with the same value system as white capitalists, I would quit this morning. What we want is white folks' technology with black folks' love." There were few better instances of that love than the uplift-oriented performance of the Adderley quintet, whose message was carried by their opener and Top 40 hit, "Walk Tall."[45]

Formed at the same time as the Association for the Advancement of Creative Musicians, Operation Breadbasket was a more extensive experiment in black self-reliance, one that aimed to regenerate black Chicago's economy and culture. By October 1969, when Adderley performed at the 500,000-person "Black Expo," Breadbasket in Chicago had evolved from a local alliance of black ministers, brought together to supplement Martin Luther King's campaign for open housing, into a broad operation that sponsored consumer boycotts, weekly services, a thousand-member choir, cultural events like "Black Christmas" and "Black Easter," free-breakfast centers, and antipoverty legislative campaigns directed at the state capital. Driving this operation was the soul capitalism of the young Jackson, who declared, typically, that "to have civil rights without economic justice is to have the right to dive into a swimming pool without water, the right to check into a hotel without the ability to check out." Jackson had the style of younger militant groups like SNCC—he sported an Afro, neck-chain medallions, and fringed buckskins, and sometimes spoke of "cracker" policemen fighting "the brothers"—but he also considered himself an heir to King's legacy. Like King after 1965, he put his greatest emphasis on how orchestrated nonviolence could confront white-dominated economic institutions and transform the underlying social arrangements between black and white communities. The slogan "soul power" captured Jackson's balancing act, his stance of nonviolent militancy. It obviously echoed the ethic behind "black power," retaining the more militant slogan's appeal to black values, while substituting righteous good feeling ("soul") for explicit separatism ("black").[46]

Breadbasket hoped to catalyze the inner city by forcing white-owned firms to employ black workers, market black products, deposit money in black-owned banks, and contract with black firms for cleaning, construction, extermination, and transportation services. Through the late 1960s, it organized rallies and consumer boycotts to put pressure on Chicago's business and political establishment—and, in contrast to King's own housing campaign, it prevailed again and again: 32 black hires at Pepsi-Cola, 30 at Coca-Cola, 183 at High-Low Foods, and so on. This success was due, in part, to Breadbasket's pro-business accent—one tenant-union activist derisively named Jackson "the Booker T. Washington of the late sixties"—but it also was a tribute to the thousands of blacks who involved themselves regularly in the boycotts, protests, and community services. According to journalist Marshall Frady, Breadbasket was "not only the single measurable success left by King's efforts [in Chicago] but one of the rare self-sustaining civil rights enterprises" of the period. *Life* reported that by 1971, Breadbasket had directly created 4,000 new jobs for blacks in Chicago and some 10,000 more indirectly. In 1974, Chicago could claim eighteen of the hundred black businesses in the United States with revenues of over a million dollars, and every one had demonstrably profited from Jackson's efforts. Starting in 1969, these successes were celebrated through the Black Expo, a black, urban version of a county fair with hundreds of exhibitions from local black businesses. Designed to show that Chicago's blacks were producers as well as consumers, the Black Expos were amazingly well attended: up to 800,000 people milled through the booths in later years, testament to the pride and curiosity stirred by Breadbasket's vision of soul capitalism.[47]

Breadbasket's successful record challenges several ingrained assumptions about the fate of the civil rights movement. Did the Movement really stall after Selma and the 1965 Voting Rights Act, when it took on the thornier issues of entrenched economic injustice, the de facto inequities in housing, education, and employment? Is the career of Jesse Jackson—arguably the major black political figure to emerge in the generation after King—a story about that failure, a parable about how the Movement, as it hit new walls, was seduced away from grassroots action and toward flamboyant media posturing?[48] And, to widen our focus and take on another central story of the sixties: If we wish to consider seriously how Movement offshoots like Breadbasket mobilized black publics, is it fair to identify America's largest "counterculture" with the young white people who affiliated themselves with rock music and antiwar protest? Why do we remember the 400,000 who gathered at Max Yasgur's dairy farm in the summer of 1969 to celebrate the arrival of the "Woodstock nation" and forget the 500,000 who gathered at Chicago's International Amphitheater a few months later to celebrate the arrival of black capitalism at the Black Expo? What story of the sixties will explain why these people returned in even greater numbers as the Black Expo became an annual fixture in Chicago, and then an event copied nationwide?

These larger questions mark the endpoint of this study, but we can suggest an answer to them by turning back to the story of Cannonball Adderley, Black Expo bandleader and jazz survivor. Adderley, who performed alongside Bill Cosby, Aretha Franklin, Mahalia Jackson, and Muddy Waters at the 1969 event, was the rare hard bopper who thrived into the late 1960s, even as the jazz community splintered into avant-garde and mainstream factions and as old venues were closed or altered their programming. Spiking his music with the experimental spirit of freer players, he nonetheless cultivated the loyalty of the soul audience, which more often treated jazz as though it were a family heirloom—valuable but not exactly relevant. Adderley wooed them back through soul-jazz hits like "Mercy, Mercy, Mercy" (800,000 copies sold), "Why Am I Treated So Bad?" (150,000 copies), and "Walk Tall," all of which shared the Top 40 in the fall of 1967. The Adderley sound on these gospel-tinged hit singles laid crisp alto-cornet lines over a funky backbeat, sometimes with meditative clarity ("Mercy, Mercy, Mercy") and sometimes with strutting fanfare ("Walk Tall"). The music drew frankly from mid-sixties soul: for instance, "Why Am I Treated So Bad?" was the rare jazz piece lifted from a gospel group (the Staple Sisters), not a Broadway musical or Hollywood film. In other parts of his repertoire, Adderley was more adventurous. While his instrumentation—brass, reed and rhythm section, and no electric guitar or electric bass—suggested the typical hard bop quintet of the mid-fifties, the band often took flight over vamping bass figures that linked its sound to the emerging fusion of Miles Davis. In fact, Adderley keyboardist Joe Zawinul, who gave the band some of its most experimental compositions ("Rumplestiltskin," "Experience in E," "Directions"), became a key collaborator with Davis, adding pieces like "In a Silent Way," "Pharaoh's Dance," and "Directions" to the trumpeter's book, the last serving as Davis's show-opener between 1969 and 1971.[49]

Much of Adderley's success might also be traced to his extroverted style of emceeing, which used good humor and black pride as main ingredients in jazz education and warmed audiences to his band's more "out" offerings. Adderley was a master of the instructive spiel, a longtime educator who had spent five years as a high school teacher and who at one point wrote a column for the *New York Amsterdam News*. His chatty interludes conveyed qualities that Miles Davis withheld when he turned his back on the bandstand: straightforward charm, emotional warmth, and an intelligence comfortable enough to expose itself. Unlike Mingus, Adderley had nothing of the Jeremiah in his personality. When his band was booed by a Parisian audience unaccustomed to his late-sixties funky sound, Adderley simply acted as if they needed a little more information and launched into his customary briefs on the importance of the blues and the compositional ingenuity of Joe Zawinul. The saxophonist had this educational bonhomie off the bandstand too, working hard to develop a rapport with younger people especially. Throughout the late 1960s and early 1970s, he toured college campuses as varied as UCLA and Birmingham's Miles College, supplementing his concerts with seminars, clinics, and dormitory rap sessions. The curriculum of his two-day seminars moved through the history of jazz from early ragtime to the latest free jazz, and then concluded with the subject of the "social factor" in "black music."[50]

Considering Adderley's aesthetics and cultural politics, it makes sense that he frequented Operation Breadbasket before his 1969 concert and endorsed the effort in his liner notes, and that Jackson so easily wove himself into the concert itself, opening it with a sermonic introduction, closing it with his "Soul Power" call and response, and serving in between as the inspiration for a new Adderley group vehicle, Zawinul's "Country Preacher." Adderley and Jackson were secret sharers, country preachers who became boosters of soul capitalism from the bandstand and the pulpit. Both men appealed to the native resources of soul, Jackson through his attempt to organize the black community into a unified power bloc, Adderley through his inventive explorations of soul's full bandwidth. Both drew on the character of the country preacher, the roughhewn minister whose cadences were the rhythms of black music and whose most powerful gestures came out of a call-and-response tradition. They were reliable crowd pleasers, lovers of the effortless flourish, garrulous and sly but not over-sophisticated.

Both Adderley and Jackson frankly exulted in black success at a moment when many radicals dismissed such success as tokenism or the work of Uncle Toms. Throughout his career, Adderley faced the charge that he had sold out jazz to the highest bidder—to which he retorted at one point, "If I knew the way to 'sell out,' I'd buy time on Huntley and Brinkley, and assure everybody that Cannonball *has* sold out." Adderley reminded his critics that jazz heroes like Duke Ellington and Count Basie were perennially forced to scuffle and suggested that in a world where struggle was a given, success was only a momentary reprieve and an unpredictable one at that. He never apologized for his long-term relationship with Capitol Records. The spirit of Adderley's remarks was seconded by Jackson, who stressed that Breadbasket's "programs are dictated by the private-enterprise economy in which we find ourselves" even as he admitted, "In my heart . . . I know that the entire system is a corruption" since "the earth belongs to everybody." Fending off the radical argument that blacks needed to sustain a separate economy, Jackson insisted that blacks "were in the system whether we like it or not." Breadbasket's main strategy was to win for black businesses and workers a rightful share of an admittedly flawed market.[51]

When Jackson and Adderley came together at the 1969 concert the result was a performance that tried to broaden the aesthetic meaning of soul power. The term "black music," Adderley told the Breadbasket audience, was an unfortunate "catchphrase, because we have a tendency to believe that it's all the same thing. It's not really the same thing—it's kind of *out of* the same thing." According to Adderley, black music shared a similar impulse but not a similar soundscape—an idea that Amiri Baraka had also elaborated in his landmark essay "The Changing Same," where he wrote, "Black Music is African in origin, African-American in its totality, and its various forms (especially the vocal) show just how the African impulses were redistributed in its expression."[52]

Jackie McLean had tested this idea of the "changing same" over the course of "Soul," which spliced together different styles of jazz and gospel in an attempt to reclaim them all. Adderley did the same over the course of his concert repertoire, which spanned a variety of genres even as it always came back to the quintet's resources, from his own fluid improvisational style to Joe Zawinul's love of crunchy outer-space clusters on his electric keyboard. At the Breadbasket show, there were up-tempo groovers like "Walk Tall" and "The Scene," a blues tag that would have seemed at home in the book of any number of hard bop outfits. There was the broad R&B comedy of "Oh Babe," adversity played for laughs, where Nat Adderley sang "Mr. Nixon, please don't cut that welfare off for me"—and drew a roar from the crowd. There was the over-the-top drama of "Country Preacher," a portrait of Jackson that built from an ambling Fender Rhodes figure up to a full-bore fanfare, then dropped back to the hushed keyboard, in loving mimicry of the country preacher's dynamic style and to the delight of the Breadbasket audience. And there was the modal and churchy "Hummin'," a piece that had the whole audience clapping to its single-note bass vamp while Cannonball took a rare turn on soprano sax.

The eclecticism of this repertoire—not to mention the glue binding it together—was showcased most extensively in the four-part, sixteen-minute "Afro-Spanish Omlet." Omelets, of course, require eggs to be broken and cooked, and the eggs in this case were various forms of music of the African diaspora: calypso, gospel, free jazz, the blues as interpreted by mid-fifties hard bop, and the "Spanish" modal music popularized by Davis's *Sketches of Spain* and Mingus's *Tijuana Moods*. The cooking was an experiment in jazz ensemble democracy, as each member of the Adderley quintet (with the exception of drummer Roy McCurdy) contributed their own segment to the suite, one that spotlighted their improvisational style.

As often was the case in hard bop, beginning with Mingus's "Pithecanthropus Erectus" and extending through Max Roach's *Freedom Now Suite* and Jackie McLean's "Soul," a larger compositional framework encouraged the freest, most digressive soloing and interplay. Nat Adderley's opener, "Umbakwen," began with his cornet soloing rubato over a minor Spanish scale, turned into a duel with Zawinul's keyboard, and ended with Nat toying with the mechanics of his instrument—buzzing around his mouthpiece, squeaking on the high end, isolating the vocal qualities of his sound. Zawinul's contribution, "Oiga," moved like "Umbakwen" toward greater and greater experimentation. After building his solo with crushed gospel chords over a pedal point, Zawinul ended with *Bitches Brew*–like dissonance, a series of furious broken-crystal glisses in the upper register. Cannonball's finale, "Marabi," returned the quintet to more familiar territory: a joyful calypso written in the spirit of the South African township jazz that gave the piece its name.[53] This last episode, which tied the freedom music of South Africa to the freedom music of black America, featured Adderley teasing out an agile, melodically expansive solo with the easeful speed that first led him to be anointed as the "new Bird." Appropriately for Operation Breadbasket, this was also calypso gone to church. A tambourine shook on every other sanctified beat.

Just after Adderley's energetic calypso, Jackson took the microphone for the call-and-response around "soul power," and Cannonball followed up the chant with these encouraging words: "Yeah, soul power, that's what the country preacher's talking about. In case you never knew what it really meant, you can understand today, brothers and sisters here at Saint Francis." To Adderley's mind, the music was the amplification, literally and figuratively, of the message at the heart of the Movement.

This book has operated from a similar premise—that if we want to understand concepts like "cool" and "hip," "freedom now" and "soul power," we should turn our ears to the music that gave these ideas expression, and we should turn our attention to the ventures, alliances, and debates that the music inspired. I have attempted to write intellectual history with the help of those usually kept on the fringes of such history—black artists and activists who have been variously hailed as the embodiments of creative excess (Charles Mingus), spirituality (John Coltrane), exuberance (Cannonball Adderley), wit (Langston Hughes), and militancy (Malcolm X, Amiri Baraka), but who have too rarely been considered thinkers in their own right, engaged in the struggle to define themselves and the fault lines of their world. It is this struggle—tense, questioning, and outward bound—that drove the jazz music of the 1950s and 1960s and spilled out to animate the cultural dramas of the civil rights and Black Power movements. I have tried to listen to this struggle on frequencies high and low and to articulate the complex ways that the music resonated for its various audiences. At once the sound of struggle and the sound of togetherness, the sound of singularity and the sound of solidarity, jazz music in the 1950s and 1960s was as powerful as the promise of freedom, and as beguiling too.

NOTES
ACKNOWLEDGMENTS
INDEX

NOTES

Introduction

1. Charles Mingus, "Haitian Fight Song," *The Clown* (1957), Atlantic 1260.

2. *Mingus: More Than a Fake Book,* ed. Sue Mingus (New York: Jazz Workshop, 1991), p. 147; Gene Santoro, *Myself When I Am Real: The Life and Music of Charles Mingus* (New York: Oxford University Press, 2000), pp. 20, 29.

3. On hard bop, see David Rosenthal, *Hard Bop: Jazz and Black Music, 1955–1965* (New York: Oxford University Press, 1992); Barry Kernfeld, "Adderley, Coltrane, and Davis at the Twilight of Bebop: The Search for Melodic Coherence, 1958–1959" (Ph.D. diss., Cornell University, 1981).

4. Samuel Floyd, Jr., *The Power of Black Music: Interpreting Its History from Africa to the United States* (New York: Oxford University Press, 1995), pp. 180–182; Nat Hentoff, liner notes to *The Clown.*

5. Santoro, *Myself When I Am Real,* p. 110; "Reissuing *Tanjah,*" liner notes to Randy Weston, *Tanjah* (1973, 1995), Verve 314 527 778-2; Hentoff, liner notes to *The Clown.*

6. Particularly formative to my thinking on the civil rights movement were Richard H. King, *Civil Rights and the Idea of Freedom* (New York: Oxford University Press, 1992); Suzanne E. Smith, *Dancing in the Streets: Motown and the Cultural Politics of Detroit* (Cambridge: Harvard University Press, 1999); and Brian Ward, *Just My Soul Responding: Rhythm and Blues, Black Consciousness, and Race Relations* (Berkeley: University of California Press, 1998), all of which try to understand the rapport between the ideology of civil rights protest and its cultural manifestations. Also helpful were Gerald Horne, *Fire This Time: The Watts Uprising and the 1960s* (Charlottesville: University Press of Virginia, 1995); Clayborne Carson, *In Struggle: SNCC and the Black Awakening of the 1960s* (Cambridge: Harvard University Press, 1981); Taylor Branch, *Parting the Waters: America in the King Years, 1954–1963* (New York: Simon and Schuster,

1988); and David Garrow, *Bearing the Cross: Martin Luther King, Jr. and the Southern Christian Leadership Conference* (New York: Vintage, 1988).

7. This critique of the affluent society—that it was stifling participatory democracy and cultivating a narrow sense of human possibility—has inspired a vast historiography. I have benefited from Howard Brick, *Age of Contradiction: American Thought and Culture in the 1960s* (Ithaca: Cornell University Press, 2001 [1998]); Daniel Belgrad, *The Culture of Spontaneity: Improvisation and the Arts in Postwar America* (Chicago: University of Chicago Press, 1998); James Miller, *"Democracy Is in the Streets": From Port Huron to the Siege of Chicago* (New York: Simon and Schuster, 1987); James Farrell, *The Spirit of the Sixties: Making Postwar Radicalism* (New York: Routledge, 1997); and a book that pays particular attention to the "antimodernism" of black artists and intellectuals, James C. Hall's *Mercy, Mercy Me: African-American Culture and the American Sixties* (New York: Oxford University Press, 2001). A summary of "prefigurative politics" appears in Wini Breines, *Community and Organization in the New Left, 1962–1968* (New York: Praeger, 1982), pp. 1–8.

8. I am greatly indebted to the current renaissance in jazz scholarship, which has offered much richer accounts of the music and its life in the broader culture. Especially useful were omnibus accounts of the music's history by Gary Giddins and Ted Gioia; wide-ranging intellectual genealogies by Eric Porter and Craig Werner; genre studies by Scott DeVeaux (on bebop), Ted Gioia (on West Coast jazz), and David Stowe (on swing); critical biographies by Lewis Porter (on John Coltrane), John Szwed (on Sun Ra), Ronald Radano (on Anthony Braxton), and Angela Davis (on blues women of the 1920s); ethnomusicological works by Ingrid Monson and Paul Berliner; and the valuable critical and historical anthologies edited by Krin Gabbard, Robert O'Meally, Robert Walser, and Robert Gottlieb.

9. My work on Mingus is indebted to Santoro, *Myself When I Am Real*, and Brian Priestley, *Mingus: A Critical Biography* (New York: DaCapo, 1983).

10. An indispensable resource for work on Coltrane is Lewis Porter, *John Coltrane: His Life and Music* (Ann Arbor: University of Michigan Press, 1998). See also Gerald Early, "Ode to John Coltrane: A Jazz Musician's Influence on African American Culture," *Antioch Review* 57:3 (Summer 1999): 371–385; and Frank Kofsky, *John Coltrane and the Jazz Revolution of the 1960s* (New York: Pathfinder, 1998).

11. In my understanding of the Black Power and Black Arts movements, I have profited especially from William Van Deburg, *New Day in Babylon: The Black Power Movement and American Culture, 1965–1975* (Chicago: University of Chicago Press, 1992); Horne, *Fire This Time;* Carson, *In Struggle;* Michelle Wallace, *Black Power and the Myth of the Superwoman* (New York: Dial, 1979); R. H. King, *Civil Rights and the Idea of Freedom;* and Ward, *Just My Soul Responding.*

12. Ward, *Just My Soul Responding*, p. 306; Coleman, notes to *Change of the Century* (1960), Atlantic 1327; Hancock quoted in Ingrid Monson, *Saying*

Something: Jazz Improvisation and Interaction (Chicago: University of Chicago Press, 1996), p. 81; Miles Davis with Quincey Troupe, *Miles, the Autobiography* (New York: Simon and Schuster, 1990), p. 274; Murray quoted in Valerie Wilmer, "Controlled Freedom Is the Thing This Year," *Down Beat,* March 23, 1967, pp. 16–17; Olive Jones, "Conversation with . . . George Russell: A New Theory for Jazz," *The Black Perspective in Music* 2:1 (Spring 1974), p. 68; John Szwed, *Space Is the Place: The Lives and Times of Sun Ra* (New York: DaCapo, 1998 [1997]), pp. 309–310.

13. Charles Mingus, *The Complete Town Hall Concert* (1962, 1994), Capitol CDP 7243 8.

14. A good history of the rhetoric of freedom in the underground arts scene is Sally Banes, *Greenwich Village 1963: Avant-Garde Performance and the Effervescent Body* (Durham: Duke University Press, 1993), pp. 137–187.

15. Eric Foner, *The Story of American Freedom* (New York: W. W. Norton, 1998), pp. 252–263 (NSC 68 quote p. 253); Kennedy quoted in Eric Hobsbawm, *The Age of Extremes: A History of the World, 1914–1991* (New York: Pantheon, 1995), p. 231.

16. Lilienthal quoted in Foner, *Story of American Freedom,* pp. 263–264.

17. Isaiah Berlin, "Two Concepts of Liberty," in *Four Essays on Liberty* (London: Oxford University Press, 1969). I have benefited from a recent essay of Quentin Skinner's, which tries to articulate a concept of liberty that goes beyond negative and positive conceptions of the term—and that in the process redacts the genealogy of the negative-positive debate. See "A Third Concept of Liberty," *London Review of Books,* April 4, 2002, 16–18.

18. R. H. King, *Civil Rights and the Idea of Freedom,* pp. 15–28; Brick, *Age of Contradiction,* p. 19.

19. Foner, *Story of American Freedom,* pp. 271–273; Karal Ann Marling, *As Seen on TV: The Visual Culture of Everyday Life in the 1950s* (Cambridge: Harvard University Press, 1994), pp. 244–252.

20. Penny M. Von Eschen, *Race against Empire: Black Americans and Anticolonialism, 1937–1957* (Ithaca: Cornell University Press, 1997), pp. 177–181; Frank Sinatra, "The Diplomacy of Music," *Western World* 1:7 (November 1957): 29–30.

21. Frank Thompson, Jr., "Cold War Jazz," in *American Jazz Annual, Newport Edition 1956* (New York: Hemisphere Press, 1956), pp. 27–28, 86–88, emphasis in original; Felix Belair, Jr., "United States Has Secret Sonic Weapon—Jazz," *New York Times,* November 6, 1955, in *Keeping Time: Readings in Jazz History,* ed. Robert Walser (New York: Oxford University Press, 1999), pp. 240–241.

22. John Miller Chernoff, *African Rhythm and African Sensibility* (Chicago: University of Chicago Press, 1979), p. 60, emphasis in original; Martin Luther King, Jr., *Where Do We Go From Here: Chaos or Community?* (Boston: Beacon, 1967), pp. 97–98.

23. R. H. King, *Civil Rights and the Idea of Freedom,* pp. 14–15.

24. Martin Luther King, Jr., *Where Do We Go from Here,* pp. 19–20; C. Wright Mills, *The Sociological Imagination* (New York: Oxford University Press, 1959), p. 174; R. H.King, *Civil Rights and the Idea of Freedom,* pp. 52–55; M. L King, Jr., *Stride toward Freedom: The Montgomery Story* (New York: Harper and Row, 1958); *Why We Can't Wait* (New York: Penguin, 1964).

25. Brick, *Age of Contradiction,* p. 21; M. L. King, *Where Do We Go from Here,* p. 54.

26. R. H. King, *Civil Rights and the Idea of Freedom,* pp. 24–26; Hannah Arendt, *The Human Condition* (Garden City, N.Y.: Anchor, 1959), p. 177.

27. Ruth Feldstein, *Motherhood in Black and White: Race and Sex in American Liberalism* (Ithaca: Cornell University Press, 2000), pp. 128–138.

28. For an influential account of African-American "musicking," see Christopher Small, *Music of the Common Tongue: Survival and Celebration in African American Music* (Hanover, N.H.: Wesleyan University Press, 1998 [1987]), pp. 310–340.

29. *New York Times* article quoted in *Keeping Time,* p. 241. Perhaps unsurprisingly, the best descriptions of the interactions within jazz performance have come out of ethnomusicology—Monson's *Saying Something* and Paul Berliner's magisterial *Thinking in Jazz* (Chicago: University of Chicago Press, 1994).

30. Szwed, *Space Is the Place,* pp. 114–122.

31. David T. Doris, "Zen Vaudeville: A Medi(t)ation in the Margins of Fluxus," in *The Fluxus Reader,* ed. Ken Friedman (London: Academy Editions, 1998), p. 98. On Neo-Dada and the Greenwich Village experiments to level the cult of artistic genius, see Susan Hapgood, *Neo-Dada: Redefining Art, 1958–1962* (New York: American Federation of Arts, 1994); Banes, *Greenwich Village 1963,* pp. 109–136.

32. Oliver Nelson, liner notes to his *Afro-American Sketches* (1961), Prestige 7225.

33. Szwed, *Space Is the Place,* p. 387; George Russell, *The Lydian Chromatic Concept of Tonal Organization for Improvisation* (New York: Concept Publishing, 1964 [1953]), p. B.

34. For an overview of the Holiness-Pentecostal line, see Cheryl J. Sanders, *Saints in Exile: The Holiness-Pentecostal Experience in African American Religion and Culture* (New York: Oxford, 1996).

35. Nat Hentoff, liner notes to Donald Byrd's *A New Perspective* (1963), Blue Note 84124; Santoro, *Myself When I Am Real,* p. 20.

36. Hentoff, liner notes to Mingus, *The Clown.*

1. Birth of the Cool

1. Oscar Brown, Jr., *Sin and Soul . . . and Then Some,* Columbia CK 64994 (1960, 1996).

2. Lenny Bruce, "Psychopathia Sexualis," in *Extreme Exposure: An Anthology of Solo Performance Texts from the Twentieth Century*, ed. Jo Bonney (New York: Theatre Communications Group, 2000), p. 45; Steven Watson, *The Birth of the Beat Generation: Visionaries, Rebels, and Hipsters, 1944–1960* (New York: Pantheon, 1995), pp. 257–261, 264, 340–341; Henry Cabot Beck, "From Beat to Beatnik," in *The Rolling Stone Book of the Beats: The Beat Generation and American Culture*, ed. Holly George-Warren (New York: Hyperion, 1999), pp. 95, 104. "Cool" and "hip" are famously elusive concepts, but see Joel Dinerstein's excellent "Lester Young and the Birth of the Cool," in *Signifyin(g), Sanctifyin', and Slam Dunking*, ed. Gena Dagel Caponi (Amherst: University of Massachusetts Press, 1999), pp. 239–276; Greil Marcus, "Birth of the Cool," *Speak* (Fall 1999): 16–25; Ingrid Monson's "The Problem with White Hipness: Race, Gender, and Cultural Conceptions in Jazz Historical Discourse," *Journal of the American Musicological Society* 48 (Fall 1995): 396–422; and Andrew Ross, *No Respect: Intellectuals and Popular Culture* (New York: Routledge, 1989).

3. Jules Feiffer, *Sick, Sick, Sick* (New York: McGraw Hill, 1958), n.p.

4. Thomas Frank, *The Conquest of Cool: Business Culture, Counterculture, and the Rise of Hip Consumerism* (Chicago: University of Chicago Press, 1997), pp. 31, 233; see also Terry H. Anderson, "The New American Revolution: The Movement and Business," in *The Sixties: From Memory to History*, ed. David Farber (Chapel Hill: University of North Carolina Press, 1994), pp. 175–205.

5. Ross, *No Respect*, pp. 83–84.

6. "Hipness" always was a dubious, if indigenous, strategy for dealing with the pleasures and responsibilities of black urban life—both the hustle of the street and the bustle of the bootstrapping black bourgeoisie. A key work that illuminates related debates over "righteous" protest is Evelyn Brooks Higginbotham, *Righteous Discontent: The Woman's Movement in the Black Baptist Church, 1880–1920* (Cambridge: Harvard University Press, 1993).

7. Wilfred McClay, *The Masterless: Self and Society in Modern America* (Chapel Hill: University of North Carolina Press, 1994), p. 234. On the genre of "social problem" literature, see ibid., pp. 226–275; and Daniel Horowitz, *Betty Friedan and the Making of the Feminine Mystique: The American Left, the Cold War, and Modern Feminism* (Amherst: University of Massachusetts Press, 1999).

8. On the gravity of the nuclear family ideal and men's flight from commitment, see Elaine Tyler May, *Homeward Bound: American Families in the Cold War Era* (New York: Basic Books, 1988); and Barbara Ehrenreich, *The Hearts of Men* (Garden City, N.Y.: Anchor Press, 1983).

9. Charles Suber, "The First Chorus," *Down Beat*, September 15, 1960, p. 4.

10. Earl Conrad, introduction to *Dan Burley's Original Handbook of Harlem Jive* (New York: Dan Burley, 1941), pp. 5–6. Calloway's *Hepster's Dictionary* and *Swinginformation Bureau* are reprinted in Cab Calloway and Bryant

Rollins, *Of Minnie the Moocher and Me* (New York: Thomas Y. Crowell, 1976), pp. 251–274. See also David Stowe, *Swing Changes: Big Band Jazz in New Deal America* (Cambridge: Harvard University Press, 1994), p. 217.

11. Calloway and Rollins, *Of Minnie the Moocher*, pp. 121, 178; Shane White and Graham White, *Stylin': African American Expressive Culture from Its Beginnings to the Zoot Suit* (Ithaca: Cornell University Press, 1998), pp. 252–255; Dinerstein, "Lester Young," pp. 244–245; Cab Calloway, *Kicking the Gong Around: Original Recordings from 1930 to 1931,* Living Era AJA 5013.

12. Calloway recalled that "Minnie"'s audience was "mainly white, outside of Harlem"; black audiences, he said, preferred straight blues. Calloway and Rollins, *Of Minnie the Moocher,* p. 121.

13. Calloway, "Minnie the Moocher" (1942), *Are You Hep to the Jive?,* Columbia CK 57645. See Calloway's "Tarzan of Harlem" (1939), also found on *Are You Hep to the Jive?,* for a similarly double-jointed song of seduction and menace.

14. Chris Erikson, "Frantic Harry the Hipster," *New York Daily News,* October 13, 1999, p. 11.

15. "The Voutians," *Life,* May 5, 1947, pp. 129–135.

16. Susan Douglas, *Listening In: Radio and the American Imagination, from Amos 'n' Andy and Edward R. Murrow to Wolfman Jack and Howard Stern* (New York: Times Books, 1999), pp. 223–255.

17. *Austin American-Statesman,* November 1, 1995, p. A1; Douglas, *Listening In,* p. 240.

18. Chris Helm, "Radio Roots," *Chicago Tribune,* February 12, 1989, p. 10; *Newsday,* October 3, 1997, p. A67; Steve Allen, "Crazy Red Riding Hood," in *From Blues to Bop: A Collection of Jazz Fiction,* ed. Richard N. Albert (Baton Rouge: Louisiana State University Press, 1990), pp. 170–174. The most readily available documentation of the Collins-Allen collaboration is Al "Jazzbeaux" Collins and Slim Gaillard, *Steve Allen's Hip Fables* (1983), Doctor Jazz FW-38729.

19. For a more substantive discussion of the connections between youth culture and rock 'n' roll DJs, see Douglas, *Listening In,* pp. 233–255.

20. Mezz Mezzrow and Bernard Wolfe, *Really the Blues* (New York: Citadel Press, 1990 [1946]), subsequently cited as *RTB; Chicago Sunday Tribune,* November 3, 1946, sec. 4, p. 9. Mezzrow and Wolfe's joint autobiography shows signs of becoming the locus classicus of white Negroism in literary studies. See Gayle Wald, "Mezz Mezzrow and the Voluntary Negro Blues," in *Race and the Subject of Masculinities,* ed. Harry Stecopoulos and Michael Uebel (Durham: Duke University Press, 1997), pp. 116–137, and her more extended discussion of related issues in *Crossing the Line: Racial Passing in Twentieth-Century U.S. Literature and Culture* (Durham: Duke University Press, 2000); see also Maria Damon, "Jazz-Jews, Jive, and Gender," in *Jews and Other Differences: The New Jewish Cultural Studies,* ed. Jonathan Boyarin and Daniel Boyarin (Minneapolis: University of Minnesota Press, 1997), pp. 150–175.

21. Nat Hentoff, "Counterpoint," *Down Beat,* February 11, 1953, p. 5; Ginsberg quote from *RTB,* back cover; Agnes Eckhardt, "Really the Blues: A Television Play," Mezz Mezzrow folder, Institute of Jazz Studies, Newark, N.J.; Orrin Keepnews, *The View from Within: Jazz Writings, 1948–1987* (New York: Oxford University Press, 1988), pp. 44–45; "Newport Jazz 1958," *Down Beat,* August 7, 1958, p. 35; Leonard Feather, "Feather's Nest," *Down Beat,* April 14, 1960, p. 43.

22. G. Wald, "Mezz Mezzrow and the Voluntary Negro Blues," p. 119.

23. Parker quoted in Eric Porter, *What Is This Thing Called Jazz? African American Musicians as Artists, Critics, and Activists* (Berkeley: University of California Press, 2002), p. 76.

24. Ross, *No Respect,* p. 80.

25. Scott DeVeaux, *The Birth of Bebop: A Social and Musical History* (Berkeley: University of California Press, 1997), pp. 1, 20–21.

26. Gillespie quoted in ibid., pp. 432–443, and in Stowe, *Swing Changes,* pp. 210–214; "Life Goes to a Party: Bebop," *Life,* October 11, 1948, pp. 138–142.

27. Dinerstein, "Lester Young," pp. 266–267, 253–258.

28. Clarke quoted in Stowe, *Swing Changes,* p. 212; DeVeaux, *The Birth of Bebop,* p. 440.

29. See also Gayle Wald's more extensive treatment of this episode in *Crossing the Line,* pp. 68–71.

30. Wolfe has generally been overlooked in critical accounts of jazz that involve Mezzrow: *Really the Blues* is often quoted as a transparent autobiographical source in histories of Chicago jazz. Andrew Ross misnames him as *Raymond* Wolfe, then drops him from his account, and Gayle Wald's fascinating essay on Mezzrow also neglects the mediation of Wolfe. Yet Wolfe was Mezzrow's literary midwife and probably the one who gave the edge to Mezzrow's sociological analysis and the blinding gloss to his jiving spiel. Mezzrow's unassisted publications in Art Hodes's *Record Changer* follow the Dixieland party line and have none of the hip daddy-o acrobatics of *Really the Blues,* even though they were also composed in the mid-forties. For Mezzrow's writing sans Wolfe, see *Selections from the Gutter: Jazz Portraits from "The Jazz Record,"* ed. Art Hodes and Chadwick Hansen (Berkeley: University of California Press, 1977), pp. 64–65, 204–205.

31. Daniel Bell, *The End of Ideology: On the Exhaustion of Political Ideas in the Fifties* (New York: Free Press, 1960), p. 287. On the shifting politics of the New York intellectuals from the 1930s to the 1950s, see Alan Wald, *The New York Intellectuals: The Rise and Decline of the Anti-Stalinist Left from the 1930s to the 1980s* (Chapel Hill: University of North Carolina Press, 1987); Alexander Bloom's prodigious *Prodigal Sons: The New York Intellectuals and Their World* (New York: Oxford University Press, 1986); and Howard Brick, *Daniel Bell and the Decline of Intellectual Radicalism: Social Theory and Political Reconciliation in the 1940s* (Madison: University of Wisconsin Press, 1986). More generally,

see McClay, *The Masterless,* pp. 226–268; Russell Jacoby, *The Last Intellectuals* (New York: Basic Books, 1987); and Ann Douglas, "The Failure of the New York Intellectuals," *Raritan Review* 17:4 (Spring 1998): 1–23.

32. Cohen quoted in Bloom, *Prodigal Sons,* pp. 166–167.

33. Howe quoted in ibid., pp. 168, 201, 299; Maurice Isserman, *If I Had a Hammer: The Death of the Old Left and the Birth of the New Left* (Urbana: University of Illinois Press, 1993 [1987]), p. 101.

34. Carolyn Geduld, *Bernard Wolfe* (New York: Twayne, 1972), pp. 11–17; A. Wald, pp. 133–135. Wolfe also seems to have been a friend of Ralph Ellison; see *Trading Twelves: The Selected Letters of Ralph Ellison and Albert Murray,* ed. Albert Murray and John F. Callahan (New York: Modern Library, 2000), pp. 197–198.

35. Geduld, *Bernard Wolfe,* pp. 84–85.

36. Wolfe's unpublished manuscripts are collected in the Papers of Bernard Wolfe at Yale University's Beinecke Library. See "Outline for a Study of the Role of the Negro in American Popular Culture," Box 187, passim; "From the Solid to the Frantic: The Somewhereness of Bop," especially the chapters "A Kleptomaniac Music," "Lust with a Giggle," and "The Calendar, the Clock, the Orgasm," passim. Wolfe's basic position on mass culture is laid out in two published articles, "Uncle Remus and the Malevolent Rabbit," *Commentary* 8:1 (July 1949): 31–41; and "Ecstatic in Blackface," reprinted in *The Scene before You: A New Approach to American Culture,* ed. Chandler Brossard (New York: Rinehart, 1955).

37. Wolfe, "A Kleptomaniac Music," "Lust with a Giggle," and "The Calendar, the Clock, the Orgasm," passim.

38. Weldon Kees, "Muskrat Ramble: Popular and Unpopular Music," *Partisan Review* 15:5 (May 1948): 621–622.

39. Henry Louis Gates, Jr., in his excellent profile of Broyard, writes, "Society had decreed race to be a matter of natural law, but he wanted race to be an elective affinity, and it was never going to be a fair fight. A penalty was exacted. He shed a past and an identity to become a writer—a writer who wrote endlessly about the act of shedding a past and an identity." Gates, "White Like Me," *New Yorker,* June 17, 1996, p. 66.

40. Anatole Broyard, "Portrait of the Hipster," reprinted in *The Scene before You;* Broyard, "Keep Cool, Man: The Negro Rejection of Jazz," *Commentary* 11:4 (April 1951): 361.

41. Anatole Broyard, "Portrait of the Inauthentic Negro," *Commentary* 9:1 (July 1950): 57, 64. I have benefited much from Richard H. King's "Jean-Paul Sartre: Between Universalism and Particularism," a chapter from his forthcoming book on theories of race and Jewishness in the postwar era.

42. Jean-Paul Sartre, *Anti-Semite and Jew,* trans. George J. Becker (New York: Schocken Books, 1976), p. 90; Broyard, "Keep Cool, Man," pp. 359–362.

43. Broyard, "Portrait of the Hipster," pp. 117, 119. See also Miles Templar's

response, which admonishes Broyard "not to let his pen get in the way of his gaze." *Partisan Review* 15:9 (September 1948): 1053–1055.

44. Broyard, "Portrait of the Hipster," p. 119; *Kafka Was the Rage: A Greenwich Village Memoir* (New York: Crown, 1996), pp. ix, 11, 69–71.

45. Pete Welding, liner notes to Miles Davis, *Birth of the Cool*, Capitol D154138; Gary Giddins, *Visions of Jazz: The First Century* (New York: Oxford University Press, 1998), pp. 340–341; *New York Times* quoted in Campbell, *This Is the Beat Generation: New Yori, San Francisco, Paris* (Berkeley: University of California Press, 2001), pp. 106–107, 134–135, 162–167, 203–204.

46. Jack Kerouac, "Belief and Technique for Modern Prose" and "Essentials of Spontaneous Prose" in *The Portable Beat Reader*, ed. Ann Charters (New York: Viking, 1992), pp. 57–59. Kerouac's co-theorist in the matter of spontaneous prose was, of course, Allen Ginsberg, whose announced guiding principle was "first thought, best thought"—and who revised *Howl* with some of the same tenacity that Kerouac brought to the many revisions of *On the Road*.

47. Campbell, *This Is the Beat Generation*, pp. 131, 203, 140–141, 81–82, 263.

48. Jack Kerouac, *On the Road* (New York: Viking, 1957), p. 227; Campbell, *This Is the Beat Generation*, pp. 174–175.

49. Gerry Mulligan quoted in liner notes to *Birth of the Cool*; Gil Evans quoted in Dan Morgenstern, "The Complete Prestige Recordings," in *The Miles Davis Companion: Four Decades of Commentary*, ed. Gary Carner (New York: Schirmer Books, 1996), p. 10; Davis quoted in Ted Gioia, *The History of Jazz* (New York: Oxford University Press, 1997), pp. 281–283.

50. Winthrop Sargent quoted in Gioia, *The History of Jazz*, p. 283; Stanley Crouch, "Play the Right Thing," in *The Miles Davis Companion*, p. 25; Giddins, *Visions of Jazz*, p. 341.

51. Dinerstein, "Lester Young," pp. 239, 259.

52. Giddins, *Visions of Jazz*, pp. 341–342.

2. Radicalism by Another Name

1. David McReynolds, "The Hipster General Strike," *Village Voice*, December 2, 1959, pp. 4, 12.

2. Ibid., p. 12.

3. Paul Buhle, "David McReynolds: Socialist Peacemaker," *Nonviolent Activist*, March–April 1999, pp. 4–5; David McReynolds, "Thinking about Retirement," *Nonviolent Activist*, March–April 1999, pp. 6–7; Norman Mailer, "The White Negro: Superficial Reflections on the Hipster," in *Advertisements for Myself* (New York: Putnam, 1959). Subsequently cited in the text as *AFM*. On the fifties left, see Maurice Isserman, *If I Had a Hammer: The Death of the Old Left and the Birth of the New Left* (Urbana: University of Illinois Press, 1993 [1987]).

4. James Miller, *"Democracy Is in the Streets": From Port Huron to the Siege*

of Chicago (New York: Simon and Schuster, 1987), p. 331; David McReynolds, "Youth 'Disaffiliated' from a Phony World," *Village Voice,* March 11, 1959, in *Kerouac and Friends,* ed. Fred W. MacDarrah (New York: Morrow, 1985), p. 215. On the sixties more generally, see the works cited in the Introduction.

5. Isaac Rosenfeld, "Life in Chicago: The Land and the Lake," *Commentary* 23:6 (June 1957): 523–534, 528, 527; James Baldwin, "Sonny's Blues," in *Going to Meet the Man* (New York: Dial Press, 1965), pp. 103–141. Baldwin subsequently cited in the text as *GMM.*

6. Alexander Bloom, *Prodigal Sons: The New York Intellectuals and Their World* (New York: Oxford University Press, 1986), pp. 172–173, 296.

7. Rosenfeld, "Life in Chicago," pp. 528–529; Rosenfeld quoted in James Campbell, *This Is the Beat Generation: New York—San Francisco—Paris* (Berkeley: University of California Press, 2001), p. 229.

8. Rosenfeld, "Life in Chicago," pp. 528–529.

9. James Baldwin, "Mass Culture and the Creative Artist: Some Personal Notes," in *Culture for the Millions: Mass Media in Modern Society,* ed. Norman Jacobs (Boston: Beacon Press, 1964), p. 123; Baldwin, "The Uses of the Blues," *Playboy,* January 1964, p. 132; Baldwin, *Nobody Knows My Name: More Notes of a Native Son* (New York: Dell, 1961), p. 180, subsequently cited as *NKMN.*

10. Holmes quoted in James Farrell, *The Spirit of the Sixties: Making Postwar Radicalism* (New York: Routledge, 1997), p. 66.

11. The City Lights book was a reprint of "The White Negro" as a stand-alone pamphlet. See Susan Gubar, *Racechanges: White Skin, Black Face in American Culture* (New York: Oxford University Press, 1997), pp. 178–179.

12. On *Dissent* editor Irving Howe's decision to publish "The White Negro," see Isserman, *If I Had a Hammer,* p. 234.

13. On existentialism in postwar American intellectual and avant-garde culture, see George Cotkin, *Existential America* (Baltimore: Johns Hopkins University Press, 2003); Daniel Belgrad, *The Culture of Spontaneity: Improvisation and the Arts in Postwar America* (Chicago: University of Chicago Press, 1998), pp. 26–28, 103–109.

14. George Steiner, "Naked but Not Dead," *Encounter,* December 1961, pp. 67, 69; F. W. Dupee, "The American Norman Mailer," *Commentary,* February 1960, p. 131; Norman Podhoretz, "Norman Mailer: The Embattled Vision," *Partisan Review,* Summer 1959, pp. 371, 383, 389. See also Diana Trilling, "Norman Mailer," *Encounter,* November 1962, pp. 45–56, where Trilling summarizes Mailer's message thus: "politics is to-day the least revolutionary aspect of social protest."

15. Nat Hentoff, *The Jazz Life* (New York: Dial Press, 1961), pp. 138–142.

16. Carlo Rotella, *October Cities: The Redevelopment of Urban Literature* (Berkeley: University of California Press, 1998), pp. 210, 300.

17. Ralph Ellison, "The World and the Jug," in *Shadow and Act* (New York: Vintage, 1964), pp. 124–125; Ralph Ellison and Albert Murray, *Trading Twelves: The Selected Letters of Ralph Ellison and Albert Murray,* ed. Albert

Murray and John F. Callahan (New York: Modern Library, 2000), pp. 197–198, 217. See also Murray's comments on pp. 199–200.

18. Lorraine Hansberry, "Genet, Mailer, and the New Paternalism," *Village Voice*, June 1, 1961, pp. 13–15.

19. Ibid., pp. 14–15; Mailer, *The Presidential Papers of Norman Mailer* (New York: Bantam, 1964), pp. 187–189.

20. Robert Lindner, *Must You Conform?* (New York: Grove, 1961 [1956]), p. 101.

21. On the sociological belief that blacks had "damaged" psyches, see Daryl Michael Scott, *Contempt and Pity: Social Policy and the Image of the Damaged Black Psyche, 1880–1996* (Chapel Hill: University of North Carolina Press, 1997), esp. pp. 71–160; and Ellen Herman, *The Romance of American Psychology: Political Culture in the Age of Experts* (Berkeley: University of California Press, 1995).

22. Mailer, *Presidential Papers*, pp. 25–61.

23. James Baldwin, *Another Country* (New York: Dial Press, 1962); Baldwin, *Blues for Mister Charlie* (New York: Dell, 1964); Louis Pratt, *James Baldwin* (Boston: Twayne, 1978).

24. *New York Times Book Review*, December 2, 1962, p. 3.

25. On a helpful and related note, Craig Hansen Werner explores the "gospel impulse" in Baldwin's fiction and essays in *Playing the Changes: From Afro-Modernism to the Jazz Impulse* (Urbana: University of Illinois Press, 1994), pp. 212–240.

26. See also Baldwin's "Notes for a Hypothetical Novel," where he writes that "freedom is not something that anybody can be given; freedom is something people take and people are as free as they want to be" (*NKMN*, p. 125). Or this passage from *The Fire Next Time* (New York: Bantam, 1963): "Freedom is hard to bear. It can be objected that I am speaking of political freedom in spiritual terms, but the political institutions of any nation are always menaced and are ultimately controlled by the spiritual state of the nation" (p. 120).

27. Sally Banes, *Greenwich Village 1963: Avant-Garde Performance and the Effervescent Body* (Durham: Duke University Press, 1993), pp. 19–23, 33–53; Hettie Jones, *How I Became Hettie Jones* (New York: E. P. Dutton, 1990), p. 172.

28. H. Jones, p. 37; Amiri Baraka, *The Autobiography of LeRoi Jones* (Chicago: Lawrence Hill, 1997 [1984]), pp. 254–261; Michael Oren, "A '60s Saga: The Life and Death of Umbra (Part I)," *Freedomways* 24:3 (1984): 167–181; Oren, "A '60s Saga: The Life and Death of Umbra (Part II)," *Freedomways* 24:4 (1984): 237–254.

29. Judith Wilson, "Garden of Music: The Art and Life of Bob Thompson," in Thelma Golden, *Bob Thompson* (Berkeley: Whitney Museum of American Art, 1998), pp. 27 (Thompson and Baraka quotes), 66, 46–48 (Haden quoted on p. 47).

30. Wilson, "Garden of Music," pp. 49, 68–70.

31. Hettie Jones remembers that Thompson himself "always wore" a porkpie hat too, adding that "after Lester Young, you had to be pretty sure of yourself to wear a porkpie." H. Jones, *How I Became Hettie Jones,* p. 135.

32. The devaluation of Beat women in books like *On the Road* should not blind us to the strong role that the women played in the subculture. See Maria Damon, "Victors of Catastrophe: Beat Occlusions," in *Beat Culture and the New America, 1950–1965,* ed. Lisa Phillips (New York: Whitney Museum of Art, 1996), pp. 141–165; Joyce Johnson, *Minor Characters* (New York: Simon and Schuster, 1984 [1983]); H. Jones, *How I Became Hettie Jones;* and *Women of the Beat Generation: The Writers, Artists, and Muses at the Heart of Revolution,* ed. Brenda Knight (Berkeley: Conari Press, 1996). On masculinity and the Beats, see Barbara Ehrenreich, *The Hearts of Men* (Garden City, N.Y.: Anchor Books, 1983), pp. 52–67.

33. Wilson, "Garden of Music," pp. 69, 80; Oren, "A '60s Saga (Part I)," 179 and passim.

34. "Killer Joe," *Meet the Jazztet* (1960), originally released as Argo LP 664.

35. Julian "Cannonball" Adderley, "Cannonball on the Jazz Scene," *New York Amsterdam News,* January 28, 1961, p. 13.

36. Steven Watson, *The Birth of the Beat Generation: Visionaries, Rebels, and Hipsters, 1944–1960* (New York: Pantheon, 1995), pp. 4, 257–261, 264, 340–341; Campbell, *This Is the Beat Generation,* pp. 246–249.

37. Tom Hayden, "A Letter to the New (Young) Left," in *The New Student Left,* ed. Mitchell Cohen and Denis Hale (Boston: Beacon, 1966), pp. 2–9.

38. David Rosenthal, *Hard Bop: Jazz and Black Music, 1955–1965* (New York: Oxford University Press, 1992), pp. 62–73, 101–116.

39. *Down Beat,* November 11, 1960, pp. 18–19; August 18, 1960, pp. 29, 26–27. See also April 27, 1961, p. 35.

40. "Jazz Singles Coming Back," *Down Beat,* August 4, 1960, p. 9; "Golden Tears," Cannonball Adderley file, Institute of Jazz Studies, Newark, N.J.; Rosenthal, *Hard Bop,* pp. 62–68.

41. "Jazz Singles Coming Back," p. 9; Rosenthal, *Hard Bop,* p. 68; Barry Ulanov, "How Funky Can You Get?" *Down Beat,* March 6, 1958, pp. 18, 50; Gene Lees, "Afterthoughts," *Down Beat,* December 22, 1960, p. 64.

42. "Nat Talks Back," *Down Beat,* August 4, 1960, pp. 9–10; Gilbert Sorrentino, "Remembrances of Bop in New York, 1945–1950," *Kulchur* 3:10 (Summer 1963): 82; A. B. Spellman, "The Next to the Last Generation of Blues Singers," *Kulchur* 2:5 (Spring 1962): 57–62; Amiri Baraka (as LeRoi Jones), "Jazz and the White Critic," *Black Music* (New York: William Morrow, 1968), p. 16; Baraka (as LeRoi Jones), *Blues People: Negro Music in White America* (New York: Morrow, 1963), p. 202; Adderley quoted in Barry Kernfeld, "Adderley, Coltrane, and Davis at the Twilight of Bebop: The Search for Melodic Coherence, 1958–1959" (Ph.D. diss., Cornell University, 1981), pp. 196–197.

43. Alex Haley and Malcolm X, *The Autobiography of Malcolm X* (New York: Ballantine, 1965), p. 94; Clarence Major, *Dictionary of Afro-American Slang* (New York: International Publishers, 1970), p. 66.

44. Golson, "Killer Joe," *Meet the Jazztet.*

45. Lewis Porter, *John Coltrane: His Life and Music* (Ann Arbor: University of Michigan, 1998), p. 325.

46. "Romance without Finance," in Charlie Parker, *Bird: The Savoy Recordings,* Savoy 2201.

47. Adderley, "Cannonball on the Jazz Scene," p. 13.

48. Ibid.; Eric Foner, *The Story of American Freedom* (New York: Norton, 1998), p. 259.

49. Hentoff, *The Jazz Life,* p. 69.

50. Langston Hughes Papers, Box 33, Oscar Brown, Jr., folder, Beinecke Library, Yale University, New Haven, Conn.

51. "They Call Oscar Brown 'Best Since Belafonte,'" *Toronto Daily Star,* April 14, 1962, p. 14; "Unusual Appeals Bring Broadway Cash," *Ebony,* June 1961, pp. 73–80. The National Movement for the Establishment of a Forty-Ninth State is covered briefly in Raymond L. Hall, *Black Separatism in the United States* (Hanover, N.H.: University Press of New England, 1978), p. 86.

52. King quoted in "Unusual Appeals Bring Broadway Cash," pp. 73–80; "Oscar Brown Signed to Host New TV Jazz Shows," *Chicago Defender,* June 23, 1962, p. 10; "Oscar Brown Jr. Steals Show from Such Greats as Bennett, Williams," *Chicago Defender,* July 7, 1962, p. 24; "Oscar Brown One of Stars in Urban League Benefit," *Chicago Defender,* June 16, 1962, p. 15.

53. "You Have to Be Halfway Hip to Dig Oscar Brown Jr. Show," *New York Amsterdam News,* February 27, 1965, p. 16; Martin Johnson, "Oscar Brown's New Cabaret Review," *Newsday,* July 25, 1986, p. 21; John S. Wilson, "Oscar Brown Jr. Seeking Audience for His Songs," *New York Times,* September 19, 1980, sec. C, p. 10.

54. Max Roach, *We Insist! Freedom Now Suite* (1960), Candid 9002. For a fine analysis of *We Insist!* that situates it in the trajectory of singer Abbey Lincoln's career, see Eric Porter, *What Is This Thing Called Jazz? African American Musicians as Artists, Critics, and Activists* (Berkeley: University of California Press, 2002), pp. 167–169.

55. Nat Hentoff, CD insert notes to *We Insist!*

56. Kathryne V. Lindberg, "Whose Canon? Gwendolyn Brooks: Founder at the Center of the Margins," in *Gendered Modernisms: American Women Poets and Their Readers,* ed. Margaret Dickie and Thomas Travisano (Philadelphia: University of Pennsylvania Press, 1996), pp. 292–293, 308. Brown was working with the Blackstone Rangers on a musical, and he introduced Brooks to the Chicago youth gang who inspired much of her 1960s poetry.

57. Taylor Branch, *Parting the Waters: America in the King Years, 1954–1963* (New York: Simon and Schuster, 1988), pp. 748, 880.

3. Riot on a Summer's Day

1. "Newport Cancels Jazz Festival and Seals Off Island after Riot," *New York Herald Tribune*, July 4, 1960, pp. 1, 3; "The Wild Newport Stomp," *Life*, July 18, 1960, p. 37; Burt Goldblatt, *The Newport Jazz Festival: The Illustrated History* (New York: Dial Press, 1977), pp. 80–86; Thomasina Norford, "Newport Freezes Jazz Festival," *New York Amsterdam News*, July 9, 1960, pp. 1, 34.

2. "Newport Revelers Caged for Mass Pleadings, Bail," Newport Jazz Festival 1960 folder, Institute of Jazz Studies, Newark, N.J.; Steve Gelman, "The Great Newport Jazz Riot," *Climax*, December 1960, pp. 27–31; Goldblatt, *Newport Jazz Festival*, pp. 80–86.

3. Leonard Feather, "Jazz Festivals: The Patient Makes It," *Show*, July 1962, p. 85; "Minutes of the Meeting of the Board of Directors of The Newport Jazz Festival Held on July 3, 1960," 1960 Newport Jazz Festival folder, Institute of Jazz Studies; Langston Hughes, "Gloomy Day at Newport," *Chicago Defender*, July 23, 1960, p. 10.

4. "Thirteen Thousand at Newport Show Jazz Concerts Have Come of Age," *Down Beat*, August 25, 1954, p. 2; "Newport Jazz Fete Gets Too Big for Its Bleachers," *Variety*, July 17, 1957, p. 45; "Newport Fete, a Hipster's Clambake, Swings, Rocks, Sputters," *Variety*, July 9, 1958, p. 53; "Beer, Beatniks, and Boffo 61,000 As 'Big Bands' Cop Newport Laurels," *Variety*, July 8, 1959, p. 75; Newport Jazz Festival 1960 folder, Institute of Jazz Studies.

5. Whitney Balliett, *The Sound of Surprise: 46 Pieces on Jazz* (New York: Dutton, 1961 [1959]), pp. 54, 149; Nat Hentoff, "Stompin' at Newport," *Esquire*, November 1960, pp. 36–40; Hentoff, "Requiem for a Jazz Festival," *Commonweal*, August 5, 1960, p. 394; Mingus quoted in Goldblatt, *Newport Jazz Festival*, p. 86.

6. On the adult concern over fifties youth culture, see Grace Palladino, *Teenagers: An American History* (New York: Basic Books, 1996); William Graebner, *Coming of Age in Buffalo: Youth and Authority in the Postwar Era* (Philadelphia: Temple University Press, 1990); James Gilbert, *A Cycle of Outrage: America's Reaction to the Juvenile Delinquent in the 1950s* (New York: Oxford University Press, 1986).

7. *New York Journal-American* quoted in Hentoff, "Requiem for a Jazz Festival," p. 346; "Newport Cancels Jazz Festival and Seals Off Island After Riot," *New York Herald Tribune*, July 4, 1960, p. 3; "Musical Events: Jazz Concerts," *New Yorker*, July 16, 1960, p. 84; "Rioting on a Summer's Day Blows Newport Jazz Festival Out of Site," *Variety*, July 6, 1960, p. 58; Ted White, "Riot at Newport," *Metronome*, 1960 Newport Jazz Festival folder, Institute of Jazz Studies.

8. O'Connor quoted in Hentoff, "Requiem for a Jazz Festival," p. 396.

9. "Why Students Riot around the World," *U.S. News and World Report*, June 6, 1960, pp. 58–60; "The Disgraceful Battle of Newport," *New York Herald Tribune*, July 5, 1960, p. 12; C. Wright Mills, "The New Left," in *Power, Politics and*

People: The Collected Essays of C. Wright Mills, ed. Irving Louis Horowitz (New York: Oxford University Press, 1963), pp. 257–259.

10. "The Disgraceful Battle of Newport," p. 12; "Self-Expression, Beat Style," *Shelby Star,* July 5, 1960, "Chaos Is King," *Olympian,* August 14, 1960, and White, "Riot at Newport," *Metronome,* all in 1960 Newport Jazz Festival folder, Institute of Jazz Studies.

11. George Wein, "The Newport Jazz Festival," *Playboy,* July 1956, pp. 19–20.

12. Marvin Barrett, "Mr. Phelps's Cows," *Saturday Review,* January 15, 1955, pp. 36–37; Lillian Ross, "You Dig It, Sir?" reprinted in *Jam Session: An Anthology of Jazz,* ed. Ralph J. Gleason (New York: G. P. Putnam's Sons, 1958), pp. 243–264.

13. John Ashton Worley, "The Newport Jazz Festival: A Clash of Cultures" (Ph.D. diss., Clark University, 1981), pp. 40–45; "Newport Counts on President to Put It Back on Map," *Business Week,* August 3, 1957, pp. 30–34; "Ike's Newest Vacation Spot," *U.S. News and World Report,* July 19, 1957, pp. 102–103; "Housing Problem," *Time,* July 6, 1962, p. 44; Robert Cantwell, *When We Were Good: The Folk Revival* (Cambridge: Harvard University Press, 1996), p. 295.

14. "Newport Counts on President," p. 31; "Waiting for a Guest," *Newsweek,* August 26, 1957, p. 31; "Ike's Newest Vacation Spot," p. 102.

15. "Newport Counts on President," pp. 30, 34; Worley, "Newport Jazz Festival," p. 43.

16. Joan Didion, *Slouching towards Bethlehem* (New York: Farrar, Straus and Giroux, 1968), pp. 209–213.

17. Worley, "Newport Jazz Festival," pp. 119, 139; George Hoefer and Gene Lees, "Newport: The Biggest Ever!" *Down Beat,* August 6, 1959, p. 15.

18. David Bittan, "Jazz Purists Razz Berry at Newport," *Variety,* July 9, 1958, p. 53.

19. Edgar Z. Friedenberg, *The Vanishing Adolescent* (Boston: Beacon Press, 1964 [1959]), pp. xxi, 9, and passim.

20. Ibid., pp. 31–33.

21. "Junior Talent in a Jazz Hit," *Life,* July 22, 1957, p. 74.

22. Ibid.; for similar coverage of the Farmingdale teens, see Dan Wakefield, "Jazzmakers' Showcase," *The Nation,* July 20, 1957, p. 32; "Trumpets Are for Extroverts," *Time,* July 15, 1957, p. 50; Nat Hentoff, "The Newport Jazz Festival Blues," *Saturday Review,* July 20, 1957, p. 29. On the Bandstand Kids and their contrast with most working-class rock fans, see Palladino, *Teenagers,* pp. 133–135.

23. Goldblatt, *Newport Jazz Festival,* pp. 45–49; Kenneth Tynan, "Some Echoes of Jazz," *Monthly Review,* May 1960, pp. 24–25.

24. Bosley Crowther, "Our Own 'New Wave,'" *New York Times,* April 10, 1960, sec. 2, p. 1; John McLellan, "Newport Fete Film Accurate," 1960 Newport Jazz Festival folder, Institute of Jazz Studies; Katz quoted in Goldblatt, *Newport Jazz Festival,* pp. 48–49.

25. On the nonpareil Giuffre, see Ted Gioia, *West Coast Jazz: Modern Jazz in California, 1945–1960* (New York: Oxford University Press, 1992), pp. 225–244.

26. Tynan, "Some Echoes," p. 24.

27. Ibid.; Bittan, "Jazz Purists Razz Berry," p. 53; Goldblatt, *Newport Jazz Festival*, pp. 52–54.

28. Kempton quoted in Hentoff, "Requiem for a Jazz Festival," p. 394.

29. Gelman, "The Great Newport Jazz Riot," p. 28; Hoefer and Lees, "Newport: The Biggest Ever!" p. 15.

30. Gelman, "The Great Newport Jazz Riot," p. 29; "Debate on Festival Closing Divides Council Alliances" and John N. Rippey, "Newport's Violence Didn't Lack Warning," both in 1960 Newport Jazz Festival folder, Institute of Jazz Studies.

31. "Riot Cancels Jazz Festival," *New York Herald Tribune*, July 4, 1960, p. 3; Worley, "Newport Jazz Festival," p. 155. On the civil rights movement generally, see the works cited in the Introduction, note 6.

32. On the "making of Caucasians," see Matthew Frye Jacobson, *Whiteness of a Different Color: European Immigrants and the Alchemy of Race* (Cambridge: Harvard University Press, 1998).

33. Worley notes intriguingly that the police "had picked up a young publicly unknown black from Massachusetts by the name of Stokely Carmichael," citing anonymous interviews with Rhode Island police, but it is difficult to assess the reliability of his sources. Worley, "Newport Jazz Festival," p. 155.

34. Hughes, "Gloomy Day at Newport," p. 10; Norford, "Newport Freezes Jazz Festival." See also previously cited articles from the *New York Herald Tribune* (from the AP wire), *Life*, *Time*, and *Newsweek*.

35. Quoted in Goldblatt, *Newport Jazz Festival*, p. 86.

36. Palladino, *Teenagers*, pp. 159–161; Gilbert, *Cycle of Outrage*, pp. 183–185.

37. "Students Riot after Resort Closes Bars," *New York Herald Tribune*, July 5, 1960, p. 10. On the redefinition of civility in the 1960s, see Kenneth Cmiel, "The Politics of Civility," in *The Sixties: From Memory to History*, ed. David Farber (Chapel Hill: University of North Carolina Press, 1994), pp. 263–290.

38. Terry Anderson, *The Movement and the Sixties* (New York: Oxford University Press, 1995), pp. 90–91; "Seven Jazz Fans Fined over Riot at Newport," *New York Herald Tribune*, July 5, 1960, p. 10.

4. The Riot in Reverse

1. Whitney Balliett, "Musical Events," *New Yorker*, July 16, 1960, p. 85; Langston Hughes Papers, Manuscript Folder 48, Beinecke Library, Yale University, New Haven, Conn.; Hughes, *The Collected Poems of Langston Hughes*, ed. Arnold Rampersad (New York: Vintage, 1994), pp. 472–531 (subsequently cited in the text as *CP*). *Ask Your Mama*, though perhaps Hughes's most formally experimental collection, has not yet assumed a central place in Hughes scholarship. I have found two treatments particularly useful: Jean Wagner,

Black Poets of the United States, trans. Kenneth Douglas (Urbana: University of Illinois Press, 1973), pp. 461–473; and Larry Scanlon, "News from Heaven: Vernacular Time in Langston Hughes's *Ask Your Mama," Callaloo* 25:1 (2002): 45–65.

2. Dick Gregory, *From the Back of the Bus,* ed. Bob Orben (New York: E. P. Dutton, 1962), p. 21. On the 1950s negotiations around the Sambo figure, see Joseph Boskin, *Sambo: The Rise and Demise of an American Jester* (New York: Oxford University Press, 1986); and W. T. Lhamon, Jr., *Deliberate Speed: Origins of a Cultural Style* (Washington, D.C.: Smithsonian Institution Press, 1990), pp. 56–86.

3. Burt Goldblatt, *The Newport Jazz Festival: The Illustrated History* (New York: Dial Press, 1977), p. 80; Balliett, "Musical Events," p. 85.

4. Balliett, "Musical Events," p. 84; Nat Hentoff, "Requiem for a Festival," *Commonweal,* August 5, 1960, pp. 394–395.

5. Nat Hentoff, liner notes to Jazz Artists Guild, *Newport Rebels* (1960), Candid SMJ 6187.

6. Balliett, "Musical Events," p. 87; Hentoff, "Requiem for a Festival," p. 395.

7. Gene Santoro, *Myself When I Am Real: The Life and Music of Charles Mingus* (New York: Oxford University Press, 2000), pp. 168–170.

8. George Hoefer, "Jazz in the Cliff Walk Manner," pp. 5–6; "Jazz Leaves the Plantation"; and Maely D. Dufty, "The Sound of Truth," all in Jazz Artists' Guild folder, Institute of Jazz Studies, Newark, N.J.

9. Hoefer, "Jazz in the Cliff Walk Manner," pp. 1–9.

10. Santoro, *Myself When I Am Real,* p. 169.

11. For more on these community arts jazz projects, see Chapter 10; for more on the *Freedom Now Suite,* see Chapter 2.

12. Brian Ward subtly analyzes this unfolding dynamic between white and black performers, celebrities, journalists, and music industry workers in *Just My Soul Responding: Rhythm and Blues, Black Consciousness, and Race Relations* (Berkeley: University of California Press, 1998). On SNCC, see Clayborne Carson, *In Struggle: SNCC and the Black Awakening of the 1960s* (Cambridge: Harvard University Press, 1981), pp. 144–145, 194–200, 236–242.

13. Anthony J. Agostinelli, *The Newport Jazz Festival: Rhode Island—1954–1971: A Significant Era in the Development of Jazz* (Providence, R.I.: Anthony J. Agostinelli, 1981), p. 48.

14. "Newport Jazz Festival," *Ebony,* October 1955, pp. 70–76; Al Nall, "Newport 'Like Penn Relays,' Few Went to Enjoy the Jazz," *New York Amsterdam News,* July 11, 1959, pp. 1, 27; Al Nall, "What They Liked and Didn't Like at Newport," *New York Amsterdam News,* July 11, 1959, p. 3; Langston Hughes, "Gloomy Day at Newport," *Chicago Defender,* July 28, 1960, p. 10.

15. "Newport Jazz Festival," *Ebony,* p. 76; Goldblatt, *Newport Jazz Festival,* p. xxvi; Brian Priestley, *Mingus: A Critical Biography* (New York: DaCapo, 1983), p. 115; Marvin Barrett, "Mr. Phelps's Cows," *Saturday Review,* January 15, 1955, pp. 36–37.

16. "Hot Time in Old Newport," *Collier's*, July 20, 1956, p. 51.

17. Agostinelli, *Newport Jazz Festival: Rhode Island*, p. 51; Goldblatt, *Newport Jazz Festival*, pp. xxvi–xxviii; "What They Liked and Didn't Like at Newport," *New York Amsterdam News*, July 11, 1959, p. 13.

18. Arnold Rampersad, *The Life of Langston Hughes, Volume 2, 1941–1967: I Dream a World* (New York: Oxford University Press, 1988), pp. 253–255.

19. See Langston Hughes Papers, Box 98, Louis Lorillard folder; Langston Hughes Papers, Box 113, Newport Jazz, Inc., folder.

20. Langston Hughes Papers, Manuscript Folder 2272, "Goodbye Newport Blues."

21. Mezz Mezzrow provides an example of the sexual use of the "Hesitation Blues" in his autobiography: he sang the tune to woo the nurses who tended him as he recovered from appendicitis. Mezzrow and Bernard Wolfe, *Really the Blues* (New York: Citadel Press, 1990 [1946]), pp. 39–40.

22. For contemporary reviews of *Ask Your Mama*, see Dudley Pitts, "A Trio of Singers in Varied Keys," *New York Times Book Review*, October 29, 1961, p. 16, which pronounces the book "stunt poetry"; Rudi Blesh, "Jazz Is a Marching Jubilee," *New York Herald Tribune*, November 26, 1961, sec. 6, p. 4; Paul Engle, "Critic Approvingly Views Seferis, Ciardi, and Hughes," *Chicago Tribune Magazine of Books*, October 29, 1961, p. 15; *Library Journal*, December 1, 1961, p. 85. The civil rights–affiliated journal *Freedomways* unsurprisingly gave the book a glowing review; see John Henrik Clarke, review of *Ask Your Mama*, *Freedomways* 2 (Winter 1962): 102–103.

23. On the dozens, see Roger D. Abrahams, *Deep Down in the Jungle . . . : Negro Narrative Folklore from the Streets of Philadelphia* (Chicago: Aldine, 1970 [1964]); Lawrence Levine, *Black Culture and Black Consciousness: Afro-American Folk Thought from Slavery to Freedom* (Oxford: Oxford University Press, 1977), pp. 344–358; and Robin D. G. Kelley, *Yo' Mama's Disfunktional! Fighting the Culture Wars in Urban America* (Boston: Beacon Press, 1997), pp. 32–36.

24. Hughes wrote to blues scholar and semanticist S. I. Hayakawa in July 1961: "You'll no doubt be interested in [*Ask Your Mama*], as for the first time so far as I know, it incorporates the 'dozens' into poetry." Langston Hughes papers, Correspondence Box 71.

25. Dollard's article "The Dozens: Dialectic of Insult" appeared originally in *American Imago*, November 1939, pp. 3–25. It is also found in Langston Hughes Papers, Manuscript Folder 47: Hughes wanted it to be seen as a crucial source of his poem.

26. See Milton Meltzer, *Langston Hughes: A Biography* (New York: Crowell, 1958), p. 111; Steven C. Tracy, *Langston Hughes and the Blues* (Urbana: University of Illinois Press, 1988).

27. Rampersad, *Life of Langston Hughes, Volume 2*, pp. 279–280, 282, 291; Langston Hughes Papers, Correspondence Box 88, Knopf folder.

28. Langston Hughes Papers, Correspondence Box 165, Randy Weston folder.

29. Langston Hughes Papers, Manuscript Folder 48. The phrase does not appear in the final version of the poem.

30. Mel Watkins, *On the Real Side* (New York: Simon & Schuster, 1994), pp. 495–497; Dick Gregory, *Nigger: An Autobiography* (New York: E. F. Dutton, 1964), pp. 142–145.

31. That the times were a-changin' is suggested by a very similar routine by black comedian "Moms" Mabley in her 1962 poem "The Dream of a Southern Governor." See Levine, *Black Culture and Black Consciousness*, p. 364.

32. Stephen Henderson, *Understanding the New Black Poetry: Black Speech and Black Music as Poetic References* (New York: William Morrow, 1973), p. xiii.

5. Outrageous Freedom

1. Gene Santoro, *Myself When I Am Real: The Life and Music of Charles Mingus* (New York: Oxford University Press, 2000), pp. 6, 145. A wonderful treatment of Mingus as a jazz intellectual can be found in Eric Porter, *What Is This Thing Called Jazz? African American Musicians as Artists, Critics, and Activists* (Berkeley: University of California Press, 2002), pp. 101–148.

2. Santoro, *Myself When I Am Real*, p. 358; Sue Mingus, *Tonight at Noon: A Love Story* (New York: Pantheon, 2002), p. 84.

3. Brian Priestley, *Mingus: A Critical Biography* (New York: DaCapo, 1983), pp. 81, 151.

4. Robert Walser, "'Out of Notes': Signification, Interpretation, and the Problem of Miles Davis," in *Jazz among the Discourses*, ed. Krin Gabbard (Durham: Duke University Press, 1995), pp. 167–168.

5. Nat Hentoff, liner notes to *Charles Mingus Presents Charles Mingus* (1960), Candid 9005; Gary Giddins, *Visions of Jazz: The First Century* (New York: Oxford University Press, 1998), p. 446. On method acting, see Lee Strasberg, *A Dream of Passion: The Development of the Method* (Boston: Little, Brown and Co., 1987). On the cultural history of emotions, see Joel Pfister and Nancy Schnog, *Inventing the Psychological: Toward a Cultural History of Emotional Life in America* (New Haven: Yale University Press, 1997), esp. Robert Walser's "Deep Jazz," pp. 271–296.

6. Janet Coleman and Al Young, *Mingus/Mingus: Two Memoirs* (Berkeley: Creative Arts, 1989), p. 43.

7. Ibid., p. 6; Mingus quoted in "The Playboy Panel: Jazz—Today and Tomorrow," *Playboy*, February 1964, in *Keeping Time: Readings in Jazz History*, ed. Robert Walser (New York: Oxford University Press, 1999), pp. 273–274; Charles Mingus, *Music Written for Monterey 1965, Not Heard, Played in Its Entirety at UCLA* (1965), Jazz Workshop JWS013/014.

8. S. Mingus, *Tonight at Noon*, p. 42; Santoro, *Myself When I Am Real*, p. 224.

9. RCA agreed to record Mingus because they had recorded an artist signed

to Mingus's Debut label; the settlement was tit for tat. Priestley, pp. 22–23, 83, 133, 112, 139.

10. Brian Priestley, liner notes to Charles Mingus, *The Complete Town Hall Concert* (1962), Blue Note COP7243; Bill Coss, "A Report of a Most Remarkable Event," *Down Beat*, December 6, 1962, p. 40; "Mingus Replies," *Down Beat*, January 17, 1963, p. 8; Santoro, *Myself When I Am Real*, pp. 200–204.

11. Santoro, *Myself When I Am Real*, p. 220; S. Mingus, *Tonight at Noon*, p. 38.

12. Nat Hentoff, "Mingus in Job Dilemma, Vows 'No Compromise'," *Down Beat*, May 6, 1953, p. 21; Priestley, *Mingus*, pp. 92–93.

13. In fact, to my knowledge, it is the only piece that Mingus ever wrote in straight waltz time, with three even beats and a rhythmic emphasis on the first.

14. Charles Mingus, "The Clown," in *The Clown* (1957), Atlantic 1260; Greenberg's "Avant-Garde and Kitsch" (1939) and Macdonald's 1953 essay appear in the Bernard Rosenberg and David Manning White anthology *Mass Culture: The Popular Arts in America* (New York: Free Press, 1957).

15. Ralph Gleason, "Charles Mingus: A Thinking Musician," *Down Beat*, June 1, 1951, p. 7; Hentoff, "Mingus in Job Dilemma," p. 21; Santoro, *Myself When I Am Real*, p. 83.

16. Priestley, *Mingus*, pp. 56–65; liner notes to *Charles Mingus: The Complete Debut Recordings* (1951–1958), Debut 12-DCD-4402-2.

17. Walser, *Keeping Time*, p. 289; Ira Gitler, "Bass-ically Speaking," liner notes to *Charles Mingus: The Complete Debut Recordings*, p. 13.

18. Howard Brick, *Age of Contradiction: American Thought and Culture in the 1960s* (New York: Twayne, 1998), pp. 18–22; Richard Pells, *The Liberal Mind in a Conservative Age* (New York: Harper and Row, 1985), pp. 249–261.

19. Coleman and Young, *Mingus/Mingus*, p. 28; Priestley, *Mingus*, p. 164; Ira Gitler, "Mingus Speaks—and Bluntly," *Down Beat*, July 21, 1960, p. 67; Mingus quoted in liner notes to *Town Hall Concert* (1964), Charles Mingus Enterprises JWS005.

20. Priestley, *Mingus*, p. 93; Charlie Mingus, "An Open Letter to Miles Davis," *Down Beat*, November 30, 1955, pp. 12–13; "Charles Mingus Interviewed by Nesuhi Ertegun," *Oh Yeah* (1961), Atlantic 1377.

21. Priestley, *Mingus*, p. 149; Coleman and Young, *Mingus/Mingus*, p. 20; Bill Whitworth, "The Rich Full Life of Charlie Mingus," *New York Herald Tribune*, November 1, 1964, p. 16; Walser, *Keeping Time*, p. 268.

22. Nat Hentoff, liner notes to Jazz Artists Guild, *Newport Rebels* (1960), Candid SMJ6187; liner notes to *Town Hall Concert*; Priestley, *Mingus*, p. 184.

23. Priestley, *Mingus*, pp. 158–159, 164, 176–177, 184.

24. Ibid., pp. 184, 164; Leonard Feather, "Jazz Festivals: The Patient Makes It," *Show*, July 1962, p. 85; Jacques Attali, *Noise: The Political Economy of Music* (Minneapolis: University of Minnesota Press, 1985).

25. Hentoff, liner notes to *Charles Mingus Presents Charles Mingus*.

26. Coleman and Young, *Mingus/Mingus,* pp. 2, 18, 24; Priestley, *Mingus,* pp. 70, 90, 91, 50–51, 138–139, 99, 165–166.

27. S. Mingus, *Tonight at Noon,* p. 127; "Ted Curson Interview," *Cadence,* July 1976, p. 4.

28. On freedom in hard bop more generally, see the Introduction.

29. Charles Mingus, liner notes to *Pithecanthropus Erectus* (1956), Atlantic 1237.

30. Nat Hentoff, liner notes to *Pithecanthropus Erectus;* on the sensory memory exercises of the Actors Studio, see Strasberg, *Dream of Passion,* pp. 123–174.

31. Hentoff, liner notes to *Charles Mingus Presents Charles Mingus;* liner notes to *The Clown.* See also Hentoff's liner notes to *Pithecanthropus Erectus;* "Caught in the Act," *Down Beat,* January 11, 1956, p. 8; liner notes to *Mingus Plays Piano* (1963), Impulse A60; liner notes to *Oh Yeah.*

32. Erkhaard Jost, *Free Jazz* (New York: DaCapo Press, 1981 [1974]), p. 35.

33. *Mingus: More Than a Fake Book,* ed. Sue Mingus (New York: Jazz Workshop, 1991), p. 4; liner notes to *Pithecanthropus Erectus.*

34. *Mingus: More Than a Fake Book,* p. 152.

35. Joe Goldberg, *Jazz Masters of the Fifties* (New York: Macmillan, 1965), pp. 74–75.

36. *Mingus: More Than a Fake Book,* p. 124.

37. Ibid., p. 147.

38. Priestley, Mingus, pp. 101, 238; *Mingus: More Than a Fake Book,* pp. 9–11.

39. Jost, *Free Jazz,* p. 36; Priestley, *Mingus,* pp. 63, 155.

40. *Mingus: More Than a Fake Book,* pp. 54–55.

41. "Caught in the Act," *Down Beat,* March 31, 1960, p. 34.

42. Priestley, *Mingus,* p. 92; S. Mingus, *Tonight at Noon,* p. 83; Santoro, *Myself When I Am Real,* pp. 147, 254; Whitworth, "The Rich Full Life," p. 13.

43. Santoro, *Myself When I Am Real,* p. 233; Whitworth, "The Rich Full Life," p. 41; Nat Hentoff, "Mingus Dynasties," *Village Voice,* March 12, 1979, p. 35; Gitler, "Mingus Speaks," p. 67; Jack Wasserman column, Box 47, Folder 13, Charles Mingus Archive, Library of Congress.

44. Diane Dorr-Dorynek, "Mingus . . . ," in *The Jazz Word,* ed. Dom Cerulli, Burt Korall, and Mort Nasati (New York: DaCapo, 1987 [1960]), pp. 14–15.

45. Nat Hentoff, *The Jazz Life* (New York: Dial Press, 1961), p. 169.

46. Dorr-Dorynek, "Mingus," pp. 17–18; Coleman and Young, *Mingus/ Mingus,* p. 26; "Mingus Mania," *Down Beat,* March 29, 1962, p. 13; Priestley, *Mingus,* p. 80; *Keeping Time,* p. 286.

47. Dorr-Dorynek, "Mingus," p. 18.

48. Mingus, "An Open Letter," pp. 12–13.

49. Charles Mingus, *Beneath the Underdog: The World as Composed by Mingus,* ed. Nel King (New York: Vintage, 1991 [1971]). Subsequently cited

within the text. Critics have finally begun to catch up with Mingus's self-conscious pummeling of African-American autobiography. See Christopher Harlos, "Jazz Autobiography: Theory, Practice, Politics," in *Representing Jazz,* ed. Krin Gabbard (Durham: Duke University Press, 1995), pp. 131–166; Porter, *What Is This Thing,* pp. 138–147.

50. Coleman and Young, *Mingus/Mingus,* p. 8.

51. Geoffrey Wolff, "Man With a Bass," *Newsweek,* May 17, 1971, p. 110.

52. Jonathan Yardley, "Agonies of a 'Mongrel'," *New Republic,* July 3, 1971, p. 29; Whitney Balliett, *Ecstasy at the Onion* (Indianapolis: Bobbs-Merrill, 1971), pp. 263–272. For a contrary review, see Felipe Luciano, "Charlie Mingus, a Nigger?" *Village Voice,* July 22, 1971, pp. 25–26.

53. "Subsoil of Black Music," *Times Literary Supplement,* September 10, 1971, in Box 47, Folder 1, Charles Mingus Archive, Library of Congress; Clive James, "Jim Crow in the Jazz World," *The Observer,* August 15, 1971, p. 28; *Publishers' Weekly* clip in Box 47, Folder 1, Charles Mingus Archive, Library of Congress.

6. "This Freedom's Slave Cries"

1. Sue Mingus, *Tonight at Noon: A Love Story* (New York: Pantheon, 2002), pp. 38, 27.

2. Brian Priestley, *Mingus: A Critical Biography* (New York: DaCapo, 1983), pp. 12–14; Mingus, liner notes to *Mingus Dynasty: Charles Mingus and His Groups* (1959), Columbia CJ 8236; Gene Santoro, *Myself When I Am Real: The Life and Music of Charles Mingus* (New York: Oxford University Press, 2000), pp. 5, 56.

3. *Mingus: More Than a Fake Book,* ed. Sue Mingus (New York: Jazz Workshop, 1991), pp. 111–112, 148–149.

4. On "Strange Fruit," see Michael Denning, *The Cultural Front: The Laboring of American Culture in the Twentieth Century* (New York: Verso, 1996), pp. 323–348; Robert O'Meally, *Lady Day: The Many Faces of Billie Holiday* (New York: Arcade, 1991), pp. 131–140.

5. *Mingus: More Than a Fake Book,* pp. 40–41.

6. Ira Gitler, liner notes to *Charles Mingus: The Complete Debut Recordings* (1951–1958), Debut 12-DCD-4402-2, p. 28.

7. Ralph Gleason, "Charles Mingus: A Thinking Musician," *Down Beat,* June 1, 1951, p. 7; liner notes to *Charles Mingus: The Complete Debut Recordings,* p. 12.

8. Eric Porter, *What Is This Thing Called Jazz? African American Musicians as Artists, Critics, and Activists* (Berkeley: University of California Press, 2002), pp. 111–124.

9. Liner notes to *Pithecanthropus Erectus* (1956), Atlantic 1237.

10. Ibid.

11. Paul Gilroy, *The Black Atlantic: Modernity and Double Consciousness* (Cambridge: Harvard University Press, 1993), p. 113; see also pp. 41–71.

12. Liner notes to *Pithecanthropus Erectus*. On the application of Hegel and Kojève to black modernity and emancipation movements, see Gilroy, *Black Atlantic*, pp. 46–58; Richard H. King, *Civil Rights and the Idea of Freedom* (New York: Oxford University Press, 1992), pp. 177–178; David Brion Davis, *The Problem of Slavery in the Age of Revolution, 1770–1823* (Ithaca: Cornell University Press, 1975), pp. 557–564.

13. Mingus's affection for Richard Strauss and his *Death and Transfiguration* is recounted in Mingus, "What Is a Jazz Composer?" in *Mingus: More Than a Fake Book,* p. 156. On Strauss's programmatic music, see James Hepokoski, "Fiery-Pulsed Libertine or Domestic Hero? Strauss's *Don Juan* Reinvestigated," in *Richard Strauss: New Perspectives on the Composer and His Work,* ed. Bryan Gillam (Durham: Duke University Press, 1992), pp. 135–175. Strauss's tone poem *Don Juan* is the story of a compulsive lover who tries to escape the routinization of sex—a figure not unlike the narrator of *Beneath the Underdog.*

14. Stanley Dance, "Mingus Speaks," *Jazz* 2:9 (November–December 1963), p. 12.

15. Nat Hentoff, "A Volcano Named Mingus," *HiFi/Stereo Review,* December 1964, p. 55; on Ellington's *My People,* see John Edward Haase, *Beyond Category: The Life and Genius of Duke Ellington* (New York: DaCapo, 1993), pp. 350–351.

16. Brian Ward, *Just My Soul Responding: Rhythm and Blues, Black Consciousness, and Race Relations* (Berkeley: University of California Press, 1998), p. 142.

17. Ibid., pp. 80, 83.

18. See Chapter 2, on Cannonball Adderley and the emergence of soul-jazz; David Rosenthal, *Hard Bop: Jazz and Black Music, 1955–1965* (New York: Oxford University Press, 1992), pp. 42–45; Samuel Floyd, *The Power of Black Music* (New York: Oxford University Press, 1995), pp. 180–182.

19. Ira Gitler, "Mingus Speaks—and Bluntly," *Down Beat,* July 21, 1960, p. 67. On Mingus and Newport, see Chapter 4.

20. Liner notes to *Blues and Roots,* Atlantic 1305; Mingus and Homzy quoted in *Mingus: More Than a Fake Book,* p. 20; Santoro, *Myself When I Am Real,* p. 210; Priestley, *Mingus,* p. 144. Impulse's motto was "The new wave of jazz is on Impulse!"

21. Edmund Pollock, liner notes to *The Black Saint and the Sinner Lady,* Impulse A35.

22. The phrase "Ellington effect" was actually coined in 1952 at Ellington's Silver Jubilee by his collaborator Billy Strayhorn. See Strayhorn, "The Ellington Effect," *The Duke Ellington Reader,* ed. Mark Tucker (New York: Oxford University Press, 1993), pp. 269–270.

23. Charles Mingus, liner notes to *The Black Saint and the Sinner Lady,* Im-

pulse A35; manuscript to "The Black Saint and The Sinner Lady," Box 3, Folder 1, Charles Mingus archive, Library of Congress.

24. Priestley, *Mingus,* p. 146.

25. Never an ace of consistency, Mingus began his program notes with an invocation of "sinner Jim Whitney"—a nod that suggests that the sinner-gentleman may have been behind the sinner-lady from the start.

26. Pollard, liner notes to *The Black Saint and the Sinner Lady,* Impulse A35.

27. Gunther Schuller, *The Swing Era: The Development of Jazz, 1930–1945* (New York: Oxford University Press, 1989), pp. 116–117.

28. See Didier Levallet and Denis-Constant Martin, *L'Amérique de Mingus: Musique et Politique: les* Fables of Faubus *de Charles Mingus* (Paris: POL, 1991) for an exhaustive look at the different recordings of "Fables."

29. Henry Louis Gates, Jr., recalls hearing this taunt in 1957 and also includes another act of "Signifyin'" on it. See *The Signifying Monkey: A Theory of African-American Literary Criticism* (New York: Oxford University Press, 1988), p. 103.

7. The Serious Side of Hard Bop

1. "A Night in Tunisia" (1946), from Charlie Parker, *The Original Dial Masters,* Vol. 1, Dial ST-CD-23; "Liberia" (1960), from John Coltrane, *Coltrane's Sound,* Atlantic SD-1419; Norman C. Weinstein, *A Night in Tunisia: Imaginings of Africa in Jazz* (New York: Limelight, 1994 [1992]), p. 63.

2. Mongo Santamaria, *Afro-Roots,* Prestige 24018; Abbey Lincoln, *Abbey Is Blue,* Riverside RLP-1153; Oscar Brown, Jr., *Sin and Soul . . . and Then Some,* Columbia CK 64944; John Coltrane, *Live at Birdland* (1963), Impulse IMPD-198.

3. Frank Kofsky, *Black Nationalism and the Revolution in Music* (New York: Pathfinder Press, 1970); Gerald Early, "Ode to John Coltrane: A Jazz Musician's Influence on African American Culture," *Antioch Review* 57:3 (Summer 1999): 373–374; Lorenzo Thomas, "Ascension: Music and the Black Arts Movement," *Jazz across the Discourses,* ed. Krin Gabbard (Durham: Duke University Press, 1995), pp. 256–258.

4. Robin D. G. Kelley, "Stormy Weather: Reconstructing Black (Inter)Nationalism in the Cold War Era," in *Is It Nation Time? Contemporary Essays on Black Power and Black Nationalism,* ed. Eddie S. Glaude, Jr. (Chicago: University of Chicago Press, 2002), pp. 69–70; Brenda Gayle Plummer, *Rising Wind: Black Americans and U.S. Foreign Affairs, 1935–1960* (Chapel Hill: University of North Carolina Press, 1996); Penny von Eschen, *Race against Empire* (Ithaca: Cornell University Press, 1997).

5. Critic Brian Priestley notes that "India" was probably named not after the county but after the daughter of his friend Cal Massey—an interesting detail that does not alter the fact that Coltrane's music tried to absorb an Indian

influence and was understood as doing so. Priestley, *John Coltrane* (London: Quartet Books, 1986), p. 46.

6. Amiri Baraka (as LeRoi Jones), *Black Music* (New York: Morrow, 1967), epigraph, n.p.

7. Early, "Ode to John Coltrane," p. 373; Sacha Feinstein and Yusef Komunyakaa, eds., *The Jazz Poetry Anthology* (Bloomington: Indiana University Press, 1991), pp. 104–105. Irony, of course, is a tricky term in instrumental music: I generally use the term to refer to the gap, performed and perceived, between what is said and what is meant. Certain styles of performance draw attention to this gap through parody, satire, and the like, while others seek to minimize it by emphasizing the virtues of sincerity, emotional transparency, and so on.

8. Carl Woideck, *Charlie Parker: His Music and Life* (Ann Arbor: University of Michigan Press, 1996), pp. 11–12.

9. Lewis Porter, *John Coltrane: His Life and Music* (Ann Arbor: University of Michigan Press, 1998), pp. 50–53, 81–83, 254–255.

10. Scott DeVeaux, *The Birth of Bebop: A Social and Musical History* (Berkeley: University of California Press, 1997), pp. 418–419.

11. Dizzy Gillespie with Al Fraser, *To Be, or Not . . . to Bop: Memoirs* (Garden City, N.Y.: Doubleday, 1979), p. 171.

12. DeVeaux, *The Birth of Bebop*, pp. 263–268.

13. Gary Giddins, *Visions of Jazz: The First Century* (New York: Oxford University Press, 1998), p. 274.

14. Ralph Ellison, *Shadow and Act* (New York: Vintage: 1964), p. 230.

15. Porter, *John Coltrane*, pp. 73–97.

16. Francis Davis, "Blue Heaven," *New Yorker*, December 4, 2000, pp. 96–100.

17. Porter, *John Coltrane*, pp. 171–201.

18. DeVeaux, *The Birth of Bebop*, pp. 424–425.

19. Weinstein, *Night in Tunisia*, pp. 61–63.

20. *The Complete Africa/Brass Sessions*, Impulse IMPD-2–168; Priestley, *John Coltrane*, p. 45.

21. Baraka, *Black Music*, pp. 64–65.

22. Ibid., p. 67. In his Obie award-winning play *Dutchman*, written the next year, Baraka pondered the fate of two urban characters, a black man and a white woman, who remain trapped in the underground purgatory of the New York subway. The play is largely a static conversation about jazz, sex, economics, and race, but it is laced with a murderous tension, the hate and desire that surges between the two characters.

23. Amiri Baraka (as LeRoi Jones), *Blues People: Negro Music in White America* (New York: William Morrow, 1963), pp. 235, 218.

24. *The John Coltrane Companion*, ed. Carl Woideck (New York: Schirmer Books, 1998), p. 218; John Tynan, "Take 5," *Down Beat*, November 23, 1961, p. 40; Tynan, "What Price Theater?" *Down Beat*, October 13, 1960, p. 19.

25. *The John Coltrane Companion*, p. 111; Leonard Feather, "Feather's Nest," *Down Beat*, February 15, 1962, p. 40; Feather, "Jazz: Going Nowhere," *Show*, January 1962, pp. 12–14.

26. *Down Beat*, April 26, 1962, p. 29.

27. A. B. Spellman, "Heard and Seen," in *The John Coltrane Companion*, pp. 219–221.

28. Howard Brick considers "the militarization of protest rhetoric" in *The Age of Contradiction: American Thought and Culture in the 1960s* (New York: Twayne, 1998), pp. 162–167.

29. Imamu Amiri Baraka, *The Autobiography of LeRoi Jones* (Chicago: Lawrence Hill, 1997 [1984]), pp. 253–254; A. B. Spellman, review of *Coltrane Live at the Village Vanguard, Kulchur* 2 (Autumn 1962): 97–99.

30. Amiri Baraka (as LeRoi Jones), "Present Perfect," review of Gil Evans, *Into the Hot, Kulchur* 2:8 (Winter 1962): 95–98.

31. "New Black Music: A Concert in Benefit of the Black Arts Repertory Theatre/School Live," *Black Music*, pp. 174, 176.

32. Werner Sollors, *Amiri Baraka/LeRoi Jones: The Quest for a "Populist Modernism"* (New York: Columbia University Press, 1978), pp. 87–94; Amiri Baraka, *The LeRoi Jones/Amiri Baraka Reader,* ed. William Harris (New York: Thunder's Mouth Press, 1991), pp. 69–75.

33. Baraka, *Blues People*, p. 65; Baraka, *Black Music*, p. 19. For a richer account of Jones/Baraka's split with earlier jazz critics, see John Gennari, "Jazz Criticism: Its Development and Ideologies," *Black American Literature Forum* 25:3 (Fall 1991): 485–496. James C. Hall is one of relatively few critics who give *Blues People* its due as a "'classic' of sixties American culture." See *Mercy, Mercy Me: African-American Culture and the American Sixties* (New York: Oxford, 2001), pp. 115–123.

34. Baraka, *Blues People*, p. 29; Hall, *Mercy, Mercy Me*, pp. 118–120.

35. Baraka, *Blues People*, pp. 139–140, 126–127; E. Franklin Frazier, *Black Bourgeoisie* (Glencoe, Ill.: Free Press, 1957).

36. Baraka, *Blues People*, p. 140; Burton Peretti, *The Creation of Jazz: Music, Race, and Culture in Urban America* (Urbana: University of Illinois Press, 1992); DeVeaux, *The Birth of Bebop;* Ellison, *Shadow and Act*, pp. 256–257.

37. Clayborne Carson, *In Struggle: SNCC and the Black Awakening of the 1960s* (Cambridge: Harvard University Press, 1981), pp. 91–95; Baraka, *Blues People*, p. 232; Askia Muhammad Touré (as Rolland Snellings), "The New Afro-American Writer," *Liberator* 3:10 (October 1963): 10; James Baldwin, *The Fire Next Time* (New York: Dell, 1963), p. 127.

38. Baraka, *Autobiography of LeRoi Jones*, pp. 259–260; Ekhaard Jost, *Free Jazz* (New York: DaCapo Press, 1981 [1974]); Timothy B. Tyson, *Radio Free Dixie: Robert F. Williams and the Roots of Black Power* (Chapel Hill: University of North Carolina Press, 1999). On the early days of Black Power, see William L. Van Deburg, *New Day in Babylon: The Black Power Movement and American Culture, 1965–1975* (Chicago: University of Chicago Press, 1992), pp. 29–62.

39. Leonard Feather, "Hierarchy of the Jazz Anarchy," *Esquire*, September 1965, p. 125; Don DeMichael, "John Coltrane and Eric Dolphy Answer the Jazz Critics," in *The John Coltrane Companion*, p. 115; Frank Kofsky, "John Coltrane: An Interview," in *The John Coltrane Companion*, p. 147.

40. Tjader quoted in Ted Gioia, *West Coast Jazz: Modern Jazz in California, 1945–1960* (New York: Oxford University Press, 1992), p. 104.

41. The best survey of Lincoln as jazz artist and intellectual appears in Eric Porter, *What Is This Thing Called Jazz? African American Musicians as Artists, Critics, and Activists* (Berkeley: University of California, 2002), pp. 149–190.

42. "The Girl in the Marilyn Monroe Dress," *Ebony*, June 1957, pp. 27–31; Francis Davis, "Leading Lady," in *In the Moment: Jazz in the 1980s* (New York: Oxford University Press, 1986), pp. 197–200; Barbara Gardner, "Metamorphosis: Abbey Lincoln," *Down Beat*, September 14, 1961, pp. 18–20; Giddins, *Visions of Jazz*, pp. 575–583.

43. Lewis Porter, "John Coltrane: The Atlantic Years," in *The John Coltrane Companion*, pp. 189, 183; Coolidge quoted in David Meltzer, ed., *Reading Jazz* (San Francisco: Mercury House, 1993), p. 251; Priestley, *John Coltrane*, p. 46. See also Ingrid Monson, *Saying Something: Jazz Improvisation and Interaction* (Chicago: University of Chicago Press, 1996), pp. 110–114, for a wonderful analysis of the quite similar groove in Coltrane's 1960 recording of "My Favorite Things"; and Frank Kofsky, *John Coltrane and the Jazz Revolution of the 1960s* (New York: Pathfinder, 1998), pp. 335–385, for an astute breakdown of the rhythmic innovations of Jones and Tyner especially.

44. Ted Gioia, *The History of Jazz* (New York: Oxford University Press, 1997), p. 304.

8. Loving *A Love Supreme*

1. Sascha Feinstein, *Jazz Poetry: From the 1920s to the Present* (Westport, Conn.: Greenwood Press, 1997), pp. 123–127; Stephen Henderson, *Understanding the New Black Poetry: Black Speech and Black Music as Poetic References* (New York: William Morrow, 1973), pp. 345–346, 274–278, 336–340.

2. Lindsay Barrett, "The Tide Inside, It Rages!" in *Black Fire: An Anthology of Afro-American Writing*, ed. LeRoi Jones and Larry Neal (New York: William Morrow, 1968), pp. 149–150, 658. See also Barrett's "The Black Artist in Exile," *Revolution—Africa, Latin America, Asia* 11:1 (March 1964): 131–138.

3. "The Screamers," in *The LeRoi Jones/Amiri Baraka Reader*, ed. William J. Harris (New York: Thunder's Mouth Press, 1991), pp. 171–177.

4. Ibid., p. 174; Lewis Porter, *John Coltrane: His Life and Music* (Ann Arbor: University of Michigan Press, 1998), pp. 91–92, 96; Amiri Baraka, "The Changing Same (R&B and New Black Music)," in *The LeRoi Jones/Amiri Baraka Reader*, pp. 186–209.

5. "The Screamers," p. 176. On Black Power, see the works cited in the Introduction, note 11. For a prescient call for "the revolution of the psyche," see

Askia Muhammad Touré (as Rolland Snellings), "Toward Repudiating Western Values," *Liberator* 4:11 (November 1964): 11, 26.

6. Larry Neal, "The Cultural Front," *Liberator* 5:6 (June 1965): 26–27; Harold Cruse, "Rebellion or Revolution? (Part Three)," *Liberator* 3:12 (December 1963): 14–17; Cruse, "Rebellion or Revolution? (Part Four)," *Liberator* 4:1 (January 1964): 14–16; William L. Van Deburg, *New Day in Babylon: The Black Power Movement and American Culture* (Chicago: University of Chicago Press, 1992), pp. 181–191.

7. C. Daniel Dawson, "The Sound He Saw," in Roy DeCarava, *The Sound I Saw: The Jazz Photographs of Roy DeCarava*, exhibition catalogue (New York: Studio Museum in Harlem, 1983), n.p.; DeCarava quoted in Sherry Turner DeCarava, "Celebration," in *The Jazz Cadence of American Culture*, ed. Robert O'Meally (New York: Columbia University Press, 1998), pp. 258–259; Peter Galassi, "Introduction," in *Roy DeCarava: A Retrospective* (New York: Museum of Modern Art, 1996), p. 13. For more on, DeCarava, see Maren Stange, "'Illusion Complete within Itself': Roy DeCarava's Photography," *Yale Journal of Criticism* 9:1 (1996): 63–92. Unfortunately, DeCarava did not grant permission to reprint his images in this book. See his website at *www.decarava.com* to view his work.

8. A. D. Coleman, "The Sound He Saw: Roy DeCarava's Jazz Photographs," in DeCarava, *The Sound I Saw*, pp. 8–9; Galassi, "Introduction," p. 26.

9. S. T. DeCarava, "Celebration," p. 251. See Galassi, "Introduction," pp. 27–29, for a discussion of DeCarava and the "available-light revolution" of related photographers like Robert Frank and W. Eugene Smith.

10. Geoff Dyer, "New Views," *Doubletake* 9 (Summer 1997): 121–123; Graham Lock, *Blutopia: Visions of the Future and Revisions of the Past in the Work of Sun Ra, Duke Ellington, and Anthony Braxton* (Durham: Duke University Press, 1999), pp. 180–181.

11. Galassi, "Introduction," pp. 19, 34–35.

12. Ibid., pp. 31–32. On the labor activism that took root in the 1930s culture industries, see Michael Denning, *The Cultural Front: The Laboring of American Culture in the Twentieth Century* (New York: Verso, 1996); on the rank-and-file insurgencies and settlements of the 1940s, see George Lipsitz, *Rainbow at Midnight: Labor and Culture in the 1940s* (Urbana: University of Illinois Press, 1994).

13. Galassi, "Introduction," pp. 31–32. On Spiral, see Mary Schmidt Campbell, *Tradition and Conflict: Images of a Turbulent Decade, 1963–1973* (New York: Studio Museum in Harlem, 1985), pp. 45–67.

14. Eldridge Cleaver, *Soul on Ice* (New York: Dell, 1968); Addison Gayle, Jr., "Cultural Nationalism: The Black Novel and the City," *Liberator* 9:7 (July 1969): 17; Hinton quoted in Larry Neal, "To Harlem with Love," *New York Times*, October 5, 1969, Sec. 2, pp. 25, 34; Van Deburg, *New Day in Babylon*, pp. 22–28 and passim.

15. Porter, *John Coltrane,* pp. 106–107, 232–233. Much of my interpretation of *A Love Supreme* is indebted to Porter's foundational work.

16. Ibid., pp. 232–249.

17. Ibid., pp. 233–242.

18. Curiously, Coltrane did not advertise that his "Psalm" performance followed the poem included with the album. In fact, he once testified that the poem did "not necessarily" contribute to our understanding of the music: "I simply wanted to express what I felt; I had to write it." The first critic to notice the correspondence between poem and solo was Gary Giddins in 1974—a decade after *A Love Supreme*'s recording. See Porter, *John Coltrane,* pp. 247–248, 332.

19. Henderson, *Understanding the New Black Poetry,* pp. 347–348; *The LeRoi Jones/Amiri Baraka Reader,* p. 271; Stephen Henderson, "Survival Motion: A Study of the Black Writer and the Black Revolution in America," in Mercer Cook and Henderson, *The Militant Black Writer in Africa and the United States* (Madison: University of Wisconsin Press, 1969), p. 110. On the difficulties of the Black Arts project of cultural unity, see Philip Brian Harper's provocative "Nationalism and Social Divison in Black Arts Poetry of the 1960s," *Critical Inquiry* 19 (Winter 1993): 234–255.

20. On Malcolm's autobiography as a conflicted conversion narrative, see Manthia Diawara, "Malcolm X: Conversionists versus Culturalists," in *In Search of Africa* (Cambridge: Harvard University Press, 1998), pp. 120–133.

21. Carlo Rotella, *October Cities: The Redevelopment of Urban Literature* (Berkeley: University of California Press, 1998); Alex Haley and Malcolm X, *The Autobiography of Malcolm X* (New York: Ballantine Books, 1965); Michael Eric Dyson, *Making Malcolm: The Myth and Meaning of Malcolm X* (New York: Oxford University Press, 1995); Ossie Davis, "Our Own Black Shining Prince," *Liberator* 5:4 (April 1965): 7.

22. Lee Rainwater and William Yancey, *The Moynihan Report and the Politics of Controversy* (Cambridge: MIT Press, 1967); Nicholas Lemann, *The Promised Land: The Great Black Migration and How It Changed America* (New York: Knopf, 1991), pp. 172–177; John D'Emilio and Estelle B. Freedman, *Intimate Matters: A History of Sexuality in America* (New York: Harper and Row, 1988), pp. 295–300.

23. Porter, *John Coltrane,* p. 232.

24. Cornel West, "Malcolm X and Black Rage," in *Malcolm X: In Our Own Image,* ed. Joe Wood (New York: St. Martin's Press, 1992), p. 49; Robin D. G. Kelley, "House Negroes on the Loose: Malcolm X and the Black Bourgeoisie," *Callaloo* 21:2 (Spring 1998): 419–435; Malcolm X, "Twenty Million Black People in a Political, Economic, and Mental Prison," in *Malcolm X: The Last Speeches,* ed. Bruce Perry (New York: Pathfinder Press, 1989), p. 27.

25. Haley and Malcolm, *Autobiography,* p. 110; Robin D. G. Kelley, "The Riddle of the Zoot: Malcolm Little and Black Cultural Politics during World War II," in *Malcolm X: In Our Own Image,* pp. 162–165.

26. Porter, *John Coltrane*, pp. 95–97, 270–272. One might say that Coltrane gave up on "the one" in his final years, when his music dropped a steady pulse in its rhythm section; but in doing so, he also drew more attention to the vocal qualities of his own improvising.

27. Kelley, "House Negroes on the Loose," pp. 420–425.

28. Adolph Reed, Jr., "The Allure of Malcolm X and the Changing Character of Black Politics," in *Malcolm X: In Our Own Image*, p. 207; Porter, *John Coltrane*, p. 275.

29. A. B. Spellman, "The Legacy of Malcolm X," *Liberator* 5:6 (June 1965): 11. Although Spellman believed in Malcolm's integrity since his conversion to Islam, he tacitly did not count his zoot-suit hipsterism among his "political years."

30. Patricia Hill Collins, "Learning to Think for Ourselves: Malcolm X's Black Nationalism Reconsidered," in *Malcolm X: In Our Own Image*, pp. 74–81; Taylor Branch, *Pillar of Fire: America in the King Years* (New York: Simon and Schuster, 1998), p. 13. See also the essays by Angela Davis, Arnold Rampersad, Ron Simmons and Marlon Riggs in *Malcolm X: In Our Own Image*.

9. "Love, Like Jazz, Is a Four Letter Word"

1. Shepard quoted in Stephen J. Bottoms, *The Theatre of Sam Shepard: States of Crisis* (New York: Cambridge University Press, 1998), p. 66; George Lipsitz, "Who'll Stop the Rain: Youth Culture, Rock 'n' Roll, and Social Crises," in *The Sixties: From Memory to History*, ed. David Farber (Chapel Hill: University of North Carolina Press, 1994), pp. 211–212.

2. See, for instance, Nat Hentoff's 1965 *Down Beat* column, where he suggested that jazz festivals might benefit from "those principles of 'participatory democracy' that are being developed by such student groups as the Student Nonviolent Coordinating Committee and Students for a Democratic Society in the course of their efforts to change society." Hentoff, "Second Chorus," *Down Beat*, July 29, 1965, p. 39.

3. Robert Santelli, *Aquarius Rising: The Rock Festival Years* (New York: Dell, 1980), pp. 22–23, 263–272; Joel Selvin, *Monterey Pop* (San Francisco: Chronicle Books, 1992), p. 8. See also Jerry Hopkins, Jim Marshall, and Baron Wolman, *Festival! The Book of American Music Celebrations* (New York: Macmillan, 1970); and Todd Gitlin, *The Sixties: Years of Hope, Days of Rage* (New York: Bantam, 1987).

4. *American Jazz Annual, Newport Edition 1956* (New York: Hemisphere Press, 1956), n.p.; Langston Hughes Papers, Box 113, Newport Jazz, Inc., folder, Beinecke Library, Yale University, New Haven, Conn. See memoranda to the Board of Directors dated July 14, 1961; August 25, 1961; September 27, 1961; October 28, 1961; and January 18, 1962.

5. Burt Goldblatt, *The Newport Jazz Festival: The Illustrated History* (New York: Dial Press, 1977), p. 93; Wein quoted in Leonard Feather, "Jazz Festivals: The Patient Makes It," *Show*, July 1962, p. 85.

6. See "Gendarmes Get Top Billing at Newport in July," *Variety,* June 14, 1961, pp. 45, 47; "All Quiet on Newport Jazz Front," *Variety,* July 5, 1961, pp. 43, 47.

7. Goldblatt, *Newport Jazz Festival,* pp. 99, 121.

8. Ibid., p. 121; "Newport Kayos Jazz Festivals," *Variety,* August 5, 1964, p. 45; John Ashton Worley, "The Newport Jazz Festival: A Clash of Cultures" (Ph.D. diss., Clark University, 1981), pp. 184–188.

9. "George Wein," *Current Biography Yearbook* (New York: H. W. Wilson, 1985), p. 437; "No. 2—French Lick," *Down Beat,* September 3, 1959, pp. 15–16; "Indiana Jazz Festival Future in Doubt," *Variety,* July 5, 1961, p. 47; "No. 3—Playboy," *Down Beat,* September 3, 1959, p. 17; "Like Man, Things Were All Mixed Up on Randall's Island," *New York Amsterdam News,* August 27, 1960, p. 14.

10. "Las Vegas Slates First Jazz Fest," *Norfolk Journal and Guide* (national ed.), April 28, 1962, p. 18; Feather, "Jazz Festivals," p. 85; "Planning Complete for International Jazz Festival," *Norfolk Journal and Guide* (national ed.), April 28, 1962, p. 18.

11. Gleason quoted in Jimmy Lyons with Ira Kamin, *Dizzy, Duke, the Count, and Me: The Story of the Monterey Jazz Festival* (San Francisco: California Living, 1978), p. 13.

12. Gene Lees, "The Monterey Festival," *Down Beat,* November 12, 1959, p. 21.

13. Lyons, *Dizzy, Duke,* pp. 72, 174.

14. Ibid., pp. 64, 96–102, 165.

15. Santelli, *Aquarius Rising,* pp. 11–15; Hopkins, Marshall, and Wolman, *Festival!,* pp. 24–28; Ralph Gleason, "The Tribes Gather for a Yea Saying," *San Francisco Chronicle,* January 14, 1967, p. 53; Gitlin, *The Sixties,* pp. 208–211; Jay Stevens, *Storming Heaven: LSD and the American Dream* (New York: Harper and Row, 1987), pp. vii–ix, 329–331.

16. Dizzy Gillespie with Al Fraser, *To Be or Not . . . to Bop: Memoirs* (Garden City, N.Y.: Doubleday, 1979), pp. 452–461.

17. Robert Christgau, "Anatomy of a Love Festival," *Esquire,* January 1968, pp. 64–66, 147.

18. Ibid., p. 147; Santelli, *Aquarius Rising,* pp. 27, 45–46.

19. Christgau, "Anatomy," p. 147.

20. Ibid., p. 154; Santelli, *Aquarius Rising,* pp. 56–57; Selvin, *Monterey Pop,* pp. 14–15.

21. William Rothman, *Documentary Film Classics* (New York: Cambridge University Press, 1997), p. 209. My analysis of *Monterey Pop* is indebted to Rothman's detailed reading of the film.

22. Lipsitz, "Who'll Stop the Rain," p. 221.

23. Santelli, *Aquarius Rising,* pp. 48–50; Rothman, *Documentary Film Classics,* p. 206.

24. Bottoms, *Theater of Sam Shepard,* p. 34. I am indebted to Bottoms's fine

work on Shepard, especially his analysis of Shepard's turn from his modernist-derived jazz plays to his later postmodern and rock-influenced plays.

25. *The Rock Garden* and *Cowboys #2* can be found in Shepard, *Mad Dog Blues and Other Plays* (New York: Winter House, 1972); *4-H Club* is included in Shepard, *The Unseen Hand and Other Plays* (New York: Urizen Books, 1981).

26. Bottoms, *Theater of Sam Shepard,* pp. 25, 33, 28; David J. DeRose, *Sam Shepard* (New York: Twayne, 1992), pp. 11–14.

27. Shepard quoted in Bottoms, *Theater of Sam Shepard,* pp. 64, 76–86.

28. Ibid., pp. 24–29, 287–288.

29. DeRose, *Sam Shepard,* pp. 42–43.

30. Shepard, *The Unseen Hand and Other Plays,* p. 203.

31. Ibid., pp. 232, 211–214.

32. Ibid., pp. 231–233.

33. Bottoms, *Theater of Sam Shepard,* pp. 62, 84; DeRose, *Sam Shepard,* p. 44.

34. Shepard, *Mad Dog Blues and Other Plays,* pp. 131–132, 149–152; Bottoms, *Theatre of Sam Shepard,* pp. 63–64.

35. Sam Shepard, *Fool for Love and Other Plays* (New York: Bantam, 1984), pp. 126–127.

36. Ibid., pp. 116, 138.

37. See Bottoms, *Theatre of Sam Shepard,* pp. 69–73.

38. Shepard, *Fool for Love and Other Plays,* p. 141.

39. For more on these "outside" plays, see Bottoms, pp. 125–140; Shepard, *Fool for Love and Other Plays,* pp. 61–62.

40. Jon Wiener, *Come Together: John Lennon in His Time* (Urbana: University of Illinois Press, 1991 [1984]), pp. 187–196 (Rubin quoted on pp. 191, 195; Dellinger and Ginsberg quoted on p. 195). The split in the New Left between media activists and grassroots organizers has been much discussed by historians, but see in particular David Farber, *Chicago '68* (Chicago: University of Chicago Press, 1988).

41. Stephen Meyers, "Finding Aid to the John and Leni Sinclair Papers," Bentley Historical Library, University of Michigan, n.p.; Herb Boyd and Barbara Weinberg, *Jazz Space Detroit* (Detroit: Jazz Research Institute, 1980).

42. Meyers, "Finding Aid," n.p.; Suzanne E. Smith, *Dancing in the Streets: Motown and the Cultural Politics of Detroit* (Cambridge: Harvard University Press, 1999), pp. 174–175.

43. John Sinclair, *This Is Our Music* (Detroit: Artists' Workshop Press, 1965); *Fire Music* (Detroit: Artists' Workshop Press, 1966); *Meditations: A Suite for John Coltrane* (Detroit: Artists' Workshop Press, 1967).

44. Sinclair, *Fire Music,* p. 40.

45. Sinclair, *This Is Our Music,* n.p.

46. Ibid., pp. 32–33; Meyers, "Finding Aid," n.p.; John Szwed, *Space Is the*

Place: The Lives and Times of Sun Ra (New York: Pantheon, 1997), p. 244; Sinclair, Meditations, n.p.

47. Sinclair, Meditations, n.p.

48. Dan Morgenstern, "A Message to Our Readers," Down Beat, June 29, 1967, p. 13; Leonard Feather, "Rock 'n' Roll: Is This Frantic Phenomenon a New School of Jazz?" Playboy 4:6 (June 1957), pp. 19, 75, 76; "Jazz'll Never Make It," Down Beat, August 18, 1960, p. 8; John Gabree, "The World of Rock," Down Beat, July 13, 1967, pp. 18–20.

49. Legs McNeil and Gillian McCain, Please Kill Me: The Uncensored Oral History of Punk (New York: Penguin, 1997), pp. 42–43.

50. Szwed, Space Is the Place, p. 244; Steve Waksman, Instruments of Desire: The Electric Guitar and the Shaping of Musical Experience (Cambridge: Harvard University Press, 1999), p. 229. See Waksman, pp. 207–236, for an expert consideration of the MC5's "politics of noise."

51. Meyers, "Finding Aid," n.p.; McNeil and McCain, Please Kill Me, pp. 48, 43–45; Sinclair quoted in Wiener, Come Together, p. 188.

52. John Sinclair, "Rock and Roll Is a Weapon of Cultural Revolution," in "Takin' It to the Streets": A Sixties Reader, ed. Alexander Bloom and Wini Breines (New York: Oxford University Press, 1995), pp. 301–303.

53. McNeil and McCain, Please Kill Me, pp. 46–49; "Statement for the White Panther Arm of the Youth International Party," in Twenty-Minute Fandangos and Forever Changes: A Rock Bazaar, ed. Jonathan Eisen (New York: Random House, 1971), pp. 222–225; "The Black Panther Platform: 'What We Want, What We Believe,'" in "Takin' It to the Streets," p. 164.

54. McNeil and McCain, Please Kill Me, pp. 35–36, 46–47, 68–73; Wiener, Come Together, p. 188.

55. Sinclair, Fire Music, p. 36.

10. The Road to "Soul Power"

1. Horace Tapscott, Songs of the Unsung: The Musical and Social Journey of Horace Tapscott, ed. Steven Isoardi (Durham: Duke University Press, 2001), pp. 105–106, 111–112; Raphael J. Sonenshein, Politics in Black and White: Race and Power in Los Angeles (Princeton: Princeton University Press, 1993), pp. 79–80; Arthur Marwick, The Sixties: Cultural Revolution in Britain, France, Italy, and the United States, c. 1958–c. 1974 (New York: Oxford University Press, 1998), pp. 572–574; Gerald Horne, Fire This Time: The Watts Uprising and the 1960s (Charlottesville: University Press of Virginia, 1995).

2. Clayborne Carson, In Struggle: SNCC and the Black Awakening of the 1960s (Cambridge: Harvard University Press, 1981), pp. 191–228; George M. Frederickson, Black Liberation: A Comparative History of Black Ideologies in the United States and South Africa (New York: Oxford University Press, 1995), pp. 286–297.

3. For nightclub information, see *The New Grove Dictionary of Jazz*, ed. Barry Kernfeld (New York: St. Martin's, 1996 [1988]), pp. 887–904, 907–908.

4. On Abbey Lincoln's career and jazz musicians' employment at universities, see Eric Porter, *What Is This Thing Called Jazz? African American Musicians as Artists, Critics, and Activists* (Berkeley: University of California Press, 2002), pp. 189, 234–238; on Cecil Taylor and the jazz downturn of the late 1960s, see Gary Giddins, *Visions of Jazz: The First Century* (New York: Oxford University Press, 1998), pp. 462, 530; for all other information on artists, see *The New Grove Dictionary of Jazz*, passim.

5. Often treated as a bleak interval in jazz history, the late 1960s have not attracted anything like the attention given to swing, bebop, or hard bop. Two notable exceptions are Ronald Radano's groundbreaking *New Musical Figurations: Anthony Braxton's Cultural Critique* (Chicago: University of Chicago Press, 1993), and Porter, *What Is This Thing Called Jazz*, pp. 191–239.

6. *Village Voice*, February 19, 1970, p. 29; Don Heckman, "Jazz: An Answer or Two," *Village Voice*, February 19, 1970, p. 32.

7. The postmodern turn in jazz—the use of parody and pastiche as tools in both creating and deconstructing an inherited tradition—is treated in Radano's *New Musical Figurations* and Ted Gioia, *The History of Jazz* (New York: Oxford University Press, 1997), pp. 354–364. On Tapscott, see Tapscott, *Songs of the Unsung*, pp. 113, 119–124.

8. See Will Friedwald, *Jazz Singing: America's Great Voices from Bessie Smith to Bebop and Beyond* (New York: DaCapo, 1996 [1990]), pp. 400–406.

9. On the riots as a function of ghetto grievances, see Robert M. Fogelson, *Violence as Protest: A Study of Riots and Ghettos* (Garden City, N.Y.: Doubleday, 1971) and William Ryan, *Blaming the Victim* (New York: Vintage, 1976 [1971]).

10. A. B. Spellman, *Four Lives in the Bebop Business* (New York: Limelight, 1988 [1966]), pp. 226, 234–235.

11. *Black Fire: An Anthology of Afro-American Writing*, ed. Amiri Baraka (as LeRoi Jones) and Larry Neal (New York: William Morrow, 1968), pp. 304–305. In reconstructing Simmons's poem on the recording, I have used the lineation of her published version in *Black Fire* while amending the text according to the recorded performance.

12. Ibid., p. 304.

13. Ibid., pp. 304, 307.

14. Ibid., pp. 306, 308.

15. Ibid., p. 305.

16. Clayton Riley, "Cheap Thrills," *Liberator* 8 (October 1968): 20; Ray Gibson, "Spiritual Voices of Black America," *Liberator* 6 (June 1966): 12–13; "Black Musicians," *Liberator* 8 (August 1968): 12–13; Harold Cruse, "Rebellion or Revolution (Part 3)," *Liberator* 3 (December 1963): 14, 17; "Rebellion or Revolution (Part 4)," *Liberator* 4 (January 1964): 14, 16.

17. Marc Brasz, "Cecil Taylor at Town Hall," *Liberator* 6 (August 1966): 20–21; Nadi Qamar, "Black Music Predicament," *Liberator* 6 (June 1966): 18–19.

18. Askia Muhammad Touré (as Rolland Snellings), "Keep on Pushin' (Rhythm & Blues as a Weapon)," *Liberator* 5 (October 1965): 6–8.

19. Charlie L. Russell, "Has Jazz Lost Its Roots?" *Liberator* 4 (August 1964): 5. On the Cooper Square scene, see Amiri Baraka, *The Autobiography of LeRoi Jones* (Westport, Conn.: Lawrence Hill, 1997), pp. 254–261, and Chapter 2, "Radicalism by Another Name."

20. Russell, "Has Jazz Lost Its Roots?" pp. 4–7; L. P. Neal, "Black Revolution in Music: A Talk with Drummer Milford Graves," *Liberator* 5 (September 1965): 14–15; Lawrence P. Neal, "A Conversation with Archie Shepp," *Liberator* 5 (November 1965): 24–25; Charlie Russell, "Minding the Cultural Shop," *Liberator* 4 (December 1964): 12–13.

21. Milford Graves and Don Pullen, "Black Music," *Liberator* 7 (January 1967): 20; *The Cricket* 1:1 (n.d. [1968?]), back cover.

22. On Pittsburgh's Black Arts Cultural Center, see Yusef Nafees, "Black Arts Cultural Center Inc.," *Liberator* 7 (March 1967): 16.

23. Tapscott, *Song of the Unsung*, pp. 78–83, 94–95, 227, 217–220.

24. Valerie Wilmer, *As Serious As Your Life: The Story of the New Jazz* (Westport, Conn.: Lawrence Hill, 1980 [1977]), pp. 213–215; Dixon qutoed in Rob Backus, *Fire Music: A Political History of Jazz* (Chicago: Vanguard Books, 1976), p. 70.

25. Baraka, *Autobiography of LeRoi Jones*, pp. 316–329; Lorenzo Thomas, *Extraordinary Measures: Afrocentric Modernism and Twentieth-Century American Poetry* (Tuscaloosa: University of Alabama Press, 2000), p. 204.

26. Wilmer, *As Serious as Your Life*, pp. 115–120; Samuel Floyd, Jr., *The Power of Black Music: Interpreting Its History from Africa to the United States* (New York: Oxford University Press, 1995), pp. 191–195; Radano, *New Musical Figurations*, pp. 77–116; Gioia, *History of Jazz*, pp. 354–355.

27. Tapscott, *Songs of the Unsung*, pp. 136–139, 122–124, 141–143, 117–118.

28. Ibid.,, pp. 114, 123–124, 214–216.

29. Sue Mingus, *Tonight at Noon: A Love Story* (New York: Pantheon, 2002), pp. 98–100, 110; Gene Santoro, *Myself When I Am Real: The Life and Music of Charles Mingus* (New York: Oxford University Press, 2000), pp. 268, 271, 247, 257, 273–275. Sue Mingus's memoir and Santoro's biography are invaluable, and very humane, explorations of this period in Mingus's life.

30. Santoro, *Myself When I Am Real*, pp. 280–282, 268–269, 286, 416–417.

31. S. Mingus, *Tonight at Noon*, pp. 114–115; Santoro, *Myself When I Am Real*, pp. 273, 279.

32. Santoro, *Myself When I Am Real*, pp. 266–267, 273; S. Mingus, *Tonight at Noon*, pp. 111, 56–57.

33. Santoro, *Myself When I Am Real*, pp. 211–212, 78, 223; S. Mingus, *Tonight at Noon*, pp. 72–74, 114.

34. S. Mingus, *Tonight at Noon,* pp. 75–78; Santoro, *Myself When I Am Real,* pp. 270–271.

35. Santoro, *Myself When I Am Real,* pp. 260, 296; S. Mingus, *Tonight at Noon,* p. 114.

36. *Mingus* (1966), dir. Tom Reichman, Rhapsody Films.

37. Brian Ward, *Just My Soul Responding: Rhythm and Blues, Black Consciousness, and Race Relations* (Berkeley: University of California Press, 1998), p. 414. For more on the Black Panthers, including a comparison of their ideology to other facets of Black Power, see William Van Deburg, *New Day in Babylon: The Black Power Movement and American Culture, 1965–1975* (Chicago: University of Chicago Press, 1992), pp. 112–191.

38. Santoro, *Myself When I Am Real,* pp. 99–100, 132, 169, 265, 270.

39. Alice Echols, "Nothing Distant about It: Women's Liberation and Sixties Radicalism," in *The Sixties: From Memory to History,* ed. David Farber (Chapel Hill: University of North Carolina Press, 1994), p. 153. For a fine synthetic history of second-wave feminism, see Ruth Rosen, *The World Split Open: How the Modern Women's Movement Changed America* (New York: Penguin, 2000).

40. S. Mingus, *Tonight at Noon,* pp. 66–70, 100–101.

41. Ibid., pp. 85, 88, 92–93, 111; Santoro, *Myself When I Am Real,* pp. 312–313.

42. Santoro, *Myself When I Am Real,* pp. 290–294; see also Chapter 5, "Outrageous Freedom."

43. On "Cumbia & Jazz Fusion," see Santoro, *Myself When I Am Real,* pp. 356–358.

44. Cannonball Adderley Quintet, *Country Preacher: Live at Operation Breadbasket* (1969), Capitol D 106286.

45. Marshall Frady, *Jesse: The Life and Pilgrimage of Jesse Jackson* (New York: Random House, 1996), pp. 256, 259.

46. Ibid., pp. 248–249; Gary Massoni, "Perspectives on Operation Breadbasket," in *Chicago 1966: Open Housing Marches, Summit Negotiations, and Operation Breadbasket,* ed. David J. Garrow (Brooklyn, N.Y.: Carlson, 1989), pp. 193–195, 223–230.

47. Frady, *Jesse,* pp. 253–257; Massoni, "Perspectives," pp. 203–211.

48. For this critique of Jackson, see Adolph Reed, Jr., *The Jesse Jackson Phenomenon: The Crisis of Purpose in Afro-American Politics* (New Haven: Yale University Press, 1986).

49. Patricia Krizmis, "Negro's Business, Culture Show Keeps Crowd of 100,000 Buzzing," *Chicago Tribune,* October 4, 1969, p. 14; Bill Quinn, "The Well Rounded 'Ball," *Down Beat,* November 16, 1967, p. 17; Leonard Feather, "Cannonball Adderley Blindfold Test," *Down Beat,* November 2, 1967, p. 34; Bob Belden, liner notes to Miles Davis, *Bitches Brew,* Columbia C2K 65774, pp. 12–13.

50. Barry Kernfeld, "Adderley, Coltrane, and Davis at the Twilight of Bebop: The Search for Melodic Coherence (1958–1959): (Ph.D. diss., Cornell Univer-

sity, 1981), pp. 201–203; Cannonball Adderley and His Quintet, *Live in Paris 1969*, Malaco/Jazz Classics RTE 1004–2; Ralph J. Gleason, "A Lesson in Jazz," *New York Post*, July 29, 1969, p. 59.

51. Quinn, "The Well-Rounded 'Ball," p. 17; Frady, *Jesse*, p. 256; "Bread-basket Maps Big Business Boycott," *Chicago Daily Defender*, October 18–24, 1969, p. 5. For earlier charges that Adderley had sold out, see Chapter 2, "Radicalism by Another Name."

52. Amiri Baraka (as Leroi Jones), *Black Music* (New York: Morrow, 1967), p. 182.

53. Marabi first emerged in the black slums of Johannesburg in the 1920s, where it was played on pianos in local bars. By the 1940s, it had cross-pollinated with American swing music and had become the music known as marabi jazz.

ACKNOWLEDGMENTS

It is a great pleasure to thank some (though, mercifully for the reader, not all) of the people who have made this project possible.

During its first five years, this book was written in moments stolen from a far more ambitious project: the organizing of Yale's graduate students into a union. As a result, my greatest debt is to the community behind the Graduate Employees and Students Organization (GESO) at Yale. From its beginnings as a baggy history of jazz during the Cold War, *Freedom Is, Freedom Ain't* evolved into a story about the redemptive power of struggle in politics and art, and I have no doubt that it bears the mark of the union struggles of New Haven, which in my time involved a year of rolling strikes and six other years of on-the-ground organizing. More concretely, I'd like to thank those unlucky souls who took on the unfortunate task of organizing and motivating *me:* Antony Dugdale, the only church deacon I know who could outwit Mephistopheles; and Wendi Walsh, the organizer with a heart of gold and a backbone of steel. I'd like to thank too Carlos Aramayo, Fran Balamuth, Ben Begleiter, Shafali Lal, Lis Pimentel, Becky Ruquist, Dave Sanders, Rachel Sulkes, and Steve Vella, all of whom supported me in ways too various to detail. And I'd like to thank my inner circle in American Studies: Joseph Entin, whose cleansing wit regularly shook me out of my psychological haze; Gaspar González, whose brand of tough love kept me learning and laughing; and Brendan Walsh, who had the unfailing ability to "keep it real" in my most ridiculous moments and to help me believe in my better self.

This book began as a dissertation in the congenial environs of the Yale American Studies Department, and I would like to thank those individuals who helped guide it to completion. Thanks to Hazel Carby, whose work steered me to often-buried questions about sexuality in jazz and whose counsel was much appreciated; to Robert Stepto, who offered helpful advice on the Chicago jazz scene in particular; to Alan Trachtenberg, whose example was inspirational; to Jean-Christophe Agnew, who gave me canny advice on how to balance the demands of intellectual, social, and cultural history; to John Szwed, whose honest and bracing comments were very helpful; and especially to Michael Denning, who was not only the director of the dissertation but also its midwife and most generous reader.

Outside of Yale and its American Studies department, I owe a great debt to Sumanth Gopinath and Peter Curtis, who lent me their subtle understanding of music theory and their finely tuned ears and who encouraged my blustery incursions into the domain of musicology; fellow popular music scholars Eric Porter and Josh Kun, who gave me helpful tips and advice along the way; Marjorie Perloff, whose no-nonsense virtuosity is a match for any jazz musician; and Craig Dworkin, whose spirit of experimentation doesn't keep him from swinging always to the beat.

I would also like to thank members of the University of Virginia community, which has been a wonderful intellectual home for the last three years. The members of the Labor Action Group and the recently formed staff and graduate student unions have made the state of Virginia seem like a place where progressive politics might actually take root: thanks to Daniela Bell, Jan Cornell, Ben Lee, Wilson McIvor, and Sylvia Strawn. Many thanks to the director and fellows of the Carter G. Woodson Institute for African and African-American Studies at the University of Virginia, where I completed a first draft of this project: Reginald Butler, Scot French, Adrian Gaskins, Joseph Hellweg, Meta Jones, and Jemima Pierre provided invaluable feedback and support. Colleagues in the Department of English have also been inspirational. I would like to single out John Charles, Susan Fraiman, Eleanor Kaufman, Jim Kim, Michael Levenson, Eric Lott, Franny Nudelman, Ken Parille, and Lisa Woolfork for their support and friendship; and I acknowledge the help of the Cary Jacobs Fund, which provided much-needed summer support.

The quest to secure permissions can be a ghastly experience. I would like to thank Sue Mingus, Thomas Owens, John Sinclair, Leni Sinclair, Craig Tenney, and the researchers at the Michael Ochs Archives, who made it ultimately a pleasure.

At Harvard University Press, I thank Lindsay Waters and Tom Wheatland, who have shepherded this manuscript from its first unruly pages on; the two anonymous readers for the press, whose comments were invaluable when I set about to revise the manuscript; and editor Donna Bouvier, whose eagle eye and sense of *le mot juste* helped save me from myself.

Finally, I would like to thank friends and family: Jay Garcia, who made our apartment at 70 Howe a perfect place to live the American Studies life; Roger Gathman, raconteur extraordinaire and sympathetic ear without compare; Dan Smith, whose sense of humor never fails to lift my spirits; and Louis Matza, who perhaps bears most responsibility for this project, since he was my co-conspirator as we plotted out our musical education over the last fifteen years. Lastly, I would like to thank my family: my brother Larry, my sister-in-law Jacqueline, my niece Rebecca, and my nephew Caleb, who have welcomed me into their extraordinary home; and my parents, whose love has been energetically and provocatively unconditional.

INDEX

Mingus, Charles *(continued)*
    Black Saint and the Sinner Lady, The;
    Jazz Workshop
Mingus, Charles, III, 284, 286
Mingus, Sue, 151, 158, 180, 323–324, 327, 328
Mingus (Reichman), 325–326
minstrelsy, 39, 50–51, 141–142
miscegenation, 67, 71, 181, 184
modal jazz, 5, 22, 58, 193, 218, 335
modernism, 181, 182, 188, 226
Modern Jazz Quartet, 59, 277
Moncur, Grachan, 306, 307, 308
Monk, Thelonious, 44, 54, 217
Monterey International Pop Festival, 9, 273–274, 277–280
Monterey Jazz Festival, 9, 273, 276
Monterey Pop (Pennebaker), 280–283
Montgomery, Robert, 41
Moore, Charles, 295
Morgan, Lee, 308
Morgenstern, Dan, 297
Moses, Robert, 62
Moynihan, Daniel Patrick, 262–263
Moynihan Report, 262–263, 267
Mulholland, Kate, 327
Mulligan, Gerry, 58, 59, 107
Murray, Albert, 69
Murray, Sunny, 10–11, 77
Museum of Modern Art, 252–253
Music at Newport festival, 274
music industry, 111, 152, 194, 272; crisis in jazz market, 311–312, 319; musicians as prostitutes, 173–174, 177–178; profits, 154–155; wage scales, 125, 155. *See also* Newport Jazz Festival
mysticism, 21–22, 182–183

National Movement for the Establishment of a Forty-Ninth State, 91
Nation of Islam, 266, 267, 317
Neal, Larry, 247, 253, 312, 314, 318
negative liberty, 14, 18–19, 159
Negro Family, The: The Case for National Action (Moynihan), 262–263
Negro-to-black conversion process, 247
Nelson, Oliver, 304; *Afro-American Sketches,* 5, 21, 197
New Deal, 4, 248
New Folk Band (Jazz Workshop), 196
New Left, 6, 83, 103, 293, 321, 370n40. *See also* liberal left

New Orleans jazz, 46–47, 162
Newport (R.I.), 109, 129, 274–275; economy, 107–109; tourism, 106, 117–118
Newport Jazz Festival, 7, 15, 123, 157, 273; aftermath of riot, 100–101; black audience, 121, 129–130; committed youth at, 110–111; consumer entitlement, 119–120, 142; corporate logic behind, 102–103, 105–106, 119, 274; cultural expectations, 105–109; directors, 101, 106–107; *Jazz on a Summer's Day,* 113–117, 280, 281, 283; lodging discrimination, 129–130; media coverage, 103–105, 110–112; musicians, 114, 116, 121, 125, 156, 195; police response to riots, 119–120; revenues, 109–110; riot as white privilege, 120–121; riot events, 99–101, 118–122, 276; security, 274–275; soul-jazz billings, 118–119; white youth audience, 111–113, 116–118; youth delinquency and, 103–105, 121–122
Newport Rebels festival, 123, 132, 143, 163, 273, 277; absence of white performers, 127–128; anticommercialism, 125–126; musicians featured, 126, 127; planning and venue, 124–125
Newport '69, 273
Newsweek, 172–173
New York Amsterdam News, 35, 88, 89
New Yorker, 107
New York Free Press, 328
New York Herald Tribune, 103, 122
New York intellectuals, 48–49, 63–64
New York Metropolitan Opera, 138
New York, New York (Russell), 197
New York Times, 52, 56, 114
nightclubs, 167–169, 303; Five Spot, 77, 169, 217, 284, 314
Nixon, Richard, 14–15
nonviolence, 17–18, 95, 268, 331
notation, 186–187
Nyro, Laura, 279

O'Connor, Norman, 104
October Revolution in Jazz, 316
O'Day, Anita, 116
Off-Off-Broadway, 232, 285–286
O'Horgan, Tom, 289
Olson, Charles, 295
Ono, Yoko, 292